09-09

VENGEANCE

George Jonas was born in Budapest in 1935, and moved to Canada in 1956. He is a successful playwright and journalist, and is TV and Radio Drama Producer for the Canadian Broadcasting Corporation, with over 150 productions to his credit. He has published three highly acclaimed books of poetry; a novel, *Final Decree*; and won the International Mystery Writers' Edgar Allan Poe Award for his previous work of non-fiction *By Persons Unknown*. He has written *Vengeance* with the full cooperation of the central figure of this story, whose identity must remain undisclosed.

George Jonas

VENGEANCE

A true story

Pan Books
in association with
Collins

First published in Great Britain 1984 by William Collins Sons & Co. Ltd
This edition published 1985 by Pan Books Ltd,
Cavaye Place, London SW10 9PG
in association with William Collins Sons & Co. Ltd
9 8 7 6 5 4 3 2 1
© George Jonas 1984
ISBN 0 330 28720 6
Printed and bound in Great Britain by
Richard Clay (The Chaucer Press) Ltd, Bungay, Suffolk

For Barbara Amiel,

and for Assi, David, Kathy, Kopi,
Milt, Tony, Smadar and Yasir,

and for those who died
from the ones who lived

Thus saith the Lord God; Because the
Philistines have dealt by revenge,
and have taken vengeance with a
despiteful heart, to destroy *it* for
the old hatred;

Therefore thus saith the Lord God;
Behold I will stretch out my hand
upon the Philistines;

And they shall know that I *am* the
Lord, when I shall lay my vengeance
upon them.

Ezekiel 25: 15-16-17

They won't believe the world they
haven't noticed is like that.

Graham Greene, *Ways of Escape*

CONTENTS

FOREWORD

In the fall of 1981 my publishers asked me if I wanted to meet a man who had an interesting story to tell. After a series of fairly elaborate arrangements, a meeting was set up in a north American city. There, in a small office, I met an individual who gave me his account of a major episode in Israel's clandestine war against terrorism: the activities of a counter-terrorist team that was set up following the massacre of Israeli athletes at Munich in 1972.

Even before contacting me, my publishers had satisfied themselves about the man's *bona fides*. After the meeting I made what inquiries I could on my own, and came to the same conclusion that they had. It was evident to us that we were talking to an Israeli agent who had 'come in from the cold' – to our knowledge, the first one.

I undertook to do further research and write a book about the agent's story. In the course of the following year, I travelled to several countries in Europe and the Middle East. I spent some time in two cities behind what used to be called the Iron Curtain. My informant and I continued meeting in different parts of the world over a period of time. Following his instructions, I interviewed six other people in Germany, France, Israel and the United States. I also interviewed a number of my own contacts – experts, officials, bystanders – who could throw some light on one aspect or another of the events. Many of the latter I feel free to acknowledge by name. Some, for obvious reasons, I cannot.

For the same reasons, I cannot identify my main source. Indeed, he took considerable precautions so as not to have to rely solely on my discretion in protecting himself from unwelcome research. And he allowed me to learn no more about him than I needed in order to complete the book.

For my better understanding of the scenario, my contacts made arrangements for me to observe some minor field operations. Accompanied by agents working in Europe, I saw something of the rudiments of routine surveillance, the purchase and use of illicit documents, the setting up of safe houses, and the methods used in contacting and paying informers. Though my studies were far from exhaustive, my research afforded a first hand glimpse into the world I intended to write about.

Most of the *events* I wanted to write about had rated a paragraph or two in the daily newspapers at the time they occurred. Though never officially 'solved', a few were described from the start as the suspected work of Israeli anti-terrorist squads. Several recent books dealing with international terror and counter-terror have alluded to some of them. Parts of the hard news had been reported in such works of documentary journalism as Richard Deacon's *The Israeli Secret Service*, Stewart Steven's *The Spymasters of Israel*, or David B. Tinnin and Dag Christensen's *The Hit Team*. Edgar O'Ballance outlined the assassinations of several Palestinian terrorist leaders in Europe in his excellent *Language of Violence*. The basic information had been available, but I hoped I would be able to gain some new insight.

Though I was inventing nothing, I could not hope to come up to the rigorous standards of the historian. Inescapably, for some of my information I was relying upon a single source whom I could not name. Certain details of his story were incapable of verification. I could satisfy myself on other details, but would have to alter some of them to protect my informant or my other sources.[1] When basing a story on confidential information, the ideal journalistic practice is to have two sources independently verifying each other: a requirement which in this book I could not always meet.[2] Similarly, in describing dialogue and exchanges of which no records had been kept, my only choice was to reconstruct

14

them from my source's personal recollections, despite the risk that human memory could be frail or self-serving.

I decided to tell the agent's story looking over his shoulder, as it were – hanging it on the double threads of his point of view and my own. I used the same method with many of the other individuals in the book. Unlike a first-person narrative, it enabled me to see events through the eyes of my sources – at times my only evidence – without forcing me to be uncritical of their vision. Like a juror, I could draw inferences from available facts.

Much in this story hangs on a third thread, of course: evidence from secondary sources, identified in the text or in the notes, in the manner of any book describing current events for the general reader. Where previously reported facts run counter to my understanding of events – as some do – I note the discrepancy.

* * *

Since this book raises, without comment, questions about which different people have different opinions, I think it is fair to outline my bias for the reader.

Like most people, I disapprove of political terror. Moreover, I do not believe in the cynical notion that one man's terrorist is another man's freedom fighter. Terrorists are defined not by their political aims but by the means they use to achieve them.[3]

At the same time, I cannot subscribe to the common fallacy that terrorism is ineffectual. I believe that such a suggestion is mere wishful thinking. While terror often fails to bring about desired aims, so does conventional war, diplomacy, or any other political endeavour. On that test one might as well suggest that war and diplomacy are ineffectual. My view is that terrorism is wrong, whether it succeeds or not.

But counter-terrorism also involves bloodshed. Inevitably, a number of ethical questions arise in telling the story of a person who, at the request of his government, ends up

15

killing twelve human beings with his own hands – seven of them deliberately and in cold blood. I will not attempt to deal with these questions here. Insofar as they can be answered, they are answered by the book as a whole.

Between Israel and her enemies, I support Israel. I do so for two reasons in addition to the fact that I am a Jew. First, I believe in the desirability of liberal democracy over any other known form of social organization, and in the Middle East Israel comes closest to being a liberal democracy. Second – though her record, especially of late, is not perfect in this respect – throughout the Middle East conflict Israel has adhered to measurably higher standards of conduct than her opponents. And while I am not without sympathy for the Palestinian cause, I *am* without sympathy for those who support it by terror.

Toronto   GEORGE JONAS
June 1983

ACKNOWLEDGEMENTS

I am grateful for comments, material and other assistance graciously provided by Mr G. Antal, Mr Frank Barbetta, Ms Brindusa Caragiu, Ms Suzy Dahan, Mr Edward L. Greenspan, QC, Dr A. I. Malcolm, Mr Michael Smith, Mr A. Soos and Mr Marq de Villiers.

I wish also to acknowledge the indirect but essential contribution of Professor Philip Anisman to the chapter notes in this book.

Special thanks are due to my patient editors, Louise Dennys and Frances McFadyen. Photo research is by Yvonne R. Freund.

This acknowledgement does not imply that any of those who helped me share my views, or my responsibility for any errors.

PROLOGUE

~~~

Munich

COMPARED TO THE mean, elegant sweep of line that characterizes most modern automatic infantry weapons, the Kalashnikov looks squat and solid. This assault rifle, officially designated as the AK 47, is said to have been invented by a Siberian peasant, at least according to the legend that grew up around it as the most popular weapon of international terror. It is simple and rugged. The 34.2-inch-long gun is made of dark blonde wood – the stock and the pistol grip – interrupted by two structures of dull grey metal. The metal centre section comprises the breech and trigger mechanism, with the magazine projecting down and forward from it in a gentle curve. It holds thirty rounds of 7.62 mm cartridges; short lead bullets with a penetrating core of steel. When set on automatic fire, the Kalashnikov is rated to spit out a hundred of them in one minute, each leaving the short muzzle with a velocity of 2,330 feet per second or about 1,600 miles per hour. It is manufactured in various models in the Soviet Union as well as in many other Communist-bloc countries. When used at short range it can literally cut a man in half.

On 5 September, 1972, several of these rifles were taken out from their greasy wrapping and handed to the eight Black September terrorists who were on their way to 31 Connollystrasse, the sleeping quarters of the Israeli athletes at the Olympic Village in Munich.

Though not recognized as such, the *fedayeen* (the Arab

19

word means 'men of sacrifice', and is often used by Islamic terrorists to describe themselves.) were first sighted scaling the six-foot wire fence on Kusoczinskidamm at 4 am. The spot where they entered the Olympic village was about fifty yards from the apartments of the Israeli athletes. A distance of fifty yards can be covered by a group of men walking slowly and cautiously in one or two minutes. However, it was not until 4.25 am that the terrorists inserted a pass-key in the lock of the door leading to the vestibule of Apartment 1 at 31 Connollystrasse. Whether or not they had any assistance during this time in the Olympic Village itself is a matter of speculation.[1]

The man who heard them first was Yossef Gutfreund, a wrestling referee, a 275-pound giant. Though he might have been uncertain for a moment whether the noise was being made by a roommate – wrestling coach Moshe Weinberger, who was expected to return late and was given a second key – the Arab voices whispering behind the door soon convinced him of danger. In fact that was the word he shouted in Hebrew – 'Danger!' – to alert another roommate as he threw his bulk against the slowly opening door.

For the next few seconds eight Arabs tried to push the door open against Gutfreund. The effort both sides expended was sufficient to twist the doorjamb and the metal hinges completely out of shape. It also gained Gutfreund's teammate, weightlifting coach Tuvia Sokolovsky, enough time to break a window and escape.

Four more occupants of Apartment 1 were not so lucky. Track coach Amitzur Shapira, fencing master Andrei Spitzer, rifle coach Kehat Shorr and weightlifting judge Yacov Springer were held at gunpoint, then slapped around and threatened by the Arabs in an attempt to make them reveal where the other Israelis were staying. Each was offered freedom if he would knock on the door of any apartment belonging to other Israeli athletes and gain entrance for the *fedayeen*. The Arabs did not even bother making such offers to Gutfreund; instead, they tied him up as the captured

Samson might have been tied up by their biblical predecessors, the Philistines.

Not getting any help from the Israelis, the terrorists decided to explore 31 Connollystrasse – which also housed the Uruguay and Hong Kong Olympic teams. They missed Apartments 2, 4 and 5 with their eight Israeli occupants,[2] but captured the six athletes staying in Apartment 3. They were wrestlers Eliezer Halfin, Mark Slavin and Gad Zobari, and weightlifters David Marc Berger, Zeev Friedman and Yossef Romano. Before they could enter Apartment 3, though, the terrorists had to deal with wrestling coach Moshe Weinberger who had been out late and just then came sauntering down Connollystrasse.

Weinberger was a man roughly Gutfreund's size, and no easier to deal with. He knocked out one terrorist, and was temporarily subdued only when another shot him through the face. But even though gravely wounded, Weinberger would not give up. After the men in Apartment 3 had been captured and were being herded back along Connollystrasse towards Apartment 1, lightweight wrestler Gad Zobari decided to make a dash for it. Though the *fedayeen* fired several bursts after him, the little wrestler, zig-zagging across the uneven ground of the compound, actually made it to safety. Weinberger used this opportunity to catch one more terrorist on the jaw, fracturing his mandible and knocking him unconscious. Another terrorist shot him immediately several times in the chest. Weinberger collapsed.

It was now weightlifter Yossef Romano's turn. Along with his teammate David Marc Berger, he attempted to break through the kitchen window of Apartment 1 before the terrorists could tie him up. Unsuccessful, Romano grabbed a knife from the counter and stabbed a terrorist in the forehead. Too painfully wounded to use his weapon, the Arab retreated but another coming up behind him fired a full burst from his Kalashnikov at Romano at close range. The weightlifter fell. When rescue workers tried to remove his body the following day, it reportedly came apart at the waist.

Weinberger, however, had not yet finished fighting. Instead of crawling away from Apartment 1 after he had come to, the wrestling coach groped his way inside the building to confront the terrorists once more. Taken aback by the bloodied hulk stumbling towards them, the *fedayeen* did not fire right away. Weinberger actually had time to hit one and, grabbing a kitchen knife, slash another on the arm before being fatally shot in the head.

The time was now around 5 am. In the initial action, lasting about twenty-five minutes, the Black Septembrists had killed two Israeli athletes and captured nine. Two Israelis had escaped. The terrorists failed to locate another eight Israelis in the building.

During the twenty-five minutes of fighting, the security authorities in the Olympic Village apparently received only vague reports about 'some kind of trouble' around Block 31 on Connollystrasse. This was not altogether surprising. Most athletes and officials had been sound asleep. The action was sporadic: shouts and bursts of fire followed by periods of silence. People awakened by the noise would not have been able to identify it immediately. They'd listen for a while, hear nothing more, and perhaps doze off again. The few who got up to investigate could see nothing. In the village few nights had gone by without a celebration of some kind. There had often been firecrackers and noisy fun. To many of the Israelis' sleepy neighbours, the terrorist action sounded like more of the same.

At any rate, it was a lone, unarmed West German security policeman who came to investigate at 4.55 am or shortly thereafter. He fingered his walkie-talkie and muttered '*Was soll das heissen?*' – a German equivalent of a British bobby's 'What's all this then?' at the hooded terrorist standing in front of 31 Connollystrasse. Without replying, the Arab disappeared behind the door.

Meanwhile, however, the two escaped Israelis turned in the real alarm – one from the building housing the South Korean team, the other from the Italians' quarters. Within the next half hour, the authorities received the terrorists' demands which had been typed up in English in several copies. The *fedayeen* also threw Moshe Weinberger's lifeless body into the street.

The demands were for the release of 234 prisoners held by 'the military regime in Israel', whose names were listed on the typewritten sheets. The terrorists named some people held by the Federal Government of West Germany as well, among them the leaders of the Baader-Meinhof gang, Ulrike Meinhof and Andreas Baader, who had been captured by the German police in June that year. The *fedayeen* also wanted three planes to take them to a 'safe destination' after their other demands had been met. There they would release the Israeli athletes. The communiqué gave the authorities until 9 am to comply with the Palestinians' demands. After that they would execute their hostages 'at once or one by one'.

The usual negotiations followed. High-ranking West German officials offered to exchange themselves for the hostages – a courageous gesture on the part of these individuals, a federal and a Bavarian minister, the Mayor of the Olympic Village, a former mayor, and the then Police Commissioner of the city of Munich. But the *fedayeen* would not accept the deal. The deadline was extended until noon. West German Chancellor Willy Brandt reportedly consulted direct with Israeli Prime Minister Golda Meir in a ten-minute telephone conversation. With predictable results. Israel's stand in matters of terrorism was well known. No deal. No deal ever, under any circumstances.

Though the Germans did not try to exert any official pressure on Israel, there is much evidence that they regarded the Israeli Government's attitude as unnecessarily and dangerously inflexible. Why couldn't they release, say, a dozen of the captured *fedayeen*? Why not let the terrorists save some face, give up their hostages, and get out of Munich? The Germans, for their part, were willing to hand over Ulrike Meinhof and Andreas Baader to them, and made a point of saying so early in the negotiations.

The talks continued. The deadline was being extended by stages until 9 pm. The terrorists had reduced their demands to one plane which was to fly them and their hostages to Cairo. There, they said, unless the Israeli Government gave up their Palestinian prisoners to them, they would execute the athletes. This, too, was a minor concession from the terrorists' original threat to shoot the athletes on the spot unless their fellow *fedayeen* were freed before they took off from Munich.

At 8 pm food was brought to the terrorists and their captives. Chancellor Brandt went on television to deplore the incident and to express his hope for a satisfactory resolution – and also to suggest that the Olympic Games should not be cancelled, which was what the Israeli Government had requested to honour the memory of the two slain athletes. In Chancellor Brandt's view, this would have amounted to a victory for the terrorists. It was certainly one way of looking at the matter – though to continue with the Olympiad, supposedly symbolizing brotherhood and peace, as if the murders were of no consequence could just as easily have been seen as a triumph for terror. The flags of all competing countries, at any rate, were ordered to be flown at half-mast by the afternoon. That is, until a delegation representing ten Arab countries protested and the Germans obediently restored their flags to the top of the poles.

At around 10.20 pm two helicopters, bound for Munich's Furstenfeldbruck airport, lifted off from a grassy enclosure near the Olympic Village. The nine hostages and the eight *fedayeen* had reached the choppers in a Volkswagen bus. Though the West German authorities, with the full concurrence of the Israeli Government, had already decided that they would not permit the terrorists to fly to Cairo with their hostages, no attempt was made to ambush the *fedayeen* during the transfer to the helicopters. In retrospect – though hindsight is always easy – this may have meant that the best opportunity was missed.

At Furstenfeldbruck airport, about fifteen miles from the

centre of Munich, events unfolded quickly. Within fifteen minutes, at around 10.35 pm, the two helicopters landed, one carrying four of the Israeli hostages, the other carrying five. The choppers touched down about a hundred yards from a 727 jet that was ostensibly being prepared to take the Arabs and their Israeli captives to Cairo. Four of the *fedayeen* got out of the helicopters to inspect the plane. Within five minutes – in poor light and from a great distance – five German sharpshooters opened fire on them.

Some of the terrorists were hit; the others returned the fire. The four German crew members of the two helicopters tried to make a run for it. Two made it. The other two were caught in the cross fire and wounded badly. The Israelis could do nothing. They were sitting, tightly bound and blindfolded, in the helicopters parked on the runway.

Perhaps surprisingly, the *fedayeen* did not kill them right away. They might have felt that this would be playing out their last card. They might have been too busy returning the sharpshooters' fire and dodging their bullets. They might even have felt a reluctance to kill nine obviously defenceless men: a kind of animal inhibition that has been known to stay the hand of the most desperate murderers. The *fedayeen* also spurned several German offers to give themselves up, even though they must have known that it would save their lives.

The exchange of fire lasted for about seventy-five minutes. At around midnight, unable to dislodge the terrorists from under the helicopters – and being limited in the fire-power they could use by the presence of the hostages – the Germans decided to launch an infantry attack under the cover of six armoured cars. Almost as soon as this attack began, one of the terrorists lobbed a hand grenade into the helicopter holding five of the Israelis. The chopper exploded into a ball of fire. Within a few seconds, two other terrorists shot and killed the remaining four hostages in the second helicopter.

Ironically, had the armoured assault been delayed for another few minutes, Zeev Friedman, Yacov Springer,

Eliezer Halfin and the gigantic Yossef Gutfreund might have survived. The four Israeli athletes had somehow managed to loosen their bonds sufficiently – there were teethmarks found on the knots of the thick ropes tying them to their seats – that they might soon have worked themselves free and surprised the two terrorists outside the helicopter. There is little doubt that the Israelis would have tried to take the *fedayeens'* weapons and liberate themselves. As for Amitzur Shapira, David Marc Berger, Andrei Spitzer, Mark Slavin and Kehat Shorr in the first helicopter, it was impossible to tell what they might have done. Their bodies were incinerated beyond recognition.

Two of the five surviving *fedayeen* continued to fight. The police and border-guard units killed one within the next fifteen minutes – the man named Essafadi or 'Issa' who was seen throwing the hand grenade into the first helicopter. At around the same time the Germans captured a badly wounded terrorist by the name of Badran. Two more, el-Denawi and 'Samir' Talafik, were also captured. They had not been hurt but pretended to be dead.

The last terrorist was a wiry, chain-smoking man named Tony who also liked to have himself referred to as 'Guevara'. Whatever human qualities he lacked, physical courage was not one of them. Tony[3] kept alternately fighting and eluding the Germans for another hour. He managed to shoot one more border guard in the neck. He was finally cornered and killed at 1.30 am. It was all over.

Next day the Olympic Games continued. That year the Soviet Union won fifty gold medals. The United States finished in second place with thirty-three.

PART I

The making of
the Agent

Chapter 1

AVNER

AVNER KNEW ROUGHLY what the letter was going to say before he tore open the brown envelope. At least, he knew who it came from and why. For such things, he could always rely on his sixth sense.

It was just as well, because his first five senses were only average. His vision, fine for everyday life, would have been only marginal for the really glamorous occupations of his dreams: fighter pilot, champion skeetshooter. His hearing was not exceptional. Nor would his touch have made him a master mechanic. But his sixth sense was something else.

Brown envelopes, like the one he was holding in his hand, tended to be standard Israeli Government issue. But the Government, even the army, would have had some marking on the outside – say, the department of such and such – while this envelope had none.

The letter itself was maybe five lines, typed on an old Hebrew typewriter that seemed to balk at the symbol for *m*. The writer suggested that if Avner was interested in a job, 'you ⊟ight wish to ⊟eet ⊟e on the corner of Frish⊟an and Dizengoff Street in Tel Aviv.' It gave the time and the name of a café, and a phone number Avner could call in case he wasn't interested or found the hour inconvenient. It was signed, 'yours sincerely, ⊵oshe Yohanan', a name that meant nothing to Avner.

It was early May, 1969, and Avner was a young man of twenty-two in good health. A *sabra*, or native-born Israeli, he had just finished his army service in a very elite unit. He had fought in the Six Day War, like everyone, and held the rank of Captain in the reserve – as had everyone who served in his particular unit. The commandos.

'Right on,' he said to himself now, and went upstairs to take a shower.

These two things – taking a shower in the middle of the day and saying 'right on' in actual English were essential Avner. To go no further, how many young men in the army would bother fixing up an empty orange crate, some string and an old bucket for a portable shower? Then strapping it to a tank, while all the other guys were laughing their heads off, and taking it along on desert manoeuvres? In addition to that other orange crate with a neat hole carved in the middle for a home-made Johnny-on-the-spot. In the Negev desert. But as far as Avner was concerned, he wasn't going to squat there on the sand like a monkey with the shit-bugs crawling up his backside.

Not that neatness was such a big deal, but he happened to be a neat person and he was not ashamed of it. If he was the only soldier in the entire Israeli army who on the day he was demobilized turned in his original mess kit in exactly the same spotless condition in which it had been issued to him four years earlier, well, what of it?

This was something of an exaggeration, no doubt, but to exaggerate was also essential Avner. Which touched upon the other thing. Up to this point, Avner had never been to the United States. But Avner's mother had always claimed that his first word as a baby – and that was in 1947, almost a year before Israel became a country – was not 'Mummy' or 'Daddy' but 'America'. This may have been just a story, but it sounded right. It certainly sounded like Avner. By the time he was old enough to run along the empty, sunbaked streets of Rehovot to catch an afternoon movie, America had become his whole inner life, his fantasy. Lana Turner. John Wayne. Rita Hayworth.

It was at the movies that Avner picked up his first words of English – or rather, American – a language he continued speaking, like many Israelis, with great enthusiasm if no particular accuracy. And unlike English at school, American in the movies was something you could taste and touch. You could make it your own and become a different person through it. Okay, mister, this is the FBI.

Not that Avner gave these things too much thought anymore. Who could afford to waste time worrying about childhood fantasies, when facing the major decisions of a young man? He had now quit the army. They had asked him, begged him, cajoled him to stay, but no. Four years was enough. Okay, but now what? Get a job? Marry Shoshana? Maybe try some kind of university?

Avner came out of the shower, cool, clean, tanned to the bone, and took a quick glance in the mirror before wrapping himself in a towel. He resembled his father – though not exactly. For that he'd have to be bigger. Blonder, though what Father had gone through had changed and aged him unbelievably. Now his hair was almost white, his muscle turned to fat, and his spirits – well, he had good days, bad days. Father must have had something to do with the brown envelope lying on the bathroom stool. Not directly, Avner was convinced of that. Father would never speak to *them* about him. On the contrary, he'd stop them if he knew. 'My son you can't have,' he'd say to them. 'Over my dead body.'

But Avner wasn't even going to tell him about the letter. He'd say no to them on his own. Just as he had to the people from *Aman*[1] a couple of months ago. 'If you won't stay on the active list in the army, fine,' they had said to him, 'but what about military intelligence?' No. No, thank you.

And he would say no to Moshe Whoever in the brown envelope. He would go to the meeting, though. He had to be in Tel Aviv on Monday anyway, to pick up Shoshana. Why not take a look at them, hear what they had to say? What harm could it do?

Avner had had his application now with *El Al*, the national airline, for two months. Everybody had said it was impossible to get in, but he had put in his papers through an aunt who knew somebody who had a close friend in the head office. There was no hope of making flight crew, of course; he'd never pass all the science tests. Besides, flight crews came from the air force. But working for *El Al* was still working for an airline. Even working as a steward or in one of their offices. There might be a chance to travel, to get out of Israel briefly once again, to catch another glimpse of the marvellous world beyond. Or, who knows, meet up with a couple of old buddies from basic training who had gone into the air force. They might be flying *El Al* by now. They might let Avner try a landing or at least a takeoff one day.

Sitting on the toilet lid, wrapped in a towel, Avner made a perfect landing with a Boeing 707. It was a greaser. The immense wheels of the big jet floated to the runway like a pair of feathers. No wonder. He had been practising landings in the bathroom since the age of ten.

Avner taxied the Boeing to the hangar, brushed his teeth and put on his shirt. Mother out visiting somewhere. Shoshana in Tel Aviv. Father – well, Avner supposed he could take the bus from Rehovot to Father's house, and maybe borrow the old Citroën. He'd have enough money for the bus. Money wasn't of much use on Saturday in Israel anyway. Country locked up tighter than a drum, as far as any entertainment was concerned. Unless you wanted to eat cold sandwiches in a restaurant.

But it would be nice to have the Citroën for Monday, even if it was the most ancient car in the Middle East. Picking up Shoshana in a car would beat the two of them hitchhiking. Not that she would care much. Shoshana, slender, pale, honey-blonde, with the narrow, aristocratic features of an Egyptian stone carving, only looked like royalty. Inside, a pure *sabra*. Nothing frail, nothing spoiled. Avner had used the wrong word that time he called at her parents' place for their first date. They had just met the night before at a mutual friend's house and he couldn't remember her name. His little cousin had opened the door.

'Yes?'

'Yeah, er . . . Is the Princess at home?'

It just wasn't the word to describe Shoshana, except for her looks. The Princess? The kid didn't even know what Avner was talking about and nearly slammed the door in his face when, luckily, Shoshana came downstairs. Avner might not have had the nerve to knock again.

She had expected him to take her to a movie, but he had to get back to his unit the same night. He had just been accepted and he wasn't going to start off on the wrong foot, princess or no princess.

'You have to get back tonight?' she had asked him. 'All the other guys are going on Sunday.'

'Well, in my unit, it's tonight.'

'Okay, let's go for a walk.'

That was it. They went for a walk. She hadn't even turned eighteen then, but she knew enough to ask him no more questions. In Israel, when it came to the army, people didn't ask. Shoshana certainly didn't. Not once.

It was always like that, from that first date, whenever he could get a couple of days' leave. A walk, a movie, on the average once a month. Say, ten times a year. In four years, that's forty dates. Twenty walks, twenty movies. Hitchhiking on a Friday pass back to his mother's house in Rehovot, arriving at 11 pm or midnight, hi Mom, I'm home, leaning the Uzi against the wall and falling into bed. After hanging up his clothes.

But now, almost three years later, there was the future to be considered. One way was simple and would have seemed natural to most of their friends. That way was right around the hot, dusty corner where Avner now stood, waiting for the ancient rickety bus. Shoshana's uncle would lend them enough money to build a house there, on an empty lot. What could be simpler? Avner and Shoshana's friendship had stood the test of time – or the test of twenty walks and twenty movies anyway. Soon she would be a qualified teacher. He? At least he had his military service behind him. A lot of happy marriages had been built on slimmer prospects.

But they did not carry the burden of Frankfurt. The miraculous city.

Frankfurt was Avner's burden alone. Shoshana was an untainted *sabra*, four generations *sabra*, though by background she was European too. But it meant nothing to her. She had never, in her twenty-one years, smelled the lush aroma of a deep, dark fairy-tale forest after two days of rain. Snow was only a word to her, something a few lucky children might encounter for a few hours in the hills around Jerusalem on a particularly bitter winter day. But she had never seen it, nor had she ever glimpsed a town that was more than twenty years old. Unless, of course, it was older than two thousand years. Unlike Avner.

What had happened to Avner in 1959, when he was barely twelve, was so exhilarating and disturbing that it was difficult to put into words. Being far more real, it was more intense than John Wayne. It couldn't be dismissed as mere fantasy. It was also inexplicable, something his father and mother could not possibly have foreseen when they decided to take him and his younger brother Ber for a visit to his grandfather in Frankfurt.

After all, what if Avner came from European stock? He was a *sabra*, a Middle Eastern child, the first precious fruit of the great ingathering of exiles from the four corners of the earth. Why should he not be at home in Palestine? Even if his parents retained some tiny bits of nostalgia, some discomfort with the tastes and smells of the Middle East, some fleeting memories of a different heritage, why should Avner feel any? Indeed, most native-born Israeli children did not. But Avner turned out to be different.

It started out as a normal holiday. It was all being done for Avner's sake, though he couldn't have cared less about it, to begin with. America was one thing, but Germany didn't excite his imagination at all. On the contrary. Wasn't Germany the place where the Nazis were always killing the Jews? Why would Grandfather, whom Avner had never seen, want them to go there now?

34

But to his amazement, during that summer of 1959, Avner found everything he loved in life – including things he didn't even know he loved because he'd never seen them – put together in one city, laid out for his amazement as if by a conjurer! Later, back in Israel, he would try to describe Frankfurt to some of his friends but it was no use. A dream, a miracle. Words just could not convey it.

It was hard to know where to begin. Imagine a city, much bigger than Tel Aviv, where everything was clean and people did not jostle each other in the streets. Yet everything was huge and busy, with the brightest neon lights and millions of cars in the streets. Avner had never seen so many cars. Just like in America. And no unfinished buildings, no heaps of broken bricks, no mounds of earth, no open ditches with wooden planks laid across them.

They had hardly been in Frankfurt a week when Grandfather gave Avner a package. Inside there was a transistor radio. A *transistor radio*! It was not that Avner didn't know such things existed, he even remembered seeing a picture in an American magazine, but to be handed one as if it were an apple was something entirely new. In Israel, it would have been a gift for Ben-Gurion!

But the most important part of the Frankfurt miracle was the air.

It was the word Avner would still use years later to describe it. It wasn't the climate. Avner loved the climate of Israel – the sunshine, the blue skies; he loved the beach at Ashdod, even though he learned to swim only in the army. He certainly preferred being warm to being cold. So it wasn't the climate. It was the air.

For Avner, there was something about the air in Frankfurt, something crisp, clean, relaxing, healthy. Or maybe there was something absent from it, something heavy, humid, oppressive and threatening. It wasn't only in Frankfurt, as he'd discover in later years, it was in the air of other north European cities, as well, in Amsterdam, in Paris. It was in the air in London and America.

'Well, are you glad we came?' his father had asked him after a week or so in Frankfurt. 'How do you like it here?'

'I love it.'

Father only laughed, but Mother seemed to have mixed feelings about his reaction.

'Remember,' she said to Avner once, without warning and much more sharply than she usually spoke, 'that all these nice people you see in the street tried to kill your father's family, and mine.'

'Let it pass,' Father said.

'I'm just trying to remind him.'

Avner needed no reminders. There was hardly a day in Rehovot when there wasn't a lesson in school about the Holocaust, or so it seemed. But Avner still loved Frankfurt – as he would the other European cities he came to know.

On the day they were scheduled to fly back to Israel, fate intervened, demonstrating to Avner how the biggest things can depend on the smallest. If it hadn't been for the bathroom scales, Avner would never have stayed in Frankfurt for another ten months. He wouldn't have gone to school there. He wouldn't have learned to speak German like a native. He wouldn't have made friends with the rich boy, Andreas. His entire life would have taken a different turn.

The mundane fact at the time was only a big thud, and then the sight of Grandfather sitting on the floor, shaking his head and hissing like a snake in pain and surprise. He had fallen off the scales. It was only a broken ankle – but they could hardly go to the airport, leaving the old gentleman to fend for himself. Avner's parents decided to stay. The boys could attend school in Frankfurt that year. They would stay and look after Grandfather until he recovered.

Strangely, even though it was her own father, it was Avner's mother who found it hardest to make the decision. Father seemed quite happy to stay in Frankfurt. It appeared to Avner – who, of course, was ecstatic for his own reasons – that Father wouldn't have minded staying in Frankfurt for ever.

'We could just stay, you know,' Avner had overheard him say to Mother one day. By that time they had rented an apartment just around the corner from Grandfather's house. Avner had been going to school for more than a month.

'You must be out of your mind.'

'Why?' asked Father in a tone of genuine surprise. 'I have to travel anyway, and you and the kids. . . .'

'I won't even discuss it.'

And she didn't, not then, not ever. For Mother, the idea of leaving Israel even for a holiday was a venal sin. Making her home and raising her children outside of Israel – and in Germany, of all places – was simply unthinkable. In all other respects a lighthearted lady with a sense of humour – even a fondness for practical jokes, which Avner inherited from her – Mother took her patriotism seriously. Let the subject of any conversation turn to Israel, and a frozen calm would settle on her lively face, an icy certainty. Israel was a revelation, a knowledge beyond right and wrong, an assurance beyond good and evil.

Avner admired her for it.

The problem was, Avner also admired his father, and Father was strangely unlike Mother in this respect. Who could tell if he was patriotic? He'd only shrug and joke. It would be many years before Avner learnt just how far his father was willing to go for his country.

Avner had no idea what his father did for a living. He was supposed to be in the import-export business, whatever that meant, but he had no regular hours. He'd always had to travel, sometimes for months at a time, for as long as Avner could remember.

Which was another thing in Frankfurt's favour: for the year they stayed in Frankfurt Father didn't have to travel at all. He had to work, of course: meeting people in restaurants and cafés, or sometimes on street corners. Once in a while he'd even let Avner come with him in the car. They'd take a leisurely drive downtown from the quiet suburb of Eschersheim, then cruise around Kaiserstrasse or Goethe Platz until

Father had spotted the man he was supposed to meet. Then he'd park the car and, while Avner waited, he'd walk up and exchange a few words with him. Sometimes Father would hand an envelope to the man who, as Avner couldn't help noticing, would always glance around nervously before putting it into his pocket. After the third time, Avner came to expect the nervous glance. The men were all different but the glance always the same. It was kind of funny.

On one occasion he decided to ask his father about it.

'Daddy, who was that guy?'

'Never mind. Business. It's only three o'clock, you want to go to a show?'

And always they'd go to see a Hitchcock movie or sometimes a western. Always an American picture; they were Father's favourites, too. It was heaven! The only pity was it didn't happen often enough.

The one curious thing that Avner noticed about his father being a businessman was that he wasn't rich. Businessmen were supposed to be rich, weren't they? Back in Rehovot it wasn't so apparent, since nobody was rich there – at least nobody Avner knew. They didn't own a car, for instance, but nor did anyone else. Here in Frankfurt they did have a car, but so had most kids' parents. Some, like the parents of his closest friend, Andreas, had three. And it was only in Frankfurt that Avner would hear his parents talk about money, or have his father reply, with a little irritation in his voice, after Avner had pointed to some toy or gadget in a shop window:

'Sorry, chum, I can't afford it. Maybe you'll make enough money and buy it for yourself one day.'

But these were only the tiniest clouds on an otherwise spotless horizon. In spite of Mother's disapproval, Avner soon decided to give himself over to Frankfurt completely. It was winter now, and after school, he'd be off to the Siedlung Hohenblick for a sleighride or take the red streetcar down the Eschensheimer Landstrasse to the American PX store on the corner of Adickesallee. That was the other special thing about Frankfurt: the NATO headquarters made it almost like America, with all the American servicemen and their families living there just on the other side of Hugelstrasse, in the suburb called Ginnheim. American cars, clubs, radio programmes, restaurants and movies. Hot dogs and French fries! And many of their children at Avner's school.

That's how he even got himself an American girlfriend – Doris, who was blonde and popular, and impressively old – almost fourteen while Avner was barely twelve. His friend Andreas had said she'd never go out with him, but he'd forgotten about Avner's persistence, or obstinacy – how he'd never take no for an answer, even back then. He would persevere with a constant, firm, quiet insistence that worked marvels with some girls. And of course Avner was handsome and handy, acting quite a bit older than his age, and he also spoke English better than most of the German boys. So in the end the blonde American Doris sat behind him on his sleigh, and he could feel her breasts pressing softly against his back as they went sliding down the steep hill at the foot of Ludwig-Tieckstrasse. Right into the bushes. Doris got scratched so badly that she wouldn't go out with him again. Well, he *was* taking chances to impress her. It was a good lesson. If you take chances and lose, people are never impressed.

The Tel Aviv bus pulled up, screeching and clattering, raising a big cloud of hot dust. Avner got on. God, where was that Frankfurt winter now? Whatever happened to blonde Doris? Or to Andreas, for that matter, his best friend then, the boy from the wealthy family, the boy whose tall good looks and polite manners Avner had admired so much. They hadn't kept in touch. A couple of letters, a few postcards, then nothing. Not that it would have been easy to keep up a correspondence from the kibbutz.

They had come back to Israel in 1961. By that time Father was more or less out of the picture. He did come back with them, even stayed with the family for a few months in

Rehovot, but then the import-export business called him away again. Not, as before, for a month or two but for good.

Avner didn't know at the time that it would be for good. Even Father and Mother didn't know it. They knew, however, that it would be for a long time. 'I can't help it,' Father had said. 'It's the business. I'll have to be away, oh, it may be for a couple of years.'

'Where?' Avner had asked.

'Don't even ask. All over the place. It's business.'

'But,' Mother interjected, 'I have some good news for you. Your father and I pulled some strings, talked to some people. There's a great kibbutz, not far from here. They'll accept you.'

'What?' asked Avner, not believing his ears.

'They'll accept you. They'll let you go to school there. Next month.'

'If that's what you want,' Father said, looking at Mother. 'I mean if you want to go.'

'Oh, how can you say such a thing?' Mother said, before Avner had time to open his mouth. 'Of course he wants to go. It's a kibbutz, the most marvellous thing in the world for a boy. Besides, I can't cope alone with two children.'

'Well?' asked Father.

Avner was shattered. He couldn't believe that his parents were serious. It wasn't the kibbutz so much as the thought of their wanting to send him away from home. Much as he would have liked to stay in Frankfurt, he would still not have wanted to stay on alone. But now, as if it weren't bad enough that they had to come back to the clammy desolation of Rehovot, they wanted to send him away. But why? Did his mother hate him so much?

Well, he wouldn't give her the satisfaction of showing how much he hated her at that moment.

'Sure,' he said, looking at the floor. 'I don't mind.'

'Well,' said Mother, satisfied, 'that's settled, then.'

It remained an open account between Avner and his mother for a lifetime. Even though Avner had realized very

40

soon after his first shock at being sent away from home that she had meant him no harm, but was convinced that the kibbutz would be good for him. His sixth sense had registered the sincerity of her passion. He sensed her enthusiasm for the idea of the kibbutz.[2] But how could she be so wrong about *him*?

Perhaps it was up to Avner to prove his mother wrong. If he put a good face on it – no, not just a good face, but really put his heart into it, worked harder and longer than all the other boys, the real kibbutzniks! That was the answer. They would recognize it, they would be forced to write and tell his mother what an outstanding boy he was. Then she would have to come and apologize. She would have to ask him to come back to Rehovot.

It had been a good resolution, but most of it had evaporated halfway through the hot, dusty bus ride to Gedera. Not that that barren little town was the final destination. The kibbutz itself was at least another hour's ride away over unpaved roads winding along low hills, cotton fields and orange groves, toward a shimmering horizon dotted with dusty eucalyptus trees. The 90-degree heat seemed almost visible in the air. And the cattle in the pastures looked so scrawny. Were those creatures meant to be cows? But cows were the fat and friendly animals he had seen in picture books at school. Or in the well-groomed, lush countryside in Germany.

What made it worse, in a way, was that the kibbutz was all right. Avner had to admit this to himself. There was nothing wrong with the friendly handshakes, the huge dining hall, the food trolleys laden with eggs and fresh vegetables, the spotless dormitories where the children slept three or four to a room, boys and girls together. All this was fine, and more power to the people who liked it, who were at home there. But Avner could see he did not belong, just from the way the kibbutzniks would look at the German moccasins his mother had bought for him in Frankfurt. All the other boys were wearing workboots. As his mother ought to have known.

There are three things an individual can do if he finds himself an outsider but is obliged to stay someplace where he feels he does not belong. He can withdraw into himself; he can try integrating with a vengeance; he can exaggerate his own isolation and present himself as an outlaw. Avner made all three choices, often within a single day.

Withdrawing was the easiest. It wasn't a complete withdrawal, visible to the others, but more an inner numbness, a haze, in which the richest fantasies could take root in the thin topsoil of reality. At 6 am John Wayne would wake up like everybody else at the sound of the old British gunboat's horn blaring from the flagpole. He would shower quickly, then put the .38 Colt in his holster and drink some fruit juice in the big dining hall. During the two morning periods in school, before breakfast, he would cast benign glances through the window at the workers in the distant fields. They were safe. Lieutenant Colonel Wayne had a perfect contingency plan in case the Jordanians attacked from the east. At his command, tanks would emerge from underground silos behind the cowshed, but instead of a frontal attack, expected by the Jordanians, they would make a flanking move into the cotton field. There the bushes would part at the push of a button to reveal the steel netting of a temporary runway, along which the huge tanks, having sprouted the wings of fighter-bombers, would rumble majestically into the air.

The hero and protector of his people, the fastest gun in the Middle East, would enter the canning factory at two o'clock to clip chicken nails. At four he would emerge as Avner the bandit, a very bad boy who made no secret about his feelings concerning the law and order of the oppressor. He and his gang – Itzig, Yochanan and Tuvia the Yemenite – would sabotage whatever they could. Look at Moshe the Muzhik putting new light bulbs into the overhead sockets in the yard. How will he reach them? These Russian immigrants are smart, just look at him. Never mind that the ladder is too short, he's hitching the old gelding to the junk wagon and he's putting the ladder *on* it. What if that horse . . . no, that old

42

gelding will never move. Yes, it will, too, if you heat this piece of wire and stick it up its tail!

Miraculously, Avner and the gang killed no one. They didn't even hurt anybody seriously in four years. Not even when Avner demonstrated beekeeping in the classroom, bringing in an active hive 'by mistake'. Not even when they led the kibbutz's borrowed bull into the big dining hall. Not even when they locked Moshe in the refrigeration room for half a day. More miraculously, they weren't even caught.

The penalty always came, ironically, whenever Avner the bandit gave way to the third incarnation: Avner the exemplary kibbutznik, the *chaver*, the good comrade. When he'd put his name down on the billboard in the dining hall to volunteer for extra Saturday work – say, helping out the neighbouring kibbutz with the harvest – only to be turned down in front of all the other boys. Come on, Mr Moccasin, what would you do there, cut off your own finger with the scythe? We've got our reputation to consider. If you're so keen to work, clip some more chicken nails.

Because, while John Wayne might whip the Jordanians and Avner the bandit might never be caught, the truth was that Avner the kibbutznik never became anything remarkable. He just wasn't a top-notch farmer. He wasn't exactly weak or slow, even if these kids – the kids who had grown up along the irrigation ditches in the middle of nowhere, the kids he both admired and despised – were a little tougher and faster. So what? He was smarter: He spoke languages, German and English. He had seen things, hobnobbed with Americans, travelled halfway across the world. For these kibbutzniks who rejected him, going in a donkey cart to Bnei Re'em would have been a big trip.

They ought to have been impressed by Avner – he had never before had any trouble impressing other boys, even in Germany, or girls for that matter – but somehow in the kibbutz it never worked out. He had brought his transistor radio along and at first all the kids had gathered around to listen to it. But someone in the office immediately wrote to

Avner's mother to come for it because this was a kibbutz where a child couldn't have something the other children didn't have. And she came the following week and took it. Grandfather's radio!

Those kids who didn't like Avner much called him a Yekke potz. Being a Yekke was another new thing Avner had learned in the kibbutz, though he would have learned it anyway sooner or later. While growing up in Rehovot Avner assumed that all Israelis were Israelis, and that was all there was to it. Maybe there was a small degree of difference between native *sabras* like himself or the old settlers from pre-independence days like his parents, and the recent immigrants who didn't even speak Hebrew. And yes, there were some Israelis, though hardly any in Rehovot, who were *religious*, who looked and acted more like Jews in the Diaspora, Holocaust Jews, even if they had been in Israel for many generations. They wore black caftans, wide-brimmed hats and earlocks. But as for being a Yekke – belonging to some sub-group instead of being simply an Israeli – this thought had never occurred to Avner.

In the kibbutz, however, Avner learned to distinguish between different types of Israelis – in terms of their own choosing. Most of the other kids in the kibbutz were Galicianers, which to Avner translated into a vulgar, pushy, know-nothing lots of East European Jews. He, on the other hand, was a Yekke. A civilized, sophisticated *sabra* of West European roots.

The two terms – at least as Avner came to understand them – described qualities associated with spirit as much as geography. Galicia, the easternmost Polish province of the old Austro-Hungarian Empire, was the breeding ground of everything that was clannish, corrupt, smart-alecky, deceitful and low-class about Jews. Undeniably, Galicianers were also clever, resourceful and determined; Avner would readily grant them that. Often they had a marvellous sense of humour. They could personally be very brave and utterly devoted to Israel. But they would always be on the lookout for an angle. They would understand nothing about the finer things. They would cheat and lie; they would be materialistic beyond belief. They would also stick to each other like glue. They would use expressions like *le 'histader* – taking care of yourself. Or 'sharing out the dumplings'. They might not all come from Galicia, of course. But if they had these qualities, they were Galicianers.

Yekkes had come to Israel mainly from Germany or other Western countries, like Avner's parents, but wherever they had come from, their main distinction was that they had been *assimilated* Jews. They had not lived in ghettoes, in *shtetls*. They had few of the survival instincts of hunted animals, the kind of eye-for-the-main-chance nature that Jews in Galicia had had to develop to stay alive. Yekkes were polite, orderly and clean. They had books in their homes, they listened to classical music. More importantly – since some Galicianers would also read books or listen to good music – Yekkes had an idea of European civilization that was different. They expected Israel to become a kind of Scandinavia for Jews, with lots of symphony orchestras playing Beethoven and art galleries exhibiting paintings by Rembrandt.

Yekkes also had a different idea about civic virtues. In times of scarcity, they expected to have things rationed, then to line up for them in an orderly fashion. They were prepared to take orders, or to give them, but not to arrange, fix, manipulate. They were punctual, methodical, maybe just a touch pompous. In the great Yekke city of Nahariya they'd built their houses in neat, uncluttered rows. In many ways they were more Germanic than the Germans.

Avner understood that the Galicianers' sense of clannishness was not directed against him personally. They would take care of their own – and in practical terms 'their own' meant other East European Jews, mainly Polish and perhaps Russian. They were the magic circle. The best jobs, the best opportunities went to them. The leadership of the kibbutz belonged to them – in perpetuity, as it seemed. When it came to the question of whose son would be sent to medical school, for instance, never mind grades, never mind ability. On the face of it it would be very democratic, of course; the entire kibbutz would vote on such questions at a general meeting, but you could bet your last *shekel* that the fellow who got the chance would be a Galicianer.

Whether it was accurate or not, this idea – or realization, as he would have called it – came to Avner in the kibbutz. And it only became stronger. It followed him through his days in the army and beyond. In Israel the Galicianers had their hands on the helm, and other Jews – German, Dutch or American – would get to do very little steering. Oriental Jews, next to nothing, if the Galicianers could help it.

The fact that Avner came to hold this belief did not mean that he would brood, sulk, or feel ill done by. On the contrary. It meant only one thing. He would compete. He would beat the Galicianers at their own game. He would become so unique, so extraordinary, so unbeatable at something that in the end he would come out on top. Ahead of Galicianers, kibbutzniks, you name it. No matter how smart, strong, determined, unscrupulous they might be. He'd win.

Maybe by following in the footsteps of his father.

Because there was a way for an outsider to win acceptance in Israel. Even for a Yekke potz, who at heart felt more at home in Frankfurt. This way was to become a hero. A real hero, a Har-Zion,[3] a boy on the burning deck. A little Dutch boy with his finger in the dyke.

It was during his last year in the kibbutz, sometime in 1964, that Avner found out that his father was a secret agent. Nobody actually told him. If anyone had, the word would not have been 'agent'. His mother might have said, well, your father is working for the Government. Most likely people would have said, unconsciously lowering their voices a little, oh he's doing something, you know, for the Mossad.

Translated, that Hebrew word meant only 'institute'. There could be a *mossad* for biochemical research or a *mossad* for traffic safety. But used by itself, Mossad meant one thing: the relatively small, closely guarded, highly respected, very secret organization that is regarded as absolutely vital for Israel's security.

There were quite a few kids in Avner's dormitory who had parents serving Israeli society on the outside in one capacity or another. Two or three were high-ranking officers in the army. One man was a member of the Knesset, Israel's parliament. And there was one boy whose father was known to be 'doing something' for the Mossad.

One day, when Avner happened to be standing with this boy outside the main gate, the boy's father drew up in a car. He had come for a visit the way Avner had hoped his own father might come sooner or later. The man got out of the car and, by way of greeting, shook his offspring by the shoulders and pummelled him on the back a few times. Then his eyes fell on Avner.

'This is Avner,' said his son.

'Glad to know you,' said the visitor, crushing Avner's hand in his own. 'You a new boy? What's your father's name?'

Avner told him.

'So,' said the man, looking at Avner with a spark of interest. 'You're his son. Well! Say hello for me when you see him.'

'You know my father?' Avner asked, a little surprised.

'Do I *know* him?' the man said, steering his son through the gate.

That was it, nothing more. Avner's head was whirling. Of course, the mere fact that a man who was said to be doing something for the Mossad knew his father was a long way from proving that Avner's father was an agent. But there was something about the way the man looked at him, that spark of recognition in his eyes, a glance that said 'one of us'. Avner's sixth sense left no doubt about it in his mind. Couple it with the 'import-export' business, the constant travelling, and the men on the street corners in Frankfurt with their nervous glances. It was only putting two and two together.

To double-check, all Avner had to do was to ask his mother, casually, the next time he saw her alone.

'Mom, is Dad a spy?'

'Have you taken leave of your senses?' said Mother, her eyes darting around.

'Come on, Mom, don't give me that. You think I'm five? There are people in the kibbutz who know Father. You want me to start asking around?'

That would have been the worst breach of etiquette, as Avner knew only too well.

'Listen, this is not the movies,' Mother said. 'We have no spies around here. Your father's in the import-export business and sometimes he works for the Government. You understand?'

'Sure, Mom.'

'Well, then,' said Mother primly.

So it was true. Avner was so excited that he could actually hear his heart beating faster. It was not only that he could now excuse his father for letting Mother send him away from home. This was important, but not everything. It was that Avner from this moment felt himself equal or even superior to the biggest kibbutznik. A chicken nail-clipping Yekke potz, equal to the biggest Galicianer wheel!

But Avner could never talk about it to anyone.

It is possible that he might have talked about it to Father, had he ever come to visit. During those four years at the kibbutz, before the army, Avner saw him only twice, both times when he was back at Rehovot for a brief holiday and Father was there too. Just for a day or two, because then he'd have to be flying out of Israel again on business. On those occasions Avner wouldn't even be alone with him, what with Mother fussing around and baby brother making a nuisance of himself, a lucky six-year-old in full flight.

But had Father come to the kibbutz where the two of them could have been alone, Avner might have talked to him. It was a pity that Father never came.

Now, in 1969, he could see his father any time. Or what was left of his father, a broken sick man. Now that Avner was twenty-two, a Captain in the reserves, with four years of service behind him in a crack unit. Now that it didn't matter any more, he could see him.

But it did still matter.

Hot after the bus ride from Rehovot, itching to take a shower again, Avner swung open the gate. Father was right there, lying in the deck chair in the garden, asleep. There were a couple of flies on the rim of the glass of orange juice beside him. It was incredibly hot. Father had put on some more weight and was breathing heavily in his sleep.

'Hi, Dad.'

'Hmm?' His father opened his eyes, first one, then the other. It was a habit from way back. Avner had never seen another person do it.

'How are you feeling?'

'Hmm.'

'You need the Citroën for the weekend? Can I take it?'

'No, take it, take it.' His father coughed, cleared his throat, and pulled himself straighter in the chair. 'What time is it?'

Avner glanced at his watch. 'About three,' he said.

'Is Wilma here?' Father asked.

'I don't know, I just got here. I haven't seen her.'

Wilma was the new wife, the one Father had married abroad, after divorcing Mother. In a way it must have been part of the business, Avner supposed, the 'import-export' business. They never talked about it. The official story was that Father had married her and then she worked with him, but it could just as easily have been the other way around. In any case, they arrested him and sent him to jail.

When he was eventually released, maybe a year and a half ago, shortly after the Six Day War, Father brought Wilma back with him to Israel. Avner rather liked and admired her. A great lady, and she wasn't even Jewish.

'How is your mother?' Father asked.

'Fine.'

Avner pulled out the brown envelope and handed it to his father. Whatever he might say about it, Avner would make up his own mind anyway.

Father put on his glasses to read the letter. It was only four lines, so he must have read it at least twice, since he said nothing for a full minute. Even his heavy breathing stopped. The only sound in the garden was of flies buzzing round the orange juice.

Then Father folded the letter and handed it back to him.

'You don't even answer it,' he said to Avner.

Hearing his father speak in this tone put Avner's back up. 'Why?' he asked. 'I can't just ignore it.'

'Don't be stupid,' said Father. 'Are you forcing me to call them? They'll have you over my dead body.'

Avner almost smiled, in spite of himself. Father had used the exact words Avner would have sworn he'd use. Well, that was it, then.

'You call them,' he said to his father, 'and I'll never speak to you again. Just let me handle it.'

'You'll say no.'

'Sure I'll say no,' said Avner. 'I just wanted to show it to you, that's all.'

'This is not a joke,' his father said. 'You may think it is, but it's not. Look at me.'

Avner looked at his father. 'Come on, Dad,' he said, putting his arm around the older man's shoulder. 'Don't worry. They may have done it to you, but let me tell you something. They'll *never* do it to me.'

Avner would always remember that conversation, down to the last detail. The heat, the deck chair, the look on Father's face, the flies diving for the orange juice. And he'd remember the drive in the old Citroën afterwards, picking up Shoshana, necking, holding hands, going to a movie, without saying anything to her. And the next day, the Monday, going to the café near the corner of Frishman and Dizengoff. Ten o'clock sharp in the morning.

Moshe Yohanan turned out to be a short man of perhaps fifty, wearing a white shirt. He was reading a newspaper, and waved Avner cheerfully to a chair the minute he saw him. They shook hands firmly, and Avner ordered two scoops of mixed lemon and vanilla ice cream.

Mr Yohanan went straight to the subject. 'Listen,' he said, 'what can I tell you? I don't even know if you're the right man – we'll have to find out. But if you are your country needs you.'

Chapter 2

---◦◦◦◦---

ANDREAS

IF HIS AUNT'S FRIEND had come through with a job of any kind at *El Al*, Avner would never have rung the bell of Apartment 5 on the second floor of a nondescript building on Borochov Street. He would have said to Moshe Yohanan, 'Forget it. I'm going home. Whatever it is, it sounds too much like the army.'

The young girl who opened the door looked like she was in the army, too, even though she wore civilian clothes. But there was something unmistakable about the trim, matter-of-fact, unsmiling way in which she handed Avner a sheaf of papers, asking him to fill them out at the wooden table. Except for a couple of wooden chairs, there was no other furniture in the room.

Avner stared at the long, printed questionnaires after she disappeared behind one of the unmarked doors. Question 36: *Do you have any living relatives in the Soviet Union?* It was certainly not too late to get up and leave. Not because answering a long list of questions, some of them very personal, would have offended his libertarian instincts – that thought would not even have entered Avner's mind – but because of the bother. And, especially, because of the bother it portended. More forms, duty rosters, orders, schedules. Commands. All leaves cancelled until further notice. Report back at 0600 hours. Hadn't he had enough of that in the last four years?

Avner never disliked the army for any of the usual reasons. For instance, he didn't mind marching nearly the

whole length of Israel, at night, carrying 50 lbs of equipment.
If half the other hopefuls who were after the same commando
insignia fainted and had to be picked up by the hospital
trucks, so much the better. Because Avner didn't faint, even
though he wasn't the biggest or the strongest. He stayed on
his feet, and he also came first in the diving course, although
he'd only learnt to swim in the army. In the end it was he who
became a commando. One of maybe fifteen out of a hundred
who had tried. He wore the second most elite insignia in the
Israeli forces. After the fighter pilots.

Nor did he dislike lowering himself into the water quietly
carrying a load of magnetic mines, under actual field conditions during the Six Day War. Of course he was afraid. Only a
fool wouldn't have been, and the commandos didn't take on
fools.

What Avner disliked were makeshift showers that would
never get you clean, no matter what. Inedible food – on
Saturdays, *cold* inedible food, by courtesy of the military
rabbi. He disliked the bureaucracy. Regulations about everything under the sun that had nothing to do with security or
fighting efficiency. Leaves cancelled for no reason – at least
none that Avner could see. Assignments, based not on what
was best for the unit, but as favours, rewards or punishments.

And he hated hitchhiking back home, trying to make the
round trip in twelve hours. Wasting precious time standing
on the side of the highway waiting for a citizen to pick you up.
Well maybe this was simply the soldier's lot, even the hero's
lot, everywhere in the world. Avner did not dispute that. He
just wanted no part of it, at least not indefinitely. Dying for
the country, any time. Hitchhiking, no way.

Avner hesitated before filling out the form for one additional reason. In spite of what he had said to his father in the
garden – *they may have done it to you, but they'll never do it to
me* – it was only words, carrying more bravado than conviction. Avner wasn't sure what 'they' might do to him. In fact
he wasn't so sure what they had done to his father.

Saying little was perhaps the habit of a lifetime, but his

53

father never really explained anything to Avner after he came back to Israel with his new wife. Marrying a new wife wasn't really bigamy, as he jokingly remarked to Avner, because the person who used to be married to his mother was not the same person who had married Wilma abroad. One of the two persons had no legal existence. Yes, he had been jailed for spying for Israel. At least, those were the charges. And the truth? Well, what do *you* think?

The relationship between Avner's father and mother, to all appearances, remained cordial. His father would come almost every week to the old house in Rehovot and spend long hours talking with Mother in the kitchen. When Avner once remarked to his mother, 'You see him more often these days than when you used to live together,' she only shrugged.

'You think the most important thing is how you *feel*?' she replied. 'Let me tell you, it isn't.'

Avner took this to mean that, for his mother, submitting without rancour to a broken marriage was just another patriotic duty. Why shouldn't she be able to sacrifice her status as a married woman, when others had sacrificed their lives for Israel? She would never say a bad word about Father, or even about Wilma, though she would avoid talking about her. In her rare references Wilma would become just another thing 'your poor father had to go through', like being captured and jailed. It was an attitude Avner understood, but he could not help feeling a little contemptuous towards her. In a way he would have preferred her to scream and yell.

Father's attitude was different. He made no secret about being bitter, though he would only hint at why. 'When it's over, it's over,' he'd say. 'Nothing's too good while they need you. You're a big shot. When it's over, they'll spit on you.'

Then he would add: 'If you're lucky enough and still around for them to spit on.'

And Avner might ask, 'What do you mean, *they*? Who?'

But Father wouldn't reply, only repeat after a few moments of silence: 'Treat you like an orange. Squeeze you dry, then throw you away.'

Though Father would add no details, in a way it was clear enough. The old man – and he wasn't even old, he was in his mid-fifties – had become a broken man after his return to Israel. Broken by something more than his interrogation, his imprisonment. 'If you look at it one way, two, three years in jail is very bad,' as he explained to Avner once, 'but if you look at it another way, it's nothing. I could do it standing on my head.' Nor was it just ill health, though he'd keep seeing doctors, or money worries, though he was pretty broke. He had no job, only a small pension of some kind. He had tried his hand at a couple of businesses after his return but they had both failed.

The real problem lay deeper.

'They let you pick up the rubies,' he remarked to Avner one day. 'They let you hold them in your hand, play with them a little. All these rubies will be yours, they say, if you do this or that. Then one more thing, then another.

'Then when the time comes for you to knock on the door, collect your rubies, they say, pardon me? What rubies? What did you say your name was?'

'What do you mean?' Avner remembered asking, but his father only shook his head.

Father was telling the truth, Avner did not doubt that. But maybe it was only the truth for him. It wouldn't have to be the truth for everybody else. If it had to be the truth for everybody and for all time, what would there be left for the little Dutch boy? A boy who had no head for buying and selling, no head for chemistry and maths? Would he have to stay outside the magic circle forever? Clip chicken nails for a lifetime? Never see Frankfurt again? Hitchhike with Shoshana to the beach at Ashdod once a week? Wait for his aunt's friend to come through with a job at *El Al*? Stay a good Yekke potz, in spite of his years in the kibbutz, his record in the army? Do nothing for himself, or for his country, ever, just because things did not work out for Father? Maybe it wasn't 'their' fault, anyway, or not entirely. Maybe Father somehow got hold of the wrong end of the stick.

Avner filled out the questionnaires on the wooden table, and handed them back to the girl. In a few minutes she ushered him through the unmarked door into another room, where a middle-aged man sat behind a plain wooden desk. There was a metal filing cabinet in the room, and one more un-upholstered chair, on castors, for visitors. The man looked Avner in the eye and shook his hand firmly before waving him to the chair.

'How are you?'

'Fine,' Avner replied, a little surprised.

'And how's your father?'

'Fine, thanks.'

'Good, good,' said the man. 'And how is . . .' here he mentioned the name of the commander of Avner's unit in the army. The names of officers in crack units, such as Avner's, were not public knowledge. Avner wasn't quite sure why the man made a point of mentioning it – to establish a rapport perhaps, or to double-check Avner's legitimacy, or maybe to prove his own. In any case, he decided to reply matter-of-factly.

'He was fine, the last time I saw him.'

'That was in, let's see . . . February, wasn't it?' the other asked casually, pulling a thin file folder closer to him on the desk.

'In March,' Avner replied, not betraying in his voice that he was either irritated or impressed. In truth he was a little of both. Irritated by the game, and impressed by the man's carefulness. They must have triple-checked him before the interview, yet they were still not taking any chances.

The man offered him a cigarette. He declined, noting that the other didn't take one himself. Non-smokers don't usually offer cigarettes, so this must have been another check to see if Avner was the person he was supposed to be. A smoker impersonating him might have unthinkingly accepted a cigarette. Oh, smart! The temptation was almost irresistible –

this was Avner the bandit – to pretend to change his mind and ask for a smoke, just to see how the other would react. But he didn't.

He listened, instead, as the man explained that, if Avner was accepted, the job would be a very interesting one. At this stage he couldn't even say if they'd invite Avner to take the entrance tests. If he passed them, he'd have to undergo a long period of training. He might flunk out, along with about half of the candidates. But if he made it all the way, the job would be fascinating.

The job would be fascinating and very important for the country. It would also mean security and a pension; it would mean insurance, medical benefits and even a dental plan. There might be a lot of exciting travel abroad. He'd find that the organization was like a pyramid, the man said, with a lot of people at the bottom and a few, very few, at the top. It would depend on him, and him alone, how far he might go.

'Look at me, for instance,' he said, warming to his subject. 'I started out at the bottom myself. I had to go through a lot before I got to where I am today.'

Yeah, and where are you today? Avner thought to himself. A fifty-year-old schmuck, sitting on a wooden chair in a sweltering little room, interviewing raw recruits. Very exciting.

But so what? This threadbare apartment on Borochov Street was clearly the bottom. The organization might still be very exciting at the top. The top, where John Wayne was heading, might be a different story altogether.

After that interview, however, the glamorous people with the dental plan did not follow up. No phone calls, no letters. But Avner's mind was far from being made up and letting things slide suited his mood best, that summer in 1969.

'You haven't heard from that guy at *El Al*?' Shoshana had asked him after one of their weekends together.

'Mmm-mm.' Avner shook his head.

'He's in no hurry, is he?'

While Shoshana wasn't exactly in a hurry herself, it was

more than just an idle question. By the fall, she'd be a qualified teacher. They didn't talk about marriage in so many words, but it was pretty much understood. They loved each other. While Avner was in the army, four years, Shoshana had gone out with no one else. If they got married, her parents would help them set up. After all, they couldn't go on seeing each other in an old borrowed car forever.

'It's not just *El Al*,' Avner said to her. 'I've got another thing on the back burner.'

'Really? What?'

'Oh, government job. Pretty good, if it comes through. I'm just waiting to hear.'

He told her nothing more about the job, and Shoshana didn't ask. It was one of the things Avner liked about her, along with her honey-blonde hair, her narrow princess features, her porcelain-blue eyes. But even they were not the main thing. The main thing was, as always, beyond the power of words.

The telegram came to his mother's house more than a month later. Avner had all but forgotten about the whole thing by then. He was, if anything, more eager to hear from *El Al*. Even a steward, a purser, any kind of flight crew, would mean travelling. Those people in Borochov Street, who could tell?

The apartment where the telegram instructed him to go this time was not in Borochov Street, though it was just as threadbare. There was a different unsmiling girl asking him to wait, before leading him into a different inner room through a different unmarked door. The wooden desk seemed to be the same, though the man sitting behind it was different, too.

'This is about the position we have been discussing with you,' the man said. 'Are you still interested?'

'Yes.'

'Good.' The man took a calendar from in front of him, circled a date, and showed it to Avner. Then he slipped a piece of paper across the desk.

'On that date report to this address. Memorize it now, then give it back to me. Okay? Don't have anyone drive you. Take public transport. At that place, you will take a short course. There will be some tests while you're taking it. At the end of the course, there will be an examination. The rest, we'll see.'

Avner hesitated.

'Do you have any questions?'

'Well – am I employed?' Avner asked. 'Do I get a salary?'

'You're accepted for training,' the man said. 'Yes, of course you'll be paid. You'll be on temporary staff with a public utilities company, I'm not sure which one. They'll send you a cheque through the mail every week. Anything else?'

'No, that's fine.' Avner stood up. 'Thanks.'

'Good luck.' The man extended his hand to him, without getting up from behind the desk. The unsmiling girl was already opening the door. In another minute the new Mossad agent was standing in the street.

Later that day, driving with Shoshana in the Citroën, acting on an impulse he could not explain, Avner asked her if she would consider emigrating from Israel. The question came out of the blue and it surprised even him. He had no idea what made him put such a question to her.

Shoshana looked at him uncomprehendingly.

'But where to?' she asked.

'I don't know. Germany, anywhere. Maybe America.'

'You mean, for good?'

'Of course for good. That's what emigrating means.'

Shoshana began to laugh, a little uneasily perhaps.

'You can't be serious,' she said. 'I start teaching in the fall. My parents . . . This is . . . this is our home.' She looked at Avner then added: 'Don't worry. You'll get a good job sooner or later.'

Avner said nothing. He didn't tell Shoshana that he already had a job, maybe even a good job. But, without knowing the expression *déjà vu*, he was overcome by the feeling that he had lived through this moment before. It was strange. He could not explain it to himself at all. That night, though, before falling asleep, the moment drifted through his memory. Of course! It was his father asking Mother if she would like to stay in Frankfurt, and her reply, 'You must be out of your mind.'

Though his appointment for the training course wasn't for two more weeks, Avner couldn't resist borrowing the Citroën again the next day and setting out – alone, of course – towards the Hakirya district of Tel Aviv. From there he took the Haifa road north.

He was intrigued. He knew the area well, but he couldn't remember any building that could conceivably be a Mossad training centre. He drove a couple of times up and down the street, seeing nothing but young people who looked like students walking or sitting in groups on porous concrete steps. The street ended in an open field, surrounded by a plain link fence, in the middle of which, sunk into the ground, there was a mushroom-shaped cupola. It looked like a generator plant, or perhaps the top of an air-raid shelter. Avner began to wonder if this was itself a test. Clearly, he couldn't start asking questions, yet he could hardly go back to the man behind the wooden desk and tell him that he couldn't find the place. In fact, there would probably be no one to go back to. Both the Borochov Street apartment and the other one looked as if they had been rented for only a short time.

An idea came to him. Turning the Citroën around again, he drove to where the street joined a main thoroughfare, then pulled into an empty parking spot and waited. The traffic was not too heavy, but within the next hour several cars turned in and out of the street. Avner looked at them but let them pass. He was waiting for a signal from his sixth sense. Something that would allow him to put two and two together.

The car that he was waiting for did not arrive until another hour had passed. There was nothing to distinguish it from any of the other cars, and the two men in it could have been young professors or teaching associates at a university. But Avner knew they weren't. He couldn't say how he knew, except, as he'd later explain it, a government car is a government car, even in Israel.

Avner let the old Citroën keep a respectful distance from the government car as he followed it down the winding side street. It was making for the chain-link fence at the end of the open field but, before reaching it, it suddenly turned right, straight, as it seemed, into the side of the last building. Except, instead of hitting a concrete wall, it continued driving down what Avner now saw was a narrow driveway between the building and the fence. At the end of the driveway there was a sliding electric door, which opened slowly, allowing the car to enter. Beyond the door, the road dipped sharply. The government car disappeared underneath the open field.

Avner did not follow it, but two weeks later he reported for training. There were twelve other people in his group, all men, most of them Avner's age, though two or three were considerably older. One looked as if he might be over forty. Avner didn't know any of the men, though it seemed to him that he had seen two or three of the younger ones before, perhaps in the army, at joint manoeuvres. There were none from his old unit.

One week later he received his first pay cheque in the mail. It was sent by the Tel Aviv waterworks to his home address, his mother's house in Rehovot, and it was for 120 Israeli pounds. A modest sum. One would have to think twice before starting a family on it. But, for the time being, it made no difference. Money, as such, was never on Avner's mind; in those days even less than later. All that concerned him was a way of life that would mean excitement, travel, doing what he enjoyed doing, and maybe cutting a good figure at the same time.

Most of the instructors were young, perhaps four or five years older than Avner. An exception was the firearms instructor, a man named Dave. He had the face of a sixty-year-old, though his body was as lean and tough as that of a twenty-five-year-old athlete. Avner had seen few men in such good shape.

Dave was an American, an ex-Marine who had never learned to speak Hebrew properly. Avner, as well as some of the others, would have been glad to speak with him in English, but Dave insisted on Hebrew. 'You learn goddamn gun, I learn goddamn language,' he said to Avner in a gritty drawl like Popeye, when they first met. For some reason, it gave a curious authority to his voice. 'We both learn good, hey?'

'Okay by me,' Avner replied.

'You army, eh?' asked the older man. 'They teach you shoot in army?'

'They gave us some guns, anyway,' Avner replied cautiously.

'You do me big favour,' said Dave seriously. 'You do *yourself* big favour. You forget you ever seen gun before. You see gun, here, for first time.'

In a way, it was true. Though he had learned a great deal about the use of side arms in the army – he had been in a commando unit, after all – Avner had never seen an approach to shooting like old Popeye's before. To begin with, he was a fanatic about physical conditioning. Not strength, but coordination. 'You think weightlifter shoot good?' Dave would ask. 'Weightlifter shoot goddamn shit. You want to throw rocks at enemy, you go lift weight. You want to shoot him, you jump rope. Like little girl.'

And for at least an hour every day the whole group of them would be doing just that in the underground gym. A dozen would-be secret service agents skipping rope like twelve-year-old girls. Dave seemed to have an almost mystical belief in the connection between rope jumping and the ability to use a handgun efficiently, expressed in the pithy maxim: 'You can't jump rope, you can't shoot.' Avner never doubted his word. Dave could certainly hammer a nail into the wall from twenty-five feet, firing with either hand.

But that wasn't the point, either. As Dave himself would

put it: 'You want to learn target shooting, you go join Olympic club. I teach you goddamn combat shooting.'

Combat shooting, in Dave's opinion, meant learning something about the weapon of the opponent. 'You think he like goddamn target, he wait for you?' he would ask Avner. 'He shoot you good first, maybe better than you. If you learn to shoot, and you lucky, you live long. But learn to *duck*, you live longer.'

This did not mean ducking a bullet, of course – that would be impossible – but it meant hour after hour in the classroom, learning weapon-recognition from colour charts and slides. Every type of gun the enemy might use. Because, as Dave explained, each one had a certain characteristic, and knowing what it was might save your life. 'A bullet not a goddamn horsefly, it don't follow you around. A bullet go in a straight line.' If you knew something about the other guy's weapon, you'd often have a split second to decide which direction the bullet was most likely to travel and duck the other way. 'You see he has revolver, maybe. You smart, you know *all* revolver pull right, a little, even if he's a goddamn champion. So you duck right. You not so smart, you duck left, and he got you. Right there. Like bingo.'

At which point Dave would poke a flat forefinger between Avner's eyes.

The other important thing was knowing your own weapon, of course. The day the old ex-Marine finally allowed them to hold an actual gun in their hands, Avner was surprised to see that the guns Dave distributed were small .22 calibre semi-automatic Berettas. Well, maybe they were simply used for target practice.

'No. In your job, *this* your gun. For good.'

As Dave explained it, in the special work of an agent the range and penetrating power of a firearm mattered less than its accuracy, quietness and concealability. Apparently this philosophy, and specifically the introduction of the .22 Beretta[1], had been Dave's original contribution to the armament of the Mossad field agent. Before his time Israeli agents

63

used army and police guns of much larger calibres, such as .32s, .38s or even .45s. 'They tell me: what is this twenty-two? You need big!' Dave recounted. 'I tell them: trust me. You don't need big.'

Dave had even insisted on reducing the load: the amount of explosive charge in the cartridges. As a result the small .22s had an even lower muzzle velocity and shorter range than usual. On the other hand, they made only a quiet popping noise – something like *pffm* – when they went off. They needed no silencers. They could also be fired inside a pressurized aircraft with less danger of penetrating the aluminium skin and setting off a reaction known as explosive decompression, which could literally blow a plane out of the sky, and which made the use of other guns inside a modern jet prohibitively dangerous.

'You worry, is little gun?' Dave would ask. 'You want big gun? Your enemy maybe elephant? Your enemy maybe *tank*? If your enemy tank, no gun big enough, you want bazooka. But if your enemy man, little gun enough.'

Nor did Dave have any patience with the view that a .22 had no range, which seemed to worry several of the men who had been trained in the army. But the field agent's job was different. For his job army training was worse than no training at all, as far as Dave was concerned. The army trained people to be sharpshooters, sit in a tree and pick the enemy off from a mile. The army trained soldiers to fire several rounds every time they pulled the trigger. 'Hell, you big agent in London,' Dave would say sarcastically, 'maybe you want machine pistol, Heckler and Koch, good gun, fire a bullet a second. Somebody look you crosseyed, you kill everybody in subway.'

The army – or, for that matter, the police – taught people to slam a cartridge into the breech, put on the safety catch, then advance, weapon in hand. Dave would say, forget the safety catch, it doesn't exist. It may not prevent a gun from going off accidentally – say, if you drop it – but it might prevent you from pulling the trigger one day when you need it. Instead, have no round in the breech. Have no weapon in your hand, unless you intend to shoot. Learn to pull your gun and pull back the slide on the top of the barrel that chambers the round at the same time, using both hands. Practise it a zillion times. Practise it until you can do it in your sleep, in one easy, fluid motion. And when it's in your hand, shoot. Never pull your gun without firing it. That's what your gun is for.

'You no goddamn cop,' was Dave's point. 'You agent. *Secret* agent. You pull a gun, you good for nobody, you blow your goddamn cover. You never pull your gun for warning. Please, mister, be good boy. No. You pull your gun, you shoot. And if you shoot, you kill.'

That was the main lesson, repeated again and again. Pull your gun only to shoot, and shoot only to kill. If a mugger wants your wallet, give it to him. Give him your shoe, give him your shirt. Let him punch you, insult you. But if for any reason you can't give up what he's after – kill him. Don't ever pull your gun as a threat. Don't shoot anybody in the leg. You're not a policeman: you're an agent. You're paid to avoid being detected. Before anything else, this is your job.

And if you pull the trigger, always pull it twice. Dave was nothing short of fanatical about that. It was as important as the skipping rope. It was the cornerstone of combat shooting with any gun, especially a .22. As the ex-Marine explained it, you cannot hold your hand in the same position if you pause after firing a gun. No matter how much you practise. No one can help moving his hand a little, even subconsciously. If you were on target the first time, you'll miss with your second shot if you pause.

But if you pull the trigger twice, immediately, no matter what, there will be two bullets in the target if your aim was right in the first place. If it wasn't, it doesn't matter whether you miss with two bullets or only one. If you miss, you can adjust your aim and fire two more bullets. If you have the time. But two. Always two. Every time you pull the trigger, you pull it twice.

'Remember it,' Dave would say. 'Remember it in your

sleep. Always *pffm-pffm*. Never just goddamn *pffm*. No good. It's *pffm-pffm*, even in your sleep.'

Once, years after he had finished basic training, Avner ran into Dave on Jabotinski Street in Tel Aviv. 'It's you, eh?' the old American said happily. 'How you doing? Remember *pffm-pffm*? See you don't forget it!'

Avner never did.

He wasn't a natural shot, but he'd practise and practise, in the way of a good, conscientious Yekke, until he'd get it right. He was never at the top of the group – for that one needed an eye, a sense of rhythm, that Avner simply did not have – but he was determined to go as far as sheer willpower could take him. And he did. He learned not to pull his gun too soon in combat practice – 'You think you fire intercontinental missile, maybe?' would be Dave's comment on that – but he also learned to overcome the fear of being too far and missing. 'Sure, you touch him with barrel you no miss, but enemy kick you so hard, you fall through your ass,' was how Dave would respond to that error, except he had no occasion to say it to Avner. At least, not twice.

It was the same with the other courses. Photography. Communications. Explosives – in which Avner needed less training than some of the others, because he had been through it once before, in his unit. Commandos had to know about the basics of demolition, it was part of their job. Not that Avner had the expertise to make or defuse a bomb – except perhaps a very simple one. All an ordinary man in the field needed to know was how to place, arm and activate an explosive device. On that level, it was simple stuff. Everything was prefabricated – the detonator, the transmitter, the *plastique* charge. A fistful would blow the door off a safe, but you didn't even have to be careful with it. You could drop it, hammer it, even use it to stub out your cigarette, it was so stable. All you had to learn was how to mould it – any desired shape, and it could even be painted any colour – then put in the detonator and connect the wires. Red goes to red, blue goes to blue. Simple.

Documents were much more interesting. That was the course in which Avner excelled, perhaps because it had to do with the sixth sense. Not the manufacture of forged documents – because that was expert stuff about which field agents were not expected to know a great deal – but their use and detection. This was a subtle science, always requiring a person to put two and two together. The instructor was an Argentinian Jew named Ortega.[2] As he put it, it was psychology more than anything else. You had to understand a little about papers, and a lot about people.

Before learning how to acquire and use false documents, Ortega suggested, field agents should learn how to detect forgeries. Though their actual job in the Mossad would never be counter-intelligence inside the country – another organization called *Shin Bet*[3] took care of that – the agent's job might well include counter-intelligence work outside Israel. Even more importantly, knowing the mistakes others make in the use of documents would teach them to avoid making similar errors.

For instance, Ortega would hand each of them a passport and tell them to make a small alteration on any page, such as gently erasing a notation with a razor blade and substituting another one. 'Do it on a different page, each one of you,' he'd instruct them, 'and when you hand me the passports don't tell me which page you've been working on.'

They did so, and discovered that Ortega could immediately tell which page they had attempted to doctor simply by allowing the passports to open in his upturned palms. The passports invariably opened at the page on which the would-be forgers had been working their hearts out for the last hour. It was logical enough that the binding should always bend at that point.

'But while I'm letting the passport open,' Ortega said, 'I don't look at it. I look at *you*.'

Because any passport, even an undoctored one, would probably open on some page. That in itself would be meaningless – without a flicker in the bearer's eye. And that

67

was the most you could expect, a flicker, since an enemy agent was unlikely to break down on the spot and cry. But a flicker could also be meaningless, or mean something totally unrelated to your concerns. Maybe the guy was trying to smuggle cigarettes. And that was where your sixth sense came in. You couldn't be a good agent without a sixth sense, whether you were trying to detect forged documents or pass with them.

As far as Avner was concerned, this was the beauty of the field agent's job. It required precisely the talents he had in abundance. True, abilities in such dread subjects as maths and science were sometimes required. Some of the equipment was unbelievably sophisticated, especially in communications. There were scramblers and descramblers. Transmitters that could fire an hour-long message in one single burst. Avner had a fair bit of trouble learning even the basics of encoding and decoding. One-time pads would always remain a mystery to him. And computers. His mnemonic skills were minimal and his physical coordination only fair. Even his driving was more fearless than skilled, as was his ability to speak English and German. He could grasp the whole picture quickly enough in any subject, but he had no patience for working with details.

But – and this was the point – in the Mossad there was room for people who did not have the talent of specialists. They had plenty of signals geniuses or chemistry wizards who would spend their lives sitting in a lab somewhere manufacturing invisible ink. They also needed whole-picture people. Men and women like Avner who may not have been particularly good at any one thing, but who could put two and two together.

Avner excelled at putting two and two together. At times it was as if an inner voice were whispering to him: never mind *that*, but watch out for *this*. Whether it had to do with papers or people, he could pick up the tiniest signs almost subconsciously. For instance, the Belgian passport at one of their practice sessions. He couldn't immediately tell what was wrong with it – the visas seemed genuine, the colours did not come off on his fingers when he rubbed them, there was no tell-tale thinness in the paper when held up against the light – but there was a warning bell ringing in his head. He had to make up his mind in less than thirty seconds, as if at an actual airport, whether to hold the passenger or wave him through. He looked again and, of course – the passport picture! The little metal clips holding it were properly rusted, as they should be in a two-year-old document carried in a sweaty pocket, but the tiny rust spots on the opposite page didn't match. They never did in the case of a substituted picture: it was impossible to put them back in exactly the same spot.

Avner was also good at the art of 'scanning', as being on the lookout for anything unusual was called. There was no separate course for this, because to be physically alert was regarded as a permanent requirement for any agent. Scanning simply meant using your eyeballs, somewhat like a radar beacon, to sweep your entire environment at frequent intervals. Never let your whole attention remain fixed on any one thing for more than a few seconds. In order to make this a complete, twenty-four-hour habit, instructors would lay unexpected traps for the trainees at the most unlikely times and places, including off-duty walks in the streets of Tel Aviv. They were being taught how to use all reflecting surfaces – store windows, car doors – as mirrors so as to be constantly aware of what was going on around them, but without giving away the fact that they had noticed anything.

Scanning did become a lifelong habit for most agents, and as a result Avner soon noticed something else: that it could also give the scanner away. For instance, agents rarely smiled. In fact, most of them had unusually expressionless faces. It was very difficult to be scanning with your eyes all the time without immobilizing the rest of your features. It was another bit of knowledge that Avner stored away in his subconscious for future use.

Being observant, not only of things that might immediately affect you, but of any information that might come your way, was central to the training of a field agent. This was stressed, perhaps more than anything else, during the six months Avner spent underneath the mushroom-shaped cupola. Their most frequent field trips had to do with observation. Take the bus to Haifa, sit in a hotel lobby until four in the afternoon, then come back and tell us what you saw. Omit nothing. Don't edit, don't decide what was important and what wasn't. Just report everything you remember – and remember everything.

Of course, this required memory and patience – not Avner's strongest points – but it also taught him a great deal about human nature. Often, unknown to the first trainee, there would be another trainee from a different group sitting in the hotel lobby in Haifa. If their reports were significantly different, the instructor might say to them: 'Listen, guys, why don't you go into the next room and sort this out for me.'

As a rule, the answer was simple. One of the trainees got bored or hungry during the observation period and went off in search of coffee and a sandwich. Agents were human, too ran out of cigarettes, had to go to the bathroom – yet this factor would often be left out of another agent's calculation. Some had a vivid imagination and were prone to exaggerate or even to invent. These exercises were not merely to train and test their powers of observation, but to find out certain things about them as human beings. Would they make up or embellish stories? Could they distinguish between observation and fancy? And, if caught in a discrepancy, would they admit it or try to brazen it through?

This was vital for another area of the training, an area in which Avner was at his best. This was the *planning*, putting together a make-believe operation; selecting the personnel, making up the list of material aids required. Whom to select for what function in the group – depending on their strengths, expertise, personalities – could be a key to success.

As the instructors soon noticed, Avner would pay attention to the nature and character of his fellow trainees and assign their roles in the operation accordingly. But he'd go considerably beyond the obvious. If, for instance, the imaginary mission was to enter surreptitiously an Arab embassy in Rome and destroy its communications room, Avner would make sure to request from the resident Roman agent a minute-by-minute report of the embassy's routine in every twenty-four-hour period over an entire week. Three days before the operation he would dispatch his dullest but most reliable agent to make a chart of the traffic pattern in all surrounding streets. If the fictional embassy was assumed to occupy a suite in an office highrise, Avner would assign to himself the task of posing as a West German businessman, interested in renting a suite in the same building, and thus getting access to all the floor plans. He would try to use the fewest possible people for every phase of the operation. He would never reserve the task of briefing all the agents under him in person, but would assign the most knowledgeable and meticulous man in each area to brief the others.

At the end, he would sign his plan with a bold, legible signature. He would be proud of it, and also sense that being proud of one's plan was important. Once, looking at alternate plans, the instructor held up a feeble, illegible scrawl and said sarcastically:

'Look. Here's the signature of a hero.'

As far as Avner was concerned, the instructor had a good point. The less legible a fellow's signature, the less confidence he had in his own plan. Avner resolved always to ask to see the signature of any plan sending him on a real mission. If he could read the name with no trouble, he'd have a better chance of coming back alive.

This was psychological stuff. In every area of his training what impressed Avner the most was always what he perceived as the psychology behind the information. He might not even retain the information for long, but he'd remember the psychology. With technical details, he could always ask somebody else or look them up. But the psychology was important. It would enable him to construct new information for himself.

For instance, Avner would never forget one thing the instructor said about documents – just a casual remark, but he would always remember it.

Depending on their quality, there were many kinds of false papers. They would range all the way from a permanent identity that a resident agent might use for years to a one-hour document – say, a passport stolen from a tourist in the washroom of an airport – that might get an agent across a border once, in an emergency. But, Ortega said, even more important than the quality of the document is your confidence in the source. Documents never work alone; they work in conjunction with *you*. If you do not trust your papers, or the person who gave them to you, you can downgrade a permanent identity into a one-hour passport. On the other hand, you might go a long way with a stolen driving licence if you believe in it.

There was some psychology in every area of a field agent's duties. Setting up surveillance in Paris or in Amsterdam, a young couple would attract less attention than, say, the lone man in a raincoat reading a newspaper on a café terrace. But in Sicily or in Corsica, assigning a lone man might be a better bet. Though elderly couples are the best operators of safe houses in most parts of the world, around the Sorbonne a young student couple would be less conspicuous. And when Avner was first ordered to follow the driving instructor in another car, he expected trick driving of every imaginable kind, but he did not expect the man he was tailing across Tel Aviv to drive like an old lady, signalling every turn. Until, at last, the instructor almost came to a stop near a yellow light, only to shoot across the busy intersection the moment it turned *red*. There was no way Avner could follow him without causing an accident. It was simple but impressive.

Many of the other trainees expected to learn firm rules, exact procedures. There were firm rules but flying invariably by the book could be the deadliest mistake for an agent. It was not a routine job – which was why Avner thought it suited him so well. Learning the rules without being bound by them was the secret. It was a job in which the person who could improvise and always do the unexpected would come out on top. Unlike the army, which ultimately belonged to the bureaucrats, *this* was finally a line of work tailor-made for mavericks. Or so Avner believed.

After the first six months, the training continued in the field. For some. This stage was not preceded by any formal examinations. Rather, each day's training assignment had been a test in which the instructors evaluated the would-be agent's performance. Avner had no idea who in his group had 'passed' or 'failed' because this information was never imparted to the others. Not seeing another trainee again might mean simply that he had been given a different assignment or channelled into some special area; though it could also mean that he had been found wanting and dropped from the course. There was always some gossip among the trainees about this, but no official questions or answers.

Before passing on to the field phase of his training, Avner was instructed to attend a set of special briefings, which had to do with working and reporting procedures, and contained interesting technical information but no surprises. However, one briefing was special. Avner didn't know whether to dismiss it as unimportant – in a way, it was almost comic – or to regard it as an ominous portent of the future. To his sixth sense, it felt like one of those dark problems to which his father had alluded. Avner decided to laugh about it in the end, though somewhat uneasily.

The man who gave this briefing had a fringe of white hair, like Ben-Gurion, though without anything charismatic about his features. He had a shrewd gnomelike face. His body was dwarfish too, probably under five feet, since his feet hardly reached the floor from the wooden swivel chair in which he sat behind an unbelievably cluttered desk. There were tobacco stains on his fingers. His bright eyes peered at Avner quizzically from his underneath unruly eyebrows, one of which was arched high on his forehead like a perpetual question mark. The original colour of his badly stained shirt was probably white.

He was not just a Galicianer, Avner decided. He was the grandfather of all Galicianers.

'So you're off to see the world,' the Galicianer began. 'That's very nice. Now sit down and listen to me. There are a few things I've got to tell you.

'First, don't be offended by what I'm going to say. It's nothing personal; I've never seen you in my life. What I tell you now, I tell to all the others.

'You want to know what these books are on my desk? They're accounting books. You want to know what I do with them? I sit here and I look at them because I want to know how much money you spend and why.

'I tell you this, because some of you guys think this is a luxury tour, operated by the State of Israel for your personal benefit. Now I'm here to remind you that it is not. I remind you only once; I remind everybody once. I'm not going to tell you again. What I want is *receipts.*

'I want receipts for every penny you spend on duty. If you have to take a taxi, fine, you bring me a receipt. If you have to charter a boat, fine, you bring me a receipt. If you have to breathe and it costs you money, you bring me a receipt. If you don't, it comes off your pay.

'And if you take a taxi, you'd better need to take it for the job. Because I'll ask you why you took it. When you can take the subway, take the subway. Take the bus, like everybody else. *Walk.* You spend money, if I'm not satisfied you needed it for the job, I take it off your pay. Don't misunderstand me: you need it for the job, take it. Your job's special; *you* are not. By me you're not a hero, whatever you do. You bring here Hitler in handcuffs, I'll say, where are the receipts? And was the long-distance call private, to your girlfriend? Because it comes off your pay, if it was.

'I say this because some of you guys think you're working for the Baron Rothschild. Nothing's too good for you. What can I tell you? You're not working for the Baron Rothschild. You're working for Israel. When it comes to money, you're working for me.'

The Galicianer stopped and cocked his head, peering into Avner's face.

'Please, don't hold me in suspense,' he said. 'If I haven't made myself clear, tell me.'

Avner stood up.

'You've made yourself clear,' he replied. What he thought was, what do you expect? People always judge by their own standards. This old Galicianer *ganef*[4] would probably steal everything that wasn't nailed down. Naturally he'd assume that everybody else would, too.

Except, as far as Avner was concerned, he would be wrong. Not only about Avner, but about most of the others as well. The kind of people who were interested in stealing – never mind *stealing*, even making money – did not join an outfit where one worked twenty-four hours a day for 650 Israeli pounds a month. It was nonsense.

The only formal series of examinations they had to undergo before being sent into the field were psychological tests. The higher-ups were evidently curious to know what made them tick. In spite of the constant joking – you must be crazy to do this, and so on – it was clear that most trainees considered themselves to be perfectly normal persons. Avner certainly considered himself normal. The others – well, maybe some were a little eccentric. But the point of the psychological tests seemed different. It was always Avner's gut feeling that some tests had to be finessed a bit to turn out right for him.

Not the examinations for stress. They were straightforward. In Avner's view, they also made a lot of sense. It was interesting to find out if he could do a problem in maths – at which he wasn't good at the best of times – after twenty-four hours without food or sleep. And the answer, that he not only could, but would do it a bit quicker and more accurately, was intriguing and gratifying.

But other kinds of tests had to be played by ear. Avner had to sense what it was they wanted from him and then try and give it to them, whether it coincided with what he actually felt or not. The main thing, as it seemed to him, was

75

that the Mossad was really unhappy about an agent having certain qualities. The very qualities without which he couldn't and probably wouldn't have wanted to be an agent. Crazy as it sounded.

His sixth sense told him that the Mossad would want no part of John Wayne, for instance. Or even the little Dutch boy. To be more precise, they'd want only the part that made John Wayne take on a whole town of bad guys by himself, but not the part that had made him look for a chance to do it in the first place. They hated heroes. 'If 'hated' was too strong a word, they certainly didn't like or trust them. Avner could sense that they didn't want people to *enjoy* their work beyond a certain point. They didn't even seem to want them to have very strong feelings about the enemy. One trainee, for instance, an Alexandrian Jew, was quite fanatical about the subject of the Arabs – not surprisingly, since a mob of them had killed every member of his family in 1949. But Avner could see from the glances of the instructors that the Alexandrian was not going to have a great future in the agency.

The ideal agent, from the Mossad's point of view, would be as precise, reliable and quiet as a well-made machine. On one level, he would have no more enthusiasm for his job than a computer chip or a magnetic compass. His performance would not depend on how he 'felt' about his assignment, though he shouldn't be merely stupid or insensitive. Then he would not be capable of either the inventiveness or the loyalty required for the job. He should be a passionate patriot – but without a trace of fanaticism. He should be a very clever person – but without an idea in his head. He should be a daredevil and a chartered accountant rolled into one. In short, he should combine qualities seldom if ever found in the same human being.

As far as Avner was concerned, it was a pipe dream. He wasn't like that. The other trainees he knew weren't like that, as far as he could tell. They were – well, frankly, they were all *different*, just like ordinary people in the streets of Tel Aviv. They were patriotic all right, but who wasn't in Israel, especially in 1969? Still, if that was the person the Mossad psychologists wanted him to be, he'd be that person. He'd sense the right answers. No psychological test would stand between him and the challenging life of an agent.

Besides, Avner knew that they'd never regret having chosen him, whether they liked John Wayne or not. He'd be the best damn agent they'd ever had. He'd save Israel a thousand times and nobody would even know about it. When, after many years of exemplary service, the Prime Minister would write him a private letter of thanks, he might show it to his mother. 'What did you do?' she'd exclaim, and he'd reply only, 'Oh, I can't really tell you. But it was nothing.'

Of course, in the end there was no way for Avner to know whether he had fooled the Mossad psychologists or not. Maybe they couldn't see the little Dutch boy in him, or maybe they could, but it suited them. In any case, they let him have his wings. Quite literally. His first field-training assignment was under the cover of *El Al*, the airline he might have joined if his aunt's friend had come through with a job in time. He became a sky marshal, one of the guards responsible for the onboard security of the aircraft.

Others might have thought of it as starting at the bottom. For Avner, at the time, it was a dream come true. Even if it wasn't being a pilot, it was still flying. It would have been marvellous even if the jet had simply taken off and circled the airport. But the jet did much more than that. It flew to places all over the world. Within a few months, Avner was flown at government expense to many of the major cities in Europe.

Though he was being trained as an intelligence agent, his assignments involved no intelligence gathering at first. Certainly no secret intelligence of the kind people associate with spying. As far as he could see, there was relatively little real spying in intelligence work, period. No doubt there were a few special agents infiltrating key government positions or photographing military secrets. A few master spies like the legendary Eli Cohen.[5] But most agents seemed to be doing exactly what Avner was being trained to do.

What Avner was expected to do – apart from acting as a bodyguard to the passengers and crew on board the *El Al* flight – was clandestine surveillance of public places. Naturally, he had to provide detailed reports on his observations. In Paris, for instance, he'd spend the entire day at Orly airport. He'd study the airport, making a note of entrances and exits. He'd describe in meticulous detail the type of service vehicles that could gain access to the runways. He'd note the location of surveillance cameras, and whether they appeared to be real or fake. Pretending to make home movies of some stewardesses, he'd film the change of shift at several customs and passport control points.

In Rome, London or Athens he'd spend a morning or an afternoon outside a designated embassy, Arab or Russian. He was expected to be inconspicuous, though how he achieved that was his business. In tourist cities it often made sense just to sit in a café – Avner's sixth sense had always warned him against elaborate disguises – though in London, walking a dog in the park across the street from one of the embassies suggested itself naturally. One time in Rome, he rented a truck, put out a detour sign, and proceeded to busy himself in a manhole in a side street outside the Libyan embassy.

Sometimes he was simply asked to report on the traffic in and out of the embassy and to note the licence numbers of the cars arriving or parking nearby. More frequently, however, he was instructed to memorize a face from a photograph and report on whether or not he had seen the individual entering or leaving the embassy in question. Avner was not expected to follow him, only to pass close enough to make a positive identification.

But there were times when the job for which he was being trained was not unlike a clerical job. Running errands, paying informers, or – as he later did – renting safe houses with a girl in London. They had to make sure that the houses

78

were located close to at least two major motorways, and always stocked with provisions. They pretended to be a married couple when they rented them, in various middle-class neighborhoods. The girl herself lived in London permanently at a different address, where she kept the keys of the houses they rented, as prescribed by the drill.

Avner performed all his tasks seriously and with enthusiasm. Frankly, he found them interesting. When he heard – as he did from time to time – about another trainee taking advanced courses in communications, photography or languages, evidently being prepared for high-level penetration, long-term residence, or more complex intelligence gathering, it did not even cross his mind to feel envious. Who would ever want to take advanced courses in forging documents or manufacturing bombs when he could be getting to a different great city every week? Though he would have tried his best in any advanced course they had ordered him to take, he was just as happy being left alone, sitting in a café in Rome or delivering envelopes in Paris. Avner calculated that, on his salary, it would take him a year of saving to pay for even one of the trips on which he was being sent every week.

By now he was nothing short of maniacal about receipts. He would have been anyway – he was, after all, a Yekke, a meticulous sort of person – but his encounter with the grandfather of all Galicianers in the bowels of the Mossad made him triple-check every penny of government money he spent. Not because the old Galicianer scared him but because he would not want to give the old man the satisfaction of catching him in an error or questioning an expense. Avner would rather have spent his own money on agency business, and at times he did. Then there was the time in Paris, when he accidentally dropped a cash tape for a glass of pineapple juice, and went back to hunt for it among the feet of the tourists sitting in the crowded café across from one of the Arab embassies. 'Like a complete schmuck,' he thought to himself. 'Good thing the enemy doesn't know how the Galicianers run the Mossad. They could catch Israeli agents just by looking for anyone scrambling for a five-franc receipt!'

In a way, it was the kibbutz all over again. He was a Yekke among the Galicianers, though it didn't bother him much. In fact, being a Yekke was probably an asset in the Mossad. In the kibbutz the Galicianers didn't really need him: they could do everything better themselves. But here, especially among field agents working in Europe, having the odd Yekke on board did not hurt. Smart and courageous as Galicianers were, they did not melt into the background. What with their peculiar manners and attitude, assimilation was not their strong point. Then there was the question of language. Though Israel as a whole was a multilingual society, young *sabras* of East European parents or grandparents seldom spoke foreign languages really well. Yekkes were more likely to have enough German or French to pass for natives, and would be less addicted to wearing running shoes with their business suits.[6]

Avner would always feel at home in Europe – much more at home than he ever felt in Israel. Shopping, crossing a street, ordering a meal, hailing a taxi in the European fashion suited him. The way people dressed or said hello, the way women returned his glance, coincided with his idea of how human beings should look and behave. Though he learned next to nothing about the art, architecture or history of Paris or Rome, he did know all about clean, inexpensive hotels, functional shopping and the quickest routes to the airport. He learned about tourist cafés and nightclubs. He was an expert on train timetables, post office schedules and cheap souvenirs. And most of all he relished being in a bustling, sophisticated European city. He enjoyed the *air*.

In addition – and unlike most native Israelis – Avner had a personal contact in Europe. His closest childhood friend from his Frankfurt schooldays. Andreas.

Frankly, on his first trip to Frankfurt, he did not even think of Andreas. It was not surprising: in the intervening eleven years so many other things had happened – the kibbutz, the Six Day War, the Mossad – that, except for the memory of Grandfather, Avner had been thinking of Frankfurt only in terms of landmarks. But on the flight back to Tel Aviv he remembered Andreas, and on his next trip, he looked him up in the telephone book.

Andreas wasn't listed but his parents were. They didn't seem to know – or wish to tell Avner – where he was to be found, but directed him to another friend, a young woman. She was very cold on the phone and disclaimed all knowledge of Andreas.

Avner, or his sixth sense, responded with, 'Look, maybe I made a mistake. But I'm staying at the Holiday Inn, Room 411. I'll be in Frankfurt for one more day.'

Andreas rang him around midnight. It was amazing: they could talk as if only a few days had passed since they had spoken last. They agreed to meet the following day in an outdoor café on Goethe Platz. Avner arrived ten minutes early. It was a routine precaution, even though he was only meeting a childhood friend. Be there early, run into no surprises. But he ran into a major surprise.

From where Avner was sitting, he could recognize Andreas as soon as he turned the corner, maybe thirty yards away. Not as his childhood friend, though. He recognized him as one of the photo subjects he had been given to memorize. A minor German terrorist. An ex-student, now a member of the Baader-Meinhof gang. A foot soldier, not a big wheel.

Avner watched Andreas stop, hesitate, and start to look at the faces of the men sitting on the café terrace. He let him look for a few more seconds, wanting to collect his own thoughts.

Andreas' glance came to rest on him then and he stepped closer.

'Avner?' he asked softly.

Avner had decided. He stood up, broke into a wide grin, and pummelled his friend on the back as in the old days. It was good luck, and only a fool would not have seen it.

Andreas knew him only by his childhood name, which

Avner had changed in the army, as everyone did in his unit.[7]
Nor would he have revealed his occupation to Andreas in any
case, not even to tell him that he worked as a sky marshal for
El Al. The simplest thing was to say nothing. Let Andreas
talk. Who could tell what kind of contacts he might establish
through him one day?

It was a prophetic thought. Avner had no way of knowing
how prophetic. In less than two years, it would change his
entire life.

But that afternoon, at the sidewalk café in the Goethe
Platz, they simply drank beer and reminisced. The talk was
about the old days, nothing else. Andreas offered almost no
information about himself – he had dropped out of university, he said, and was thinking of becoming a writer – and
Avner was equally vague about his job. He was doing a lot of
travelling in Europe, he explained, for an Israeli leather goods
firm. Their conversation did not touch on politics. Before saying goodbye, Andreas gave him a phone number. Avner could
always get in touch with him there, or leave a message.

From then on Avner always looked Andreas up whenever
he found himself in Frankfurt. Sometimes they'd meet for a
beer; at other times they'd only talk on the phone. The main
subject was always old times, as though they were middle-
aged men, not 23-year-olds. Avner felt that Andreas was
cautiously trying to renew their old camaraderie. Without
pushing, he let him do it. Once, when he told Andreas that
he was flying to Zürich, Andreas asked him to post a letter
for him from Switzerland.

'It's to a girl,' he explained to Avner. 'I told her I was
going to be out of town.'

Avner took the letter and posted it, without inquiring into
the contents or investigating the address. It was a favour: a
letter of credit with Andreas on which he might collect one
day. He had decided right after their first meeting – though
not without some hesitation – that he would not report his
contact to the Mossad. It wasn't a question of conflicting
loyalties. It was something his father had said.

His father had found out about his new employment when Avner had barely begun his training. He didn't ask him how he knew – Father's old contacts in the Mossad might have told him or he might simply have put two and two together. 'How do you like the waterworks?' he asked Avner one day. Then he added, without waiting for an answer: 'You're stupid. But it's your life.'

'Is that your best advice?' Avner asked. His father shook his head.

'You wouldn't take my best advice,' he replied, 'so there's no point giving it to you again. But I'll give you my second-best advice. Once you're in, work your ass off. Fly by the book. Be the blue-eyed boy. But don't show them your whole hand. Always have one card up your sleeve.'

So Avner decided to say nothing about Andreas. It was safe enough. If anyone had seen them together – and recognized Andreas – he was simply a childhood friend whom Avner failed to associate with a smudgy Mossad photograph of a Baader-Meinhof terrorist. Negligent perhaps, but nothing else. A small risk for a potential joker in his pocket.

The next two years in Avner's life passed quickly and uneventfully. He continued enjoying his work, and his superiors seemed satisfied with his performance. He remained a low-echelon agent, not involved in any real intelligence gathering, but his assignments were gradually being upgraded. Once in a while he'd be instructed to fly on a service passport to a European capital – Athens or London – where the local Mossad station chief would provide him with another passport and identity, say that of a West German businessman. He would then use this passport to fly to another city, like Zürich or Frankfurt. There he would meet an Israeli agent working in an Arab country – generally an Oriental Jew – whom it would be Avner's assignment to brief or debrief. As a rule, agents working in Arab countries under assumed Arab identities were not brought back to Israel for routine briefings. This was to minimize the risk of the agent being seen by Arab agents, either in Israel or in Europe, as he was boarding an aircraft bound for Israel. The intelligence services of most powers operated this way. They would exchange three-quarters of all their secret information in the great tourist capitals of the world.

Avner developed a somewhat cynical theory about this. For brief, surreptitious meetings Birmingham would have been as good a place as London, Nancy as good as Paris. But – spies were human too. Who'd want to spend a week in Nancy when he could spend it in Paris? Avner certainly didn't object to the practice. It was one of the perks that went with the job.

Many of Avner's assignments during that period involved defensive operations against terrorism, either directly or indirectly. The current cycle of international, and especially anti-Israeli, terror that began shortly before Avner joined the Mossad in the summer of 1969 was fast becoming a regular feature of life in many countries. By the fall of 1972 there had been over twenty major incidents involving the various Palestinian terrorist organizations alone.[8]

Prior to the autumn of 1972 Palestinian terrorists concentrated their major attacks on air transport and facilities belonging to Israel as well as to various Western nations. On 21 February, 1970, forty-seven people were killed when the 'General Command' – a faction of the Popular Front for the Liberation of Palestine – bombed a Swissair jetliner taking off from Zürich. The same day an explosion damaged an Austrian plane carrying mail to Tel Aviv. These attacks came only a few days after another Palestinian terrorist group had lobbed hand grenades into an *El Al* bus at Munich airport, killing one passenger and wounding eleven more, including the well-known Israeli actress, Hannah Marron, who had to have her leg amputated. Then, between 6 and 9 September the same year, five planes were hijacked in a spectacular operation by the Popular Front for the Liberation of Palestine. Only one plane – an Amsterdam-bound *El Al* Boeing 707 – escaped when sky marshals shot a hijacker dead and captured his comrade, the female terrorist, Leila Khaled.

The terrorists flew another plane to Cairo and destroyed it, while three more were held at the old military strip of Dawson's Field in Jordan, together with 300 hostages, who were eventually released in exchange for Palestinian terrorists captured earlier in Switzerland, England, and West Germany.

Successful as this operation was, the Palestinians soon had cause to regret it. Within weeks, King Hussein of Jordan drove all of their terrorist groups out of his country, massacring a number of them in the process. This in turn led to the formation of Black September, possibly the most fanatical of Palestinian terrorist organizations.

But terrorism was invented neither by Palestinians nor in the late 1960s. The weapon of political terror may be disregarded for a few decades, only to be rediscovered by a new generation, and many otherwise respectable nations or movements have made use of it at one time or another in their history. The only new discovery made by Palestinian groups in the late 1960s was that Israel – a tough nut to crack through conventional warfare or direct guerrilla attacks on its territory – did have a soft underbelly in the West. In spite of his denials, an individual who shared this discovery was a one-time engineering student at the University of Stuttgart in West Germany, named Aba a-Raham (Yasser) Arafat. Though not officially endorsing terrorist acts outside Israel and Israeli-occupied territories, Arafat soon began making use of such acts, first through Al Fatah itself, and then chiefly through the surreptitious use of Black September, all the while publicly denying any association.

1971 saw the first attacks by Arafat's Al Fatah, directed in a try-out sabotage operation against some fuel depôts in Rotterdam, then – in revenge for King Hussein's massacre of their countrymen – against Jordanian airline and government offices in Cairo, Paris and Rome. Emboldened by Fatah's success, Black September mounted its first operations later that year. In November its gunmen assassinated Jordan's Prime Minister on the steps of the Sheraton Hotel in Cairo.

Less than three weeks later, in London, they shot and wounded the Jordanian ambassador, Zaid Rifai.

Black September terrorists were much less successful in their first attack on Israel. In May, 1972, they attempted flying a hijacked Belgian jetliner to Tel Aviv and exchanging it for the release of 317 Palestinian guerrillas held in Israeli jails. Instead, the number of jailed Palestinians rose to 319 when Israeli paratroopers stormed the plane and captured two of the Black September hijackers.

The successful operations against Israel that year continued to be carried out by the Popular Front for the Liberation of Palestine, the oldest and largest of the Palestinian groups of international terror, founded by Dr George Habash[9] and commanded at the time in its terrorist operations by Dr Wadi Haddad.[10] It was Dr Haddad who first established international links in terror. On 31 May, 1971, he sent three kamikaze killers from the Japanese Red Army to Lod Airport in Tel Aviv, where they proceeded systematically to murder people with hand grenades and assault rifles in the busy terminal. The death toll from this operation was twenty-six, with another seventy-six wounded – ironically, most of them Christian pilgrims from Puerto Rico.

Some of Avner's assignments involved quite literally hanging around European airports, trying to identify would-be terrorists before they could get on a plane bound for Israel. It was not pure guesswork, though it could be close to it. Informers would tip off the Mossad sometimes about an impending terrorist operation, but they would be vague about such details as the exact embarkation point, the intended airline, or the number and identity of the terrorists. Though terrorists were often young Arabs, in theory they could be any age or nationality. They could be male or female, or travel as a mixed group. They could also be unwitting accomplices.

Not all terrorist operations involved sabotaging or hijacking the plane itself. Some terrorists were travelling on various missions within Israel; others were going to recruit Palestinian Arabs living in the occupied territories for spy or sabotage operations.

The Mossad developed a certain profile of a likely suspect, and while few terrorists fitted it in every detail, they had some traits in common. From questioning captured terrorists, for instance, the Mossad could piece together the way a young Palestinian guerrilla would often spend the forty-eight hours immediately preceding his mission. A common tendency was to live it up, stay at the best hotels and, very frequently, have only enough money left for a one-way ticket to Israel. Most would not think of making a hotel reservation in the country they were supposedly visiting and could name no friends or relatives with whom they planned to stay. It was also a common practice to take a very circuitous route to Israel. Therefore, a one-way ticket to Tel Aviv via Paris–Rome–Athens, purchased by a young man who claimed to be a student, but was living at the most expensive hotel in Geneva and had no plans for staying anywhere in Israel, would be viewed with some suspicion.

Terrorists might also behave in other predictable ways, as people often do under stress. They usually travelled with little luggage, but tended to clutch their duffle bag or small suitcase or cradle it in their lap, rather than put it on an empty seat or on the floor in the airport lobby. They might smoke a lot and go to the washroom frequently. They were unlikely to immerse themselves in a book or magazine, though it would be usual for them to flip through the pages of one. They seemed to find it hard to concentrate. If on a hijacking operation, they travelled in groups of three or four. While waiting for departure they never sat together, but were likely to maintain eye contact with each other at very frequent intervals. (A Mossad agent who recognized one terrorist from a photograph at Schiphol airport in Amsterdam, had no trouble identifying two others simply by following the first one's nervous glances.) Terrorists also seemed to show a great preference for window seats, even when aisle seats would have made more sense from an operational point of view.

All this was quite uncertain, even though Mossad psychologists dignified it with the expression 'projected profile'. In fact, there was nothing particularly scientific about it. Some of it was common sense, but it would have been very hard to rely on it without that special feeling, that peculiar ability some people have to put two and two together. Avner himself, out of dozens of such assignments, turned in the alarm twice. On one occasion all the signs were present – but the young couple in question had nothing more deadly to hide than a large quantity of *keef*. The other occasion was paydirt: his suspect proved to be a major recruiter of terrorists on the West Bank. Even though he had a round-trip ticket, didn't smoke, never went to the washroom, and was maintaining eye contact with no one in the departure lounge. Avner could not explain what made him phone Tel Aviv and suggest they detain the man on arrival for questioning. True, he was an Arab – but so were many other passengers.

It would not have been accurate to say, though, that Avner became a specialist in anti-terrorist work. Throughout this period he was being sent from one low-level assignment to another as the need arose and this suited him. For one thing, he did not think of his assignments as low-level. For another, the work was generally abroad, which meant travelling. By the end of 1971 he had even made it to New York. The ultimate trip; a dream come true.

Avner was no longer flying as a sky marshal but he was still given security assignments from time to time. Once he took part in an operation where an East German defector – he was never told who – had to be smuggled out of West Berlin. It was a complex mission, but in the end Avner's job amounted to nothing more than driving an *El Al* catering truck from a break in the fence at the airport's perimeter to a waiting Boeing 707. He never even caught a glimpse of the fugitive. On another occasion he acted as a bodyguard to Golda Meir on an uneventful trip to Paris.

There was no longer any reason for Avner and Shoshana

not to get married. They did so in 1971, while Avner was still doing his field training. As an unmarried woman who had finished university Shoshana ran the risk of being called up for military service, and while this was not the main reason for their decision to marry, it did influence the timing. Avner, like many men, had been comfortable enough in a relationship without formal ties.

Avner had never been unfaithful to Shoshana while travelling, though not because he had no eye for other attractive women or because having affairs was against Mossad regulations. Most of the time he was simply too preoccupied and busy. Then, there was a little intangible resistance, perhaps having to do with Father. *Let's not do what Father did; let's have a normal family life.* However, the main reason why Avner resisted temptation might have been his feeling that he had nothing with which to impress women. They needed to be impressed, didn't they? And they would have been if they had only *known* what Avner was really doing for a living. But this was the last thing he could talk to them about. Some guys might be able to impress women by talking about other subjects, but Avner never could. All he'd do when meeting a gorgeous girl in those days was to stand there like a fool. It was frustrating – having an ace in your hand, and not being able to play it.

In defence, Avner developed a somewhat sour grapes attitude towards women. Whenever the other guys in a flight crew would go ape over some stunning blonde, Avner – though his eyes might be popping out – would only shrug. 'Oh, she'll do,' he'd say, 'under field conditions.'

Shoshana was different. She was beautiful, too – not stunning, perhaps, but beautiful in a quieter sort of way. And she was a *sabra*. She didn't need to be impressed. She understood Avner without words. And though she never asked questions, she no doubt had some idea of what Avner's constant travelling was about. But whenever she was asked, she'd be content to reply, 'Oh, Avner's doing something for the Government.' In Israel, it was good enough.

The wedding was a very happy affair. The photographs afterwards would show Avner with a wide grin on his face, deeply tanned, in a white blazer. Shoshana looked mysteriously demure in her long, white dress. There were neighbours, friends, even three or four of the fellows from Avner's old unit in the army. There were elaborate cakes on the long table, and many bottles of honey-coloured sweet Israeli wine. Mother was there, of course, and so was Father, charming as always in company. He came with Wilma, his new wife. Everyone was being very cordial. Mother, Father and Wilma even appeared in some of the pictures together – along with Shoshana's parents – though Mother and Wilma would always be looking in different directions.

PART II

Changing Jewish History

Chapter 3

❧❧❧❧

GOLDA MEIR

AVNER HAD BEEN IN PARIS during the Munich massacre – glued to the television like most Israelis wherever they happened to be. He flew back to Israel just as the victims were being buried. Though it was a solemn state occasion, Golda Meir, the Prime Minister, did not attend the ceremony. Her sister having just died, the official reason for her absence was her private grief, though some people in Israel suspected that she wanted to avoid being spat on or having stones thrown at her at the athletes' funeral. Though there was little reason to blame her for the tragedy, the grief and outrage of her countrymen were unprecedented.

Avner spent hardly twenty-four hours in Israel; he was sent almost immediately on a minor courier mission to New York. Normally he would have looked forward to the trip, but this time he had got caught up in the mood of national mourning.[1] For once, he felt uncomfortable in New York, surrounded by the bustling indifference of Americans. On the Friday, two weeks after the terrorist attack on the Olympic athletes, Avner was glad to be heading home.

As usual, he was laden with inexpensive souvenirs – T-shirts for Shoshana, keyrings and saltshakers for Mother and the in-laws. Even Charlie, their German shepherd pup, was getting a box of chewy milkbones from New York. Shoshana and Avner doted on him. Charlie had been a wedding present from the fellows in Avner's old unit, who had remembered him talking about his favourite childhood pet, Bobby, also a German shepherd.

It was late when the plane landed. Avner had been hoping to take Shoshana out for dinner, but you couldn't get any hot food on Friday after sunset in Israel so he wasn't too happy to see his section chief waiting for him at the airport.

'Did you have a good trip?' the section chief asked.

'Yeah, fine,' said Avner. He wasn't usually greeted by his superiors at the airport, unless one happened to be there on other business. 'Is anything the matter? I'm trying to get back home before dark.'

'Sure, that's fine,' said the section chief. 'I just came out to tell you, make no plans for tomorrow. Someone will be around to pick you up at the house at nine.'

'What's up?'

'I really don't know,' the other man replied. 'Just be ready at nine.'

Avner wasn't happy. 'Oh hell,' he said, 'I'm bone tired. It's a twelve-hour flight. I wanted to get a little sleep.'

'So, go sleep already,' said his boss. 'Who's stopping you?' That was it.

Avner had almost forgotten the conversation and was already putting his swimming trunks in a bag the next morning – Saturday was beach day in Tel Aviv – when he suddenly remembered. 'Forget it,' he said to Shoshana, 'I can't go. Dammit, it's nearly nine. Somebody's picking me up in two minutes.'

As usual, Shoshana asked no questions. She didn't even show that she was disappointed. She just stood by with the cup as Avner tried to drink his coffee and tie his shoelaces at the same time.

The downstairs bell rang at one minute after nine. Avner clattered down two flights of steps from their second-storey apartment, still buttoning his shirt. At the entrance he pulled up short, recognizing the man in the doorway; they were nodding acquaintances. The other man was a security agent, like Avner himself, except on a permanent assignment. He was chauffeur to the *memune*, the boss, General Zvi Zamir, the head of the Mossad.

Avner's first thought was that it must be some kind of mistake.

'You rang my bell?' he asked, still fumbling with the last button on his shirt. The chauffeur nodded, and held the door open for Avner. Then he followed him into the street and opened the door of the car parked by the kerb. The man sitting in the back seat was Zamir.

Avner hesitated.

'Get in, get in,' the General said, waving his hand impatiently.

Avner got into the back seat next to the head of the Mossad. His thoughts were in a jumble. He had met Zamir twice before: once when he was briefly introduced to him at a training session along with a number of other young agents, and once when they happened to share a flight to Rome. Zamir was a passenger and Avner a sky marshal. On that occasion they even exchanged a few words.

And now Zamir was sitting next to him in a car! Just like that.

At the same time, this was Israel, a small, egalitarian, informal country. Surprised as Avner was, he was not nearly as surprised as a low-ranking FBI agent would have been to find himself sitting next to J. Edgar Hoover. The social and professional distance between any two persons was simply not as great in Israel as in most other countries. They were all Jews, rowing in the same lifeboat together, doing what had to be done.

The car drove along Hamasgar Street. Then, past the Derekh Kibbutz Galuyot, it swung east on to the highway. 'We're going to Jerusalem,' said Zamir. Avner nodded. There was no point in asking questions. He'd find out soon enough what this was all about. It crossed his mind that he might have done something wrong but it would have had to be something enormously wrong for Zamir to be dealing with it in person. Avner could think of nothing like that and so he relaxed.

The highway to Jerusalem was nearly deserted that Saturday morning. The late September sun was still scorching when they started out from Tel Aviv, but within half an hour, as the car began the long climb into the hills surrounding Jerusalem, the air got perceptibly cooler. Avner always enjoyed the winding road through the thin forests of the Jerusalem hills, the rusty rocks, the gentler, drier air: its smell reminded him of crisp summer days in Europe. The highway was dotted with the wreckage of 'sandwiches' – trucks protected by homemade armour. They were the remains of convoys that had kept the supply lines open between Jerusalem and the rest of the country during the War of Independence, vehicles frequently ambushed by guerrillas as they travelled through long stretches of hostile Arab territory. Many areas of the country were filled with mementoes like that. Most Israelis were so used to them that they didn't give them a second glance, but they always had a strong effect on Avner.

Zamir seemed friendly but preoccupied. He didn't say much during the drive, except to ask Avner about his father. Avner was used to that. Father had become famous after his arrest and trial, almost as famous as Eli Cohen. There were articles written about his exploits on behalf of Israel; there was even a book. Of course, the writers knew little about his private life, not to mention his private feelings. The name under which he was publicly known was not the name he used when they had lived in Rehovot; and Avner had changed his own name in the army anyway.

'He's doing okay,' he replied to Zamir. 'His health is so-so.'

The General nodded.

'Tell him I asked,' he said to Avner. 'Tell him I'm going to drop by to see him one of these days.'

'He'd like that,' Avner said, politely. He had no idea whether his father would or not. He rather suspected that Zvi Zamir might even be among the mysterious 'them' his father talked so darkly about.

They drove the rest of the way in silence. The entire distance between Tel Aviv and Jerusalem, across the narrow waist of Israel, could be covered in about an hour of brisk driving. They did it in less than an hour that Saturday. It was not yet 10 am, Avner remembered, when they pulled up in front of a building on the outskirts of the city.

Avner thought he knew where they were – though he could hardly believe it. First General Zamir, and now this. He glanced at the *memune* questioningly, but he was already getting out of the car, beckoning Avner to follow him. A policeman was standing outside the gate, swinging it wide as they approached.

He followed the General in a daze. The apartment, the living room were very nice in an old-fashioned sort of way, though not luxurious. Avner had absolutely no doubt about where they were, yet he refused to give in to the knowledge until he saw the pictures on the wall. Of herself. Cutting some ribbons. Bowing at Nehru. Standing beside Ben-Gurion.

Golda Meir came into the living room. As she opened the door, Avner could see that she was coming from the kitchen. A little bent, wearing a housecoat, going clip-clop in her sturdy black shoes. She extended her hand to Avner.

'How are you doing?' said the Prime Minister of Israel. 'And how is your father?'

Avner had no idea what he mumbled in reply.

'Good, good,' said Golda Meir. 'I'm glad to hear it. Do you know everybody?'

Avner noticed only then that beside the bodyguard and General Zamir, there was another man in the room. He was in uniform, wearing the Israeli insignia – a slender stalk of wheat across an engineer's measuring rod – on his shoulder. Avner knew him from his army days as Major-General Ariel Sharon.[2] One of his early heroes. They shook hands.

'Will you have some tea?' asked Golda Meir. 'Coffee? Maybe some fruit?'

General Sharon and the *memune* pulled out chairs for themselves. After a second's hesitation, Avner followed suit. He couldn't for the world imagine what he was doing in Golda Meir's living room. Even his sixth sense deserted him temporarily. He watched in amazement as she went back into the kitchen, then came out again with a tray and started setting cups and saucers on the table. The bodyguard had disappeared. General Zamir and General Sharon were talking softly to each other, not offering to help. Avner got up, then sat back again, as Mrs Meir shook her head at him. He stared in fascination at her unruly grey hair, her strong, somewhat squat fingers, the old-fashioned square watch – a man's watch – on her wrist. Though he had met her once before, as a security agent on her flight to Paris, he had never really looked at her. She reminded him of his grandmother – but then, Avner supposed, Golda Meir reminded everyone of their grandmother. Especially when she started cutting up an apple and handing it out to them, slice by slice, starting with General Zamir, as if they were children.

Then the Prime Minister began to speak.

Avner couldn't decide at first to whom she was addressing her remarks. For a second he thought she was speaking to him, but she was not looking at his face. He could see, though, that she was not looking at Ariel Sharon or at General Zamir either. She seemed to raise her eyes to a point on the wall above them, as if she were speaking to someone outside, to an invisible audience somewhere beyond the room. Perhaps she was speaking to the entire city of Jerusalem, the entire country, although she never raised her voice. Perhaps she was only speaking to herself.

Avner's puzzlement grew as he listened to Golda Meir. It was not because of what she was saying. She spoke simply, movingly, powerfully, and Avner agreed with every word she said. She talked about history. She talked about how, once again, Jews were being ambushed and slaughtered all over the world, simply because they wanted a home. She talked about innocent airline passengers and crew members being murdered in Athens, in Zürich, in Lod. Just like thirty years ago, she said, Jews had been tied up, blindfolded, and massacred on German soil, while the rest of the world was busy playing volleyball. Brass bands, Olympic torches, while the Jews were carrying home coffins. The Jews were alone, as they had always been. Others, at best, were making pious noises. No one would defend them. It was up to the Jews to defend themselves.

The State of Israel existed to defend Jews, Golda Meir said, to save Jews from their enemies, to provide them with one haven in the world where they could live in peace. But even while fighting, Israel had always tried to draw a line in the past. She would not descend to the level of her enemies. She would try to observe restraint even in the defence of her children. She would try to save them while keeping her own hands clean, to save them while obeying every command of civilized conduct. Without unnecessary cruelty. Without risking a single bystander's life. Israel was one country that did not have the death penalty even for terrorists, saboteurs or spies.[3] For her own part, Golda Meir said, she had always opposed anyone who would take Israel from this path. She had vetoed any plan that would breach even a single moral commandment.

For the first time, the Prime Minister looked directly at Avner.

'I want you to know,' she said, 'that I've made a decision. The responsibility is entirely mine.'

She got up from the table.

'It's my decision,' she repeated. 'You can talk it over among yourselves.'

Golda Meir left the room.

Avner was flabbergasted. As far as he was concerned, everything Mrs Meir had said about Israel and history was absolutely true. But why would she find it necessary to say it to him? Or to Ariel Sharon, or to General Zvi Zamir? Why would the head of the Mossad bring Avner to Jerusalem on the Sabbath so that he could hear from the Prime Minister's mouth all the things that he, or most people in Israel, had always taken for granted? As for a decision, what decision? What was there for them to talk over in what she had said?

The silence was broken by General Sharon.

'As you can probably gather,' he said drily, looking at Avner, 'what is happening here is very important. I don't have to tell you. You know you wouldn't be sitting here if it was not important.'

Avner nodded, as he was clearly expected to.

'The question is,' continued Sharon, 'will you undertake a mission? An important mission, I don't have to tell you. But I will tell you that it's a dangerous mission. It will totally disrupt your life. You'll have to leave the country. You won't be back – who knows? Maybe for years.'

Avner said nothing.

Sharon glanced at Zamir, then continued. 'You won't be able to talk about it with anyone, of course,' he said. 'We might make arrangements for you to meet your wife occasionally, in another country. But you won't be able to tell her what you're doing.'

Avner was silent. For a few seconds, so were the other two. Then General Sharon spoke again.

'I only wish,' he said quietly, 'that they were asking me to do it.'

Avner came out of his daze. Most of his mind was still a blank, but some thoughts began to take on a coherent shape. A mission – of course, it had to be a mission. He ought to have guessed it. What other reason would they have for bringing a bottom-rung agent to Golda Meir's apartment? And important – of course it had to be important. But why him? And what could it possibly be?

He had to say something, so he asked the first question that came into his mind:

'Would I be doing it alone?'

The *memune* spoke for the first time. 'No,' he said. 'But that's not relevant now. What's your answer? Are you volunteering?'

'I'll have to . . .' Avner began, '. . . I'll have to think about it. What if I tell you in a week?'

He had no idea what made him hesitate. Maybe it was his sixth sense. It certainly wasn't the danger. Avner still didn't care about that, not even at twenty-five, not even after four years in the army, the Six Day War, the assignments abroad. So why was he hesitating? Shoshana – Shoshana was in fact pregnant, which Avner had learned a few months earlier. She was such a slim creature, in her fifth month it hardly showed on her. But it wasn't Shoshana. There he was, in Golda Meir's apartment, being asked by the head of the Mossad to go on a mission – and he was hesitating!

General Zamir shook his head.

'You have one day,' he said. 'Think it over. Anybody who can't make up his mind in one day can't ever make it up.'

General Sharon extended his hand.

'You probably won't see me again,' he said to Avner, 'so . . . let me wish you good luck.' He looked into Avner's eyes. 'Good luck whatever you decide.'

If he could only ask them questions! But he knew he couldn't. Would it be a mission like Eli Cohen's? Like his father's? Would it mean becoming a 'mole', assuming another identity? Would it . . .?

Golda Meir came back into the room. Avner's mind turned blank again.

'Well, how are you doing?' she asked. 'Is everything settled?'

'It's settled,' said Zamir curtly. Then he added: 'We'll know by tomorrow, but . . . it's settled.'

In spite of his own confusion, Avner noted a glance between the *memune* and the Prime Minister, a little shake of Golda's head, as if she were saying, 'I told you, it's not so easy,' and the General's glance replying, 'Don't worry, this one or another, we'll do it!' But it could have been his imagination.

Golda Meir – and this wasn't Avner's imagination – stepped closer and put her arm around him, walking him slowly out of the room, speaking as they were going along the hallway. 'Say hello to your father for me,' Golda said, 'and to your wife – what is her name again? – to Shoshana . . . I really wish you good luck.' And as she shook hands with him at the door she added: 'Remember this day. What we are doing is changing Jewish history. Remember, because you are part of it.'

Avner did not attempt to reply. He was dazzled, he was awed, he was impressed but he also longed to know what she was talking about. He hoped the fixed grin on his face wasn't too foolish. He looked on as Golda Meir shook hands with the *memune* and General Sharon, then disappeared behind the door.

General Zamir's cool voice interrupted the spell. 'Naturally you understand,' he said, 'that you say nothing about this meeting to your father. Or to your wife, or to anyone else. Whatever you decide. What happened in here concerns only the Prime Minister and the three of us.' He paused. 'All right, wait for me in the car,' he said. 'I've got a couple of other things to discuss.'

Avner waited in the car. He could still not quite believe what was happening. In modern times agents do not expect to receive a request directly from a head of State, in Israel or anywhere else. In older societies rulers might have addressed their subjects directly if the matter was significant enough, but such contacts are almost unthinkable in today's complex and impersonally organized communities.

In all likelihood – though this is necessarily speculation, and Avner had no way of knowing it at the time – Golda Meir chose, or was advised to choose, such an unusual approach to underline the extent to which the request would be unusual. She herself may have felt – and certainly succeeded in making Avner feel – that he was going to be asked to do something no Israeli soldier had ever been asked to do before.

One reason for this might have been the ambivalence Israelis have always felt about any covert action of violence. True, Israel had engaged in isolated acts of counter-terror, deception and destabilization long before the Lod and Munich massacres. In 1956 for instance, after Egypt had inspired the first *fedayeen* incursions into Israel, parcel bombs had killed Lieutenant Colonel Hafez and Colonel

Mustapha, two Egyptian intelligence officers in charge of *fedayeen* terror. But such operations have always appeared far more controversial for Israel than for other powers. Great powers – not only the Soviet Union, but even the United States and Great Britain – have always had a certain acceptance of the use of force in the national interest: a tradition Israel has never fully shared. The agent who is 'licensed to kill' would not have found ready acceptance in Israeli (or Jewish) folklore.

The second reason for Golda Meir's presence – though Avner would not have known it either at the time – might have been internal Mossad politics. By the fall of 1972 General Zamir was under something of a cloud for being unable to prevent such terrorist attacks as Lod and Munich. Military intelligence specialist General Aharon Yariv was being appointed as 'Special Assistant for Terrorist Affairs,' reportedly taking away some of the *memune*'s control over his organization. Yariv was said to be a personal favourite of Golda Meir.[4] Her presence at the meeting might have been on his recommendation – or General Zamir might have insisted on it himself, either to involve the Prime Minister, or to demonstrate to her the efforts he was making, as head of the Mossad, to counter terrorism, a most acute threat and one that, in the fall of 1972, was sapping the nation's morale.

From the window Avner could still see Sharon and Zamir standing outside the gate, talking quietly but with animated gestures. He took a deep breath and tried to relax. Counting up to a hundred seemed the best thing. Slowly. Thinking about nothing.

He was at eighty-seven when General Zamir got into the car. General Sharon had disappeared. 'I'm staying in Jerusalem for the day,' the *memune* said. 'The driver will drop me off, then take you back to Tel Aviv. Tomorrow . . .' he glanced at his watch, '. . . tomorrow at noon, report to my office.'

Avner looked at his own watch. It was twelve noon. General Zamir was giving him exactly twenty-four hours.

He didn't really need it any more. He knew already what he was going to say.

Still, as they pulled up to the kerb in Tel Aviv, he couldn't help wondering if the passers-by would notice him opening the door of the big, chauffeur-driven Dodge. And if they did, would they recognize that he was getting out of General Zvi Zamir's official car? It might have been an unworthy thought for someone about to play a part in changing Jewish history, but there it was. At that moment it happened to be the only thought in Avner's mind.

Chapter 4

———— ❧ ————

EPHRAIM

ABOUT TEN DAYS LATER, in the afternoon of 25 September, 1972, Avner was sitting on a bed in a modest hotel room in Geneva. The Hotel du Midi, respectable and discreet, had a pink and white façade overlooking the place Chevclu in the centre of the elegant shopping district. Through his window Avner could catch a glimpse of the sombre buildings in the business section on the opposite bank of the Rhône, whose narrow neck widened into magnificent Lake Geneva a few hundred yards further to the east.

The Swiss city was like a glass house: people staying in it were careful never to throw stones. The out-of-bounds rule was seldom violated. By mutual, unspoken agreement Geneva had become an orderly place in which the forces of international disorder could plot, regroup and recuperate.

Shifting his glance into the room, Avner's eyes came to rest on four men who were looking back at him in a relaxed, confident way. They were waiting for him to speak.

Only a week ago Avner did not know that these men existed. Now they were his partners – his team. He was their leader. He was – though he could still hardly believe it – in charge of their mission.

Until that mission was completed, these four strangers were expected to be closer to him than any other human being had ever been. Closer than his mother or his father. Closer than Shoshana. Closer than his oldest friends; closer even than his *chaverim* in his army unit. He would have to trust them with his life. They would have to trust him with theirs.

In the space of ten days, more significant events had crowded into Avner's life than in all his previous years combined. His life had changed from one moment to the next, though not entirely unbidden. After all, he had put himself in line for something like this by every one of his choices since his commando days in the army. Still, from the moment Golda Meir had wished him luck, Avner felt totally out of control. It wasn't that he was frightened. He simply noted, with an almost clinical detachment, that he had finally done it. He had slipped overboard. He was in the water, and the tide was taking him out to sea. Like it or not, there wasn't a thing he could do. Swimming against the tide was clearly pointless.

When he had reported to General Zamir in Tel Aviv on the dot of noon that day after the meeting in Golda Meir's apartment, the *memune* seemed cool and almost uninterested. 'Yes?' he asked Avner, looking up from his desk.

'I'm volunteering,' Avner said.

The General nodded. He nodded in a distant, matter-of-fact way, as though he had heard the only response possible. Avner wasn't surprised – people in Israel did not jump up and down whenever someone volunteered for unusual or hazardous duty – but he was, nevertheless, deflated.

'Wait outside for a minute,' said the General. 'I want you to meet someone.'

The man to whom Avner was introduced about half an hour later was tall and somewhat professorial. He was middle-aged, with prematurely greying hair and stooping shoulders. There was a mournful cast to his mouth, though his dark eyes were lively. He was pleasant. More than that, from the minute they first shook hands he had a knack of talking to Avner as if they had known each other for years. He did not exactly inspire any feelings of kinship in Avner – he was clearly another Galicianer – but Avner liked him.

'Call me Ephraim,' he said to Avner. 'I'm going to be your case officer. Listen, we're all just feeling our way through this. You must have a lot of questions, and I may not have all the answers yet. You'll have to be patient. Umm . . . have you eaten? Why don't we start with some lunch?'

They had lunch, and afterwards went for a long walk along the beach. Ephraim talked.

Later it occurred to Avner that even though Ephraim had told him within the first five minutes what his mission was to be, he did not really understand it for about two more days. He understood it in one sense, but in a deeper, more fundamental sense, he did not.

When Ephraim said, 'We have decided to put together a team to destroy the terrorists in Europe,' Avner nodded in full agreement. It was about time. He was even a little relieved that the mission for which he had volunteered was not turning out to be a lonely spying assignment, like his father's, involving endless preparatory work in languages and cryptography. A team – that was just fine. It was pretty much like his army unit. Europe – well, that was perfect too. As for the word 'destroy' – *lehashmid* in Hebrew – it was a natural word to use. It was a normal army word, a word used in briefings a thousand times. It could mean a raid, a reconnaissance in strength, the blowing up of a radar installation, a supply depôt, a communication centre. It was a commando word. It might mean a surprise attack, the capture of a few prisoners. It was not a word to shock or surprise a one-time soldier from a special unit.

'Anyway, before we talk about this,' Ephraim told him, 'let's talk about procedure.'

The procedure involved Avner's explaining to Shoshana that he would not be home for a few days, then reporting to an address in downtown Tel Aviv. There, in a downstairs apartment – the upper floors were occupied by a clothing firm – he stayed alone with Ephraim for forty-eight hours. Once in a while Ephraim would leave for an hour or two, during which time another man would stay with Avner – 'to keep you company,' as Ephraim put it. The man wasn't much company though, since he never said a word: he was clearly there

107

to see that Avner did not leave or use a phone while being briefed.

Avner's first major mission for the Mossad required his resigning from the Mossad. The first 'contract' Ephraim asked him to sign did not outline any tasks for the contracting parties to perform, but simply listed all the things the two parties would contract not to do. The Mossad would not employ the party of the second part. It would not give him benefits, or pension, or legal aid. It would not acknowledge in any way that he was working for it. It would provide him with no consular assistance or medical help. As for Avner, he would forever discharge the party of the first part from any claims. He would not seek its assistance or hold it responsible for any of his actions or their consequences. He would not reveal that he was in its employment – or that he had contracted not to reveal it.

'Do you understand what this says?' Ephraim would ask Avner whenever he shoved a new piece of paper under his nose. 'Read it. I don't want you to sign anything you haven't read.'

Avner would nod and sign though it flitted through his mind once or twice that, contrary to his father's advice, he was not keeping any cards up his sleeve. But what should he do, ask for a lawyer? After Golda Meir had put her arm around him and said that he was part of Jewish history?

Also, whatever one might say about Galicianers, they would not leave a comrade in the lurch. In that sense Avner had complete trust in his compatriots – even in those he would otherwise not have trusted as far as he could throw them. In spite of all the *le'histader*, all the looking out for themselves. No matter how busy they might be sharing out the dumplings, if a comrade were in trouble they'd move heaven and earth to rescue him. They would cheat, lie, flatter, threaten, and ultimately they would kill or die rather than leave a comrade in the hands of the enemy. Contract or no contract. Look at Eli Cohen, what Israel did to save his life, when other countries would simply have disowned him, as most other countries did once an agent's cover had been blown. While Israel even risked the lives of some commandos just to get Cohen's body back from Syria.[1] That was one thing Avner felt he did not have to worry about.

He said as much to Ephraim, who smiled wryly.

'No, but let's worry about your live body, for the time being,' he said to Avner. 'Sign this. You're just saying goodbye to your dental plan.'

'Goodbye,' said Avner and he signed.

When the paperwork was complete, Ephraim handed him a cheque for slightly under two thousand Israeli pounds. It represented a refund of Avner's contribution to the government pension plan during the three years of his employment. 'Congratulations,' said Ephraim. 'You're a free man. I'm serious,' he added, 'because if at any point you change your mind while we're discussing this in here, and you tell me you don't feel like doing it, fine. Until you leave here, you're free to change your mind.'

'And after I leave here?' Avner asked.

Ephraim looked at him and laughed. 'I'm glad you have a sense of humour,' he said.

The idea behind the mission, as Ephraim started explaining it, was to cut off terrorism at its source. Unlike armies, which were extensions of their countries as a whole, terrorist movements, pervasive as they seemed, could be reduced to a few identifiable sources. The whole point about them was that they involved relatively few people who were utterly dependent on a handful of organizers and leaders. They were underground. They had to operate from mobile bases behind enemy lines. Secrecy and invisibility might have been their strength, but were also their weakness. Unlike regular military forces, they had no life or power of their own. They had to be artificially supplied through a few clandestine channels with everything they needed for survival: money, weapons, papers, hideouts, training, recruits. With a single lifeline severed, a whole network of them would wither.

'Terrorism is a monster,' Ephraim said, 'but luckily it has

only about a dozen heads. We may be able to cut them off, one by one.'

'Can't it grow new ones?' Avner asked.

Ephraim smiled, and looked at his fingernails. 'I'm sure it can,' he said, 'but look at it this way. It takes time. A terrorist is a fanatic. A top terrorist is a skilled and clever fanatic. Most people are not fanatics; and most fanatics are neither skilled nor clever. If you eliminate one top terrorist, it may take a year or two for another to emerge. The old network has gone to pieces in the meantime; it may take the new guy another year to rebuild it. While he's doing it, he has to show his hand. We may be able to identify and eliminate him, too, before he can do much harm.

'Meanwhile, you have saved hundreds of innocent lives. Isn't it worth it? Also, the best terrorist is only like a match. He needs a powder keg before he can make a big bang. Well, right now the world is like a powder keg; I don't have to tell you In a year or two, who knows?'

Ephraim stopped talking. He looked up from his finger-nails and held out his hand for Avner to see.

'Look,' he said. 'Look at my nails. Maybe it's time to cut them. Are you going to tell me, why bother, they'll only grow out again?'

'You're right,' Avner said.

'Anyway,' said Ephraim, 'that's philosophy and we're not here for that. We're here for operation. I'm not saying, don't ask me any questions. If you have a question, ask. But for now, let me talk operation for a few minutes.'

They talked operation. The Mossad had given the matter much consideration, Ephraim said, and decided that the best way to proceed was with a small, self-contained group. One that could survive on its own in Europe for months or even years. A team that would not depend on Israel for any support. A team that was composed of experts in various fields – weapons, explosives, logistics, documents – and would therefore not have to rely on any of the Mossad's usual sources. This was not only to keep them at arm's length –

though this was a factor, as Ephraim freely admitted – but also for their own safety. Agents were usually detected at times when they had to 'touch base' with the headquarters that supplied their instructions, weapons, documents. But a team that was able to generate its own papers, find its own weapons, build up its own network of informers; a team whose members would never have to go near an embassy, a resident agent, a source of contact used for other Mossad work or even a dead-letter drop; a team that would never have to send a signal or a dispatch through any channel of communication – such a team would be close to invulnerable. It would be like a team of terrorists but with infinitely more strength. It might even patch into the terrorists' own networks for its needs and supplies. Ideally, it would. Why not? Kill two birds with one stone. There were many terrorist groups, one knowing very little about the other, but all needing safe houses, passports and explosives. To become like one of them would be the ideal cover.

'We don't need communication,' Ephraim said. 'What do I know when the *mechablim*, the terrorists, blow up a plane? I read about it the next day in *Le Monde* or in *Corriere della Sera*. Maybe even the *New York Times*, if there are Americans on board. So now, when I open *Le Monde*, I see that a *mechabel* is blown up. What else do I need to know?'

The longer Ephraim talked, the more interested and enthusiastic Avner became. This was big. This was the real thing. He could organize *this*. With such a mission, he could show them his mettle. But he was careful to reveal none of his enthusiasm to Ephraim. A poker face. Remember the psychological tests. They don't want a happy-go-lucky guy, coming on with the big hero stuff. It was better to look thoughtful, even gloomy.

It was just as well. Because, at this point, Avner still did not understand what the mission was really about. He did – but he did not. Understanding came only when, after a short break for lunch, Ephraim told him to start asking questions.

'This team,' said Avner, 'do I put it together?'

'No. We have already selected the men.'

'When can I meet them?'

Ephraim smiled. '*Shvoye*,' he said in Arabic, 'patience, everything in good time. They're . . . they're not in the country yet.'

For some reason, Avner's sixth sense told him that Ephraim was not telling the truth about this, but it didn't seem to matter. 'All right, what are they experts in? One guy is explosives?'

'Right,' Ephraim said.

'Another is documents?'

'Uh-hmm.'

'Then one or two for the job itself,' Avner continued, noting that Ephraim was wrinkling his eyebrows in puzzlement. 'Well – the hit, I mean. Push the button.'

'What do you mean, push the button?'

It was Avner's turn to be puzzled. 'I mean a specialist in – you know, pulling the trigger. A guy trained to do the – the actual hit.'

Ephraim looked at Avner, as it seemed, in utter amazement.

'A *specialist* in pulling a trigger?' he asked slowly. 'You mean . . . you don't know how to pull a trigger? Four years in the army, you've never learned to pull a trigger?'

Avner was silent.

'*Trained* to do a hit?' Ephraim continued. 'Who's trained for that? You know a place in Israel they train people for it? It's news to me. How do you train people to do a hit, anyway? Practise on dogs first, then say to them, see that old guy crossing Dizengoff Street, now you go ahead and shoot him?'

Avner said nothing.

'We train people to use a gun,' said Ephraim after a pause. 'We train soldiers to do commando work, to plant a bomb, to use a knife, anything. The way you have been trained. But we don't train anybody to do a *hit*. We have no experts in that.'

Avner cleared his throat. 'I see,' he said, then stopped. 'I asked only because . . . ' he started saying, then stopped again. Ephraim was leaning back in his chair, looking at him. Whether he was pretending or not, he seemed to be as puzzled as Avner.

Finally Avner found his voice. Never mind if he was being naïve; never mind if he should have expected it. The fact was, he did not. Was that why they had chosen him? He was going to get to the bottom of it, once and for all.

'Let me get one thing straight,' he said, his voice hardening. 'Why me?'

'Why you what?' asked Ephraim, a little impatiently.

'Why did you select me?'

'Why, what's wrong with you?' Ephraim asked.

'There's nothing wrong with me,' said Avner. 'I know Europe, I'm a good organizer, I . . . I think I can finish what I start. But why me? I've never done this kind of thing before.'

'Who has?' Ephraim leaned forward, his voice becoming gentler. 'Don't misunderstand me; if you don't want to do it, say so. Nobody's forcing you . . . But who should we have selected? All we have is guys like you. Young, trained, good condition, good record, speaking languages . . . If you want to know, it's no big secret, maybe nobody selected you. Maybe it was a computer. We put in some questions, it gave us some names.

'So, what do you expect us to ask the computer? Give us all the bank robbers in the country, all the maniacs, the *ganef*s, the psychopathic killers? We're going to ask criminals to save Israel, because all our Mr Nice Guys are too squeamish?'

The computer. It could have been true. It made sense. When you thought about it, it made perfect sense. Yet . . .

'Listen,' said Ephraim, 'I know it's not easy. Don't for a minute think I don't know . . . Let's talk about it for a few seconds now, so we don't have to talk about it again.

'Did you know Yossef Gutfreund, the wrestling referee they killed in Munich? Huge guy . . . as it happens, I knew him. Two daughters, ran a little shop in Jerusalem. Saved

113

about a dozen Egyptian soldiers in the Sinai who were dying of thirst . . . Doesn't matter. They trussed him up like a chicken. Head to toe, the ropes nearly cutting through him, before they shot him four times. Okay.

'Now, you see the man who ordered them to do this to Yossef. The man who gave them the guns, the instructions. You see him, I don't know, maybe having coffee in Amsterdam. He killed Yossef. There's a girl in Tel Aviv, a pretty girl, she hobbles on crutches, they nearly blew her leg off at Lod . . . and this guy ordered them to do it. He's sitting there drinking coffee, thinking about who to blow up next.

'You stand there, and you have a gun. You may tell me you don't care, you can't pull the trigger. I understand. I don't blame you. I mean it: I really don't. We shake hands, goodbye. I don't think less of you for that. It's very hard to shoot a man.

'But don't tell me about training. Don't tell me about *specialist*. If you can't do it, you can't do it. I couldn't train you in a hundred years. I wouldn't want to. I wouldn't try to convince you to do it. Why? Because it would be useless.

'But if you can do it, believe me – you can *do* it. You have all the training in the world. You have all the training you'll ever need.'

'I don't know,' said Avner. 'Maybe I can do it.' He was silent for what seemed to him a long time, then he spoke again. 'You're right,' he said. 'I can do it.'

'I know you can,' said Ephraim. 'Do you want to know something: I wasn't worried about it. You wouldn't be here if you couldn't.'

It was a good thing Ephraim wasn't worried about it, Avner thought, because *he* was. Very worried. He had never been more worried about anything in his life. His heart was beating so loud during the entire conversation, it was a miracle that Ephraim couldn't hear it. But he didn't seem to. He changed the subject to logistics. The philosophy was settled.

The following day, 20 September, Avner made his first

trip to Geneva. He took a room at the Hotel du Midi, then drove his rented car across the pont du Mont Blanc and along the quai Général Guisan. He found a parking garage around the rue du Commerce, in the city's business section, then walked to the somewhat old-fashioned building of the Union de Banques Suisses. He opened two accounts and rented a safe-deposit box. In one account he placed a nominal sum, but in the other he deposited a letter of credit for a quarter of a million dollars. Then he immediately drew fifty thousand dollars in cash and put it into his safe-deposit box.

The first account was where his salary and personal living allowance would be deposited from time to time. The amount would come to nearly three thousand dollars every month – not a princely sum perhaps, but more than twice his previous salary. Better still, he was not expected to touch it. He could look at it every time he happened to be in Geneva – watch it grow, was how Ephraim put it – because his meals, his hotel bills, his ordinary living expenses would come out of operational costs. This was one of the perks of being on a mission where he was expected to be on duty for seven days a week, twenty-four hours a day. 'That means every expense,' Ephraim had told him, 'within reason, of course. We don't pay for hookers or diamond rings. But if you need a shirt, a pair of shoes, a raincoat – buy it. Just make sure you keep the receipts.'

The operational costs were unlimited. They had to be, since no one could possibly foresee how much an informer, a trip, a document, a vehicle, or quantity of gelignite would cost. Strict accounting was never expected for operational expenses – logically enough, since one couldn't very well ask a snitch or a black-market arms dealer for a receipt. That wasn't surprising at all. Avner had always found it much more curious that the same agent who could be trusted, no questions asked, with tens of thousands of operational dollars, would be expected to submit a two-dollar receipt for an order of spaghetti with meat sauce.

The operational account would always be kept at the level

of a quarter of a million dollars. Funds would be transferred to it from various other banks at regular intervals as it was being depleted. Avner wouldn't have to concern himself with this. It would be handled by regular agents who would not even know why the account was being maintained.

The safe-deposit box served a number of purposes. First, in it the team would keep a portion of the operational funds in cash. Payments would often have to be made in cash and at a moment's notice, and it would be simpler to take it out of a deposit box than to draw it from the account every time. In some cases cash was also better than bank drafts or transfers when they needed to move sums of money into banks in other cities. It made the source of the funds far more difficult to trace.

Finally, the box was for communication. Ephraim would keep one of its two keys. He could leave a message for the team in the box or they could leave messages for him, though this was unlikely to happen often during the mission. In any case, it was to be the only means of contact with head-quarters.

After he had finished at the bank, Avner left his car in the garage and walked back to his hotel across the pont de la Machine. It wasn't strict procedure and he didn't think he was being followed, but banks were obvious places for a casual stakeout. On previous assignments he had frequented banks himself, as they were good places for spotting other agents. Avner always made a point of alternating between walking and driving, if he had the time, or entering and leaving buildings through different doors. It was a matter of being unpredictable, doing the unexpected whenever poss-ible, until it became a habit. Someone waiting to follow him in a car, for instance, would now have difficulties. The pont de la Machine is a pedestrian bridge. Whoever might be inter-ested in Avner's destination couldn't drive across it, nor could he just abandon his car on a busy street to follow him on foot.

Ephraim was doling out information to him bit by bit, saying only *shvoye*, patience, whenever he wasn't ready to answer a question. Who will be the others on the team? *Shvoye*, you'll meet them when you come back from Geneva. What if we're the wrong mixture, we can't work together? Relax, the way we selected you, you'll work together fine. What if we can't generate documents, we can't buy weapons? I've never bought any weapons before. Don't worry about it. The guys who'll be with you, they'll know. That's their training. Fine, so what do they need me for?

'They need you,' Ephraim had said. 'They need you to lead the team.'

The next day on his return to Tel Aviv he'd meet the rest of the team. What about the other unknown factor? Obviously they were not being sent after the foot soldiers, the little guys, the young *fedayeen* from the refugee camps, the left-wing students, the unbalanced girls who were somehow pressured or brainwashed into murdering and putting their own lives on the line. But who exactly were the targets? And how many? One, maybe two, were self-evident. He had brought up their names to Ephraim himself, but his case officer had only shrugged and waved his hand at him.

'*Shvoye*,' he had replied. 'All in good time. We give you two things, money and a list. The money you have. Go deposit it, then come back. Before you leave again, don't worry. You'll have the list.'

Don't worry. Easy to say. What if we get the wrong guy?

'Don't even say such a thing,' had been Ephraim's reply to that.

The following morning Avner checked out of the Hotel du Midi, after reserving a room for himself for the 25th. Then he sauntered over to the Hotel Ambassador and reserved two more rooms for the same date. He picked up his car from the garage on the other side of the river where he had left it the day before, drove back across the pont du Mont Blanc to make sure he was not being followed, then returned the car to a rental office in the city and took a taxi to the airport. About four hours later he landed in Tel Aviv.

The apartment to which he drove with Ephraim around

5 pm was on the outskirts of the city. The young, serious-looking girl who opened the door reminded Avner of the one at the Borochov Street address where he went for his first interview three years ago. She led them into another room, then closed the door behind them.

The four men in the room looked up as they entered. One put down the book he had been reading. The second uncrossed his legs and leaned forward, without actually getting up. The third stopped knocking the bowl of his pipe against a metal ashtray. The fourth, who had been standing, took a step forward.

There was a split second of silence. The four men and Avner were looking at each other.

'Well,' said Ephraim. He stopped and cleared his throat. 'Guys, I want you to meet Avner . . . Avner, this is Carl . . . this is Robert . . . Hans . . . and, of course, Steve . . .'

They shook hands. Firmly, army style. Avner had no idea what the four men were thinking. For his part, he was utterly taken aback. He was shocked. These men were *old*. The youngest-looking of them – Steve – appeared to be ten years older than Avner. Carl, the oldest, must have been over forty.

It wasn't that they might be too old for the job – Avner had no opinion on that – but that he was to be their leader. Yet they must all have been far more experienced than he. They must all have fought in the Sinai campaign. Carl looked old enough to have fought in the War of Independence. Was he supposed to be leading a team of men, some of whom could have been his father?

Would they allow him to lead them?

'OK, we haven't got all the time in the world,' said Ephraim. 'Let's sit down and go over some details. This will be our only meeting together. The next time you see each other will be on the mission, in Geneva.'

Avner was too tense to sit. He watched Carl refilling his pipe, wishing for the first time in his life that he was a smoker. Hans, Robert, Steve – they all seemed completely relaxed.

Carl was patting his pockets, concerned only with finding a match. Avner took a deep breath.

All right. Steady.

'The schedule is as follows,' Ephraim said. 'Two more days of refresher courses for everyone except Carl and Avner. That takes us up to the 24th. That will be a day off; I expect everyone to settle his personal affairs. On the 25th you pick up your service passports and go to Geneva. Choose your own routes and times individually, but get there before evening. Avner has reserved hotel rooms for you; he'll give you the details. After you've checked in and got your passports back, deposit them in a safe. While you're on the mission don't ever use them again.

'While you're doing your refresher courses,' Ephraim continued, 'Avner and Carl will look at the list of targets we have prepared. By the time you meet in Geneva they will know as much about them as we do, and they will brief you there.

'All right. We will give you the list of the *mechablim* in order of importance to us, as we see it, but the sequence in which you get them is up to you. Just find them and get them. First come, first served.

'Now it seems to me that this covers everything. After the 25th you're on your own. If you do okay, I'll read about it in the paper. If you don't – but you'll do okay. I have every confidence in you.'

Ephraim had been standing, but now he pulled up a stool and lowered himself onto it in a somewhat awkward, loose-limbed way. He took a paper napkin out of his pocket, as if he were about to blow his nose, but then he just stared at it thoughtfully, crumpled it, and put it back. The others were silent except for Carl who seemed to be having some trouble keeping his pipe going. He'd been making noises like a water buffalo, then he looked up and smiled apologetically.

Avner had no instincts about the others yet, but Carl, yes. He could bet that he'd get along with Carl. Even if he was old enough to be his father.

Ephraim was speaking again. 'There are two principles,' he said, 'that we may not have touched on yet, or not enough. They're both important. Let me just go over them.'

'First, you know the terrorists' motto: punish one, frighten a hundred. Well, how do you frighten terrorists? If you just shoot one while he's out in the open, exposed, going from A to B, it may not be enough. The others might say, "Oh, they got Ahmed while he was sticking his neck out, but me, I'll be more careful." You'll kill one but the rest will carry on as usual; they won't be scared.

'But if you get a *mechabel* when he's surrounded by his own people, when he really feels safe, when he least expects it – it's a different story. If you do it ingeniously, unexpectedly, I . . . I can't give you an example, but if you do it at an unlikely time or place, or in some unlikely way, then . . . then the others will be frightened. "Oh, the accursed Jews are smart," they'll say. "The Jews have long hands. If they could get Ahmed *there*, in such and such a *way*, they could get me." '

Avner noticed that Carl was looking at Robert while Ephraim was saying this. Robert was not looking back, but had his eyes closed, with his chin resting in his hand, as if he were deep in thought. Quickly, subconsciously, Avner's mind was putting two and two together. He knew nothing about his team yet – but Robert must be the specialist in unusual weapons, probably explosives. He and Carl must have worked together before. Good.

'The second principle,' Ephraim went on, 'is something that Avner brought up at an earlier point. What if you get the wrong guy? Or what if you get the right guy, but you get an innocent bystander as well?

'I want to make myself very clear. The answer is, you don't. It is as simple as that. You don't.

'Now there's always a risk, but you're there to minimize it. Zero risk: that's part of your job. You're not terrorists, throwing hand grenades at buses or machine-gunning people in a theatre lobby. You're not even like the regular air force,

120

bombing a target – and too bad if a couple of civilians are in the way.

'Yours is the cleanest operation there is: one person, one homicidal criminal, and no one else. If you're not one hundred per cent sure it's him – you let him go. That's all there is to it. You identify him as if he were your own brother. You let him identify himself. If you're not absolutely certain, you do nothing. You let him go.'

Ephraim stood up.

'I want you to remember this, because this is one of the few things you could do wrong on this mission. There will be eleven names on your list. If you get only three, we'll be disappointed, but you did nothing wrong.

'If you get no one, of course, the whole mission's a failure and we'll be very unhappy. But still, you will have done nothing wrong. On the other hand if you get them all but you also hurt one innocent person, you'll have done wrong. Remember this.

'Everything's a question of priorities. In this operation, this is your first priority. If he's got his girlfriend with him – you let him go. If the taxi driver's standing behind him – you let him go. I don't care if you tailed him for months and today's your first chance. You'll get him tomorrow. If you don't, you don't. You'll get the next one. Relax. You're not doing piecework, you're on salary. This mission was authorized on certain conditions. We don't want another Kanafani affair.'

Ghassan Kanafani was a Palestinian writer and spokesman for the Popular Front for the Liberation of Palestine. Five weeks after the kamikaze attack at Lod airport, Kanafani's car blew up in Beirut. According to some rumours Avner had picked up at the time, people from his old unit might have played a part in the explosion, along with the Mossad. There was some question as to whether Kanafani had any real involvement in the Lod massacre other than being an apologist for the terrorist organization and its aims. There was no question that his niece, a girl named Lamees,

121

who perished in the blast along with Kanafani, had no involvement.[2] It was the first time Avner had heard the case mentioned since. People did not like to talk about it.

Clearly Ephraim didn't like talking about it himself.

'I don't want to hear any philosophical discussions about how things like Kanafani could or could not be helped,' he said, even though no one else was about to say a word. 'At this juncture I'm not interested in anybody's views on right and wrong. I'm simply giving you the ground rules for this particular mission.'

Carl blew out a huge ring of smoke and looked at Avner. The others followed his glance. Avner felt uneasy, but the men were right. The question had to be asked because of what Ephraim had said. And since Avner was the leader, it was up to him to ask it.

'What about self-defence?' he said. 'What if a bystander pulls a gun? Or tries to arrest us?'

Ephraim grimaced.

'If, if,' he said, glaring at them. 'If you plan it well, it shouldn't happen. If it happens, well . . . what can I tell you? If a bystander pulls a gun, he's no longer a bystander, is he?'

He sat down on the stool again and pulled the crumpled napkin out of his pocket. 'Listen,' he said, speaking very softly, 'in this . . . this kind of mission, who can plan for everything? Who doesn't wish we didn't have to do any of it? I'm just setting priorities, I'm telling you what we want. The rest?' Ephraim spread his hands. 'I've no doubt you'll do the best you can. That's all we can ask.'

It was the right note. Even though Avner felt he knew exactly what Ephraim was doing – using a hard-and-soft routine, playing on them a little good-cop/bad-cop ritual all by himself – he admired him for it. He was good. He was a leader to learn from. Look how the men relaxed, easing all tension, becoming anxious to live up to everything Ephraim might expect of them.

It was a trick, Avner felt, he had better learn himself.

'All right,' Ephraim said. 'Now the way we set up the team – we've discussed that before – everybody does everything, as the need arises. Total flexibility. No one specializes in just one thing. Still, one guy obviously knows more about certain things than the others, so why don't we quickly run through our various skills for Avner. I'm sure he'd be interested.'

'Let me start,' Avner said promptly, because it was the traditional Israeli way. The leader should establish his credentials first. 'My background is army – a commando unit. I was born in Israel but went to school in Germany for a while. I'm married, no children yet.'

Ephraim nodded approvingly. 'Hans?' he said.

The man who seemed the second oldest in the group cleared his throat. He was the only one wearing a tie. He was slim, with thinning dark hair and long, bony fingers. If there was an object he resembled, it would have been a pencil. Avner was not altogether surprised to hear what his speciality was.

Hans was to be in charge of documents. Born in Germany, he had come to Israel as a young boy before the war. After his army training, he had been a businessman before joining the Mossad. His previous assignment had been in France, where his wife, an Israeli woman, also made her home with him. They had no children.

'I'll need some money for materials,' Hans said, 'and preferably a place to myself. Then I can look after the documents. Retouching stuff is easier, of course, but I can probably make them up from scratch.

'I'll need a few details from everyone for identities, but I think we can settle that later. We'll have plenty of time.'

This was important. Names and one or two other details were easy enough to memorize, but agents generally selected a basic set of data for their various identities. It wasn't just a question of remembering the age, address, or occupation of an assumed person; he also had to come from a background with which the bearer was familiar. It would have been foolish, for instance, to manufacture papers for someone showing that he was from Bilbao if he had never been there and spoke neither Spanish nor Basque. Depending on their memories, language skills and general sophistication, most experienced agents could manage between three and six permanent identities – though it was not unknown for some people to handle fifteen. For a quick emergency border crossing, of course, just about any 'twenty-four-hour' passport would do if the gender was right and the picture bore at least a superficial resemblance to the person carrying it.

'I speak German and English,' Avner said to Hans. 'You?'

'German and French.'

'Okay.' Ephraim pointed to the next man. 'Robert?'

Robert was also tall and thin, though not quite as thin as Hans. He was in his late thirties perhaps. He had calm grey eyes set wide apart and wiry light brown hair. Avner was surprised to hear that he spoke Hebrew with a noticeable English accent. As to Robert's particular skill, he had guessed correctly. Robert specialized in explosives. He had come from a family of toymakers in England, and tinkering with unusual, ingenious devices had been his hobby long before he joined the Mossad. Robert was married to a French-Jewish woman and they had several children.

'If you want it to go bang, I suppose I can put it together for you,' said Robert. 'I know where to get everything I need, but depending on what it is, we may have to work out logistics. And, of course, money.'

'Languages?' asked Avner.

'Only English, I'm afraid.' Robert smiled. 'And Hebrew, if you really press me.'

Avner smiled, along with everybody else. Robert's Hebrew was, in fact, quite fluent. 'When did you come to Israel?' Avner asked him.

'Only four years ago,' Robert replied. 'After you guys had had all the fun.'

Avner wasn't quite sure he would have described the Six Day War in quite this fashion, but he smiled and nodded. Ephraim turned to the youngest man. 'Steve?'

'Cars, chum,' said Steve. 'And how to get them from one place to another in an awful hurry.' Steve also had a very slight foreign accent, but Avner couldn't place it. He looked like a pilot, not very tall, but handsome and muscular. And cocky. He couldn't have been less than thirty-five, ten years Avner's senior, but beside him, Avner felt himself the elder. It was a feeling he didn't mind.

'Is English a good guess?' he asked him.

'Yes,' said Steve. 'And German. Also a bit of Afrikaans, though I don't suppose there will be much call for that. I'm from South Africa, originally.'

'That leaves me, I guess,' said Carl, after a glance at Ephraim. He stood up and struck the empty bowl of his pipe against his palm. 'I'm afraid I don't have any special skills. But – I've been around for a long time. I'll figure a way to make myself useful. I propose to be the handyman.'

'Sweeping?' Avner asked, respectfully. This was possibly the most dangerous – certainly the most highly exposed – part of any operation. The man who was sweeping would be the last to leave the scene of action. He would prepare the way for the others to escape, but would not make his own getaway until he had looked at the scene, found out the drift of the immediate investigation, and collected all potentially damaging evidence. It required a man whose blood was a few degrees colder than liquid air. It also took quick thinking and a great deal of experience.

Not surprisingly, Carl was the senior agent in the group, a Mossad veteran since the earliest days of the Israeli security service. Like Hans, he had been born in Germany and came to Israel as a boy. He had a Czech-Jewish wife and an adopted daughter, living in Rome, where Carl had been stationed before his assignment to the mission.

'I have German and Italian,' said Carl. 'The German is native. I'll do my best to pick up the pieces.'

125

'We'll do our best,' Avner said, 'to have some pieces for you to pick up. Glad to have you around.'

This was going to work. This was just like the army. They were great guys, far better than he could ever hope to be – but as he was talking to them the reason he had been chosen to lead the team came to him in a flash.

For a European mission, the Mossad, very sensibly, selected Europeans. All Yekkes, by God; not one Galicianer in the lot. Israeli citizens, of course, but – Avner seemed to be the only *sabra* among them. Being native-born was far from being the only thing that mattered in Israel, but it was a big plus. It was a kind of symbol, in every walk of life. It still had a special meaning for Jews, after millennia of being aliens everywhere, to be able to boast of native-borns like any other country. *Sabras* were precious.

'Just one word about chain of command,' Ephraim said, as if sensing the drift of Avner's thoughts. 'In this kind of operation, everybody depends on everybody else. You all discuss everything together it goes without saying. The leader is simply the first among equals. That, as you know, is Avner. The second among equals is Carl.' Ephraim finally decided to put the napkin to use and he blew his nose. 'Okay. Questions?'

No one had any, but as they were filing out of the room Carl glanced at Avner, then turned to Ephraim. They were the last ones inside; the others had already left. 'A matter of curiosity,' said Carl. 'You will give Avner and me a list of eleven names tomorrow. That is a fair number. Are we the only team targeted to take care of them?'

There was a little pause. 'I can't respond to that question,' said Ephraim. 'I do not know the answer.'[3]

The following day Avner and Carl received a list along with some biographical and intelligence data. They spent the entire day committing it to memory, as they would not be taking the written material with them to Geneva, though they would take available photographs to show to the others and then destroy. 'I hope your memory is better than mine,'

Avner said at one point to Carl, who only shrugged and grinned.

The identities of the eleven targets were not surprising. They were not the generals – like Arafat, Habash, or Jibril – but the top lieutenants of anti-Israeli terror. First on the list was Ali Hassan Salameh, a handsome Palestinian in his early thirties, who was generally regarded as the main architect of the massacre at Munich. Second was Abu Daoud, the explosives expert of Black September. Third was Mahmoud Hamshari, an intellectual, diplomat, and spokesman for the Palestinian cause, who at that time was not generally known to be a terrorist leader as well. The same was true of Wael Zwaiter, a poet, who was fourth on the list. Fifth, the law professor Dr Basil al-Kubaisi, was a purchaser of weapons for Dr Habash's Popular Front. Sixth, Kamal Nasser, another intellectual, was the public relations chief for Al Fatah and, by 1972, the official spokesman for the PLO. Unlike Hamshari, Zwaiter and al-Kubaisi, Nasser made no secret of his connection with terrorism. Neither did Kemal Adwan, the number seven target, who was in charge of sabotage operations for Al Fatah in Israeli-occupied lands. Number eight, Mahmoud Yussuf Najjer, known as 'Abu Yussuf', was one of the highest-ranking officials in the Palestinian movement, responsible for the liaison between Al Fatah and Black September. Number nine, the Algerian Mohammed Boudia, was an actor, theatre director, and man-about-town, well known in Paris, though by most people only as an artist and ladies' man rather than an important figure in international terror. Number ten, Hussein Abad al-Chir, was one of the PLO's main contacts with the KGB. The last man on the list, Dr Wadi Haddad, was the universally acknowledged mastermind of terrorism, second in importance only to his friend, Dr George Habash.

With the exception of two or three names, it was a list with which any Mossad agent – and many ordinary Israelis – would have been quite familiar.

Avner spent the next day with Shoshana.

It was difficult. As they were lying in bed in the afternoon – pregnancy had given Shoshana a fuller figure and firmer breasts, but otherwise it still hardly showed on her – Avner caught himself wishing that she would cry. But Shoshana was Shoshana, and she wouldn't oblige. She was running her fingers along his chest, looking at him with her porcelain-blue eyes.

'It may only be a few months,' Avner said to her. 'It may be a year. I simply can't tell you when I will be back.'

'I didn't ask,' Shoshana replied.

'I'll write as often as I can,' Avner continued. 'You won't need to worry about money.'

'I'm not worried.'

The less she objected, the more defensive Avner felt himself becoming with her and he was furious at himself for it. 'I told you this might happen,' he said. 'We've discussed it before.'

'I know.'

'Well, then, if you know,' said Avner, quite illogically becoming furious with her, 'what do you keep at me for? I can't help it.'

Shoshana laughed and held his head between her hands. Her honey-blonde hair fell forward and she blew it away from her face. 'The trouble with you,' she said, 'is that you really don't understand.' She kissed him. 'Try to make it home for the birth of your child, will you?'

'I promise,' said Avner enthusiastically. 'I give you my word.'

In truth, he had no idea whether he would be able to make it or not. The next morning, after he had showered and packed his bag, he tiptoed into the bedroom. Shoshana was still asleep, or seemed to be. Avner bent down and kissed her. They had always made it a point that she did not come with him to the airport to say goodbye.

Now, in the late afternoon of 25 September, Avner was looking through the window from behind the pink and white façade of the Hotel du Midi. He could see the first lights coming on along the quai Général Guisan on the other side of the Rhône. The lights danced and sparkled as they glanced off the rippling waves. Geneva never looked more like a glass house.

Shifting his glance, Avner's eyes came to rest on Carl, then on Hans, Robert and Steve, all looking back at him in a relaxed, confident, expectant way. Seeing them sitting there, Avner suddenly had the feeling that he had never known anyone but these four; never felt as intimate with anyone as he did with these men he was seeing for only the second time in his life. He could feel the vibration of their presence on his skin, he could guess every one of their thoughts and emotions. They were waiting for him to speak.

Avner spoke to them. He spoke easily, casually, with an occasional glance at Carl, who was puffing on his pipe, confirming what Avner was saying with a nod or correcting it with a word or a gesture. Hans doodled on a piece of paper, Robert leaned back on the chair with his eyes closed and his hands in his pockets. Steve emitted a little sharp whistle once in a while, like a twelve-year-old kid.

He became silent, though, when Avner started reeling off the names of the eleven targets. Hans stopped doodling for a minute, and even Robert opened his eyes. The silence continued after Avner had stopped.

'Yes,' said Hans finally, and started doodling again, 'we don't seem to know so much about them. The background information is a bit scanty.'

'We know what we need to know,' Avner said. 'I'm not sure if I want to know whether any of them likes playing chess.'

'I see your point,' Hans nodded. 'Well – on the basis of what Ephraim said about innocent bystanders, it would seem to rule out explosives in most cases.'

Robert looked up. 'You're wrong,' he said. 'It doesn't

129

necessarily rule out anything. It just takes a little more thought, that's all.'

'Tomorrow,' Avner said. 'Tonight we settle in.' It was working. They were his team. They were his *chaverim* his comrades.

Avner had booked rooms for Carl, Hans and Robert at the Hotel Ambassador, but Steve was staying at the Midi. After the meeting the two of them went for a walk. The traffic streamed by; the after-dinner crowd around the place Chevelu seemed cheerful and elegant. Almost instinctively, Avner and Steve directed their steps towards the river.

Halfway across the pont de la Machine, Steve stopped and leaned against the diamond-patterned railing of the quiet pedestrian bridge. The city's light, like reflections from a giant Ferris wheel, twirled hypnotically in the waves. 'I have a feeling, chum,' said Steve, after taking a deep breath and letting it escape, as though he had been lifting an enormous weight, 'I have a feeling that not all of us will come out of this alive.'

Avner said nothing.

'Don't worry, though,' Steve said. He paused and flashed a sudden, boyish grin. 'I also happen to feel that you and I will.'

PART III

The Mission

Chapter 5

WAEL ZWAITER

THE LEONARDO DA VINCI is a moderately-priced Holiday Inn-style hotel in the Via dei Gracchi on the Vatican City side of Rome. As such, it was entirely to Avner's taste.

The rooms on the top floor afforded a vista of St Peter's and a good glimpse of the Castel Sant' Angelo. Even more important from Avner's point of view, the hotel was clean, modern and had three-star showers in the bathrooms. There was also a restaurant almost next door, called the Taberna de' Gracchi, with an enormous pig's head in the window which Avner had always found irresistibly comic. The food was excellent.

Avner and Carl moved into the Leonardo da Vinci on a Sunday, 15 October – almost three weeks to the day since the team first left Israel for Geneva. By that time they had spent several days in the vicinity of the Eternal City. Steve and Carl had been staying at the Holiday Inn just outside Fiumicino since 10 October, while Hans, Robert and Avner had made their headquarters at a hotel in Ostia, a popular resort on the Mediterranean a few miles from Rome. On the same Sunday – just before they had checked out of their hotel in Ostia to move into Rome – Robert met one of his contacts in a parking lot facing the beach. He was handed a sturdy shopping bag which contained five Beretta .22 handguns with two full clips of ammunition for each.

On the following day, Monday, 16 October, around 8.30 pm, a car driven by a young Italian picked up Avner Robert a couple of blocks from their hotel, just where the Via dei Gracchi ends at a pretty little park called the Piazza della Libertà. Driving at a leisurely pace – by Roman standards – the car crossed the Tiber over the Ponte Margherita, circled the Piazza del Popolo, picked its way along the edge of the magnificent gardens of the Villa Borghese, then sped down the Corso d'Italia until it reached the Via Nomentana. Two left turns – the second of them illegal – brought the car to the Corso Trieste, where it began following the quiet residential boulevard's gently twisting course north towards the Piazza Annibaliano.

Though hardly ten minutes' drive from the bustling tourist centre of the Via Veneto, the Piazza Annibaliano is completely off the beaten track, one of Rome's many undistinguished piazzas which, unlike her notable ones, can boast of no antique temples, Renaissance fountains or historic palaces. The Piazza Annibaliano has, in fact, nothing but a tiny park in its middle with half a dozen unkempt trees sprouting from the asphalt-rimmed soil, ringed that evening by as many small Fiats, Renaults, Volkswagens and Lambretta scooters as could be squeezed, Roman style, into its non-existent parking pattern.

Six streets converge haphazardly on the square. The two that run north, almost parallel to each other, are the Via Massaciuccoli and the Viale Eritrea which changes its name to the Viale Libia further along. These two streets form a wedge whose southern tip fronts the Piazza Annibaliano. The body of the wedge itself consists of a sprawling, mournful seven-storey apartment complex, renting to Romans of moderate income. It has entrances from both sides as well as from the tip of the wedge. The one facing the Piazza Annibaliano is entrance C. Tiny businesses eke out a living on the ground floor of the building: a barber's shop to the left of entrance C and a neighbourhood restaurant, called the Bar Trieste, to the right.

Avner touched the driver's shoulder when the car reached the corner of the Via Bressanone. The Italian pulled over, let Avner and Robert out, then rounded the Piazza

Annibaliano and sped off in the direction from which he had come. His job was finished. The time was a few minutes after 9 pm.

Avner and Robert sauntered across the square, noting that Hans was already sitting in the passenger seat of a car parked between entrance C and the Bar Trieste. Hans noticed them too, but did not acknowledge them. Instead, he said something to the Italian girl who was sitting at the wheel. Avner and Robert watched as she got out of the car, walked slowly to the corner of the Viale Eritrea, turned, and walked back to the car.

Though the Italian girl did not know it, the signal meant that the man Avner and his team preferred to think of as the 'target' and who lived in one of the apartments above entrance C had been at home and had gone out again. If he had still been upstairs in his apartment the girl would have stayed in the car. If Hans had noted a problem that indicated to him that the mission should be aborted at this point, on seeing Avner and Robert he would have told the girl to drive off. In that case they would have walked over to the other side of the square, maybe twenty-five yards away, where Steve was waiting in a rented green Fiat 125 with Milan licence plates. Steve also had an Italian woman in his car, though she was sitting in the passenger seat. If Hans had given the 'abort' signal, Avner and Robert would have got into Steve's car and driven away.

But, at this stage, the mission appeared to be on. Avner and Robert continued walking around the square, talking quietly to each other, keeping Steve and Hans in their line of sight. They knew that by this time Carl would have checked Avner and himself out of the Leonardo da Vinci – the others had checked out of their hotels earlier – and would also have deposited a new set of passports, driver's licences and some cash for each of them at various prearranged places in Rome, in case they got separated and had to make their way out of the city on their own. By now Carl was probably having a quiet Campari and soda in one of the many working men's bars in the neighbourhood, sitting by a window, keeping an eye on the key streets converging on the piazza. The major part of his job would not begin until later.

At this time of the evening – 9.30 or so – the streets were still fairly busy, though the traffic was only a fraction of what it had been earlier in the day. Most parts of Rome were bumper to bumper during daylight hours. The evenings, however, were never too busy in residential suburbs. Apart from Rome's innumerable cats, the streets were mainly filled with young Romans of both sexes put-putting along the boulevards on their Vespas. But people of all ages were strolling or standing on street corners talking to one another, as Robert and Avner were doing, without attracting a glance from other passers-by. Rome is anything but an inquisitive city.

Another thirty minutes had elapsed when Avner saw Hans get out of the car parked in front of entrance C. Hans looked at his watch, walked over to the driver's side, leaned against the door, and chatted casually for a few seconds with the girl behind the wheel. Then he waved goodbye to her and started walking across the piazza in the direction of the corso Trieste, without a glance at Robert or Avner. The girl drove off. Steve was still sitting with the other girl in the green Fiat parked a few dozen yards away.

Evidently it was time to take up positions. The target appeared to have regular habits. If this particular evening was typical, he would be walking home within the next few minutes from his girlfriend's apartment several blocks away. Before turning into entrance C he was likely to stop at the Bar Trieste to make a brief phone call or two. Though he had a telephone in his apartment, the team's information was that it had been disconnected for nonpayment of charges.

The fact that Hans had sent his car away meant that he had spotted, not the target himself, but a young Italian couple sauntering towards the piazza, the girl hanging on to the boy's arm with both hands. Their job was to precede the target by about a minute as he made his way home. Though the young couple knew that their presence on the piazza Annibaliano would signal that the man they had been watching and following for the past three days was approaching, they did not know whom they were signalling or why.

Having spotted the couple, Hans would now be taking up his position beside the second getaway vehicle, a dilapidated van with an elderly Italian driver waiting patiently behind the wheel, parked a few hundred yards from the piazza. At a leisurely pace, Avner and Robert began crossing the square towards entrance C of the apartment building, keeping an eye on Steve in the green Fiat. It would have been unwise to loiter in the hallway longer than necessary. Until, or unless, the girl sitting beside Steve got out of the car, Avner and Robert would not enter the apartment lobby.

If she got out of the car only to walk away, Avner and Robert would not enter at all. This would be the final signal to abort the mission. It could mean that the target was accompanied by another person, or had changed his direction altogether. The man would be coming from around the corner, invisible to Avner and Robert. All they could see was the girl in Steve's Fiat – the back of her blonde head.

Avner could feel his stomach muscles tighten.

He stole a quick glance at Robert, but his partner's face betrayed no tension. If anything, there was a slight expression of boredom in the slack muscles around his mouth, the half-lowered lids over his grey eyes.

It was time for the blonde girl to make a move, one way or the other.

She did. She was getting out of the car. And she did not walk away, but ran, with the awkward, high-heeled run of a young girl, to the couple who had just come around the corner. She shouted 'Ciao!' at them, hanging on with both hands to the boy's other arm. Laughing, talking, clinging together, the threesome passed by the Bar Trieste.

Presumably one minute ahead of the target.

Quickly, decisively, as if he had meant to do nothing else all his life, Avner walked into the hallway of entrance C. He did not, by word or gesture, signal Robert to follow him. He had no doubt that Robert would be right behind, but he would have entered the hall anyway. Ordering others into action was not the Israeli army's tradition. Leaders simply proceeded to wherever they expected the others to follow them. And it was rare for one to move forward only to find himself alone on the killing ground.

Inside the foyer the air was cool and a little damp. The lobby was pitch dark, in the European tradition of inexpensive apartment buildings. The lights in lobbies, stairwells or hallways would, when turned on, switch off again automatically after a couple of minutes. There was no point in wasting electricity.

Avner and Robert had looked into the lobby the previous day, just long enough to obtain an idea of the layout. The stairs. The iron grille of the old-fashioned elevator whose door could be operated only by inserting a coin. A kind of reflecting glass, like a mirror, on one wall – which now gave Avner a turn even though he ought to have remembered it was there. Catching a glimpse of himself as his eyes were getting used to the dark, his heart nearly stopped. For a second he thought there was someone waiting in the lobby. Shit! Jumping at his own shadow. It was a good thing Robert seemed not to notice.

Looking back towards the entrance they could see people walking by; silhouettes framed for a split second in the narrow doorway. A woman. An older couple. A dog, stopping, looking back, wagging its tail, bounding away again.

Then, without any doubt, the man they were waiting to kill.

Though he had passed by the entrance in less than a second – just another silhouette, carrying a grocery bag – both Avner and Robert knew that it had to be him, on his way, as they had expected, to the Bar Trieste next door. Just at this moment the dash-dot of a car horn reached their ears – Steve signalling them from the green Fiat – but it wasn't necessary. They knew.

The man would be making his phone calls now. Four,

five, maybe six minutes. Ten, if there was somebody else using the phone. Or only two. The exact time was impossible to predict, but it wasn't important. Eventually he'd be coming through entrance C, on his way home, alone.

Of course, other people might come walking through entrance C at exactly the same moment. Or come down the stairs, on their way out. In which case, they'd do nothing. Abort for the day. Perhaps abort altogether, if the situation gave the target a chance to take a good look at their faces.

What would happen if people walked in after they had already begun what, in the team's vocabulary, was called 'the action'? The best idea Avner could come up with was to dismiss such a possibility. Zero risk could only mean near-zero risk, not absolute zero. Even Ephraim had acknowledged that in such operations it was impossible to plan for absolutely everything. Real zero risk was staying at home and watching television and even then the roof might fall in.

The target was coming through the door.

Except – Avner could hardly believe his eyes – a man and a woman were following right at his heels. A couple of innocent bystanders. Robert saw them too. They were about to walk through the door, just a few paces behind the man with the grocery bag. He was fumbling for something in his pocket as he walked, perhaps for the coin that opened the door of the elevator.

At this point Robert made a sudden move, possibly because of the couple walking behind the man. Later he wasn't certain himself why he moved; perhaps he considered the mission aborted and he was starting to head out of the building. In any case, he moved – and the couple behind the target might have sensed the movement, caught sight of a dim figure they did not know in the dark lobby. Or they might simply have changed their minds about entering the building. They stopped.

Then the man seemed to pull at the woman's hand, and they both walked away.

Ahead of them, the man with the grocery bag noticed

nothing. He continued walking into the lobby towards the elevator. With firm, familiar steps, not worrying about the darkness. His free hand was still fumbling in his coat pocket. A slim, slight man, sensing no danger. Avner could see the neck of what looked like a bottle of wine sticking out of his bag.

Robert reached out and switched on the light.

Caught in the sudden glow, which wasn't at all bright, the man looked up but he did not slow down or stop. His expression wasn't frightened. He wasn't even startled, only a little puzzled, perhaps. He seemed ready to brush past Avner and Robert. His attitude seemed to imply that whatever two strangers might be doing in the darkened lobby, it was none of his business.

Robert spoke to him in English while he was still a couple of steps away from them.

'Are you Wael Zwaiter?'

The question was mere operational formality. The minute the lights had come on, both agents recognized the slender Palestinian poet who had for years been the PLO's representative in Rome. They had studied photographs of him in detail. They knew his official biography by heart: age, late thirties; born in the city of Tchem, on the west bank of the Jordan River. A literary man, popular in left-wing intellectual circles, very poor, moving from one modest job, one modest apartment to another. Currently employed as a translator at the Libyan Embassy in Rome. Low-key. Even his ladyfriend was an older woman, a little on the heavy side, though very well dressed, who seemed to have a fondness for spending her vacations in the Soviet Union. No crime in that, of course. Nor was it a crime to have a younger brother expelled from Germany after the Munich massacre. It was not a capital offence to express, as Zwaiter did, patriotic sentiments in articles and literature, or even to promote the works of other patriotic Arab writers, like the Syrian poet Nizar Qabbani who would celebrate *Al Fatah* with such lines as 'Bullets alone, not patience, open the lock of deliverance . .'. These were standard sentiments expressed even by many Western intellectuals of the new Left. Or the older Left. Or, for that matter, the even older Right. No crime.

Zwaiter was, in fact, Yasser Arafat's cousin, though even the Mossad did not know it at the time. But that was no crime, either.

The reason Zwaiter's name appeared as Number four on Ephraim's list was different. The Mossad had reason to believe that Wael Zwaiter was one of the major organizers and coordinators of terrorism in Europe. He was the man responsible, in the Mossad's view, for the Palestinian hijacking of the *El Al* plane from Rome to Algeria in 1968 – the one that had launched the terrorist decade. Zwaiter was the author – or so the Mossad held – not only of a modern translation of *A Thousand and One Nights* but also of the August 1972 attempt to blow up another *El Al* jet by means of the tape-recorder bomb carried aboard as a gift by an English woman.[1] The captain of that plane had managed to turn back and land safely in Rome and two Palestinian terrorists had been arrested. The captain of the next plane might not be so lucky.

'Are you Wael Zwaiter?'

Robert's voice was casual, even courteous. For a fraction of a second Zwaiter might still have been unsuspecting. Robert and Avner had no weapon in their hands. 'Pull your gun only to shoot' – and there could be no shooting until the question of identity had been firmly established. 'Identify him as if he were your own brother,' Ephraim had said. 'Let him identify himself.'

Zwaiter began identifying himself. His eyes, his head, started describing the arc of an affirmative nod in response to Robert's question. But something – some premonition, some warning – stopped him. He never finished inclining his head. Afterwards Avner would often wonder what it was that made him realize, in that fraction of a second, the mortal danger.

'No!'

Avner and Robert moved together. Half a step back with the right foot, knees bending in combat crouch. Right hand held close to the body, sweeping back jacket, fingers curved for the pistol grip. Left palm down, moving in a short semi-circle over the right coming up with the Beretta. The slide being pulled back and snapping forward. Cocking hammer and pin, raising the first round from the clip into the breech.

Less than one second. Just as Avner had practised it a million times for old Popeye.

One second for the enemy to fire first. If, for instance, he had a gun in his hand hidden behind the grocery bag. With a round already chambered. The Mossad's one second trade-off for zero risk, for never having a weapon in your hand, for never having a bullet raised from the clip into firing position. Until you intended to use it. Then, no more warning, no more waiting. 'You pull your gun, you shoot,' as the old ex-Marine had said.

'And if you shoot, you kill.'

Wael Zwaiter would not be ready. If the background information on him was correct, he would not even be carrying a gun. No bodyguards, no weapons. For security, Zwaiter would be relying on deep cover alone. A penniless poet. A harmless intellectual. A displaced person, a home-less immigrant translator, maybe with some natural sym-pathy for the cause of his people. A man who could not even pay his telephone bills. Carrying his supper home in a paper bag.

What if that was all he was?

An unarmed man crying 'No!' Clutching a grocery bag and a bottle of wine. A man who looked the way anybody else would look at such a moment. Frozen in fright, with only his eyes opening wider and wider. What if somebody back home had made a mistake?

It would not be accurate to say that these thoughts actually passed through Avner's mind during the next second. And he had no idea what might be passing through Robert's mind. They never talked about it afterwards. But one thing was certain. For another second nothing happened.

The first second – making sure, before pulling a gun – was

regulation. But after they both had their Berettas in their hands there was one more second that had nothing to do with the drill. An unrehearsed pause. A moment's silent grace to honour a commandment that was about to be broken. 'How do you train people,' Ephraim had asked, 'to do a hit?'

Later Avner thought that they had each simply been hoping that the other would fire first.

Zwaiter moved. He started turning away.

Avner and Robert pulled the trigger at the same time. Twice. Aiming, as always, at the body, the largest target. Knees bent, left hand extended for balance, like fencers, though their Berettas had hardly any recoil. Twice, twice, then twice again, their aim following Zwaiter's body as it fell. Avner could not tell whether the bottle in the grocery bag broke or not, but he could recall rolls spilling on to the floor.

Their rhythm was not perfectly synchronized. Robert was getting his shots off faster, which made Avner fire the last two rounds alone. There was a little pause. Then Robert fired again. Twice.

Zwaiter was already lying motionless on the floor.

If neither of them missed – at the range of four or five feet they were not likely to miss – there should have been fourteen bullets in his body. The Beretta's clip was designed to hold eight cartridges but both Avner and Robert always squeezed in two extra ones. It was quite safe, especially if one did not expect to keep the spring depressed for days on end. Avner had fired six times, so he should have four bullets left. Robert's magazine might still hold two.

Avner saw Robert bending down for some unaccountable reason. At first he thought his partner wanted to look at Zwaiter's body, but in fact he was starting to pick up the ejected shells. There was no point in doing that, as Robert ought to have known. Though he felt almost numb with tension, seeing what appeared to be Robert's confusion had the effect of making Avner comparatively calm. 'Leave that,' he snapped as he tucked his gun into his belt, starting to move towards the exit at a fast walking pace. Looking back, he could see Robert straightening up and following him. Robert seemed dazed. He was trying to put his gun away, but in the end he just held it under his jacket.

They walked out through entrance C on to the piazza. Behind them the lights were still burning in the lobby. Less than three minutes must have elapsed since Zwaiter had entered the building – maybe less than two.

They walked towards the green Fiat, quickening their pace as they went. Fixing his eye on the car, parked only two dozen yards away, Avner did not even notice whether they had been passing other people on the sidewalk or not. The Fiat's nose was pointed away from them, facing the traffic circle, but Avner was sure Steve would be watching their approach from the rear-view mirror. The closer they got to the car the faster they walked, and for the last few steps Avner could feel himself breaking into a run. Without meaning to. He tore open the rear door, and let Robert dive into the back seat ahead of him.

Steve turned back.

'What happened?' he asked anxiously just as Avner was slamming the door shut. 'Why didn't you do it?'

It was amazing. Inside the lobby the crackle of the two Berettas had sounded so loud that Avner was convinced people would hear it on the other side of the earth. He was worried about it; he couldn't understand why the normally muffled pop-hiss of a .22 should sound like all hell breaking loose. Now it seemed that Steve, parked only a few yards away and no doubt straining to listen, had heard nothing.

'It's done,' Avner replied. 'Let's go.'

The Fiat shot forward. It leapt into the flow of traffic around the Piazza Annibaliano, forcing another car to brake and swerve so hard it nearly spun around its axis. It was unbelievably close. Avner could already hear the crunch of metal and was surprised when it didn't come. The next few hundred yards along the Corso Trieste were only a blur.[2]

In contrast Hans seemed totally calm, waiting for them as they pulled in behind the van, a few blocks away. He motioned the Italian driver to pull forward and give Steve some room, then opened the side door of the van for them, but kept his eyes on the traffic coming from the direction of the Piazza Annibaliano as Steve parked the Fiat. There was nothing to indicate that they had been chased.

'You got everything?' Avner asked Robert, climbing into the van. Robert nodded, but looked a bit dubious. He had put his Beretta away but kept patting his pockets, as if he were looking for something. Avner decided to let it go. Whatever Robert had lost, Carl – who would be approaching the scene of the hit just about now – could sort out later. That was part of his job.[3]

No one spoke after that. The elderly Italian drove the van at a moderate speed, unaware, like the rest of the Italians, of whom he was driving or why. There were some garden tools rattling in the back of his van, and he had a little Madonna statue on his dashboard. When Avner, Steve and Robert jumped into the van, he didn't even glance at them.

After about twenty minutes of driving the van pulled into what looked like a stonemason's yard, somewhere in the southern part of Rome. Avner could feel himself becoming tense again as the van stopped. Both he and Robert had slammed fresh clips into their Berettas while they were still in the green Fiat. Hans and Steve were armed, too. Still, they were now all entering the most vulnerable phase of the mission, completely in the hands of others of whom they knew nothing except that they were not their own people.

The van drove away, leaving them standing on the soft, sandy soil, in front of some low sheds filled with half-finished tombstones. A little distance away, on the open ground, two small Fiats were parked, perpendicular to each other. The driver in the second Fiat was smoking. Avner could see the glow of his cigarette in the dark.

Instinctively they fanned out as they approached the two cars. As Avner walked slowly, about ten feet from Hans, the idea that flashed through his mind was that the concept of

145

'zero risk' was really a bad joke. Certainly as it applied to them, at this moment.

On the other hand, they had done the first job.

The engines of the little Fiats came to life. Steve and Robert were already getting into the first one. The driver of the second was stubbing out his cigarette and opening the door for Avner and Hans. Whatever might yet happen would not be at this spot or at this time.

Outside the city limits, the two cars turned south in the direction of Naples. Avner could see that they were not taking the main highway – the Autostrada del Sole – but a smaller secondary road running closer to the Mediterranean coast. He caught a glimpse of a sign. They were on Route 148, driving towards the little town of Latina.

Neither Hans nor Avner spoke for a while. Avner was busy watching the lights in the rear-view mirror, making sure the other Fiat was right behind them. Finally Hans broke the silence.

'Well – that's one,' he said, speaking in Hebrew. 'As a matter of curiosity, would you like to know the cost?'

It occurred to Avner that Hans had never looked more like a pencil.

'Give or take a few cents,' Hans said, 'it was three hundred and fifty thousand dollars.'

Chapter 6

LE GROUP

THE QUIET FARMHOUSE on the outskirts of Latina was a perfect place to sit and think for a few days. The late October sky was nearly cloudless. Walking among the stunted apricot trees in the backyard, Avner could smell the sea. If he had gone for a short stroll he could even have looked at it, but it was safer not to leave the house. Latina wasn't Rome. In a small place strangers might attract unwelcome attention.

The figure Hans had mentioned in the car didn't surprise him. Killing people was turning out to be an expensive business. Avner tried to remember where the money had gone. It was an exercise to bring into focus the events of the last three weeks.

It was easy to remember what had happened to the first fifty thousand dollars. It went to Andreas. In one lump sum. In exchange for nothing tangible, at that point.

During the first days in Geneva, Avner and his partners hadn't had the beginning of an idea how they should start on the mission. It was all very well for Ephraim to say that they would be completely autonomous. They had all agreed that they should be on their own, self-assigning, not being sent on wild-goose chases dreamed up by the people in Tel Aviv. They should not be burdened by red tape, by contradictory instructions. In theory, this was just fine.

In practice, they had sat gloomily in a Geneva café for hours on end for the first two days, buttering their hard-crusted Swiss rolls, watching the rain beating down on the gabled roofs. The worst thing about it for Avner was that the others were waiting for him, as the leader, to speak. And he was not yet sure where to begin.

In the end he began with the list of targets. What, in fact, did they know about the eleven terrorist chiefs who added up to the heads of Ephraim's monster? The list had been compiled in order of descending importance to the Mossad, so that both Avner and Carl were surprised to find Dr Wadi Haddad assigned the least important spot. He was the most notorious target. Of course, the team was not expected to go after the targets in the order listed. There would have been no point in wasting months chasing one terrorist, while missing three or four others right under their noses.

The list could also be divided in a different way. Numbers one, two, six, seven, eight, ten and eleven were what Avner and his partners described, in the quasi-military parlance of their preference, as 'hard' targets. Salameh, Abu Daoud, Nasser, Adwan, Najjer, al-Chir, and Dr Haddad were open, self-confessed, armed revolutionary leaders and organizers, about whom everything was known – except their current whereabouts. They would carry weapons and be physically protected by bodyguards, even when travelling incognito. They could be expected to take every precaution to avoid being detected and ambushed, not only by their Israeli enemies, but even by fellow revolutionaries belonging to a rival faction of the 'armed struggle'. They would be completely alert, stay in strongholds, change their travel plans all the time. Some might never sleep under the same roof twice.

Numbers three, four, five and nine were 'soft' targets. Like Wael Zwaiter in Rome, Hamshari, al-Kubaisi, and even Boudia might expect to be protected mainly or solely by their cover. They did not hide their sympathies for the Palestinian cause – or expect to be known as terrorists. Living openly in Western European cities, they were seen to be involved merely with the educational, cultural or diplomatic side of their political convictions. If they had a clandestine existence, it occupied only half of their lives. While even the ordinary French, German or Italian police would have been after known terrorists, gunrunners or explosives' smugglers – if only to expel them from the country – writing articles or maintaining information centres in support of any cause was no crime in a Western democracy. Indeed, such a terrorist could rest secure in the knowledge that the Israelis themselves would not regard mere political support of the PLO as an activity exposing anyone to physical reprisals. As long as they thought that was all he was doing.

'You're not going to hit a person,' as Ephraim had put it to Avner, 'because he thinks the Palestinians should have a home. Hell, *I* think the Palestinians should have a home. You hit him because he blows up schoolchildren or Olympic athletes.'

For that reason 'soft' targets took fewer security precautions. In fact, the current Paris address of one of the targets was included with the rest of his biographical data. This did not mean that the team could assassinate them without any preparation. Indeed, it was the setting up and, especially, the getting away that were difficult, no matter how 'soft' the intended victim might be. The logistical problems were enormous.

Still, soft targets were easier. At least they were easy to find. And having found one, the team would not have to fight their way into a fortress to get at him.

'Softies' were also less prone to being misidentified. Unlike hard targets, terrorists operating under good permanent covers would have no reason to bother with disguises or fake identities. They would permit themselves to be photographed and even have their nameplates on their doors. If asked, they would probably introduce themselves. No possible mistake could be made about them. Unless it had been made back in Mossad headquarters, and they were exactly what they were representing themselves to be.[1]

There was one more reason for selecting a soft target first. Time. The Munich massacre had occurred at the beginning of September. The hard targets might not come out of hiding for several months, by which time the world would have forgotten about the slaughter of the Olympic athletes. If the team missed one terrorist, they might not come across another for a few more months. By then, public opinion or even the *mechablim* themselves might fail to make the emotional connection; an assassination might even appear unprovoked. Avner was not acquainted with Lord Byron's remark about revenge being a dish best eaten cold. But if he had been, he would not have agreed.

'To hell with this,' Avner had said to them in the middle of the second rainy day. 'Let's forget about Geneva. It's too quiet, we don't even have contacts here. We'll make Frankfurt the headquarters. First we spread out. Open bank accounts, pick up the news, each in the place he knows best.

'Steve, you go to Amsterdam. Carl, obviously to Rome. Hans to Paris, Robert to Brussels. I'll meet you all in Frankfurt in five days.'

'Let's get the first *mechabel* in two weeks.'

It sounded impulsive, but it made sense. They would obviously need bank accounts, contacts, lockers, safe houses in major European cities. Any of the targets could be here one day, there the next, and they needed escape routes and prepared hiding places themselves, in case they made a hit. Ideally they should have new passports, new identities waiting for them in different European towns; certainly enough money to see them through a couple of weeks. They would never use the same identity leaving a country after a hit as they had used at the time of entry; they would never carry weapons on their persons across international borders. At least, they shouldn't have to, if they had been well prepared. They shouldn't even have to carry two different sets of identities at the same time.

Rome used to be home ground for Carl; Paris for Hans; Amsterdam for Steve. Their old informers – and just as in ordinary police work, four-fifths of all intelligence comes from disgruntled or greedy snitches – might have picked up a rumour about one or other of the targets. As for Robert's

150

destination, Brussels was still one of the world's major centres for illicit explosives and weapons. Avner didn't know much about the technicalities – that was Robert's speciality – but it was common knowledge that, with the right contacts and for the right money, you could acquire a fair arsenal from a Belgian dealer *and* have it delivered anywhere in Western Europe. Maybe even to points beyond.[2]

After his partners left, Avner made his fifty-thousand-dollar phone call to Andreas, from a public booth outside the Geneva café.

It was a phone call made by his sixth sense. It was also something Ephraim had said, something that had stuck in Avner's mind, about patching into the terrorists' own network. Killing two birds with one stone. After all, Avner and his team were now a tiny, watertight cell, just like many others in the underground of international terror. They had no official connection with any government. They were not bound by the procedural rules of any secret service. They were on their own. They were working for a country – but they were not.

In this respect, they were not unlike the seemingly spontaneous bands of armed anarchists that had sprung up, from Uruguay to West Germany, in the wake of the great drug-culture-anti-Vietnam-War-environmentalist-feminist-New Left movements of the turbulent 1960s. Such terrorists were working for a country too: the Soviet Union.[3] But in 1972, few people made this association.

There were numerous reasons why most liberal commentators and politicians in the Western democracies refused to inquire into the possibility of the Soviet connection until the end of the 1970s. First, the 1960s generated an immense and, in some instances, not undeserved sympathy for many of the causes and ideas espoused by the terrorists. Though the overwhelming majority of the Western public would have had no sympathy for terrorist methods or 'tactics' – meaning murder, robbery, hijackings and kidnappings – many people easily saw violent fanatics as somewhat unstable, immature individuals spontaneously carried by a commendable *Zeitgeist* to unfortunate extremes.

Second, the Soviet Union always tended to condemn, or at least failed to applaud, most forms of terrorism in its official pronouncements. Speaking at the United Nations Assembly, Soviet Foreign Minister Gromyko found it 'impossible to condone acts of terrorism by certain Palestinian elements leading to the tragic events in Munich'.[4] Experts in Sovietology could point, with some justification, to the traditional gulf between anarchists and orthodox Communists, the latter regarding the former as 'petit-bourgeois romantics' who would 'objectively' only hinder the 'victory of the proletariat'. In fact, some terrorist groups would occasionally go public themselves in expressing their opposition to 'Soviet imperialism' as well as to 'Western colonialism' – though with regard to their anti-Soviet feelings they were always very careful not to back up their words with action.[5]

Third, the mushrooming terrorist groups in Europe, in the Americas, in the Third World and in the Middle East presented such a chaotic, incoherent jumble of confused, contradictory philosophies that it was difficult to think of them as the manifestations of any single policy or design. Some were religious fanatics; some ultra-nationalists; some Marxists or quasi-Marxists of all shades; some simply 'anti-authoritarian' or 'anti-imperialist' – though never actively objecting to the considerable authoritarianism or imperialism of the Communist bloc. Even the groups calling themselves 'Communist' subscribed to ideas that, inside the Soviet Union, would have been promptly labelled 'left-deviationist' and landed them in a pyschiatric hospital or worse. Moreover, they took their ideological differences very seriously and spent nearly as much time ostracizing, shooting and blowing each other up as they spent terrorizing the people and governments of the West.

The Soviet bloc and, in the early days, the Chinese Communist forces that launched, trained, armed and partially financed terrorists were not interested in the day-to-day details of their activities. No one inquired into their orthodox Communist credentials. They were exempt from having to toe the party line. The terrorists' function, in the eyes of the Soviet organs of state security, was to disrupt and destabilize the Western democracies, and it was a matter of indifference to the Kremlin by what means and on the basis of what ideas they achieved it. The only thing that mattered was their terminal militancy – and the degree to which they could provoke democratic governments to respond to them in an equally intemperate fashion. They were there to invite, to actually create, the repression against which they were ostensibly fighting; and whether they based their acts of violence on ideals of religion, national liberation or social or racial justice, was quite immaterial to the KGB.[6] It was also immaterial whether their causes were merely bizarre or did, in fact, contain a measure of justice or a grain of truth.

The terrorists themselves – certainly in the lower echelons, but sometimes even in the higher ones – were often not aware of the extent to which they were being used as instruments of Soviet policy. Or, ironically enough, they might be lulled into an illusion that *they* were using the Soviet Union for their own ends. The genius of this approach lay in the fact that the Soviets could do fundamental harm to liberal democracies – indeed, in countries like Turkey or post-Franco Spain, prevent or retard the growth of democratic government altogether – while washing their official hands of any involvement. The same hands in which they were holding out the olive branch of *détente*.

And here, perhaps, was the final reason behind the West's refusal to acknowledge the Soviet Union's role in international terrorism throughout the 1970s, even after many of the facts had become public knowledge.[7] In an age of nuclear weapons, to many statesmen it seemed wiser not to rock the boat for little matters. Terrorism wasn't such a problem, really; the odd diplomat, business leader, journalist or airline passenger not such a high price to pay to avoid endangering the thaw in East-West relations or the Helsinki

153

accords. Especially since the Soviet Union seemed courteous and diplomatic enough to achieve much of its support of terrorism through proxies: many of the instructors were Cuban or Palestinian; many of the training camps were in Czechoslovakia or South Yemen; many of the weapons were manufactured in and shipped from East Germany; many of the briefings were held in the Bulgarian capital of Sofia rather than in Moscow. The reason was not simply, as many otherwise well-informed people believed, to keep the Soviet Union at arm's length from the wet business of blood in the streets. The Kremlin did not particularly intend to deceive the public, let alone the government leaders or intelligence services of the West – terror isn't terror unless its source is crystal clear – but merely enable them to close their eyes if they so chose. It was an excellent test of their will. The perfect way to add insult to injury, to demoralize and humiliate Western leaders, to make one ambassador lick the hand that shot the other, until the great democracies lost all confidence in their own values and strength.

The Soviets did not, of course, invent the ills and tensions of the world.[8] They merely identified and exploited them. They would leave no scab unpicked. They would allow no wound to heal, if they could make it fester. If there was a conflict, they'd turn it into a war; if a cause emerged – legitimate or not – they'd wait for a fanatic to surface and take an extreme position in it, then supply him with weapons. If none emerged, they might create one. The KGB calculated, accurately enough, that if it supplied and trained a sufficient number of violent extremists, it could let them loose without any detailed instructions or supervision. Havoc was certain to follow.

In 1972, however, this was not yet common knowledge. People with access to intelligence data strongly suspected it and were gathering the evidence, sometimes discrediting themselves by speaking out too soon.[9] Others, like Avner, with little classified information but some experience and much common sense, suspected it anyway. Without being familiar with the expression *cui bono*, Avner posed it to himself very quickly. Who benefits? With all that lovely troubled water around, somebody must be doing a little fishing.

And if so, Avner might do some fishing himself. In the same water.

In Frankfurt the phone was picked up by Yvonne, Andreas' girlfriend. She was the suspicious lady to whom Avner had spoken when he first called Andreas years ago. Yvonne had long since stopped being suspicious. She had even cooked dinner for Avner once. She was a striking brunette – Avner was actually a little envious of Andreas because of her – with large green eyes. An inch or two taller than either of them.

Avner decided to play the whole thing by ear.

'Listen, Yvonne,' he said, 'I'm calling from Switzerland. Is Andreas there? I'm . . . in a bit of a spot.'

There was a little pause on the other end of the line.

'Just a sec,' Yvonne said. 'Don't go away. I'll find him for you.'

Andreas came on the phone about a minute later, sounding a little breathless: 'Sorry,' he said, 'I was on my way out. What's up?'

'I may be in trouble,' Avner replied. Then he waited. His sixth sense told him that the less he said, the better.

'Do you want to come here?'

'That's the point,' Avner said. 'Going there's going to another country.' He took a breath as if he were going to say more, waiting for his friend to interrupt him.

Which he did.

'Okay, you don't have to talk about it on the phone,' Andreas said. 'Have you got any money?'

'Yeah,' said Avner. It was working. 'Money's the one thing I've got. Lots.'

'Are you in Zürich?' Andreas asked. 'Never mind, go to Zürich, wherever you are. Call a man named Lenzlinger.'[10] He spelled the name and gave Avner a number. 'Tell him I

155

told you to call. He'll help you.' Andreas paused again, then he asked, 'When you say you've got lots of money, you mean you've got *lots* of money?'

'Oodles,' said Avner. 'Don't worry about it. And thanks. I'll be in touch.' He rang off before Andreas could ask any more questions.

The same afternoon Avner called the number Andreas had given him, and then took the train to Zürich. A uniformed chauffeur was waiting for him and, twenty minutes later, Avner was walking through the gates of a handsome villa in a quiet, expensive suburb. The house was surrounded by a low stone wall, with wrought-iron gates set in the middle, and two enormous weeping willows casting their drooping branches over it.

Lenzlinger owned an ocelot. Avner knew what it was only because he asked Lenzlinger, the minute he got over his shock at seeing what he took to be a young leopard raising its head from the rug in the study.

'She's harmless,' Lenzlinger answered, smiling. He was a small man with small hands and eyes. One wall in his sombre, wood-panelled study was lined from floor to ceiling with African masks and weapons. His ocelot may have been harmless, but Avner guessed Lenzlinger was not. He wanted a thousand dollars for each .22 Beretta with three clips, and two to three thousand dollars per passport, depending on the country of issue, on two days' delivery. In 1972 it was a great deal of money, even in black-market terms. Avner paid him without a murmur.

He did not need the seven guns and five passports that he had bought, but they could do no harm sitting in a locker in Geneva. The point was that he had made the first contact. He had bought documents and weapons within hours of placing his first phone call, and with little more trouble than going to the supermarket for eggs. From one of the terrorists' own sources.

He had made the purchase, putting down half the money in cash, and arranging delivery at a patisserie off the place

Kléberg in Geneva forty-eight hours later, because he wanted Lenzlinger to tell Andreas about it. The real entry into this world was not just through contacts, friendships or clever stories. Having actually done business was the necessary first step from which all the other steps would follow.

Avner decided not to make up any explanation ahead of time when, three days later, he rang Andreas from Frankfurt airport. He could always think faster on his feet. By this time Lenzlinger would have told Andreas that his friend had needed certain things and had easily come up with nearly $20,000 in cash. This would no doubt prompt Andreas to make up a story in his own mind about what Avner might be doing; if it was a useful story for his purposes, Avner would go along with it.

'Lenzlinger is telling me,' Andreas said later, fingering his coffee cup, 'that you want to start a small army.'

Avner laughed. Yvonne had cooked them another dinner – gourmet-style on short notice, as she put it – and was in the process of clearing away the dishes. Statuesque, green-eyed, she seemed somehow out of place in the modest, one-bedroom apartment with its few pieces of Scandinavian furniture. There were two suitcases near the door and Avner had tried moving one with his foot when he first came in; it was obviously full, packed and ready for a quick getaway. The place contrasted not only with Yvonne, who would have seemed more at home in a villa like Lenzlinger's, but also with Andreas' childhood home, which Avner remembered well.

'No, not an army,' he said to Andreas, who also laughed but kept watching Avner. Then he gave Yvonne a glance to show that he wanted to be alone with his old friend.

'And, apparently, you gave a handsome tip to the messenger,' Andreas continued.

Avner nodded. News certainly travelled fast. He did give five one-hundred-dollar bills to the young man who delivered Lenzlinger's suitcase to him in Geneva. He wasn't sure of the going rate, but couriers took a lot of chances.

'If you've got your own printing machine,' Andreas said, 'I wouldn't mind borrowing it for a few hours.'

'If I had one,' Avner replied, 'I'd give it to you for a whole day.'

They both laughed.

'Tell me, old friend,' Andreas asked, 'are you running from the law?'

'Sort of,' Avner replied.

'Did you rob a bank?' Andreas asked, without a smile this time.

Avner's reply was also serious. 'No.'

'You embezzled?' Andreas clearly had an idea of his own, and Avner would have given a lot to know exactly what it was.

'Well, some other guys and I,' he replied, 'we all . . . had to leave the places we were working at and . . . I don't know if it's going to hit the papers or not. It's . . . it's very big.'

'Don't tell me,' Andreas said, his eyes lighting up. 'Son of a gun. You're Lichtenstein.'

Avner heaved a deep sigh, quite openly. So that was what Andreas thought! At the time the newspapers were spilling over with stories about some shady dealings involving a major financial institution in the tiny principality of Lichtenstein. There were banks threatening to collapse all over France, and some Israelis were said to be involved. It was a big scandal.

Avner pleaded guilty to it right away. And now it was obvious. Avner did not even have to call on his sixth sense for it. Andreas needed money.

'Listen, old friend,' Andreas said, rolling a thin smoke of marijuana for himself, 'we met a few times in the last years, but . . . we didn't really talk. You did your own thing, and I . . . well, Yvonne and I were doing our own thing, too. You guessed something. Or you didn't guess, I don't know . . . but you called me. You must have had a reason, right?'

'I needed help,' Avner said. 'Don't think I'm not grateful.'

'Never mind that, I was glad to do it.' Andreas lit his joint

158

and inhaled deeply. 'But maybe you can help me too . . . You have something I need. Correct me if I'm wrong, because if you don't have it, we'll still be friends and I'll still try and help you . . . but I think you're flush and I need some money.'

Avner pretended to think.

'How much are you talking about?' he asked.

'You mean, immediately?' Andreas took a deep drag again. 'I need between fifty and a hundred thousand dollars.'

'I can let you have a hundred thousand,' Avner replied promptly, looking straight into his friend's eyes. Let him regret that he had not asked for more. Let him believe that he could, in the future. If he remained useful. 'I can give you fifty right away.'

He was amused as Andreas slapped his back, and even offered him, absent-mindedly, a drag from his joint, though he knew Avner neither smoked nor drank, except for a glass or two of beer. Not surprisingly, Andreas was excited. The Baader-Meinhof people, like most terrorist groups, always needed funds. If Lenzlinger's prices were any indication, their expenditure would be enormous. Even their lifestyle would cost a great deal of money. Security was expensive. So was travel. Maintaining safe houses, paying informers, buying communications equipment, buying or renting vehicles – all were likely to run to immense amounts.[11]

These were things Avner knew, in a general way, from operational profiles on terrorist groups. It was part of his training as an agent. But when it came to his friend Andreas, his sixth sense told him something more.

Here was a rich, adventurous, spoiled, yet rather sensitive boy who had been drawn into a world where he did not really belong. Andreas was good-looking and in good shape, but at the same time, a little too earnest, too easily excited. He had a habit of every so often wiping his granny glasses in a white batiste handkerchief. Avner remembered those handkerchiefs; Andreas' mother must have bought him dozens of them when he was still at high school. The Baader-Meinhof Red Army Faction would not automatically accept a young man like this. His admission price was undoubtedly money, or some of the things it would buy.

For a while, Andreas might have fulfilled the demands of his role from his own allowance, by raiding some trust fund set aside for him, or by extorting or borrowing money from his parents or relatives. But in time his sources would run dry, leaving Andreas terrified of being rejected by the group.

Or worse.

If Avner was right, Andreas would never question too closely his reasons for supplying him with funds and asking for some favours, contacts or information in exchange. Even if he suspected that Avner might not be just a fugitive, a smuggler, an embezzler; even if it should cross his mind that Avner, an Israeli, might be in the same line of work as himself, though on a different side, he would probably turn a blind eye to his own suspicions. If Avner was right, he would be the life raft that would permit Andreas to ride the rapids of the revolution a little longer. He would do nothing to upset it.

'Some friends of mine will be arriving in the next few days,' he said to Andreas. 'I'll need three apartments – something like yours. Do you think Yvonne could find a few for me to look at? I don't want her to rent them yet, just give me the addresses. Very, very quiet places – you know.'

'Sure,' Andreas said.

'Say, tomorrow,' Avner said, and stood up. 'After we meet for lunch and I give you the money.'

By the following evening, Yvonne had seven safe houses for Avner to choose from. He needed only three: one for Steve and Robert to share, another for Carl and himself, and a third for Hans, alone. There were several reasons for splitting up the five of them in this particular way – some operational, others private.

Avner knew just from looking at Steve, and especially Robert, that he could never share a place with either of them without going crazy in a day. Life with Steve would be overflowing ashtrays and socks in the refrigerator, while Robert had an even more disconcerting habit. He collected mechanical toys and would play with them for hours at a time. He would not call it 'play' though, because for Robert toys and novelties were serious business. His family owned a toy factory in Birmingham, and Robert had designed and built the most elaborate and ingenious of their products until he went to Israel. Toys were still his main hobby, and he was forever collecting and researching them.

Carl, on the other hand, had the quiet, clean and orderly habits that were Avner's own. Though he smoked his pipe incessantly, there was never any ash around him and even the smoke did not seem to hang in the air. Carl was forever opening windows and arranging pillows in a symmetrical pattern. Fortunately, it made sense for Carl and Avner to room together, since they would be working out the plans and logistics for the mission.

Hans had to be alone for security. His place would be the only one to contain anything incriminating. He had also stated his preference for a quiet place to himself when he was working on his documents.

Avner's partners would not arrive in Frankfurt for another two days. Meanwhile he went with Yvonne to look at the safe houses. She obviously knew her job because they were all highly suitable, in respectable residential neighbourhoods, close to major arterial roads. The following day Avner went back alone to rent three of them – though he told Yvonne that he had rented only one, for himself and a friend, because the rest of his friends had changed their minds about coming to Frankfurt. There was no point in giving away the location of all their safe houses. The one he chose for Carl and himself was in a medium-sized apartment building on Hügelstrasse, just around the corner from where he had lived with his parents as a child. Little psychological insight is necessary to see why Avner would have selected it for a safe house.

The places he picked for Hans, Robert and Steve were near a street called Röderbergweg, about twenty minutes from Hügelstrasse by car, and in a similar neighbourhood.

Both apartments were near an immense, Teutonically organized and manicured city park. Steve had a fetish about physical fitness and would run five miles every day, while Hans – who would run, as he claimed, only if someone chased him with a butcher's knife – was fond of solitary walks. At this stage, Avner had no idea how much time they'd be spending in their 'headquarters' during the mission. Maybe very little. But it was just as easy to choose places that suited their personal tastes and habits.

The last evening before his partners were due in Frankfurt Avner let Andreas take him to a meeting. Andreas already seemed eager to earn the money Avner had given him, along with his good will.

The small smoke-filled apartment seemed to serve as a kind of clubhouse for one cell of Baader-Meinhof sympathizers, and from the way he and Andreas were received, Avner could tell that his friend was the most important person there. This made the rest of them, and the evening itself, pretty uninteresting from Avner's point of view. Although the five men and two women in the apartment were roughly his contemporaries, Avner felt sixty in comparison. He could hardly keep his eyes open during the endless political chatter. So these were some of the dreaded terrorists of Western Europe – at least in their incipient stage. They looked and sounded like undergraduates discussing books and ideas that rang only the vaguest bell for Avner, but which sounded to him like a mixture between ordinary Communism and plain nonsense. And who were their gurus? Frantz Fanon and Herbert Marcuse, yes, he had heard something about those two, but who on earth were Paul Goodman and Regis Debray? And could any of these glib young men or women actually fire a weapon or place a bomb? But then Avner remembered with a pang how easy it is to set an explosive charge. Red goes to red, blue goes to blue.

In any case, there was no discussion that evening relevant to any terrorist operation, past or present, or to the Palestinian question, even in theory. Avner only nodded and smiled when the others tried to draw him into the conversation, and he tried to store their faces in his memory.

'I thought some other people might turn up,' Andreas said on their way home, by way of apology. 'These fellows on the fringes talk a lot, you know,' he added, 'but you don't pay attention to all the nonsense. They're okay for taking a briefcase from here to there, renting a car, lending a cottage. Personally, I don't even consider myself a Marxist. But that's not important. There will be plenty of time to eliminate all the chatterboxes after the victory.'

Avner nodded. It was not necessary to express an opinion on who would eliminate whom after whose victory.

Neither could Carl, Robert, Steve nor Hans report anything encouraging when they all met the following day. They had done their preparatory work, as had Avner – there were deposit boxes, money, documents and safe houses waiting for them in Paris, Amsterdam and Rome, and one phone call from Robert would get any hardware they needed for an operation delivered to them within forty-eight hours. Anywhere in Europe. 'Except for ordnance,' as Robert put it to Avner, 'but you don't see a call for that, do you?'

'I don't see a call,' Avner replied, 'for a slingshot at this point. No news, any of you?'

They shook their heads. Not only could their usual informers offer nothing on the current whereabouts of any of the 'hard' targets, they couldn't even say for certain if the organizers – the 'soft' targets – listed in the phone book were actually staying in town. Avner's partners could pick up no word on the schedules or habits of anyone on their list. 'The way it looks right now, chum,' Steve offered, 'we're all dressed up with no place to go.'

Which just about summed up their situation in the afternoon of 2 October, 1972.

The next day Avner took Andreas for a walk.

'I told you I would give you a hundred thousand,' he said, 'and I can give you the second half in a few days. But I need something, too.'

163

'Anything,' Andreas replied. 'You want another like Lenzlinger, right here in Germany? I can . . .'

Avner shook his head. It was a moment of great danger – and the test as to whether or not he had 'read' Andreas correctly.

'No,' he said, almost gently. 'I want someone who is in touch with the Palestinians. Somebody who knows them, knows things about them. Do you understand?'

Andreas walked silently beside Avner for a while. 'I don't know if I need another fifty thousand that badly,' he said at last.

'It's not only that,' Avner said. 'When you put me in touch with this person, whoever he is, I don't pay him. I give you the money for him, too. You pay him, whatever he wants.'

Andreas laughed softly. Avner could see that he understood he was being offered the role of the middleman with a chance to skim off any fee other informers would ask for, and to enhance his role in the underground. He would be the man with a source of funds – the thing that made the world of terror go round as it did the rest of the world.

'You look at it the right way,' Avner continued, a little faster now, 'you're just getting a bit of your own money back. Don't the Palestinians charge you for training, for weapons? You pay through the nose. You're fighting for the same revolution, but they're still making you pay. Now a little of it comes back to your cause. It's not as if you were keeping it for yourself. Yvonne doesn't need any fur coats.'

The reference to Yvonne was a good touch. She certainly wasn't with Andreas for material reasons. No man would be able to impress her with jewellery or furs. But she would have to be impressed with *something* about a man – all women had to be impressed, as far as Avner was concerned – and Yvonne was probably impressed with the idea of the revolutionary, the romantic urban guerrilla. Did she realize, though, how much money a man like Andreas would have to come up with for such a position? And where he might end up, after the money was gone?

Andreas knew. He stopped laughing.

'You're not a free-lancer, old friend,' he said. 'You don't deal in Lichtenstein leather.'

'I am a free-lancer,' Avner replied. 'I deal in information, sometimes. Information is money. You're getting paid for it. I may get a higher resale value, that's all.'

It sounded perfectly plausible. 'And listen,' Avner continued, 'remember that we're old friends, as you keep saying. I'd never do anything to harm you. But I already have some information.'

That was plausible, too. And a threat.

'Believe me, even if I wanted to do it,' Andreas said, 'there's no one in Frankfurt . . . I don't know anybody.' He began wiping his granny glasses. 'You need a man like Tony. But he's in Rome.'

'Rome, you say?' asked Avner. It was in the bag. It had been in the bag the minute Andreas started wiping his glases. 'Set it up for me.'

On the morning of 3 October, the two of them took a Lufthansa flight to Rome. They rented a car after they landed, but Andreas drove only to the village of Fiumicino, a few miles from the airport. They sat in a little trattoria just off the via Molo di Levante. From the window Avner could see a flock of noisy gulls wheeling and diving for garbage in the sea.

They had just finished their first glass of beer when a short young man came up to their table. He wore a crumpled light suit, jacket and tie, a raincoat flung over his shoulder. His hair and eyes were dark, but his skin was very white, almost pasty. At a guess, an office manager in a shoe factory, turning thirty, but looking older.

'Hello, Tony,' Andreas said, in English.

Tony smiled, nodded, pulled out a chair and sat down. He threw a quick glance at Avner, a neutral glance without hostility or friendliness. But even before he spoke, Avner could sense that Tony was a step up the ladder. Whether he proved to be useful or not, Tony was in a different league. 'Have you ordered?' he asked, in fluent English with a strong Italian accent. 'I'm famished.' He scanned the menu and gave his order to the waiter, carefully considering the wine. Avner could see that he had a little paunch. His eyes were intelligent, sardonic. Tony was not acting or dressing any part.

'Avner is the friend I was talking to you about on the phone,' Andreas said, when the waiter had finished serving their lunch. 'One of us, of course, and . . . he has the questions.'

'Yes,' said Tony. He began to eat, without haste, obviously enjoying his meal. 'There's a lot of movement in the Arab community right now. A lot of recruiting, and so forth. Especially on the part of one person.'

Avner could practically feel his hair standing on end. Tony looked up at him for a second, cocking his head slightly, as if to ask, 'Wasn't that what you wanted to hear about?'

It was. There was no point in being anything but equally direct in reply. 'What is that person's name?' Avner asked.

Tony wiped his mouth, just tapping the corners, then he put down his table napkin. 'Now you're talking business,' he said.

There was a little pause. Andreas looked at Avner, then turned to Tony. 'Listen, I guarantee the money,' he said. 'You don't have to worry about that. But you appreciate that Avner has to know if what you have is of interest to him or not. Fair?'

Tony continued looking at Avner while Andreas spoke. Then he nodded. 'Zwaiter,' he said to Avner, without a pause. 'The person's name is Zwaiter.' He spoke very quickly. The name would have been hard to catch for anybody who didn't know it already.

'Wael Zwaiter,' Avner said immediately, and quickly so

that Andreas could not catch it, as if it were a password. In a way, it was. A soft target, right here in Rome. Number four on Ephraim's list. Tony was clearly the man.

Tony must have thought so, too, because he took a sip of his wine, then said to Avner: 'Well – is there anything else you want me to do?'

Avner thought for a few seconds. 'Within the next five days,' he said, 'can you find out his schedule, his routine? Where does he live; where does he go and when; who does he meet? That's all we're interested in.'

Requesting such information gave nothing away at this point. There could have been any number of reasons to ask for it. Andreas had introduced Avner as 'one of us', that is, Baader-Meinhof. Different groups would often be keeping an eye on each other's activities. Terrorists might wish to make sure that another organization was not being infiltrated before a joint mission; or suspect that a key organizer like Zwaiter, who might have approached them, was a double agent. In the underground, surveillance was routine.

'Yes,' Tony replied. 'Five days is okay. You're talking about fifty thousand dollars.'

Avner stood up. 'Andreas will meet you here in five days,' he said, 'with the money.'

Andreas was full of enthusiasm during the flight back to Frankfurt. 'How did you like Tony?' he kept asking. 'I've known him for a long time. A very radical person. From Milan, originally. But he never talks politics. He has been past that stage for years.'

Avner agreed that Tony was a long way past that stage.

Meeting with his partners the same evening, Avner proposed a step-by-step operational plan. They would move Zwaiter to the Number one spot on their list, in point of time. By 8 October they would all move to Rome, except Steve, who would fly to West Berlin to check out a lead concerning their prime target, Ali Hassan Salameh. (This lead had come from one of Carl's old Arab informers; one of the several regular contacts used by the Mossad.) If the lead turned out to be solid, they'd abandon Zwaiter for the time being. If not, Steve would join them in Rome.

Avner's next meeting with Tony would be step two and he would take Andreas along. But there was no reason for Andreas to meet the others. If Tony's information led to step three in the operation, Avner would phase Andreas out, simply telling him that he now had everything necessary for the moment, and would be in touch again, later.

Step three would be for Tony's surveillance team to take them through a simulated hit at least twice, without knowing that was what they were doing. This meant Tony's people driving Avner's team (except Carl) to and from the scene of the hit, going through a set of prearranged signals, as if surveillance were the entire purpose of the exercise. (In the surveillance of an experienced, suspicious subject it was sometimes normal practice to use as many as a dozen different people, handing the subject from one observer to the other, as in a relay race.) Tony's pre-hit observers would be moved away from the scene before the action began, and his post-hit escape team would be staggered, with the closest one situated several blocks from the scene. No outsiders would be present at the actual hit, or know about it until they saw or heard it on the news. At which time they would consider themselves to be implicated, and would not be anxious to talk to anybody about it. Even if they did talk, there wouldn't be much they could tell.

The only phase for which Avner's team would have to make its own arrangements was the first getaway car, driving whoever had done the hit to where the second car was waiting. Afterwards, Carl would 'sweep' the scene on his own, and meet the rest of them later.

If they ever got as far as step four, that is. The hit.

As it happened, the plan worked out so well that they hardly had to alter it at all. Tony's report was meticulous, and Avner instructed Andreas to hand over to him fifty of the fifty-five thousand dollars in crisp American one-hundred-dollar bills. Then he let Andreas fly back to Frankfurt, and arranged a further meeting with Tony on his own.

Without asking any questions, the Italian agreed to continue Zwaiter's surveillance, this time with the participation of Avner's team. He also agreed to have a safe house prepared for them near Rome. Tony wanted an additional hundred thousand for this work, which sounded reasonable. In this fashion the team did a 'dry run' on Zwaiter even before Steve joined them.

Steve's tip on Salameh proved to be without substance – a *canard*, as Hans called it, with Avner picking up enthusiastically the French newspaper expression for false rumour – so the team rehearsed Zwaiter's assassination again, this time with Steve. Tony provided different drivers for each dress rehearsal, though the spotters remained the same. Zwaiter himself turned out to be a cooperative target; his routine, which never seemed to vary in any detail, was the greatest help a victim could give to his assailants.

The team made its own arrangements for living accommodations in Rome for the period before the hit. Carl insisted on this, for security; Tony would not know where to find them, and his people would simply pick up Avner and his partners at a prearranged spot in the street, dropping them at a different place after each rehearsal. (Later Avner came to believe that Tony could have found them in Rome within hours in spite of all these precautions: he seemed to have the entire city under surveillance.)

The only person neither Tony nor any of his people would meet for the time being was Carl. He would hover in the background at all times in order to keep an eye on whoever might be following Tony's surveillance team, watch the watchers, prepare alternate escape routes, safe houses and documents. He was to be the team's security net. If anything threatened to go wrong, he would have a chance to spot it and warn the others.

After the hit, Carl would be the first on the scene, before

the police arrived. He would dispose of anything incriminating, or plant false clues. He might move the original getaway car to a different parking place. He would try to find out what the authorities were thinking at the scene, or what direction the initial investigation or pursuit might take.

All of which would make Carl the busiest as well as the most exposed man on the team.

By 13 October, all that remained unresolved was the first getaway car, the one that would be driven only a short distance by one of them, probably Steve; the car that would be abandoned near the scene. Obviously, such a car could not be registered to any of Tony's people. It could be a stolen vehicle, but that seemed an unnecessary risk, and to rent a car would lead to the sacrifice of one set of documents as well as the description of one member of Tony's or Avner's team at the rental agency's office.

'We need one more car,' Avner said to Tony. 'It's a car that might be abandoned.'

Tony took the request in his stride, as he had all previous requests. He continued purposefully spooning his ice cream in the small sidewalk café where they were sitting, near the Piazza Navona. 'It can be arranged,' he replied, mentioning the name of a major American car rental agency and the address of one of its branches. 'They will rent you a car with out-of-town plates, and you don't have to worry about papers. If the police ever question the rental agent, he or she will describe a tall Texan with a Diner's Club credit card renting it in Milan. It'll cost you ten thousand dollars.'

Then came the surprise.

'But you won't owe it to me,' Tony continued. 'I will give you a number in Paris. When you're next there, you call that number and ask for Louis. Tell him I told you that you owe him something, then just pay him. No hurry, but do it within a month or so.'

This was interesting. Did Tony have a boss? Or a senior partner who was collecting a franchise fee from him for operating in Rome? Or did he simply owe 'Louis' ten thousand dollars and find sending it by Avner simpler than flying to Paris himself?

Or, as Carl mused when he had heard about it, could it be a set-up? But Avner dismissed this possibility. His sixth sense signalled no warning.

Arms dealers, informers, and other privateers have always existed in international spying, smuggling, crime, and terror. Sometimes they form loose organizations – more a network of contacts than a strict hierarchy – within which they pass customers to each other for whatever services they cannot provide themselves. A few have political motivations, others are completely apolitical, but in any case their first interest is money. Serving one side only – especially considering the quickly shifting alliances within the terrorist and criminal underworld – is generally against their own interests. Though at times one dealer or another will draw a line at a certain type of activity or merchandise – some may never touch drugs or explosives, some may specialize only in industrial espionage; some will not knowingly work for a specific country – as a rule they will sell information and services to all good clients. However, at least in the short run, they will not sell one client to another, any more than private detectives or other legitimate businessmen do. 'Whatever Tony thinks or suspects,' Avner said to Carol, 'he knows that we pay him in clean money.'

There was only one more question to be decided, which in operational jargon was called 'Who, what?' It concerned only four of them, since Carl's duties would always be the same. Steve was clearly the best driver, so it made sense for him to be behind the wheel of the first getaway car. Being a leader in the Israeli army tradition, it would have been unthinkable for Avner not to assign himself as one of the gunmen, especially in their first action. In fact, the rest of the team would take this for granted. But should the other gunman be Robert or Hans?

'I'm not trying to push myself,' Robert said when they started discussing the assignments, sounding rather English

171

even in Hebrew, 'but I'm familiar with the weapons and I . . .'

Hans smiled. No one doubted Robert's preeminence in explosives, but they were all familiar with small handguns. 'Be my guest,' said the older man, picking up a magazine and putting on his reading glasses, 'you can take my turn any time you want. Just tap me on the shoulder when it's over.'

It was one-upmanship in reverse, very much as in Avner's old unit in the army: protesting that the last thing you ever wanted to see was the firing line but making sure by your tone that no one would believe you. Though in this instance, who could tell? Perhaps Hans was really just as happy not having to do the job. Perhaps they would all have been.

Nevertheless, in two more days, the job was done. Zwaiter was dead.

And now Avner was walking among the stunted apricot trees in the backyard of a farmhouse on the outskirts of Latina, smelling the sea, soaking up the late October sun, and feeling – well, not happy, but certainly not unhappy. Feeling – feeling very little, one way or the other. There was no point in lying about it. They had proved they could do it, starting from nothing, in just about three weeks to the day. Five Yekkes on their own. On the other hand, while Avner couldn't tell what might be going on in Robert's or any of his other partners' minds, *he* certainly hadn't enjoyed shooting a guy in a doorway who was carrying rolls in a paper bag. Nor would he do it again, if he didn't have to. But – it wasn't as bad as he had thought it might be. It wasn't even as bad as thinking about it had been, beforehand. He hadn't lost his appetite; he hadn't lost any sleep. No nightmares, and in the morning he ate a full breakfast. But enjoy it? No normal person could.

The matter was not a subject of conversation between the members of the team, anyway. Not before or after the first hit, not at any time later in the mission. True, as time wore on, they would be talking more and more 'philosophy', but never directly about such feelings. And they had to talk about hits all the time, they talked about little else, but not in such terms. The unspoken feeling might have been that having to do these things was difficult enough, and talking would make it only more difficult.

Perhaps one indication of a guilty conscience about what they were doing was that in their daily lives they would go out of their way to be unusually polite and helpful to anybody who crossed their paths. Any bellboy, waiter, taxi driver, bank teller could testify that their language was nothing but 'please' and 'thank you'. An old lady couldn't cross the street without Steve stopping his car, jumping out and helping her. A stranger couldn't drop anything without Hans bending down and picking it up. Like regular Boy Scouts. Avner and Carl would be buying souvenirs and sending postcards home at every chance they got, just like any other loving husband on a business trip. In Rome, just a few days before the hit, Avner saw Robert give a new mechanical toy to a street urchin who had stopped by their table to gawk. Of course Robert was good-natured, Avner thought, but maybe he was painting the lily just a little bit.

Carl arrived in Latina early in the afternoon of 17 October in Tony's car. As agreed, Carl had contacted Tony for the first time after the hit. Tony himself had driven Carl to the safe house and the arrangement was that if everything seemed in order, Carl would hand over his last payment. This seemed to suit Tony.

By the time he got out of his car in Latina Tony must have known not only what had happened to the man his people had been keeping under surveillance, but that Avner and his friends had had something to do with it. Yet Tony made no comment. The subject was not discussed at all. The Italian presented his account and received his money in cash. Before leaving, he reminded Avner about delivering the $10,000 for the rented car to Louis in Paris at his earliest convenience.

Which was how Avner came to meet Louis, Papa's eldest son, the number two or three man in *Le Group* – though

173

Avner would learn nothing about Papa or his children for some time to come. It was a very gradual process.

The meeting itself didn't take place for another month. The team stayed in Latina for a few more days, Carl collecting all their weapons, their documents, even their clothes for disposal, and bringing them new papers and clothes in exchange. He reported that the Italian police had arrived on the scene of the assassination within minutes, probably just as the team was transferring from the green Fiat to the van a few blocks away. Carl said he had glanced into the getaway car before the police had discovered it, but couldn't see anything incriminating that needed to be picked up. (Robert thought he might have dropped something while he had been changing magazines in his gun.) Carl had overheard some witnesses talking to the policemen at the scene – Italian investigations, at least in their initial phases, were not difficult to overhear – but they seemed to Carl unable to contribute anything that might jeopardize the team.

When the time came for them to leave Latina, Carl was to go to Rome where he would collect all the weapons, money and documents they had left in various hiding places. However, he would begin to do this only when he knew the rest of the team were safe in Frankfurt.

Robert and Steve flew to Zürich, from where they would make their way to Frankfurt by train. Avner and Hans left the day after, flying to Frankfurt directly from Rome. Passport control hardly glanced at their papers. The first reprisal – including the most difficult part, the escape – was complete.

In the next couple of weeks they could pick up no rumours concerning the whereabouts of any of the known terrorists on their list. Some of them could have been in Europe, but it was equally possible that they would not emerge from their Middle Eastern hiding places – where Avner's team was not supposed to operate – for months or even years. Some might have been in Eastern Europe or Cuba, also outside their designated area.

Which left the soft targets – Numbers three, five and nine on Ephraim's list. In fact, it left only Number three, Mahmoud Hamshari, because the present whereabouts of Numbers five and nine, the law professor, al-Kubaisi, and the theatre director, Boudia, were also unknown.

Mahmoud Hamshari, however, was in Paris.

After some discussion they all agreed that the smartest move would be for Avner to travel to Paris. Though Hans had the best knowledge of the French capital and language – Avner's own French was next to non-existent – he would be better occupied working on documents in the little 'laboratory' he was setting up in his Frankfurt safe house. Avner did know his way around Paris reasonably well, and whoever Louis was, it was about time to pay him. It would have been very poor policy not to live up to any obligation they had incurred through Tony. In a business where debts could not be enforced by law, they tended to be enforced outside the law in an uncompromising fashion. In any case, Louis might turn out to be as useful in Paris as Tony had been in Rome.

Avner decided to travel with Andreas and Yvonne. Although he did not think the meeting with Louis would turn out to be a set-up, he agreed with Carl – Cautious Carl, as they had already dubbed him – that it would be safer to let Andreas make contact with Louis first. Andreas had, apparently, dealt with Louis once or twice before in connection with Baader-Meinhof business, and he described him to Avner as 'a little like Tony'. That is, a very radical young man who was 'past the stage' of talking about politics. For his part, Andreas did not mind doing another favour for his old friend – he had already travelled to Rome again with the money owed to Tony – because the commission for the Frankfurt cell of the Red Army Faction was turning out to be generous. In fact, as Hans grumbled, 'We're keeping half the terrorists in Europe in milk and honey. Soon they'll quit the Russians and come work for us.'

Avner could see Hans's point, of course. It was ironic: Israel was helping to fund the Baader-Meinhof gang which

175

had often helped the *fedayeen* to terrorize Israel. A senseless, vicious circle. But what else could they do? Their job was to get the *mechablim*. 'Patch into the terrorists' own network,' Ephraim had said. He must have known that the only way to do that was by paying the terrorists money.

The others agreed with Avner. 'Ours is not to reason why, chum,' Steve said. 'We leave that to the bigwigs. Besides,' he added, 'this kind of thing cuts both ways. Look at that Andreas fellow. He must know by now that he's helping us to wipe out his friends.'

Avner was not so certain about this. Andreas had left Rome well before the hit, and he had never even caught the name of the man Avner had asked Tony to keep under surveillance. Zwaiter's death was not front-page news in Italy, and in Germany it had hardly been reported at all. Andreas might not have heard about it or made the connection even if he had. The various Palestinian groups were often assassinating one another.

Even if he had made the connection, Andreas could still have accepted Avner's explanation that he was a kind of mercenary, gathering information on terrorists for resale, and he would have assumed that Avner was selling it to rival terrorist groups. It need not have occurred to him that his childhood friend was doing any hits himself – and Tony was not likely to tell him. Tony was no fool.

But Hans was right. The whole thing did sometimes seem insane. It was probably smarter not to dwell on it too much. They were only agents. Perhaps if they had the kind of information the *memune* and even Ephraim were privy to, it would all become obvious. Perhaps on a higher level it all made perfect sense.

In Paris Avner let Andreas call the number Tony had given him for Louis, evidently that of a bistro on the Left Bank. Andreas left a message for Louis in his own name, suggesting some alternate times when he could call him back at his hotel.

Louis returned the call the following evening shortly after

six. Avner was with Andreas in his suite when the call came, and he picked up the extension.

'*Comment ça va*, Louis?' Andreas asked, switching immediately to English for Avner's benefit. 'A friend of mine is in Paris with a message for you from Tony.'

'Yes, I was expecting something from Tony,' Louis replied. His voice was light but very masculine, almost like a television announcer's, his English slightly accented. 'Tell him to meet me here tonight at nine. If it's convenient.'

Andreas glanced at Avner. 'I'm sure nine o'clock is fine,' he said, 'but I think he'd prefer to meet you in front of the Royal Monceau Hotel. On, you know, the avenue Hoche.'

'Indeed I know it,' Louis replied, sounding a trifle sarcastic. The Royal Monceau was one of the better-known hotels in Paris, and far from inexpensive. 'Is he staying there?'

Avner shook his head at Andreas.

'No, I don't think so,' Andreas replied, 'but that's where he'd like to meet you.'

'Fine,' Louis replied curtly. 'Tell him I'll be there at nine. I'll pull up right in front in a . . . oh, in a black Citroën. I'll have Fifi with me.'

'That's his dog,' Andreas explained after Louis rang off. 'He often takes it along to meetings. Well, at least you won't have any trouble recognizing him.'

Avner could understand such habits easily; he wouldn't have minded taking Charlie along with him either, perhaps even for the entire mission. He was, in fact, staying at the Royal Monceau, but for the time being Louis did not have to know that. Even Andreas didn't know it: Avner had told him that he would be staying in a private home with friends. The less people knew at this point, the safer it was, though the word 'safe' was really a joke. Zero risk! They were sailing in uncharted waters. But there was no point in making it easier for the Kalashnikov crowd.

The man who opened the passenger door of a black Citroën promptly at nine was in his early thirties. He was well dressed in a casual sort of way. Good-looking, too; a little chubby like Tony, but with much stronger features. 'Shut up, Fifi,' he said to his growling alsatian in the back seat, 'this gentleman is not going to take anything from us. On the contrary, no?' he added, turning to Avner, who was still standing on the sidewalk.

'I hope your dog understands English,' Avner replied, taking a thick envelope from his pocket.

Louis laughed and reached for the envelope. He looked into it, but made no attempt to count the wad of hundred-dollar bills before slipping it into his briefcase. 'Thanks,' he said. 'Were you planning just to give this to me, or would you also like to have a drink?'

'If you make it a bite to eat,' Avner said, 'you've got yourself a date.'

'Done,' the Frenchman replied. 'Any favourite place in Paris?'

It sounded all right. If he had an ambush in mind, Louis would have suggested a place himself – and he obviously knew that Avner knew it. 'There's a little restaurant just down the street,' he said to Louis. 'It looks fine to me.'

Louis looked in the direction Avner was pointing, then nodded. 'I'll join you there in twenty minutes,' he said, then slammed the door and drove off. Avner wished he hadn't – but he could understand that Louis would not wish to sit at a restaurant table clutching a briefcase with $10,000 in it.

The little brasserie called le Tabac Hoche was just a couple of blocks from the place Charles de Gaulle. From its sidewalk tables, there was a view of the Arc de Triomphe which suited Avner's picture-postcard approach to the great cities. However, on this November evening, he took a table inside the restaurant.

Louis arrived in exactly twenty minutes, without the briefcase and without the alsatian. He certainly wasn't lean but he was tall, much taller than he had appeared while sitting behind the wheel of his car. His face resembled that of Yves Montand – a sophisticated, somewhat world-weary face, but very *simpatico*. Avner liked him right away. For some reason

178

he felt that Louis might be his kind of man – more so than Tony, and much more than Andreas.

Louis seemed to take to Avner as well. Their first conversation, though it was about nothing tangible, lasted for hours. After finishing supper, they strolled to the Arc de Triomphe, then all the way down the Champs Élysées to the place de la Concorde and back again. Louis did most of the talking.

It was only much later, remembering this conversation, that Avner understood what the Frenchman might have been talking about. At the time he was fascinated, but he understood very little. Louis seemed well educated, and once in a while he would make references to events, writers or ideas that Avner had never heard about. The gist of what he was saying appeared to be that the world was a pretty horrible place. Full of wars, suffering and misery. A lot of people seemed to believe that the world was in bad shape for this reason or that; and that if only humanity became religious, or communist, or democratic, it would become better. Some thought it was just a question of Algeria being liberated, or women becoming equal, or Canadians stopping the slaughter of baby seals. But all this was total nonsense.

The world, according to Louis, couldn't be put right until every existing institution in it had been erased – a *tabula rasa*, as he put it – and people could start building it up again from scratch. Therefore, he said, for the group of people who understood this, it didn't matter whether other people were fighting for this cause or that cause; whether they were blowing up a place for the socialist future or for the glory of the church. As long as they were blowing it up, Louis explained, they would be helping humanity. The small group who understood this – a very small group, *Le Group*, more like a family – would help such people, whether they agreed with their cause or not. To be more precise, Louis said, *Le Group* agreed with every cause. If you stopped to consider it, there was really no unjust cause in the world.

It wasn't, of course, that *Le Group* rejoiced in places or

179

people being destroyed – only madmen would rejoice in that – but they understood that the more quickly and thoroughly people blew up everything, the sooner they could stop blowing things up altogether. It was that simple.

Avner was not remotely swayed by anything Louis was saying. If he had talked pompously or with great fervour, Avner would have regarded it as even greater nonsense than whatever Andreas' Baader-Meinhof undergraduates had been frothing at the mouth about in Frankfurt. But Louis had a shrugging, self-deprecating, humorous way of saying everything, a kind of take-it-or-leave-it anecdotal manner. Like a very smooth stand-up comedian, he would often make Avner laugh. Even when he was being serious, he would not be earnest. 'Look at the so-called great powers,' he would say. 'Look at the CIA, tripping over its own tail, or the KGB goons in their floppy pants. They're barbarians. Then look at Paris, look around: a thousand years of history. Why should we entrust ourselves to *their* hands?

'If you forgive me for saying so, we're smarter than they'll ever be. We even have a slightly better taste in women.'

It would take another year before Avner fully understood what Louis was saying during their first walk through Paris – or why he was saying it. Avner's sixth sense was flashing a green light, but real understanding would come only two more hits and several thousands of dollars later. It would come only after he had met Papa himself – Louis' father – the ex-*maquis* with his grey hair and ruddy face, who looked a little like Avner's own father, except for his old-fashioned black suit and the thick gold chain dangling from the fob in his vest. Papa, the French patriot, who in his time blew up a lot of *Boche* trucks and trains in occupied France – until, as he explained with a big wink, he had acquired a taste for it. Papa, who as a shrewd and rational Frenchman – a simple peasant, as he called himself – realized after the war that there was a lot of money to be made out of the incurable passions of the world. Papa, who had sent Louis and his two younger brothers to the Sorbonne, not to be taken in by all the books they would have to read at the famous university – books, *merde*! – but to keep their eyes open for other passionate and daring young men and women who might be useful one way or another for *Le Group*.

Avner may never have understood everything about Papa and his family – three sons, including Louis, an elderly uncle and two or three cousins – who were running such a brilliant terrorist-support organization in Europe. For instance, he never really understood Papa's politics. They didn't seem to have much to do, in fact, with the vaguely anarchistic ideas expounded by Louis during their first walk along the Champs Élysées. True, Papa appeared to have nothing but contempt for all governments, including the French, and said that he'd never work or allow anyone in *Le Group* to work for them. He would shrug and grimace, even spit on the floor, when the conversation turned to the American, Soviet or British secret services. Eh, *merde*! The Mossad, *merde*! The *sales arabes*, *merde*!

But his special dislike seemed to be reserved for the Anglo-Saxons of the world, whom he believed to be engaged in some gigantic conspiracy against the people of continental Europe. The Russians, though he didn't like them, did not seem to bother Papa nearly as much. He didn't hate even the Germans as much as he did the Anglo-Saxons. In fact, he appeared to blame the English for the Germans, the Russians, the two World Wars, the unrest in Africa, the Middle East. It was hard to tell whether Papa blamed the English more for building an empire, for snatching one away from the French, or for dismantling it in such a hurry after the war. As a European continental patriot, perhaps as a Catholic, possibly even as a peasant, a common man, considering himself to be an heir of the glorious French Revolution, Papa seemed to be waging a war far more ancient than any conflict current in the world. A war whose origins were lost in the mists of European history as well as in his own mind; a war against the snotty Queen of England and the perfidious British aristocracy who had put arsenic in Napoleon Bonaparte's soup on the island of St Helena.

But if Papa had some trouble seeing the woods – at least as far as Avner was concerned – he had none in seeing the trees. On the contrary, he and his sons seemed to be on first-name basis with every tree in the dense forest of clandestine activity in the 1970s. Certainly in France, probably in Europe, and possibly throughout the world. It would have been an exaggeration to say that *Le Group* had information on the whereabouts of every agent, terrorist, recruiter, organizer or spy involved with the vast and incredibly complex network of anarchist revolutionaries in the world, but it was no exaggeration that they had information on a substantial portion of them, which they would sell to any others willing and able to pay the price. Though never – at least, never knowingly – to any government, as both Louis and Papa were proud to point out to Avner, after they had got to trust him enough. Dealing with governments was against their principles, for one thing. For another, they considered it too dangerous. Governments and secret services were far too treacherous and unscrupulous, in addition to being inefficient and riddled with office politics. They wouldn't even know the meaning of a certain *code d'honneur*, an honour among thieves.

In addition to selling information, Papa was also selling services. One of the first things he had learned during his years in the *maquis* (the French resistance in World War II) was that guerrillas needed safe houses, safe transportation, supplies of food, clothing and weapons, supplies of documents, and people to dispose of everything after the work had been done. Including, sometimes, the bodies. Such jobs – as well as the work of surveillance – were generally better and more easily performed by ordinary men and women, natives of the country where the clandestine operation was being set up – people who might have specialized in such work anyway in the course of their legitimate occupations. It was just a question of money. 'What do you know about locks?' Papa would ask Avner, once they got to know each other better. 'But, I – I will send you a locksmith. Why would you dig a grave? I'll send you a gravedigger. For a small fee, *n'est-ce pas*?'

The great discovery of Papa's peasant genius was that for a small fee some people would do anything, many people would do many things, and almost everybody would do something. For instance, just about everybody would do more of what he or she did for a living anyway. A driver would drive, a gunsmith would make or fix a weapon. For their 'small' fee, all they would be asked to do in addition was not to talk to the authorities, which – outside of the unreliable Anglo-Saxon countries – most people were loathe to do in any case. It did mean maintaining a lot of different people on a payroll in a lot of different countries, but *Le Group*'s fees were large enough to cover the expense.

Another of Papa's great discoveries was that agents, like all other foreigners, would generally enter or leave a country via scheduled airlines, trains or ships, or sometimes by private cars. Very few agents would bother fighting their way across bush or mountain country between unmanned border points in peacetime, or take off from secluded airfields in private planes. Once inside a country, they would favour certain cities, and inside those cities, certain hotels, banks, rental agencies and restaurants. Therefore, having someone on a modest payroll in those places, at those key crossroads, whose sole job was to report on the arrival of a known – or unknown but suspicious – foreigner, would probably bring a fair number of terrorists and agents within Papa's radar-scope. Not all, by any means, but a fair number. Enough for continuing business.

The details of all this, however, were for future discovery. No mention at all had been made of Papa at the point when Avner said goodbye to Louis under the Arc de Triomphe around 1 am, promising to keep in touch. 'My car's that way,' Louis said, pointing towards the avenue Victor Hugo, 'unless you need me to walk you back to your hotel.'

Avner smiled. 'I'm not staying at the hotel where we met,' he said. 'I'll just grab a taxi.'

Louis smiled as well. 'How stupid of me,' he said. 'Of course, you're not staying at the Royal Monceau in Room 317. I forgot.'

Avner raised his eyebrows and nodded. Fair's fair. Louis was very good. Also safe, for the time being. He would not give away that he knew Avner's room number if he were planning to harm him.

'It was a pleasure meeting you,' Louis continued. 'Tony tells me it was a pleasure doing business with you. Remember, if you need anything, let me know – whatever it is. I can't promise I will always have what you want – but it's possible. Keep it in mind.'

'I will,' Avner replied. They shook hands. Then, as Louis started walking away, Avner said: 'Oh, Louis, one more thing.'

Louis turned.

'Do you happen to know,' Avner asked, 'a man named Hamshari?'

Louis took a step closer to Avner.

'I know Mahmoud Hamshari,' he said. 'He lives in Paris, but I don't believe he is in town right now.'

'In a few days I'll call you at the number I have for you,' Avner said. 'Will you let me know if Hamshari is back?'

Louis nodded. 'Let me give you a better number, though,' he said to Avner. 'I may not be there, but if you call at 6.15 pm, Paris time, you don't have to leave your name; I'll know it's you. Just leave me a number where I can call you back.'

Avner memorized the number, hoping he wouldn't forget it before he could give it to Hans. Remembering numbers was not one of his strong points, though he was better at numbers than names. It was one of his nightmares that he would check into a hotel one day under a new identity – and wouldn't remember who he was supposed to be. According to company legend, it did once happen to a young Mossad trainee.

Avner always envied people like Hans or Carl who could remember anything.

But he was elated about his meeting with Louis. So elated, in fact, that a mischievous spirit overcame him as he was walking along the deserted hallway of the Royal Monceau. He wanted to do something, some kind of prank, out of sheer exuberance. Avner had always been fond of practical jokes: it was something he must have inherited from his mother. But in the end he pulled himself together and did nothing. It would have been the height of lunacy to jeopardize the entire mission for a prank.

A curious thing about the team was that they were all pranksters at heart, addicted to practical jokes, which often they had to make conscious efforts to resist. Steve, for instance, had a coin that was 'heads' on both sides, which – knowing that Robert would invariably choose 'tails' – he'd always use when flipping for such chores as shopping or cooking. Robert, for all his mechanical inclinations, took months to discover the trick, and then only because the others burst out laughing. But Avner was the worst, and when in an unguarded moment he told the others that as a child he used to be called *shovav* or imp, he was soon dubbed 'Mother Imp' by Steve – combining his fondness for practical jokes with his penchant for worrying about the neatness or the eating habits of the others in the group.

The next morning Avner checked out and, after calling Andreas and Yvonne, who had plans of their own in Paris, flew back to Frankfurt. The same night he reported to his partners on the meeting with Louis.

'Well?' Hans asked, looking at Carl.

Carl lit his pipe. 'Sounds as good as Tony, anyway,' he said. Robert and Steve nodded.

It was one of the things Avner liked about his team. Different as they might have been from him, or from one another, they shared one important characteristic: no fuss. No endless 'ifs' and 'buts', no endless chatter. Careful planning, yes; but no useless belly-aching about all the pros and cons fertile human minds could conjure up, especially if fuelled by the kind of caution that really amounted to cowardice. They were not like that, any of them. They could see the odds at a glance, and if they seemed right – time to act! Perhaps it was not the attitude people in the Diaspora, the old Holocaust Jews, would have called 'Jewish', but it was the attitude without which Israel would never have come into being. At least not as far as Avner was concerned.

So it was to be Mahmoud Hamshari. The Number three target on Ephraim's list.

Chapter 7

MAHMOUD HAMSHARI

IF THE STATUS of the PLO had amounted to that of a country, Mahmoud Hamshari – Dr Hamshari, as he was sometimes called, because of a PhD in economics from the University of Algiers – would have had the status of an ambassador. As it was, he was the PLO's official representative in Paris. He had a desk in the offices of the Arab League. He published a newsletter called *Faht-Information* and maintained liaison with various Arab delegates to UNESCO in the French capital. Casual acquaintances would describe him as a cultured, well-mannered man who tended to dress and behave like any other diplomat. In a way Mahmoud Hamshari was more French than a Frenchman, leading a conservative – indeed bourgeois – existence in a modest, bourgeois neighbourhood, keeping middle-class hours in a middle-class apartment, living with Marie-Claude, his French wife, and a little daughter named Amina.

A soft target.

What Mahmoud Hamshari's casual acquaintances did not know was that – at least according to the Mossad – he was also one of the chief organizers of terrorism in Europe. From behind his façade as a diplomat, a legitimate public relations man for the Palestinian cause, he was said to have coordinated elements of such celebrated acts of terrorism as the attempt on Ben-Gurion's life in Copenhagen and the mid-air explosion of the Swissair jet.

As well as the massacre of the Olympic athletes in Munich.

According to the team's information Dr Hamshari was not about to retire from these activities. On the contrary. Along with two other soft targets on Avner's list, he was in the process of organizing an entire terror network involving many native French and other non-Arab anarchists, often referred to as the *Fatah-France*.[1] Hamshari was said to be one of the leaders of Black September, the terrorist organization with which Yasser Arafat's Al Fatah denied any contact at the time. Al Fatah's official position in the early 1970s was to oppose guerrilla activity outside Israeli-occupied territory. Unofficially, however, Black September became Al Fatah's 'fighting arm', spreading the extremists' indiscriminate brutality all over the Middle East and Europe. Such a division was in the time-honoured tradition of revolutionary movements of the anarchist-nihilist type, with roots going back to Russia's nineteenth-century Ishutinites, whose movement consisted of an outer circle of respectable theoreticians, activists and apologists designated as 'The Organization' and an inner circle of assassins called simply 'Hell'.[2]

'What about a hand coming out of the shower and shooting him?' asked Avner, who had never heard of Ishutin and his followers, but was much preoccupied with showers.

The others shrugged, but didn't laugh. Avner was not joking. They had all agreed that, unlike Zwaiter, Hamshari should be killed in some spectacular way. Speed was not as essential as it had been the first time. It might be weeks before Hamshari returned to Paris, and by then they should have a plan that no one could mistake for a chance killing. His death should not be merely an act of revenge, but serve as a warning to other terrorists that 'the Jews had long hands' – as Ephraim had put it – and no cover, no façade of respectability, would ensure their personal safety.

At the same time it was imperative that no harm come to Hamshari's wife or his little daughter, or to anyone else in his home, car, or office. Even if the other victim turned out to be a fellow terrorist or sympathizer, it would not relieve the team from the responsibility of having done wrong. Not to mention if they hurt a truly innocent by-stander. There must be no victims apart from the eleven on Ephraim's list.

Privately, Avner often wondered if it was possible to ensure this. It was certainly possible to try but would mean, in all likelihood, no explosives again.

'I don't know why you chaps keep saying this,' Robert remarked in some irritation. 'Explosives can be highly controlled. They can be every bit as focused and limited as a bullet. They don't have to spread any further than the immediate target, if you design them with some intelligence.'

'Okay,' Avner replied. 'Don't get upset. We're listening.'

'I haven't come up with anything yet,' said Robert. 'I just don't want you to exclude me from the start.'

'Oh, we'd never do that, chum,' Steve countered. 'What about a bomb in his toilet? Presumably he's all by himself when he's taking a crap.'

'Please, don't be disgusting,' Hans grimaced, obviously offended.

All of which did not bring them any closer to having a plan when, around 20 November, Louis reported to Avner that Hamshari was back in Paris, according to his information. But, he continued, *Le Group* had some other information which might interest Avner. Within the next few days Louis understood that there was tò be a meeting in Geneva of three people involved in the Palestinian movement. Would Avner be interested in their names?

'Yes, I would,' Avner replied.

Louis coughed discreetly. 'I take it,' he said, 'that we're having this conversation on a business basis?'

'Of course,' Avner replied, waiting for Louis to name a figure, which he did not. Apparently he would be satisfied with the understanding and submit his account later, very much like a lawyer, doctor or other professional. 'Have you heard of a man named Fakhri al-Umari?'

'Umm,' said Avner noncommittally. In fact, he had not.[3]

189

'He'll be meeting, I believe, with Ali Hassan Salameh and Abu Daoud,' said Louis.

Avner's heart skipped a beat. Hard targets. Numbers one and two on their list. *The* men behind Munich, especially Salameh. The ultimate heads of Ephraim's monster.

'In Geneva, eh?' he asked Louis, making an effort to control his voice.

'That's my understanding,' Louis said.

'We're interested in Geneva,' said Avner. He was trying to think fast. 'We're also interested in Paris. Can you keep on top of both situations, on a business basis of course, and I will call you back the same time tomorrow?'

'Will do,' replied Louis.

The next day Avner flew to Geneva with Carl and Steve. Hans and Robert joined them two days later. They decided to stay away from the centre of town, booking rooms in a hotel on the route des Romeles, not very far from the Palais des Nations. Geneva had never been a very comfortable place in which to operate, especially for the Mossad. Safe houses were difficult to rent, and hotels were highly undesirable as bases for agents. The Swiss secret service, to put it mildly, was uncooperative. They welcomed foreigners but only as long as they conferred, shopped and banked – stayed on their best behaviour and departed as soon as possible. The Swiss did not object to rough traders inside their borders, only to rough trade.

However, Ali Hassan Salameh and Abu Daoud[4] were worth the risk. If the team could get no one but these two, the mission would be a success. All five had agreed from the beginning that the minute they had a solid lead on Salameh's whereabouts they would abandon everything else and go after him. Salameh was the one the Mossad regarded as mainly responsible for the deaths of the eleven Israeli athletes.

But the Geneva meeting between Salameh and Abu Daoud turned out to be another *canard*.[5] Actually Louis used an English expression when he talked with Avner on the telephone two days later. 'I'm sorry,' he said, 'if I sent you on a wild-goose chase.'

Hamshari, on the other hand, was staying on in Paris. By 25 November, when Avner contacted Louis again from Geneva, he could report on Hamshari's routine in much the same way as Tony had reported on Wael Zwaiter's. Just as in Rome, there was no discussion about the reason for the surveillance. Though Louis may well have surmised Avner's intentions right from the beginning, talking about it would have amounted to a grave breach of etiquette, might even have resulted in Louis withdrawing from the operation altogether. It was oddly hypocritical – but there it was. Avner felt sure that if he had asked Louis to bring him a gun, then have a grave dug and ready an hour later, he would have complied; but if he had asked him to help kill someone, Louis would have said no. Louis was there to supply information and services only. The use to which they might be put was no longer *Le Group*'s business.

Hans referred to it as the Pontius Pilate factor.

In discussing this or any other assassination among themselves, Avner and his partners always did so in purely technical terms. And this time it was Robert who came up with the plan that seemed best designed to satisfy the requirements of both flamboyance and safety. It grew out of a discussion about Hamshari's chief method for recruiting and organizing terrorists and their projects.

'Isn't he on the phone all the time?' Robert asked. 'His house must be like a switchboard, phoning all over Europe and the Middle East. Well! Let him die by the telephone.'

The following day Avner, Carl and Steve left Geneva for Paris. Hans took the train back to his Frankfurt laboratory to prepare additional documents. Robert flew to Brussels.

For some reason, between the latter part of the nineteenth century and World War II, a thriving armaments industry developed in the small and relatively pacific country of Belgium. This was especially true of the region north-east of Liège, the upland of Hevre, where during that period handguns, automatic weapons and explosives were being manufactured not only in factories, but often in small workshops around villages and on private farms. The art of handcrafting weapons and infernal machines was frequently handed down from father to son, making Belgians – along, perhaps, with the craftsmen of Spain, where a similar development had taken place – the internationally acknowledged masters in concealable instruments of bloodshed. Curiously enough, it was the advent of Nazism and Fascism, both in Belgium and in Spain, that put an end to this cottage industry, because the victorious armies of Hitler and Franco naturally insisted on putting the manufacture of all armaments under their own control. By the end of World War II the Belgian small-arms industry had been all but wiped out, while in Spain Generalissimo Franco permitted only three factories to make pistols, one of them also being allowed to manufacture revolvers.[6]

In Belgium only a handful of individuals practised the traditional craft, working from isolated farmhouses. However, they still managed to supply a not insignificant portion of Europe's illicit arms market. Some of their products were among the most sophisticated in the world and Robert knew he could count on them.

As the PLO's representative in Paris, Mahmoud Hamshari had frequent contacts with the press. He would not have found it unusual, during the first week of December, 1972, to receive a phone call at his apartment in No. 175, rue d'Alésia, from an Italian journalist requesting an interview. What might have surprised him on meeting the journalist in a small neighbourhood café the next day was that, even for an Italian, he seemed curiously uninformed about Palestinian affairs. The journalist kept fussing with his pipe, and finally suggested to Hamshari that he might be better prepared to interview him after he'd read the press kit the diplomat had brought along for the meeting. They agreed that the Italian would telephone him again in two or three days.

Carl felt that his performance as the Italian journalist had been, if not flawless, at least good enough not to arouse their target's suspicion. It also gave him a chance to acquaint himself with Hamshari's voice. Meanwhile Avner and Steve had meticulously explored the bustling, crowded, cosmopolitan but respectable neighbourhood in the 14th *arrondissement* of Paris where Hamshari lived. Driving in a small Renault supplied by Louis, they practised the approach and escape routes for two days, starting from the church of St Pierre de Montrouge on the place Victor Basch, roughly the midway point of the rue d'Alésia, and about four blocks from No. 175. They experimented with the morning traffic pattern from the Jardins du Luxembourg all the way to the Hôpital St Joseph, and from the Gare Montparnasse to the Hôpital Cochin, deciding that the best escape route after the hit would take them along rue Vercingétorix to the boulevard Lefebvre, past the Palais des Sports, across the pont du Garigliano, then along the boulevard Exelmans to their safe house on the Right Bank. The way the operation was set up there would be no need for them to abandon any cars.

Louis' surveillance team had in the meantime reported on Hamshari's routine, which was fairly predictable. Though he spent much time in the company of other Arabs, some of whom may well have been connected with the 'armed struggle', he had, contrary to previous reports, no bodyguards.[7] It was the early part of his days, in particular, that tended to follow the same pattern. His wife and little girl would leave the apartment shortly after 8 am, Madame Hamshari dropping Amina off at a kindergarten, then generally pursuing her own activities for the rest of the day. As a rule, she would not return to No. 175, rue d'Alésia until after she had picked up Amina again in the early evening.

Hamshari himself would be alone in the apartment until some time before 9 am, when he would receive a phone call from a woman named Nanette, who may have been his mistress, and who had an apartment in the Right Bank's more elegant 17th *arrondissement* off the avenue Niel – not far from one of the team's Paris safe houses. Nanette would make her morning phone call to Hamshari from a post office on the corner of rue d'Alésia and rue des Plantes, just a few blocks from No. 175. Presumably she'd be checking to see if Hamshari was ready or whether his wife and daughter had left the apartment. Receiving an affirmative answer, she'd get back into her Renault and pick up Hamshari, who by that time would be waiting for her in the street. Finding a parking spot around rue d'Alésia, which had a fire station as well as several covered market stalls, was never an easy business.

Avner and Carl agreed that the best time for the hit would be the period between 8 and 9 am, after Hamshari's wife and daughter had left the apartment, and before the arrival of Nanette. He would not only be alone then, but, expecting Nanette's call, could be counted on to pick up the phone instead of just letting it ring. The exact date of the hit would be predicated on how soon Robert's explosive device could be designed, manufactured, smuggled into France, and put in place inside Hamshari's telephone.

The making of bombs, where safety and selectivity were not factors, was relatively simple. The main explosive would be a comparatively stable substance, often commercially available, like dynamite or *plastique*, which could then be fitted with a small detonator – a tiny amount of very unstable explosive often of the nitric or sulphuric acid family – which could be set off by anything from percussion to a small amount of weak electric current. It could be activated mechanically by, for instance, an alarm clock or even an egg timer, or by any wireless signal from a radio transmitter or a simple TV remote-control switch.

The problem with a mechanical trigger – say, the ignition switch or gear lever of a car – was that it would respond to being operated by anyone at all, and could not be deactivated if the target was unexpectedly accompanied by others. This was an even greater problem with timing devices, which would obviously explode the bomb whether or not the target, or anyone else, happened to be in the vicinity. While this could be a matter of total indifference to terrorists who often did not have specific targets anyway, it ruled out the use of automatic triggers for Avner's team.

Triggers operated by a human agent, who could visually determine that the target, and only the target, would be affected by the explosion, were the only solution – but in most urban situations it was impossibly dangerous to run wires from the bomb site to wherever the assassin was to lie in wait. Radio signals could overcome this problem, but would create a different one: anyone operating a radio on the same frequency in the vicinity might set off the explosion at any time.

With the proliferation of powerful walkie-talkies, citizen-band radios and other remote-control devices, the danger of accidental detonation became so acute that careful explosives experts like Robert would not even work on the installation of a receiver, unless the bomb was deactivated by a separate switch, for fear that it might blow up in their hands. The only solution, in fact, was such a separate switch. One that would arm the bomb, often with the intended victim operating it unwittingly. Then, and only then, could the bomb be set off by an observer using a radio signal.

As Robert explained the plan. The bomb would be installed in the base of Hamshari's telephone. It would be perfectly harmless until the receiver was lifted off the cradle, but once Hamshari lifted the receiver, the bomb would be armed. At that point a radio signal could be sent to trigger the explosion.

Avner thought the device, as described, was almost accident-proof. Almost. Since it would clearly have to be installed at least half a day before the hit, what if Madame Hamshari decided to settle down for a long telephone chat that evening with one of her friends? A radio-ham somewhere in the neighbourhood might decide to start transmitting on the same frequency as the bomb's receiver at the same time. What would happen then?

Robert shrugged. It was clear what would happen. There

was no such thing as absolute zero risk. His device would reduce the risk to as near zero as possible; but if even this was too much risk for Avner, they would have to think of an entirely different way. There wasn't enough room in the base of a telephone for *two* receivers, each on a different frequency, one to arm the bomb and the other to explode it.

'All right,' said Avner, after a little hesitation. 'Make sure you don't make it so big we kill everybody in the whole damn building.'

'I have a different problem,' Robert said. 'I'll have to make sure it'll pack enough punch for the *mechabel* standing right next to it. There isn't much room in a telephone.'

The bomb was smuggled into France from Belgium on 6 December, a Wednesday. It looked very small and light, as Avner held it in his hand. Hardly enough to harm a man, except Avner remembered seeing the damage an ounce and a half of *plastique* could cause inside a letter bomb – a favourite device of the terrorists. It was less than three months earlier, just a few days after the Munich massacre, that a Black September letter bomb killed an Israeli diplomat in London.[8] 'Let's hope it works,' Avner said as he handed the box back to Robert.

That same day the team split up into two new safe houses provided by Louis, who had also arranged for the earlier safe house where they had been living.

On Thursday, 7 December, there was an unexpected hitch. The plan was to wait in the morning until Madame Hamshari had left with Amina, and Nanette had picked up Hamshari in her Renault. Then, shortly after 9 am, Robert and Hans, dressed as telephone repairmen in uniforms provided by Louis, were to enter the apartment and install the bomb. Robert estimated that the work might take twenty to thirty minutes, less rather than more. Avner, Steve and Carl were to wait outside the building – Carl, as the Italian journalist, very much out of sight – to warn Robert and Hans if a member of the Hamshari family should return. In the event, Louis provided a young French couple whose only job would be to engage Madame Hamshari in conversation until Avner or Steve could get the other two out of the apartment.

However, Nanette did not show up that Thursday, and even Madame Hamshari returned to the apartment before long. Hamshari himself did not leave at all.

Avner, Carl, Hans and Robert soon left the area. There was no point in waiting in front of No. 175, rue d'Alésia for hours, when they knew the routine had been interrupted for some reason. It could even have been dangerous. Only Steve and Louis' couple remained in the vicinity. But it wasn't until shortly after 6 pm that Steve called to say that Hamshari was leaving the house on foot and that he was going to follow him.

The partners drove back to the 14th *arrondissement* immediately. With Hamshari gone, there was a good chance that Madame Hamshari would also leave to pick up the child from the kindergarten – unless that was what Hamshari had gone to do himself. Robert and Hans, still dressed in their uniforms, drove their van to the nearest parking space across from No. 175. Avner stationed himself in the post office on the corner of rue d'Alésia and rue des Plantes – the same one that Nanette always used – and waited. Carl kept out of sight.

Steve rang almost as soon as Avner had taken up his place. Apparently Hamshari had gone to 'an Arab-League-type building' (Steve, whose French was no better than Avner's, couldn't say which one) on the boulevard Haussmann. If Madame Hamshari herself left shortly, the team would have at least three-quarters of an hour before either of them returned.

By the time Avner had walked the three blocks from the post office to Robert's van, across from No. 175, rue d'Alésia, he could see Hamshari's wife coming out of the brightly lit ornate main door of the apartment building. She was almost certainly going to the kindergarten for Amina. Here was a chance. It was perhaps a little late in the day for making telephone repairs, but the Postes Télégraphes et Téléphones might always respond to an emergency call. Besides, Avner trusted the phenomenal indifference of urbanites in any big city. Concierges were ceasing to be watchful, even in Paris, and neighbours would hardly ever ask questions. Anyway, the team had no choice. The bomb would not get into the telephone by itself.

Robert and Hans disappeared under the archway of the entrance, carrying their toolboxes.

For about fifteen minutes Avner stood alone next to the van on rue d'Alésia. He wished he had some chewing gum. Once he thought he caught a glimpse of Carl crossing the street a block or so away, but in the dark he couldn't be sure. Avner wondered if he would even see Hamshari or his wife in time to warn Robert and Hans if they came back before his partners had finished.

Then, almost before they could even have had time to pick the lock, Robert and Hans came sauntering back across the street.

'You're joking,' Avner said. 'All set?'

'Well, I don't know,' Robert replied. 'I guess we'll find out tomorrow morning.'

On 8 December, a Friday, they took up their posts across the street from Hamshari's apartment building shortly before 8 am. Robert, Avner and Carl in the van, parked about 200 yards away; Steve and Hans in a car, parked a little closer to the main entrance. The latter were acting as guards, and it was also their job to make sure Madame Hamshari or the child did not return to the apartment at the wrong moment. Louis had no operatives on the scene that morning.

It was almost 8.30 when Hamshari's wife and little girl emerged from the building. They were making for the bus stop, not very far away. As Nanette could be phoning any minute, it was important to act quickly.

Carl got out of the van and walked to a public phone in a nearby bistro about fifty yards away, turning around to check that there was a clear line of sight through the window between himself and Avner. Then he lifted the receiver and started dialling.

Avner glanced at Robert sitting beside him in the van.

Robert's head was also turned in Carl's direction. He held a small box in his hand, one finger resting lightly on a toggle switch.

Carl was still standing by the phone, holding the receiver to his ear. His lips seemed to be moving, but from that distance it was impossible to hear him or even be sure he was speaking. It didn't help matters that even now he was holding the stem of his pipe between his teeth. But Avner was not watching Carl's mouth; he was watching his right hand. Slowly, deliberately, with a movement that was just a little unnatural, Carl was raising his right hand and bringing it to the crown of his head. His fingers wiggled a little. It was the signal.

Avner could feel Robert tense beside him. He must have seen Carl giving the signal, too – but he would move only on Avner's command. 'Go!' Avner snapped, his eyes shooting instinctively up along the façade of No. 175.

He could not hear the click of the toggle switch beside him. He could not hear any explosion. But he could see a sudden shimmering of the air along the front wall as if a little shiver had run through the entire building. And he could see a criss-cross pattern of cracks appearing in one of the large windowpanes that the percussive force had shattered.

A few passers-by stopped and looked up.

Someone was opening the French windows on a second-floor balcony, coming out and first glancing down into the street, then craning round trying to look up at the windows above him.

Carl was walking purposefully back towards the van.

They had done it.

They had done it again.

In the evening they were not so sure, sitting in one of the safe houses, watching the news on TV, looking at the late editions of the papers. Hamshari was still alive. Hurt badly, without any doubt, but it was impossible for them to tell from the reports whether or not he would survive. He had been taken to the Hôpital Cochin on rue du Faubourg Saint-Jacques – the other hospital, St Joseph, would have been a little closer, but the ambulance was probably pointed the other way – and by now he might even have told the police about the Italian journalist who had phoned him just before the explosion.

Hamshari had sounded a little strange on the phone, Carl told the others, a little hoarse, as if he had just been wakened from his sleep. Carl wasn't even sure of his voice, so after explaining that he was the Italian journalist calling for his interview, he asked him if he was, in fact, Dr Hamshari. Carl scratched his head only when he heard the reply – yes, that's me – coming from the other end of the line.

Robert seemed especially upset, even defensive. He could have made the explosive stronger, he explained, but they were all so insistent that no one else be hurt that he had tried to make doubly sure the blast would be contained in the room where it occurred. According to the early news reports, the authorities were baffled by the source of the explosion and mentioned 'sabotage' as only one, remote possibility. Avner was not unduly concerned; even if Hamshari should survive, they had taken him out of action for a long time, perhaps forever, and it didn't seem to matter what he could tell the police about the 'Italian journalist'. They might eventually make the connection between the journalist and the bomb – in the end they would probably have discovered that it was a telephone bomb even if the explosion had been much stronger – but by that time Carl would be long gone and the team would not use the same method again anyway.

They spent two more nights in their Paris safe houses. They returned the van and the car, as well as some handguns, to Louis. They paid the balance of their bill – some two hundred thousand dollars, of which by that time they had given Louis about one hundred and fifty thousand the preceding weeks – then, each taking a different flight, and with passports different from the ones used to enter France, they flew back to Frankfurt on 10 December. It was Sunday. The police seemed to be swarming all over the Paris airports, but no one had challenged them. At that point, as far as they knew, Hamshari was still alive.[9]

Avner did not fly to Frankfurt. He flew to New York.

His ostensible reason for the trip was a rumour – picked up not by Louis this time but by one of Hans's old Paris informers – that Ali Hassan Salameh or some other high-ranking PLO terrorist might be going there soon to coordinate a raid with the Black Panthers on an *El Al* aircraft at Kennedy airport. It was a rumour worth checking out, though Avner did not really believe it. Salameh, a rather aristocratic terrorist in his own way, was unlikely to have much in common with Black Panthers.

In any case, Avner also had a personal reason for going to New York. He wanted to find an apartment for Shoshana.

In his own mind, he enumerated the reasons. One, he missed her – actually missed her more than he had imagined he would. During the mission, which might last for years, he would probably have no way of visiting her in Israel. He should not be returning to Israel at all during that time, except in some dire emergency – after which it would be doubtful if he would be allowed out again to continue the mission. The others – except Steve, who wasn't married – already had their families outside Israel, and had already visited them once or twice.

Two, he had some vague feeling, a kind of warning from his sixth sense, that he might not be returning to Israel to live, even after the mission. There might be a reason – maybe operational, maybe not – that could prevent him from returning. Well, in that case, why not New York? After all, Avner had always wanted to live in America (wanted to *be* an American, his mother would have said) and the few times he had visited New York had certainly not changed his mind. As for Shoshana, perhaps if he moved her to New York – as a temporary arrangement, during the mission, so that they could see each other from time to time – she might grow to like it. Perhaps she would not insist on going back to Israel to live.

There was also a third reason. Avner *needed* Shoshana. He was twenty-five years old, and he had not been to bed with a woman since September. He was certainly looking at women, but he never did anything about it. Perhaps he wanted to stay faithful to his wife; perhaps there was simply too much pressure. The others, except for Steve, did nothing for sex, as far as Avner could tell. Of course, *they* could visit their wives once in a while, or perhaps they didn't need it – the subject never came up in conversation. But Avner certainly needed it; he needed it badly. He made arrangements to rent a one-bedroom apartment in Brooklyn, in a building where they allowed pets, so that Shoshana could bring Charlie. He gave them a down payment for occupancy in April. By that time the baby should be three months old.

On 20 December – Avner would never forget the date – when he was already back in Frankfurt, he telephoned Shoshana. It was incredible. She said something to him on the phone, something that he would never have expected to hear from her. Not from a *sabra*, not from an Israeli wife, whose husband was on a mission. 'The baby's due on the twenty-fifth,' Shoshana said, 'and I want you to be here.'

Avner didn't even know what to reply for a second. Then he said, 'I'm coming over.'

'No, you can't,' Shoshana said, obviously shocked by her own request more than by Avner's response. 'Don't be stupid. I didn't mean it. I've got everything here. I'm going to the hospital on the twenty-fifth; everything's being looked after . . . I was only joking, you have nothing to worry about.'

'I'm coming over,' Avner repeated. Then he added: 'Don't say anything to anybody.'

Two days later, using a false German passport, without saying a word to his partners, in total contravention of operational instructions, Avner sneaked into Tel Aviv. He knew that what he was doing was inexcusable and if he had been seen by anyone on his own side, God knows what would have happened. The best he could have hoped for would have been complete disgrace. If the other side had spotted him, he could have jeopardized the mission, his own life, and his partners' lives. He had never been more terrified about crossing a border illegally, partly because of what was at stake, but also because, like most of his compatriots, Avner had a somewhat exaggerated idea of Israeli security. It was not a baseless idea – Israeli counter-intelligence being top-notch – but Avner, like many people, believed it to be better than that. Which it was not. But believing it to be near-infallible, as he did, Avner had to be pretty desperate to risk breaching it. Which he was.

Avner spent four days in Tel Aviv, seeing no one but his mother and Shoshana. He did not even dare to visit his father – or go with Shoshana to the hospital. However, after the baby was born, late at night, playing the role of an uncle, he asked the night nurse to let him take a look. The baby, so the nurse assured him, was a girl. It was the ugliest thing Avner had ever seen.

Shoshana surprised him again. Avner expected something of an argument, but it seemed now that she wanted to go to the United States. 'I don't care if I'm going to be alone most of the time,' she said. 'I don't care if I'm going to see you only twice a year. I don't want the grandparents to bring up our daughter.'

They made a date for April in New York.

Chapter 8

———◇◇◇◇———

ABAD AL-CHIR

THE TERRORIST ORGANIZER Hussein Abad al-Chir spent a great deal of his time in Damascus, outside the team's operational area. This was the main reason Avner and Carl designated him as a hard target; otherwise al-Chir was not known to be armed or guarded. By occupation he was a teacher specializing in Eastern languages. His occupation in the 'armed struggle' was as the PLO's contact man with the KGB operation in Cyprus. He was Number ten on Ephraim's list.

Al-Chir came to Avner's attention in Paris through a conversation with Louis. People on *Le Group*'s payroll in Nicosia had picked up some rumours about a possible commando action being planned by the Palestinians: terrorists were to board a Greek ship which would call at the Cypriot port of Kyrenia, near Nicosia, as part of its normal schedule before continuing to the Israeli port of Haifa. At Kyrenia, automatic weapons and maybe explosives would be smuggled on board for the terrorists. Once in Haifa, the terrorists would take over the ship and wreak as much havoc as they could, in the manner of the kamikaze attack at Lod airport.

'This, by the way,' Louis said, 'is on the house.'

'Can you tell me anything more,' asked Avner, 'on a business basis?'

'I can try and find out more,' said Louis. 'The only other thing I heard was that the people doing the raid would be travelling on Afghan passports. The guy coordinating in Cyprus is apparently called al-Chir.'

This happened a few days before the Hamshari hit. Avner

discussed it with the others. If Louis' information was correct, al-Chir would have to turn up in Nicosia before long. Cyprus was not outside the team's operational area.

Before leaving for Israel, Avner had given Carl the number he had for Louis. (Until then Avner had been the only one maintaining direct contact with Louis, though the others had met some of Louis' operatives.) Now Avner arranged with Louis that Carl would phone him every day. If anything developed concerning al-Chir in Cyprus, Carl was to call Avner after 27 December at a number in Athens.

On that date, having said goodbye to Shoshana, he flew from Tel Aviv to the Greek capital.

Avner knew Athens well, though his memories of this cradle of Western civilization were anything but pleasant. It was in Athens that, as a Mossad trainee, he had encountered for the first time a hint of that dark, mysterious aspect of the work which his father muttered about. It was in Athens, too, that he realized that little Dutch boys were also civil servants, working in a bureaucracy, filled like any other bureaucracy with personal loyalties, enmities, intrigues and office politics.

The incident itself was simple. Quite unremarkable, really. The older Mossad man who was at the time the station chief in Athens got drunk one night. He got drunk in public, in a restaurant, in the company of his considerably younger wife, Avner, and another young Mossad operative. The station chief, needless to say, was not known to be an Israeli agent; his cover was that of an Athens businessman, and as such it was not necessarily a great breach of security for him to get drunk in a restaurant. However, he happened to be an ugly, obnoxious drunk, and at the height of his inebriation he had climbed on the table, unzipped his fly, and if Avner and the other young agent hadn't stopped him, he would have urinated on some other patrons. His wife, who was apparently used to her husband's occasional displays of vulgar pugnacity, simply got up and left the restaurant, leaving the two young agents to cope with their drunken boss.

They did so without any further mishap, but Avner was

205

quite shocked by the affair. He was a raw trainee with certain illusions; he had just arrived in Athens; and he took it for granted that his station chief would be a man to respect. Also, while Jews may have as many vices as any other ethnic group, being drunk and disorderly is the rarest of them. Avner could not recall ever seeing another example of it – and this man was supposed to be a Mossad station chief. It was inexcusable.

He decided to write a report on the incident, after discussing it with the other young agent. He, too, had said that he was going to mention it in his report. After all, it was their duty: their boss might be a man in need of psychiatric help. It even crossed Avner's mind that the whole thing might have been a test, something staged for him as a trainee just to see if he would hush it up out of some misguided sense of loyalty to the older man. Well, they wouldn't catch him out on that!

However, to Avner's utter amazement, after he got back to Tel Aviv about a month later, he was told to report to the Mossad equivalent of a personnel department. There, sitting in an office, three men were waiting for him. Looking very sour. Typical Galicianers, as far as Avner was concerned.

'You've made some very grave allegations in this piece of paper,' said the first one, shoving Avner's Athens report at him across the desk. 'We advise you to withdraw them.'

Avner was stunned. 'What are you talking about?' he asked. 'That's what happened. Look at the report of the other guy who was there with me.'

'We've looked,' said the Galicianer smugly. 'There's nothing in it about this alleged incident. Maybe it was just your imagination.'

'Even if it wasn't,' said the second man, 'look at it this way. The man you're writing about did important things for Israel when you were still wet behind the ears. Now he's only a year from retirement. A thing like this, it could have bad repercussions. And you – you're not perfect either. I could show you *his* report about *you*.'

'But,' said the third Galicianer, 'maybe it's not necessary. Maybe it's just a personality conflict. We forget about his report; we forget about your report. Then everybody's happy.'

It happened to be the wrong note for Avner; it reminded him of some people he'd known in the kibbutz. The Galicianers looking out for their own. He stood up. 'You have my report,' he said. 'I don't care what else you have. What you forget and what you remember is your business. Is there anything else?'

The Galicianers didn't reply, and Avner walked out of the office. He was seething. No one said anything to him about the incident again, but it left a very bad taste in his mouth. When his next Athens assignment came, about eight months later, the Mossad in Greece had a different station chief.

The interesting thing about it was that now, two years later, arriving in Athens from his highly irregular visit to Tel Aviv, Avner would have had more understanding for the station chief. Today, he might not have written a report.

In any case, that was all ancient history.

Carl called as soon as Avner arrived in Athens. He called, moreover, not from Frankfurt but from Nicosia. He and Hans had already been there for a day, keeping al-Chir under observation.

Almost as soon as Avner had left for Israel, Louis reported that al-Chir had turned up in Cyprus. In Avner's absence Carl decided to join Louis' operatives in Nicosia with Hans, dispatching Robert to Belgium for a conference with his bomb-designer friend. (Steve was in Spain, checking out another lead.) Robert wanted to go to Belgium anyway for a post-mortem, as it were, because he felt very unhappy about the performance of his exploding telephone.

Within hours Avner was with his partners in Nicosia. They were staying in a safe house arranged by Louis, keeping al-Chir under surveillance. They reported happily that he had met with the man known to be the KGB resident in Cyprus. Unfortunately, they also decided to celebrate Avner's arrival by having lunch with him, leaving the terrorist organizer in the hands of Louis' Nicosian surveillance team. By the time they had finished lunch, al-Chir had checked out of his hotel and taken off from the airport for some unknown destination.

There was nothing to do but return to Frankfurt; they could accomplish nothing by staying in Cyprus. Al-Chir would eventually come back to the little Mediterranean island which the Soviet Union had selected as one of its fixed points from which to move the earth. The island's geographical location made it a perfect place from which to fan the flames of the Middle East – not to mention the chronic conflict between the Greeks and the Turks.[1] Avner was uncomfortable in Cyprus anyway; it was altogether too Mediterranean a place, combining the elements of climate and temper that he could well do without. Let Louis' people keep a lookout for al-Chir in Nicosia.

Steve's Spanish lead fizzled out in the meantime, so he also returned to Frankfurt. As did Robert. 'Listen,' Robert said to Avner as soon as he saw him, 'you have to let me try again if we do that Cyprus hit. My friend and I have worked out a new system.'

'Yeah, I know,' Steve said irreverently to his roommate, 'an invisible bomb that gives him liver disease and shortens his life by ten years . . . Why don't we just shoot the bastard?'

'You're jealous,' Carl said to Steve, 'because he won't let you play with his rubber duck.'

They all laughed, including Steve. Even though Robert stopped short of rubber ducks for the bathtub, the safe house the two of them shared was filled with amazing toys that he would not let Steve touch. It was a source of minor friction between them. Once when he came home unexpectedly to find Steve trying out a remote-control car, Robert got quite testy. Steve retaliated by using his rigged coin to make Robert lose a flip deciding which of them would get his ear pierced for a hippie disguise to penetrate a safe house and make contact with an Arab informer. Robert never forgave him for that.

'Oh, settle down,' Avner said. 'Obviously the way we do it depends on the location and the target's routine. So far he has always stayed at the Olympic Hotel in Nicosia. Assuming that's what he does the next time,' Avner turned to Robert, 'how would you do it?'

'Six little bombs,' Robert replied promptly, 'under his bed.'

'Why six?'

'To make sure we get him,' Robert said, 'without getting anybody else.'

This brought up a somewhat touchy subject. Avner took Robert's and his Belgian contact's expertise for granted – and the telephone bomb was an ingenious design – but the fact was that it did not kill the target, at least not outright. The last time Avner talked on the phone with Louis, the Frenchman very tactfully recommended an explosives man he could supply for a price if Avner thought he needed one. Avner mentioned this to the others. Robert wouldn't hear of it. He wouldn't touch any device he didn't help to make himself.

'But if you're so keen on Louis,' Robert said, 'I tell you what he could do. He could bring the stuff to Cyprus for us, from Belgium.'

This made sense. In a way, the most risky part of any operation was taking illicit material, such as weapons or explosives, across international borders. Many terrorists solved the problem, at least for less bulky packages, by using the diplomatic couriers of Arab or Eastern bloc countries whose official pouches were exempt from ordinary customs control. Since Avner's team could not employ such methods, *Le Group* was clearly better equipped for smuggling.

For more than two weeks there was no news on al-Chir or any of the other targets. Hans used the time to work on a pet project – setting up an antique furniture dealership in Frankfurt. Hans loved antiques and understood a great deal about them. He also had a very good head for business, unlike Avner or Steve. He actually enjoyed buying and selling.

Carl – Cautious Carl – fully approved of the idea. An antique business could give the entire team, with their constant travelling and irregular hours, at least some rudimentary cover, as well as a way of shipping larger objects across various borders, should the need arise. Avner appreciated the idea, though the only cover he had ever worked out for himself was playing the German lotteries and the British football pools. He started even that as a trainee; it was an excellent way to provide an innocent explanation for having the communication code numbers, which he could never learn or remember, in his possession on various bits of paper.

Avner used the waiting period to fly to Geneva and leave two messages for Ephraim, using for the first time the prearranged method of communicating through the safe-deposit box. One was a message about the possible raid on Haifa. The second was a personal message, asking his case officer to facilitate Shoshana's trip to New York in April. It had been understood from the beginning that Ephraim would help Avner meet his wife abroad during the mission, and Avner did not find it necessary to spell out that Shoshana would not be returning to Israel.

Since he was in the Geneva bank anyway, Avner did one other thing. He took a look at his personal bank account, the one in which his monthly salary was being deposited while he was on the mission. It was still a modest amount, but it was growing nicely. It amused him to think that he already had more money in a Swiss bank than he had ever managed to save before.

The phone call from Louis came on Monday, 22 January. Abad al-Chir would be arriving in Cyprus within a day or two. It was impossible to know how long he was planning to stay.

That night, the team landed in Nicosia. Avner and Robert went to a safe house, while Carl, Hans and Steve checked in at the Olympic Hotel. It was Carl's idea that some of them should stay at the hotel where they expected the target to be. For one thing, it would help them identify him positively. For another, it would enable them to study the layout of the building. Finally, though they would check out as soon as al-Chir arrived, their presence later in the hotel would arouse no suspicion among the hotel's service or security staff. They would be recognized as guests the staff had seen before.

By Tuesday lunchtime Louis' people had delivered a package for Robert from Belgium.

Later the same day, Abad al-Chir checked into the Olympic Hotel.[2]

Steve and Carl reported – the first with some amusement and the second with some concern – that the target was apparently occupying a room next door to a newly-wed couple from Israel who had come to Cyprus to get married because the girl was not Jewish. This was quite common, because the religious authorities in Israel would not solemnize mixed marriages.

'Well,' Steve offered, much to Hans' dismay, 'sounds as if there will be some banging in both rooms.'

'I take it there is no way they could get hurt?' Avner asked Robert.

'No way,' Robert said firmly. Then, less firmly, he added: 'Of course, I'm not giving you a written guarantee. If it's a written guarantee you need, call it off.'

'Or warn them, maybe?' asked Hans, then shook his head to give his own reply. In an operation of this kind no one could be warned. The team would either assume the risk or not. Which was up to Avner.

'We'll take a chance,' Avner said.

'You mean, we'll make *them* take a chance,' Hans said unexpectedly. 'Would you like to be next door when Robert's six little bombs go off?' It was a surprising statement for a team member to make after Avner had spoken, but Hans' concern was genuine and everybody felt it. After a little silence Robert said: 'Oh, for heaven's sake! I'm *giving* you a written guarantee.'

That settled it.

This time Robert's infernal machine was essentially a

pressure bomb, consisting of six small explosive packages connected to a double frame. The two frames were held apart by four powerful springs with a metal screw running down the middle of each. Placed under a car seat or a mattress the springs would prevent the screws in the top frame from touching four contact points in the bottom. However, the weight of a human being would depress the springs sufficiently for contact to be made. In a simple pressure bomb, the explosives would be detonated at this stage.

However, in Robert's device the weight would serve only to arm the bomb. Once armed, it could be exploded by a human agent using a radio signal. If no signal was sent, the device would remain inactive. Similarly no stray signal could explode it accidentally or prematurely, until the target had put his weight on the object under which the bomb was hidden. The safety feature meant that the rigged bed would blow up only when the team was certain that al-Chir himself was in it.

On the morning of 24 January, a Monday, Ephraim's Number ten target left his hotel room around 8. He was picked up in a car by the KGB resident and another person, who also looked Russian, or at least did not look like an Arab or a Cypriot. The car was being followed by several different vehicles from Louis' surveillance team – six people in all – who had instructions to call Carl immediately if the Russians seemed ready to bring al-Chir back to the hotel. In fact, the terrorist-organizer stayed all day in a house known to be rented by the Russians in Nicosia.

Shortly after noon, when the cleaning staff had finished their work, Robert and Hans let themselves into al-Chir's hotel room with the help of another one of Louis' men. They placed the bomb on the metal spring netting in his bed under the mattress. They also disconnected the main light switch of the room, leaving only the bedside lamp functional. When that light went off at night, al-Chir would almost certainly be in his bed.

The Russians drove al-Chir back to the Hotel Olympic

shortly after 10 pm. They walked him to the main entrance where, just before he entered, one of them handed him an envelope.[3] One of Louis' operatives went up in the elevator with the man he did not know was about to die to make sure no one else entered al-Chir's room.

No one did. In about twenty minutes the lights went out in his window. (The Israeli newly-weds' window next door had been dark for some time.) Outside, Avner and Robert were sitting in one car; Hans and Steve in another. Carl, as usual, was on his own.

Avner waited for about two minutes after al-Chir's lights went out before giving Robert the order. Just in case the Arab turned out the light before getting into bed. In fact, Avner was still too early. When Robert pressed the button on his remote-control box, nothing happened. Al-Chir might have been sitting on the edge of his bed, taking off his socks, not putting enough weight on the mattress to depress the springs.

Robert pressed the button a second time after a count of ten. He pressed it with gritted teeth, with an enormous force, nearly crushing the fragile bakelite box in his hand. The force was quite unnecessary, since it would have made no difference if al-Chir had still not been lying in his bed. But he was.

The explosion was tremendous. It blew a tongue of flame along with a shower of glass and masonry into the street. Clearly, Robert was making up for the weaker bomb that did not kill Hamshari outright. After such an explosion, Avner had little doubt about Abad al-Chir's fate.

As they drove away, lights were coming on in every window of the hotel and in buildings along the street. On this unfortunate island the Greeks must have thought the Turks were attacking, while the Turks would be entertaining similar suspicions about the Greeks.

Chapter 9

BASIL AL-KUBAISI

On 17 March, 1973, Carl and Avner were sitting in Avner's room at the Hotel du Midi in Geneva. There was a third person sitting across from them in an armchair, propping his long legs up on the bed.

Ephraim. His unexpected visit was the result of office politics, intelligence-agency style.

After the al-Chir hit, the five partners regrouped in Frankfurt. They had left Cyprus one by one, using different routes, with Avner travelling via New York, in order to conclude his living arrangements for Shoshana. Carl was the last to leave.

He had gone into the hotel right after the explosion to make sure that the assassination had been successful without hurting anybody else. Much to his relief he found that, except for their target, everyone in the hotel had survived without a scratch – including the Israeli newly-weds. On the other side of their thin wall, however, al-Chir's body and bed had been blown to pieces.

Back in Frankfurt, the team remained without leads for about three weeks. However, on 25 February, Louis left word for Avner to meet him at Frankfurt airport where he would be spending an hour in transit.

At the meeting Louis gave Avner precise information on four more of his targets. (After Zwaiter and Hamshari, Avner saw no point in maintaining the Baader-Meinhof fiction he had originally used with Tony, and had told Louis, even before the assassination of al-Chir, that he was in the market for information on Palestinian terrorist leaders. He did not specify their names – his function was to gather intelligence, not to give it away – and said nothing about his connection with the Mossad. The Frenchman, as always, acknowledged Avner's request without asking any questions.)

Now Louis told him that one terrorist leader would be arriving in Paris early in March. For the other three he had a current address: an apartment building in Beirut.

The one in Paris was the Number nine 'soft' target on Ephraim's list: Dr Basil al-Kubaisi. The ones in Beirut were hard targets; known terrorist leaders who could never travel in Europe under their own names. They were Kamal Nasser, official spokesman for the PLO; Mahmoud Yussuf Najjer, also known as 'Abu Yussuf', the man responsible within Al Fatah for the activities of Black September; and Kemal Adwan, then in charge of terrorist activities in Israeli-occupied lands. On the team's list, they were Numbers six, seven and eight.

This was vital information. Avner had no way of knowing whether the Mossad would be independently aware of the Beirut address or not. He felt that it was his duty to let Ephraim know – asking permission at the same time for the team to be allowed to go into Lebanon to assassinate the targets. Without special permission they were not supposed to operate in any of the 'confrontation states', as the countries bordering Israel were called.

Somewhat to Avner's surprise, Carl put up a strong argument against letting Ephraim know about the Beirut lead. Cautious Carl, having many years of 'company' experience behind him, felt that other people within the Mossad would immediately make a grab for the job. The team was an independent entity, Carl argued, not obliged in any way to pass on information to Tel Aviv. They were, by the very terms of their mission, no longer 'working' for the Mossad. For its part, Carl said, the Mossad would never allow them to extend their operation into Beirut, but would simply use the information the team got to mount a regular Mossad-type operation and reap all the glory. Sharing information was not the way to get ahead.

It was also unnecessary. The team was doing just fine. If they assassinated enough field men in Europe, the headquarters men in Beirut would eventually be forced into the open. Terror did not organize itself; with Zwaiter, Hamshari, al-Chir and maybe one or two others eliminated, sooner or later Adwan, Najjer and Nasser would be forced to come to Europe.

Avner was astounded. Although he did not have a real argument with Carl, he did remark to the older man that Carl was doing exactly what he suspected Tel Aviv would do with the information: play politics; try to hog the glory. Who cared about 'glory'? Who cared about 'getting ahead'? They were not civil servants climbing their way up some bureaucratic ladder; they were soldiers in a life-and-death struggle. How could they withhold information from Israel?

Carl shrugged. It was always better to have a few cards up one's sleeve. Especially when playing with the *le'histader* crowd back in Tel Aviv – the ones who were busy sharing out the dumplings.

Avner looked a little shamefaced at this, perhaps because Carl had hit on Father's expression: having a card up one's sleeve. Maybe it was the simple truth. Besides, who was Avner to lecture Carl on patriotism? And how could he, the little Dutch boy, say with a straight face that he didn't care about glory?[1]

In any event, Carl turned out to be right. Ninety-five per cent right, anyway.

Avner flew to Geneva to leave the message, and about ten days later flew back to pick up Ephraim's reply from the safe-deposit box. Ephraim's message was: do nothing. Hold tight. He would be in Geneva to meet Avner and Carl on 17 March.

Now, sitting in the Hotel du Midi, they spent the first few minutes exchanging pleasantries and congratulations, though it seemed to Avner that their case officer wasn't going overboard on praise for what they had done so far. It's all very good, Ephraim would say, but it's taking a little time, isn't it? And it's certainly taking more than a little money. Admittedly it's a great morale builder back in Israel, the news that the *mechablim* don't just have the run of the whole world, murdering travellers, children, athletes with impunity; that nowadays they, too, have to be looking over their shoulders. Very good. But – it would be hard to assess whether or not it was having the effect of slowing down terrorism. Judging by some recent cases, it might be doing just the opposite.[2]

'Anyway,' Ephraim continued, 'that's none of your concern at this point. We're still one hundred per cent behind the operation but we have another problem.'

'You may not realize this, but your existence is a big mystery. Not just to the enemy – may it remain a mystery to them forever – but to our own people. The ones who do know about you, you can count on the fingers of one hand.

'Now there's beginning to be a lot of pressure. Inside, you understand. People are beginning to say, what gives? Terrorists being knocked down all over Europe, and we don't know anything? Department heads, at the Thursday meetings.[3] Must we get the information from the newspaper, they say, don't you trust us anymore?'

'Oh, come on,' Carl said edgily. 'I'm sure you can cope.'

'We're coping for now, you don't have to worry,' Ephraim replied. 'But we're trying to think ahead. As I say, there's some pressure. Other people have their own ideas on how to deal with terrorism and maybe their ideas are not so bad. We can't say to them "hold off" forever. We can't say "our big secret stars in Europe need more time".'

'Well,' asked Avner, 'what's the point of what you're saying?'

'Only this,' Ephraim said. 'This information you have on Beirut, we know it already. We've known it for a long time. There have been plans. Not just our people, but the army and so forth. The decision may be to move in, in a much bigger

217

way. Not just Mossad, but a joint operation. Do you understand? So these three *mechablim* are off your list. We don't need you for them.'

Avner looked at Carl. Carl looked back at him. They both shrugged, then Avner said, 'Fine. You don't need us – you don't need us.'

Ephraim said, 'So, give me a complete briefing. Not just the address, we know that already. Everything you've got. The whole set-up.'

'Oh, come on,' Avner said, getting annoyed. He looked at Carl again, but the older man smiled and waved his hand, as if to say, that's exactly what I was warning you about, now deal with it on your own. Avner turned to Ephraim. 'What do you mean, the whole set-up? We're to find out their movements, their routine, everything, use all our sources, but not do the job?'

'We're doing the job, don't you understand?' said Ephraim. 'You guys are not even working for us, remember?'

'Fine, we're not working for you,' Avner replied. 'You said it. So go get your own information.'

He was astonished to hear himself, and Ephraim looked a little astonished as well, but then he started to laugh. 'What is this,' he said, 'kindergarten time? I don't believe it! Never mind who you're working for, you're army reservists, you're Israeli citizens: I'm asking you for some information. Are you forgetting what this is all about?'

Arguments like this always brought out a stubborn streak in Avner. It was perhaps the same quality that made him walk the length of Israel with fifty pounds of gear on his back, despite the athletic guys collapsing around him. 'We're not forgetting,' he said. 'Maybe you're forgetting, what with all this talk about pressure, and other people having their own ideas. Anyway, don't you guys have enough to do? You need to spread the work around? If you need *our* information, why can't *we* do the job?'

'Listen, maybe this thing is getting to you,' Ephraim said,

still making light of it. 'Maybe you need a rest. Why can't you do the job? Because that's what we decided. From now on, you want us to submit all decisions to you, so you can tell us whether it's reasonable or not?' He went on, 'And what's this about your information? You think your informers fell in love with you? You got information because you paid a lot of money. Maybe you want me to tell you whose money?'

Ephraim had a point. But it was still a frontal attack, and as such, would only make Avner dig in deeper.

'Forgive me, I forgot,' he said. 'It was your money. Well, there's still a lot of it in the bank. Why don't you just go and take it? See how much information it'll buy you.'

Carl intervened at this point, as both Avner and Ephraim clearly hoped he would. 'Look, you know exactly how it is. In this business a lot of things depend on personal relations.

'Our informers don't know exactly who we are. Maybe they don't want to know – partly for the money, partly for other reasons – so they don't ask. If we just told them, now you go work for the Mossad, you go run around with the paratroopers in Lebanon, probably most of them wouldn't. For any money.'

'And what's more,' Avner added, 'they might even have second thoughts about *us*. I'm not taking that chance.'

He felt like adding, 'And maybe I'd advise them not to work with you anyway, because they couldn't trust you.' But he quickly thought better of it.

Ephraim said nothing for a while. He got up, walked to the window, spent some time looking at the sombre buildings on the other side of the Rhône, then lowered himself back into his armchair. 'You guys stick around Geneva,' he said, 'I'll contact you in a couple of days, and we'll talk some more.'

Carl and Avner did not stay in Geneva awaiting Ephraim's return. They flew to Paris where Robert, Hans and Steve had already been making arrangements for the surveillance of Basil al-Kubaisi. On the question of Beirut, the five of them reached an agreement very quickly. Whatever proposal Ephraim might come back with, they would not hand over the services of *Le Group* to the Mossad. Later Avner would admit to himself that, in part, the reason for this decision was childish. Petty pride. Being miffed at being excluded.

But it was mainly for reasons of security, their own as well as the security of Louis' people in Beirut. Avner and his partners could not guarantee that there would be no slip-ups, no infiltration, no double agents around an operation which they did not handle themselves. The risk would simply be too great.

Ephraim came back to Geneva on 23 March. His suggestion was a compromise. The team would go into Beirut and prepare the hit, using their own contacts and resources and operating entirely on their own, without direct instructions or supervision from anyone. Then, when everything was prepared, special commando units would take over and do the actual assassinations. It would be a joint operation between the Mossad and the Israeli army. It would extend in scope much beyond the killing of three terrorist chiefs.

When Ephraim outlined the details of the plan, even Avner and Carl had to agree that such an operation could not be done by five people and a support team of French privateers. It was big.

It was also unbelievably audacious.

Ephraim was to inform them as soon as possible of the actual target date. Time was of the essence, since they could not know how long the *fedayeen* leaders would stay in their Beirut stronghold. The operation would probably take place some time before the middle of April. This, however, raised another problem.

The timing might interfere with the team's plan for the al-Kubaisi hit in Paris.

Avner came up with a solution.

'As soon as we have the date,' he said, 'Carl and Steve can go to Beirut. Robert, Hans and I will deal with Kubaisi here in Paris. As soon as we're finished, we join you in

Beirut. So, it's going to be a tight couple of weeks in April. So?'

Avner had no idea at this point how tight a schedule it was going to be.

On 1 April word came from Ephraim. The target date in Beirut was 9 April. Carl and Steve immediately prepared for their rendezvous in the Lebanese capital with some members from *Le Group*.

On the same day Louis had some new information for Avner. The man who was Black September's replacement contact with the KGB would be arriving for a meeting in Athens, probably around 11 April. The successor of the late al-Chir was a Palestinian named Zaid Muchassi, also known as 'Abu Zeid'. The team knew very little about him, except that he was a terrorist organizer who until recently had been working out of Libya. Carl thought an 'Abu Zeid' might have been the victim of a letter-bomb explosion sometime in October, 1972 in Tripoli. If this Muchassi was the same man, he had obviously recovered from his injuries. Of one thing there was no doubt: Muchassi was the *fedayeen*'s new link to the Soviets. *Le Group* had picked him out some time ago by keeping al-Chir's old KGB contact under surveillance.

Muchassi, of course, was not on Ephraim's list.

For Carl, this made the matter very simple. 'He's not on the list, we don't touch him,' he said. 'It's academic who he is and what he is. Anyway, between Kubaisi and Beirut, what else do you want to do? Don't we have our hands full?'

Avner had a different view.

'He's not on the list, that's true,' he said to Carl. 'Believe me, I'm the last person to start looking for people, just in case we don't have enough to do. It would be crazy.'

'And it would be wrong,' said Hans.

'I agree,' Avner said. 'But think about it for a second: *why* was al-Chir on the list? Maybe Ephraim didn't like the colour of his eyes?'

'He was on the list for one reason. One reason only. He was the contact in the Soviets' main staging area, Cyprus.

221

Right? Now the new contact is Muchassi. So what do we say? 'Do we say, if al-Chir organizes a big raid on Haifa we stop him, but if Muchassi does the same thing, hands off? Al-Chir can't do it, but Muchassi's welcome?

'That list's just a piece of paper. The names were on it for a reason. Do we go by the paper, or do we go by the reason? Just think.'

Avner had a point, not only in the abstract, but in the Israeli tradition. Everywhere – in the kibbutz, the army, the Mossad – the stress was always on everybody thinking for himself. Don't just follow regulations. Show initiative. *Think*. This didn't mean blithely disregarding orders or not giving a damn about the drill. But it did mean saying: The drill isn't everything. It's there for a reason. Look to the reason behind the drill. If there is a conflict between the letter and the spirit of a rule – if you are certain there is a conflict – follow the spirit. Act like a man, not like a machine.

In practice, however, it was not so simple.

'Before you decide,' Carl said, 'think about it this way. If you do Muchassi, and it's okay, you're a hero. If you leave him alone, you're still a hero. If you do him and it's not okay, you're a bum.'

'That's a two to one chance,' Hans added, 'to be a hero by doing nothing.'

This remark stirred Steve sufficiently to take Avner's side in the dispute. 'The way you guys talk,' he said to Hans and Carl, 'is enough to make me sick. Is that what happens when you reach forty? All you think about is covering your ass?'

This was enough to bring Carl and Hans around. In truth, they rather wanted to be brought around anyway. Carl would still have proposed the compromise of checking with Ephraim first – going beyond the list, even for the best of reasons, was a major departure – but there obviously wasn't time for that. It would have involved two trips to the Geneva safe-deposit box with a waiting period of five or six days in between.

'The way we do it,' Avner decided, 'Carl and Steve leave

for Beirut tomorrow. Hans, Robert and I make sure we finish Kubaisi here by the sixth. Then I join Carl and Steve immediately, but Robert and Hans go to Athens to set up Muchassi. They don't need more for that than maybe a day. Then they join us in Beirut.

'When Beirut is over, which is the ninth, we go to Athens. As many of us as we need for the job.'

Later, looking back on the events of April, 1973, Avner would admit that he had had an additional reason for pushing to do three major operations in three different cities within days of each other. The truth was that Ephraim's reaction in Geneva to what the team had done up till then worried him. Ephraim didn't exactly say: What's taking you guys so long? He didn't say: Do you think you are on a luxury cruise? But, somehow, Ephraim didn't seem too impressed. He wasn't enthusiastic enough. It was not that their case officer should have treated Avner and Carl like heroes – Israelis couldn't expect to be treated like heroes just for doing a hazardous assignment; half the country was doing hazardous assignments; just *being* an Israeli was a hazardous assignment, in a way – but Ephraim's attitude seemed so equivocal, so low-key, that Avner was afraid it might be signalling a change of heart in Tel Aviv about the entire mission. Some people back in the bureaucracy, in the Mossad, in the cabinet, who knew where, might be saying *why*? Why are we doing this, sending five men on a trip around the world for six months for millions of dollars, just to get rid of three terrorists? It's stupid!

And if this was so, Avner would never become the little Dutch boy. On the contrary, his name would forever be associated with a mission that was cancelled because it was stupid. 'Oh,' people might say, 'you mean that guy who did that wild-goose chase we aborted halfway through because a bunch of commandos could do better in Beirut in five hours for half the money? And half the fuss?'

Perhaps what Ephraim wanted to convey in Geneva, without actually saying so, was: Step on it. Do better. If you don't, we might have to forget about the whole thing.

Carl must have guessed what was going through Avner's mind, because after the decision was taken to try for all three of the operations, he told him privately, 'Look, maybe you're right, and we'll do it. But don't ever let yourself be pressured. Remember, if you fuck up, people will never admit they've pressed you. They'll say, "What, *us*? We never said a word to him."'

The coordinator of the support team Louis had assigned for the surveillance of al-Kubaisi was a young woman approximately Avner's age. It was the first time Avner had seen a woman doing a bigger job than that of a spotter, housekeeper or a decoy. He knew, of course, that there were many women involved in every echelon of intelligence gathering, and the *mechablim* used women as terrorist foot soldiers with some frequency. A few, like Leila Khaled, Rima Aissa Tannous or Thérèse Halesh, had achieved much notoriety.[4] But as it happened, Avner had never worked with a woman in a higher position before.

'Kathy' was very good at her job. A slim woman, with dark eyes and short dark hair, Kathy could have been pretty if she had not gone to some lengths to make herself look dowdy. She was obviously well educated, speaking both French and English like a native – not unusual for a middle-class Quebecoise, which Avner believed her to be by birth. Like a substantial minority of French-Canadian university students, Kathy probably became involved with the FLQ – Front de la Libération du Quebec – in the 1960s, possibly only as a sympathizer at first. It was from there that she graduated to the point where, like Tony or Louis, she would have been 'past the stage' of talking about politics.

As a matter of curiosity, Avner began wondering what Kathy's politics might be, or if she had any politics left. Why would any woman want to do what Kathy was doing? This question would not have occurred to him regarding a man. The obligation of having to make a living, of having to do *something*, could land a man in the strangest of professions (the way Avner always felt he had 'fallen' into his job as an agent). But a woman whose job was unusual was more likely to have gone out of her way to choose it. In which case, why had Kathy made this choice?

But she could provide Avner with no insight. She was quick, reliable and polite, with an easy laugh, often displaying old-fashioned comradely warmth towards people in the underground. She had a habit of making a stiff little bow, almost like a Prussian officer of the old school, when she shook hands. Kathy shared Papa's dim view of the English. Her dislike manifested itself in little asides and chance remarks. And there was no mistaking the smile on her face when, for instance, the talk turned to Geoffrey Jackson, the British Ambassador to Uruguay, who had been held for eight months in a 'people's prison' by the Tupamaros.

Kathy may have had a certain fondness for 'patriots' in general, which for her meant people engaged in physical combat for their countries, even if they happened to be fighting each other, like the Palestinians and the Israelis. That, at least, was all Avner could ever discern about her feelings. For all other people she appeared to have only contempt. Her habit was to call them 'donkeys'.

'He's not difficult to follow,' she'd say to Avner, referring to Basil al-Kubaisi, 'because he's always walking up rue Royale around ten. There are not too many donkeys around.'

Indeed, being a man of regular habits, Dr Basil al-Kubaisi was not difficult to follow. The Iraqi law professor, one-time lecturer at the American University in Beirut, and (according to the Mossad) by the spring of 1973 an efficient organizer of the logistics and weapons supply for the Popular Front[5], had made it especially easy for *Le Group*. He had done so by way of an unlucky conversation with a pretty ground hostess at the airport when he first landed in Paris on 9 March. 'You see, I'm not a rich Arab,' al-Kubaisi had apparently told the girl. 'I'm just a tourist, a simple tourist. What I need is an inexpensive hotel.' The ground hostess, who supplemented

225

her modest income by being on Papa's payroll, recommended several cheap hotels in the heart of Paris, then (having no idea who Kubaisi was) gave a routine report of the incident to her contact in *Le Group*. From there, a simple check of the three or four hotels she had mentioned led to al-Kubaisi's being spotted by Kathy's surveillance team.

The hotel al-Kubaisi chose for himself is in the rue de l'Arcade, a narrow street in the 8th *arrondissement*. Rue de l'Arcade runs between the boulevard Malesherbes and the boulevard Haussmann, less than a minute's walk from the top of the rue Royale where the Madeleine, one of the most spectacular churches in Paris, forms the centre of a Y-junction. Rue Royale, the stem of the Y, leads to the place de la Concorde. The left arm of the Y, the boulevard Malesherbes, leads to the almost equally spectacular church of Saint-Augustin. The right arm, the boulevard de la Madeleine, leads to the Paris Opéra.

Al-Kubaisi would split his time between the bistros and sidewalk cafés of the Left and Right Banks, often meeting his morning contacts in the vicinity of the boulevard Saint-Germain, while favouring the rue du Faubourg Montmartre or the Champs Élysées for his evening appointments. If his evening meetings found him in the Montmartre, he would stroll along the boulevard des Italiens and the boulevard des Capucines, right by the Opéra, on his way home. (This walk, ironically, would lead him all but past the front door of the safe house used at that point by Hans, Robert and Avner.) If his last appointment took him to the Champs Élysées, al-Kubaisi would walk back to his hotel either by taking the avenue de Marigny past the Palais de l'Élysée and turning right at the rue du Faubourg Saint-Honoré, or along the avenue Gabriel, passing the American Embassy and the elegant Hotel de Crillon, to the place de la Concorde. Both routes would eventually take him into the rue Royale – at a point either below or just above Maxim's, the world-famous restaurant – from where another five minutes' walk past the great church of the Madeleine would see him safely home.

On the evening of 6 April, Dr Basil al-Kubaisi chose the latter route.

Being a careful man – or, perhaps, sensing danger – al-Kubaisi would turn around from time to time, as if to see whether he was being followed. However, he would have been unlikely to notice two different cars passing and re-passing him in the stream of Paris traffic as he was walking along the Champs Élysées. In the avenue Gabriel, Kathy's spotters left him alone. There would have been no point in alerting a target whose route, by then, was known to them anyway.

Avner, Robert and Hans were waiting for a phone call in their safe house – not far from the boulevard des Capucines, near the top of the right arm of the great Y-junction – to tell them that the target was approaching rue Royale. The plan was for them to pick up al-Kubaisi near the Madeleine, at the centre of the Y, then follow him on foot as he walked along its left arm towards his hotel.

The phone call came at a few minutes past 10 pm.

At this precise point al-Kubaisi, walking along the quiet avenue Gabriel, was not under direct observation, except perhaps by the Paris police guarding the American Embassy. Al-Kubaisi might have chosen this deserted street for that very reason: no one was likely to attack him under the watch-ful eyes of the well-armed *gendarmerie*. At earlier and later points along his route he would feel sufficiently protected by the much denser pedestrian traffic. He was isolated only during the short walk from the top of rue Royale to his hotel.

After it rounded the obélisque on the Place de la Con-corde, the first of Kathy's surveillance cars observed al-Kubaisi already walking up the rue Royale. This car didn't stop or even slow down. Reaching the top of the broad, elegant shopping street it turned right on to the boulevard de la Madeleine, flashing its lights once to alert Avner and his partners who were walking at a fast pace in the opposite direction.

The second car – with Kathy herself sitting next to the driver – followed al-Kubaisi at a slower speed, eventually passing him as he had nearly reached the top of rue Royale. This car did not turn right. Instead, it rounded the church, stopping at the far side of the Madeleine at the corner of a smaller street named rue Chauveau Lagarde. It waited parallel to the kerb, in front of the large indoor 'Parkings Garages de Paris', its lights out and engine idling.

Avner and Hans, with Robert following about fifty paces behind them, were crossing the top of rue Royale – from the right arm of the Y-junction to the left – just as al-Kubaisi was crossing the boulevard Malesherbes perhaps a hundred yards ahead of them. Since the Arab was walking at a brisk pace, it was not easy to close that gap within the next block or two without betraying their intention to catch up with him. But any further on would have been too late. Between the third and fourth block, al-Kubaisi would already be at his hotel.

At that point there were hardly any pedestrians in the broad boulevard, and even the traffic was light. From the way al-Kubaisi glanced over his shoulder on reaching the opposite side, it looked as if he might be easy to spook. Should he decide to break into a run, Avner thought, they might not be able to catch up with him at all. One more short block would take him to the rue de l'Arcade where he'd turn right; then an even shorter block to the passage de la Madeleine. From there he had only one more block and a bit to go. Once al-Kubaisi had crossed the traffic lights at the rue Chauveau Lagarde, they would probably have lost him.

Avner and Hans tried to quicken their pace without giving the appearance that they were doing so, which was not easy. If al-Kubaisi did not start running until they had halved the distance between them, it would be too late for him. At this point the quartermaster of the Popular Front was clearly no longer oblivious of being followed. He, too, had quickened his pace and started glancing back at Avner and Hans. Still, he wasn't running. Avner found himself hoping that his target might be a courageous man of steady nerves.

To his misfortune, al-Kubaisi was courageous. He didn't break into a run as he turned into the rue de l'Arcade. He didn't run as he passed the flower shop, the elegant 'Au Lotus' cigar store, and the small Hotel Peiffer on the corner of the passage de la Madeleine. He merely walked faster and faster, looking back over his shoulder one more time. Avner and Hans, giving up all pretence of strolling casually, were by now less than thirty yards behind him. Robert was following them a little more slowly on the other side of the narrow street. Avner and Hans could thus concentrate solely on their target, knowing that Robert would keep everything secure behind them.

Though al-Kubaisi didn't run, Avner and Hans might still not have caught up with him in time if he hadn't decided to stop at the red light on the corner of the rue Chauveau Lagarde. This was strange behaviour for a man who knew he was being pursued. There was absolutely no traffic in the street, yet al-Kubaisi halted at the kerb, looking at the automatic traffic signal, hesitating in front of a large drugstore called Pharmacie de la Madeleine.

Avner and Hans passed him on either side, stepping off the kerb into the street. The reason they gave themselves for this was that they wanted to face al-Kubaisi to make absolutely sure they had the right man. In addition they both had an aversion to gunning someone down from behind.[6]

A few seconds earlier Avner had glanced up to see if anyone might be watching from a window, and he noted with satisfaction that they were passing underneath some awnings which would obscure the view from the windows directly above them. This still left the windows on the other side of the rue de l'Arcade, but it was already cutting in half their chances of being seen. Not zero risk by any means, but better than nothing. There was no zero-risk method of shooting a man in the street.

'Now,' Hans said, in Hebrew, and in the next second they had both turned, facing al-Kubaisi, left hands rising in an arc, ready to pull back the slides of their Berettas. Al-Kubaisi was staring at them, his eyes unbelievably wide, saying 'La! La! La!' then repeating the Arabic word in English: 'No! No!' As Avner and Hans had walked past him, al-Kubaisi must also have stepped off the kerb. Now, as he tried to back away, his heels caught the edge of the pavement and he started falling backwards, his arms windmilling wildly. For some reason the thought that crossed Avner's mind was that if they missed, their bullets would crash through the large plate-glass window of the Pharmacie de la Madeleine. He didn't want to damage the window. Adjusting the angle of his gun slightly, he started following al-Kubaisi's falling body, squeezing off the first two rounds before he hit the pavement. Twice more he pulled the trigger, then twice again. He was hardly conscious of Hans' gun pop-hissing in the same rhythm beside him, but from the corner of his eye he caught a glimpse of Robert on the other side of the street. He was standing behind a parked car, waiting.

Al-Kubaisi's body was lying on the sidewalk as he fell, his head almost touching the traffic-light standard, but his feet still dangling over the kerb. He made no sound, only his shoulders were squirming. Then, like a person trying to rise, he pulled up his knees and turned to his side. Avner almost fired again, but at that moment al-Kubaisi gave a series of short, sharp, rasping sounds as if he were clearing his throat, and in another second Avner could see his body relax. The man whom the Paris press next day would call Dr George Habash's roving ambassador was dead.[7]

When Avner looked up, the first thing he saw was a cigarette glowing in the dark. In a doorway, on the other side of the street. A man seemed to be standing there, or maybe two men, with a girl. Eyewitnesses.

Without a word, Avner started walking along the rue Chauveau Lagarde back towards the place de la Madeleine. By now Robert had turned around, and Avner knew he would be walking to Sainte-Madeleine the same way they had come, without passing the spot where al-Kubaisi's body lay.

Hans was following Avner. They could only hope that the eyewitnesses were not.[8]

Kathy's cars picked up all three of them on the place de la Madeleine in front of the elegant Caviar Kaspia. They drove back to the safe house, then directly to the airport. By the following day Hans and Robert were in Athens.

Avner was in Beirut.

The speed at which events were happening at this point precluded thinking. Later, looking back, Avner would feel that, if he had only had a moment's time to reflect, he would not have done much of what he did between 1 and 15 April, 1973. Or, at least, he would have done it in a different way. He would have been far more careful. To begin with, he would not have set up a hit in the heart of Paris, in the middle of the street, with only three people plus a couple of getaway cars parked a block away. He would certainly not have had his team fly out of Paris the same night. Brazening their way through an airport swarming with police.

Then again, had he been more careful, perhaps they would all have been caught.

Perhaps the secret was to just *do* it, without thinking about it too much. And if it worked it was professional and brilliant.

Chapter 10

⌒⌒⌒

BEIRUT AND ATHENS

THE RAID ON BEIRUT was certainly regarded as professional and brilliant – at least after the event. It was not nearly as easy to be certain about it on Sunday the 8th.

Carl and Steve had already been in Beirut for two days when Avner arrived. Carl was staying at the Atlanta Hotel, having travelled on a British passport under the name of Andrew Macy. Luckily, Avner had no trouble remembering that. If he hadn't remembered it, he would have had to sit around for half a day in the lobby of the Sands Hotel, until Steve came in. Because Avner had drawn a complete blank on the name that Steve was supposed to be travelling under, even though Hans had made sure that it rhymed: Gilbert Rimbert, a Belgian, because Steve could pass off his Afrikaans as Flemish, at least in Lebanon.

Avner had no trouble remembering his own identity. He was Helmuth Deistrich, a German businessman. He did not check into any hotel, but went directly to a safe house provided by Louis.

Robert and Hans arrived from Athens – via Rome – a day later. Robert also had a Belgian identity as Charles Boussart. Hans preferred to travel under a German name, as Dieter von Altnoder. They both joined Steve at the Sands Hotel.[1]

In 1973 Beirut was not yet the ravaged, burned, strife-torn hulk it was to become two years later when the Lebanese civil war broke out between the country's Muslims and Christians. In April, 1973 Beirut was still a city of tall apartment buildings, casinos and nightclubs, elegant shopping districts and beautiful, well-dressed women. As such, it was perhaps the one city in the entire Mediterranean basin that was to Avner's taste. He thought with pleasure of the exquisite strip of bikini beaches, or the Aden Rock Club of West Beirut, where a valid American Express card would allow anyone to enter a world of modest private pleasures – modest, since Avner would neither drink nor gamble. He would, however, have loved to lie on the beach in a deck chair, soaking up the sun, watching the girls, taking a sip once in a while from a tall glass of crushed ice and Coke.

Instead, Avner and his partners used their credit cards to rent a small fleet of cars – three white Buicks, a Plymouth station wagon, a Valiant and a Renault 16. With *Le Group*'s local contacts acting as drivers, they used Sunday and part of Monday to explore six particular locations. Two were in Beirut itself, three on the outskirts of the city, and one about thirty miles south of Beirut, near the coastal town of Sidon. This last location, and the three just outside Beirut, were guerrilla camps and supply depôts, storing and maintaining arms, vehicles, boats, records and documents. Of the two locations in Beirut proper, one was the headquarters of the PLO.

The other one was the four-storey apartment building where Kamal Nasser, Mahmoud Yussuf Najjer and Kemal Adwan lived.

Since some of the planning, preparation and surveillance had already been done by local agents of the Mossad who would be expected to stay in Beirut after the operation, Avner's team was required only to do the work that the local agents could not do without blowing their cover. This included renting the vehicles that would be abandoned after the raid, and guiding the raiding parties to their destinations. Some local employees of *Le Group* would also be involved, though this was a great – and expensive – concession on the part of Louis to which he very nearly did not agree. However, since Avner gave his word that no Mossad agents or army commandos would meet Louis' people, whose sole job was to allow a small convoy of civilian cars to follow their own vehicles as they drove past certain locations, Louis said yes. The risk to his organization would be minimal under those conditions.[2]

The eight cars were parked near the beach at Ramlet-el-Beida shortly after midnight. Though the area was totally deserted, a few American-made cars along the beach would not have attracted much attention. The natives of Beirut, like most people in the Middle East, went to bed early, but everybody was used to tourists keeping later hours.

It was a moonless night. The sea was black. At 1 am Steve saw the pinpoint of a flashlight in the dark and turned on the lights of his car a couple of times. The flashlight went out. A few minutes later, emerging black from the pitch-black waves, a group of frogmen waded silently ashore. They carried their weapons and civilian clothes in watertight bags.

The forty commandos squeezed themselves into the eight cars – which Steve would later say was the toughest technical problem of the entire mission – and, splitting into two groups, made for the centre of Beirut. Carl and Robert were guiding their raiders to PLO headquarters; Avner, Steve and Hans were leading the way to the apartment block of the terrorist leaders. The raids on the other four locations were organized from different staging points.

Three armed but unsuspecting Palestinian guards in front of the apartment building on the rue el-Khartoum were killed by the commandos as soon as the cars pulled up. The Israelis used handguns and knives so as not to alert the occupants of the building. Avner, Hans and Steve stayed by the cars as the commandos rushed upstairs. The partners were not needed. They might, in fact, have been in the way.

Kamal Nasser, a forty-four-year-old Christian Palestinian, lived in the third-floor apartment. He was unmarried. An intellectual, with a doctorate in political science from the University of Beirut, he became public relations chief for Al Fatah in 1969, and the official spokesman for the PLO a year later. It was a position he managed to retain in spite of a 1971 quarrel with Yasser Arafat, who had found Nasser's stand too militant. When the commandos burst into his apartment he was sitting at his dining-room table next to his typewriter. A couch behind him burst into flames as the phosphorus bullets riddled his body.

On the second floor Kemal Adwan also sat at his desk, writing. Unlike the unarmed Nasser, he had a Kalashnikov within easy reach. An engineer, Adwan was a founding member of the Kuwait branch of Al Fatah; in 1973 he was the head of all sabotage operations in Israeli-occupied lands. He was good at his job and the success of some of his operations may have precipitated the Beirut raid. He was a married man, with two small children. He managed to fire one shot from his automatic rifle before the commandos cut him down.

Mahmoud Yussuf Najjer, known as 'Abu Yussuf', had the responsibility for Black September within Al Fatah; and as the head of the PLO's military-political affairs he was at the time probably third[3] in the constantly shifting hierarchy of the Palestinian movement. He lived on the fourth floor of the building with his wife and fifteen-year-old son. Afterwards the commandos told Avner that Najjer's son was not hurt – though according to other reports he had also died in the shooting. There was no question about Najjer's wife. Trying to shield her husband with her body, she perished with him in a hail of bullets.

A woman in a neighbouring apartment had the misfortune of opening her door. She, too, was immediately killed. The woman appeared to be a truly innocent bystander, no suggestion having been made, then or later, that she was involved in any way with the Palestinian terrorists.

At the PLO headquarters and the other four locations short battles developed between the Palestinians and the raiders. Though outnumbered, the Israeli commandos had the element of surprise entirely on their side. They were also far better trained. Since these two factors are generally decisive in any but the most protracted engagements, the firefights at all locations ended in complete victory for the Israelis. Reportedly over a hundred Palestinian guerrillas lost their lives within the next two hours.[4] The Israelis' casualties were one dead and two or three wounded, who were eventually evacuated by helicopter. The Lebanese authorities, far from being kept in the dark about the fighting, were immediately notified by the Israelis from various public phone booths that gun battles seemed to be developing between rival Palestinian factions at several locations in Beirut. Hearing this, the Lebanese police kept meticulously away, just as the Israelis had expected they would.[5]

By around 3.30 am it was all over. The rented cars – none of which, according to Steve, had as much as a dent – were neatly parked on the beach again. The commandos were evacuated by sea, as were Avner and his partners. The only difference was that they did not get into the Israeli landing craft. A boat took them, as well as two of Louis' people, to a fishing vessel anchored a quarter of a mile offshore. Chartered by *Le Group*, the fishing boat landed in Cyprus shortly after daybreak.[6]

All was not quiet in Cyprus. Coincidentally, the *fedayeen* had scheduled a raid on the residence of the Israeli ambassador and on an *El Al* aircraft in Nicosia for the same day, 9 April. However, the commando action of the Palestinians was far from successful. At the ambassador's home the three commandos managed to wound a Cypriot policeman, while at the airport an Israeli sky marshal killed one of the six raiders – from Abu Nidal's National Arab Youth splinter group – and wounded two others. These terrorists had tried to get at the *El Al* Viscount by driving a Landrover and a Japanese compact on to the runway, but caused no damage to the passengers or the plane.

Still, as Carl remarked, it was not for want of trying.

Israeli Ambassador Rahamim Timor, along with his family, had just happened to leave their residence minutes before the *fedayeen* attack. So after putting the Cypriot policeman out of action, the terrorists packed enough explosives in the ground floor of the house to shatter windows in Florinis Street, in the centre of Nicosia, half a mile away.[7] Had Timor and his family been on the first floor, as the commandos believed they were, there was every likelihood that they would have been killed in the explosion. The Palestinian raid on Cyprus only increased Avner's determination to press on with the team's plan to assassinate Zaid Muchassi in Athens, whether he was on the original list or not.

It was an attempt that very nearly ended in disaster.

In retrospect Avner wondered whether the first mistake might not have been to split the team again, as in Paris. But three of them had managed to handle the al-Kubaisi hit with so little trouble that it did not seem rash to try for a repeat performance in Athens. As before, Avner, Robert and Hans could do the job. In the meantime Steve could follow up any new leads that might have developed, especially in relation to their Number one target, Ali Hassan Salameh. As for Carl, he would be far better employed looking after their various safe houses and accounts. This would enable the team to move quickly again should any of their remaining targets surface in Europe. At the rate they were going, they might even get all eleven *mechablim* on the list. 'Wouldn't that be something!' Avner said, and the others agreed.

It was also a fact that, so far, the mercenaries of *Le Group* had performed faultlessly. In Rome, in Nicosia, in Beirut, and twice in Paris. With the one exception in Geneva, Louis' information had invariably turned out to be accurate, which was a better track record than that of any of their usual Mossad informers. His surveillance people were professional, as were his safe houses. Hans preferred not to rely on Louis' documents, but the team had by now relied twice on his people to deliver them weapons and explosives, and to dispose of their handguns after a hit. Everything had worked without a hitch. It was little wonder that, using such a top-notch support organization, the various terrorist groups of Europe had been performing so well in the past three or four years. If anything, it was surprising that they had not been performing even better.

In Athens, all the team would have to do was rely on Louis one tiny bit more than had been necessary in the past. Since there was no time for Robert to go to Belgium and have the explosives prepared by his usual source, they would use whatever Louis' man could supply in Athens. It was taking a chance – as Robert put it, terrorists blow themselves up with boring regularity – but it was not an unreasonable chance. Terrorists also managed to blow up their intended targets often enough; and, according to Louis, his man in Athens had supplied explosives for Baader-Meinhof's urban guerrillas on several occasions.

As in the past, Avner, Robert and Hans also intended to use Louis' safe houses and surveillance teams.

They arrived in Athens on 11 April – a Wednesday – to find the safe house in which they spent that first night filled with Arab terrorists. Believing Avner and his companions to be from the Red Army Faction of the German underground, the Arabs talked freely in front of them, not only because of their presumed ideological affinity but also because they did not expect the German comrades to understand Arabic. The topic was the recent Israeli raid in Beirut and the Arabs seemed gratifyingly afraid as they talked about lying low in Cairo or Baghdad for the time being. Though Avner had no doubts about the efficacy of counter-terrorism, the way the Arabs were talking helped reinforce his conviction that his team was doing the right thing. Thanks partly to their efforts, the *mechablim* were on the run.

The following day they moved to another safe house, run by a Greek girl who had only a few words of English. She had prepared a very good dinner for Avner and Hans – Robert was with his explosives man at the time – and they were still sitting at their meal when, a little after 6 pm, a call came from Louis' stakeout at the Hotel Aristides in Sokratous Street.

Apparently Zaid Muchassi had just left the hotel; he had been picked up by the KGB man's black Mercedes.[8]

Their plan was to take the Greek girl's car and pick up Robert, along with the explosives. Another of Louis' contacts had arrived with handguns for them – .22 Berettas, as specified – and Avner and Hans quickly selected one each, and one for Robert. Then they piled into their hostess' green Chevy Impala and set out for their rendezvous.

It was a long trip from their safe house off the Imitou to almost the other end of town – the corner of Trius Septembriou and Omonia – where they picked up Robert with his travel bag. (Their second safe house was near a cemetery; as Hans remarked: 'Good, at least we don't have far to walk.') At Omonia the Greek girl, who had been driving until then, left them and took the underground, the *electrikos*, back home. Avner took the wheel and attempted to cope with the traffic at Omonia Square – Athens' Piccadilly Circus – which rivalled that of Rome. A middle-aged Greek from *Le Group*, who had been driving Robert in his own car, changed places with Hans and sat beside Avner. The Greek and Avner in one car, followed by Hans and Robert in the second, covered the short distance to Sokratous Street in a few minutes.

They arrived in front of Muchassi's hotel shortly after 8 pm. Louis' Greek accompanied Robert and Hans into the lobby; Avner stayed outside. While alone with Hans in the other car, Robert had transferred some of the contents of his travel bag into a small suitcase. Naturally, he did not want to do it in front of their Greek companion. It was a firm rule never to disclose the nature of the operation to any of the support team beforehand. This was primarily to protect themselves, but also to protect their helpers from being implicated in a murder charge if anything went wrong. With the sole exception of the man supplying the explosives in Athens, all the others, there and elsewhere, could and possibly did believe – initially – that they were assisting Avner and his partners only in surveillance or sometimes in bugging a hotel room or an apartment.

At the Hotel Aristides, Louis' Greek engaged a porter, for a modest fee, to take a small suitcase on a room-service wagon to the fifth floor and, by way of his pass key, allow two foreigners – Hans and Robert – to enter a certain guest's room. What they might do there was their own business. Neither accomplice would ask them any questions.

What Robert and Hans did was to plant eight incendiary bombs in Muchassi's room. These bombs, filled with a flammable, magnesium-like substance, were not designed to go off with a high explosive force. On being detonated, somewhat like fireworks, they'd blow up with a swoosh and immediately suck up the available oxygen. Though they would almost certainly kill anyone in a room, they would be very unlikely to set the room itself on fire, because their effect would amount to a flash, extinguishing itself through its own force after a couple of seconds. The bombs were originally designed to be thrown, in the manner of hand grenades, and Robert hated them. But they were the only explosives available.

The bombs had no safety feature. If someone had accidentally sent a signal on the right radio frequency, they would have gone off at that moment. But Robert's main concern about them was the incendiary material itself, which he judged to be old, unstable and unreliable. He was worried that it might go up by itself – or not go off at all. He had bought a dozen of the bombs from the Greek supplier, but used only the eight he thought were in the best shape for wiring radio receivers, leaving the other four unaltered in his travel bag. If the fire bombs worked, eight would be enough.

It was shortly after 9 pm when Robert and Hans left the hotel. Unlike the far more sophisticated infernal machines in Paris and Cyprus, these 'home-made' fire bombs were very difficult to place and conceal. Time was not a real problem, though, because the KGB liked working late into the night. As the surveillance team had reported, on all previous occasions the black Mercedes had not brought Muchassi back to his hotel before midnight.

It didn't matter much. The team's parked cars wouldn't attract any attention. Athens is a late-night city where some restaurants – especially in the Plaka, Athens' Soho – do not even start serving dinner until after ten.

However, hours passed and Muchassi still didn't return. Around 3 am Avner, Robert and Hans walked a little way down the street for a short conference. In a couple of hours it would be daybreak. The man inside the hotel who worked for Louis – the one who let them into Muchassi's room – would no doubt be going off duty. They needed him to go up with Muchassi in the elevator, then come down and signal them that Muchassi had entered his room alone. (There were other Arabs staying in the hotel, and even though Muchassi was unlikely to go to their room or invite them into his at this hour of the night, Avner did not want to take a chance on it.) Soon they would have to make up their minds whether to abort the mission or not.

If they decided to abort, what should they do with the explosives in Muchassi's room?

Leaving them was impossible.

Going back and dismantling the bombs was very dangerous, not only because Muchassi might walk in on them, but because they might blow themselves up.

Which left, as the only alternative, triggering an explosion in an empty room.

Avner hated the idea, because it would mean signalling their failure – and with the one target who was not on the original list. To have an unauthorized success was one thing; an unauthorized failure was quite another. It was the kind of thing the Palestinians would do: blowing up an empty room, because of bad planning. It could be rationalized as a warning to Muchassi, but in reality, terrorists – or the KGB – could not be 'warned' off their designs; they could only be forced off them. They'd make peace only if they were forced to see that making peace paid better dividends than making war. That was at the very bottom of Israeli thinking and experience. Warning shots across their bows would accomplish

241

nothing. On the contrary, Muchassi and his masters would regard such a thing as a victory for themselves, and would only be emboldened by having foiled the Jews.

Hans and Robert agreed. They would wait for one more hour. After that, they would have to act.

At 4 am – one hour later – they decided that they could wait for another half hour. That was the absolute maximum. If Muchassi wasn't back by 4.30, they would have to do something.

The black Mercedes drove down Sokratous Street at 4.25.

But it didn't stop in front of the main entrance. Slowing down, it pulled up to the kerb about thirty yards away. Avner couldn't hear whether the engine had stopped or not, but the driver switched off the lights.

For about a minute no one emerged from the Mercedes. It was too dark to recognize the people sitting in it; too dark even to be certain whether there were two or more. But when the door finally opened, the interior light in the car came on for a couple of seconds. There was no question about it. The man getting out of the car was Zaid Muchassi. Another man remained seated in the back. A third one, sitting behind the wheel, was wearing a chauffeur's cap. The interior light went off when Muchassi slammed the door, but the driving lights did not come on. They still hadn't come on as Muchassi walked through the main entrance into the hotel lobby.

Evidently, the Russians were waiting. Why? Did they expect Muchassi to come back?

It was possible.

Muchassi might be going up to his room for something to give to his KGB contact. He might even be going up to pack his bags and check out. The Russians might be waiting to drive him to a safe house or to catch an early flight at the airport.

In a few seconds Louis' operative in the hotel would be coming out to signal them as to whether Muchassi had entered his room alone. That would be the signal for Robert to set off the explosion. On this occasion Avner knew that

Robert would not wait for a separate signal from him. If Avner wanted the mission aborted, he would have to let Robert know before the Greek came out of the hotel.

Avner put his hand on the door handle. Should he stop Robert? The Russians waiting a short distance away were an unexpected development. But did it really make any difference? And if he stopped Robert now, what could they do about the bombs in Muchassi's room? They clearly couldn't remove them, but if they just left them there, the explosives might kill some innocent people. Or, if the bombs were discovered intact, it would give the authorities a far better chance of tracing their source. With all the complications *that* might entail. The man who had sold them had seen Robert. He could be arrested and . . .

The choice was no longer available to Avner. The Greek hotel employee was walking out of the main entrance, stretching, yawning, taking his hat off and scratching his head. Then he turned and walked back into the hotel.

Avner's eyes instinctively ran up the wall to the row of windows on the fifth floor. Muchassi, like many Arabs, preferred the fifth floor for *chamza* – good luck. Avner wasn't quite sure of his particular window but, though there had been no need this time to set up the explosion with the kind of precision Robert needed for his six little bombs in Cyprus, the sudden flash would be unmistakable. Even if he wasn't looking at the right window, he'd see it.

He saw nothing.

Nothing, even though a minute must have passed since the Greek employee went back into the hotel.

Still nothing.

Avner tried to see what Robert and Hans were doing in their car, but it was impossible. Could Robert have misunderstood? Could he be waiting for Avner's signal? It was unlikely.

The Russians' Mercedes had not moved. An ominous black shape, it sat silently next to the kerb about fifty yards away.

Suddenly the door of Robert's car opened and Robert – no, it was Hans! – emerged from it, carrying the travel bag Robert had used for the explosives. To Avner's utter astonishment, Hans was making for the main entrance. With the bag in his hand. He was walking straight into the hotel. What earthly reason would he have for doing that? It looked almost as if Hans had gone crazy, even from the way he walked. Usually he'd move in a somewhat stiff, deliberate way, like a much older man. Now he was taking long, determined, almost flowing strides, holding his chin high in the air. Avner was so taken aback that he hesitated for another few seconds. Hans had not even glanced in his direction when he walked into the hotel. He was clearly not signalling Avner to take any kind of action, but under the circumstances, Avner couldn't just stay in the car.

'Start it up,' he said to the Greek, who had been looking at him uneasily. 'Understand? Don't do anything, just start the engine.'

Then he jumped out of the Impala and strode across the street.

In the hotel lobby everything was quiet. There was no one behind the reception desk. No sign of Hans, no sign of their Greek contact. Looking at the elevator, Avner saw that the indicator was pointing to the fifth floor. For another second or two he looked around the deserted lobby, trying to recall the layout. There was a door leading to the employees' entrance. Another door to the stairwell, the fire exit. If the elevator was on the fifth floor, Hans must have taken it. If he did, it might be dangerous to call it back. Avner started for the stairwell.

At this point he heard an explosion. It was not very loud but it was unmistakable. A deep, muffled thud, with no reverberation. A low-frequency shudder in the floor which he could feel through the soles of his feet.

The elevator was coming down. Avner could see the indicator swing above the door. He flattened himself against the wall, his hand moving back to his hip.

The automatic doors opened. Hans was coming out, pale,

244

his face set. The Greek behind him was going berserk. Shaking his fist at Hans, jabbering at him in Greek. He was carrying the travel bag.

'Fucking Robert with his fucking remote control,' Hans said, on seeing Avner. 'I had to do it.'

'Come on,' Avner replied, pointing to the door leading to the employees' entrance. 'Through here.'

He grabbed the Greek by the shoulder, shoving him after Hans.

The hallway to the employees' entrance led through a semi-basement, down half a flight of stairs, and along a dimly lit corridor to the street. Hans was striding in front, the Greek following, still babbling and gesticulating. Avner brought up the rear. Just before reaching the exit, there were another few steps. As Hans opened the door, Avner could see the pavement from a low angle. And something else.

The black Mercedes. Parked right in front. They were coming out of the hotel exactly at the point where the Russians were waiting. Avner could not have guessed that. They could just as easily have left the hotel through the main doors, the way they came in. But no, he had to play it smart. Never leave the same way you enter. Confuse the enemy. Smart.

Too smart by half, this time.

Hans saw the Russians' car too, and he stopped. The KGB man in the back seat had already half opened the door, and was about to get out of the car. He must have heard the explosion, must have seen a flash. He was probably getting out to investigate. Now, men were bursting through a side door right in front of him, seconds after the blast. The Russian would make the connection.

He did. Still standing behind the half-opened car door, he began to move his right hand towards his left armpit. The KGB man was going for his gun.

Later, thinking about it, Avner felt that he might have been mistaken. Perhaps the Russian – who was, after all, an agent, with his own cover to consider – was not reaching for a weapon. Being totally uninvolved at this point, why should he have wanted to interfere? However shrewdly the Russian might have guessed, he had no way of knowing for certain that whatever happened at the hotel involved him in any way. He would have had no reason to try to stop three strangers running past him. Going for his gun could have been a totally reflexive, unthinking act on his part, too. Like Hans or Avner, the Russian would also have been trained to have hair-trigger responses. Unlike an unsuspecting witness, an innocent passer-by, he would have been tense as he waited, sitting in his car. Perhaps this was the one drawback of professional training. It might make a person a bit too alert, condition him to act too quickly. His reaction time would be honed to an edge just a touch too fine. He would lose the normal human capacity for freezing in surprise, hesitating, doing nothing. That little catch, that little delay, which – curiously enough – might add a margin of safety to everyday existence.

And if Avner was mistaken about the Russian going for his gun, Hans was mistaken too, because he assumed the same thing when he saw the KGB man's right hand move.

Hans shot first. As he had been trained. Twice.

Then Avner fired twice as the Russian was holding onto the door frame with his left hand, his right hand still groping for his holster. Avner was firing from the bottom of the stairs, at an angle, trying to hit his target through the open car window, because he knew the low-velocity slugs would not penetrate the steel door of the Mercedes. He could actually see Hans' shots finding their mark, but he wasn't certain about his own. In fact, he rather thought he had missed. In any case, the Russian was slumping back into his seat, and his companion in the driver's seat was reaching back to pull him further inside by his shoulder. The chauffeur must have been a powerful man because he somehow yanked the wounded man inside the car with one hand, then slammed the door. The next sound came from the black Mercedes' tyres, screeching as they spun, sending the KGB car fishtailing down the street.

Avner was putting his gun away, holding the Greek hotel employee by the collar with his free hand. It was unnecessary, because the Greek had lapsed into a stupor. Further up the street Robert's car was coming to life with a roar, a second later spinning in a U-turn right in front of them. Avner took the travel bag the Greek was still clutching, and pushed the man into Robert's car after Hans. Then he ran across the road to the green Impala where the older Greek had already switched on the headlights. 'Just drive,' Avner said to him when he got into the car, 'but not too fast. Understand? *Nicht sehr schnell.*'

The Greek nodded. Unlike his compatriot, he was totally calm. But then, Avner reflected, he had not seen a group of incendiary bombs go up right in front of him. Even if he had witnessed the shooting.

Back at the safe house they began to sort things out, everyone making a tremendous effort to be calm. First, they had to pacify the hotel employee, who spoke only Greek. The man was completely shaken. He would alternately sit and stare, muttering '*bomba, bomba*', or get up and start shaking his finger at Hans, heaping on him what was presumably a string of choice Greek invective. Avner decided to take him aside with the older Greek, pressing hundred-dollar bills in his hand. This seemed to affect the man as a stream of water would a spluttering fire. Eventually, after being doused by the fifth or sixth bill, the fire went out. Then Avner handed the same amount to the older man.

After the Greeks left, Robert said: 'Look, I know how you guys feel. How do you think I feel? Believe me, I checked out the transmitter and it worked. There was nothing more I could do. That old stuff they sold us was simply no good.'

Robert should have kept quiet, because this started a major argument, the first one they had had since the mission began. Hans was adamant that if Robert had had real doubts about the explosive material, he should have recommended that the mission be postponed. If they had then overridden his recommendation, Robert could not be blamed. As it was, he should be. Just to mutter under his breath 'I don't think this stuff's much good' – which, Hans said, Robert did every time anyway – did not amount to a recommendation to cancel.

Hans had a point, but Avner had a more serious quarrel with *him*. There was, after all, a chain of command – but even common sense would have demanded that Hans consult the others before involving them in a brand-new plan of action. Because that's what he had done, by grabbing the travel bag with the four bombs which still contained the original contact-fuses and rushing upstairs to Muchassi's room. Apparently Hans had the unsuspecting Greek come up with him in the elevator and call Muchassi to the door. Then – waving the Greek aside while the Arab fumbled with the lock – he took one of the bombs from the bag. When Muchassi opened the door, Hans kicked it in, throwing the fire bomb inside like a hand grenade. Without telling Robert or Avner that that was what he intended to do.

'Well, if I had told you,' said Hans sullenly, 'you would have said no. At first. Then I'm sure you would have said yes, because that was the only solution, but we would have wasted more precious time. I took a short cut.'

'Why the only solution?' Robert asked. 'Anyway, once you had that Greek call him out of the room, you could have shot him.'

'*Shot* him?' said Hans, outraged. Then he turned to Avner: 'You see? He's simply not thinking!'

Avner had to agree with Hans. Shooting Muchassi would not have solved the problem of the unexploded bombs in the room. Once Robert's remote control had failed, the only solution might well have been Hans' – but he should still not have acted on his own. At least, he should have alerted them.

'What if you'd got hurt in the explosion?' Avner asked him. 'What would we have done, just left you, or hung around trying to find out what happened until we all got caught? You acted irresponsibly. And why did you have to shoot that Russian?'

'Because he was going for his gun,' Hans replied indignantly. 'Should I have waited for him to shoot me first? And why did *you* shoot him? You shot him for the same reason!'

'I shot him because I saw you shoot him,' Avner replied, but without conviction. It was becoming a childish argument. 'Anyway,' Avner added, 'I probably missed him.' He certainly hoped he had missed the Russian. The last thing he wanted was to tangle with the KGB – or to tangle with Ephraim and the rest of the Galicianers for killing a Soviet agent. Yet, if the Russian was about to pull a gun, what else could they possibly do?

He was also amazed at Hans. Hans, with his reading glasses; Hans, who looked like a pencil. Calm, methodical, you-can-take-my-turn-any-time Hans. It would have been a different story for Steve to suddenly rush off with a bag of bombs, or Robert. Maybe even Avner himself. But Hans? Dashing off impulsively, kicking in doors, shooting at Russians? You really could never predict a thing about people.

Yet Avner had the uneasy feeling that insane as Hans' action seemed, it was probably right under the circumstances. Hans had simply had the courage to face it. If the booby traps could be neither blown up nor safely removed, what else could they have done but blow them up by manually throwing another bomb into the room, with the *mechabel* still inside? Nor was Hans wrong that if they had stopped to have a conference about it, they might have been too late.

'All right,' Avner said in the end, 'let's not talk about it anymore. The job's getting to all of us. When we get back to Frankfurt, we'll put it to Carl.'

The others accepted this. Though Avner was the leader, Carl had from the outset become – partly because of his age and experience, but mainly because of his personality – the Solomon, the field rabbi, the conscience of the group. And being uninvolved this time, Carl would also be impartial and objective. If they should have acted in any other way, Carl would tell them.

They stayed in Athens for another week, then flew out one by one. The explosion in the hotel, according to the papers, must have been like the Fourth of July. It did start a fire, but the only person killed was Muchassi. Some reports mentioned a German tourist who was slightly injured. There was no word of any kind in the press about the shooting of the Russian.[9]

In Frankfurt, they put the case to Carl. He said nothing for a long time, just kept puffing on his pipe, raising his eyebrows, and rolling his eyes to the ceiling. Steve's reaction was just the opposite. He looked at them in utter astonishment. simply because they seemed so upset about what they had done. 'So what,' Steve said to Avner. 'So we got him. Fucking Russsky, we got him too. What's the matter, chum, you scared?'

'Oh, keep quiet, Steve,' said Carl finally. 'Look, I wasn't there. I can't be the judge. Main thing is, you're all here. Let's look ahead.'

That was clearly the only thing to do. But Avner was worried. He couldn't say why. Everything had gone smoothly so far. For the eleven Israeli athletes, they had exacted vengeance on Zwaiter, Hamshari, al-Chir, and al-Kubaisi, as well as Najjer, Nasser and Adwan in Beirut. Also on Muchassi and the KGB man. In the final analysis, it was very easy.

Maybe too easy. For the first time since the mission had started, Avner could feel a painful pressure in the pit of his stomach.

Chapter 11

~~~~~~

MOHAMMED BOUDIA

THE TRUTH WAS that, for the first time since they had set out from the Hotel du Midi in Geneva at the end of September, perhaps for the first time in his whole life, Avner became afraid. He could not recall ever having experienced the same feeling before. Not in the army, not during the Six Day War, not while he was being trained, and not while he was working as an ordinary agent. Not even during the mission, until the middle of April. Of course, he had always known what it was like to be tense or startled. Or scared. But the feeling he began experiencing in April was entirely different. It wasn't a fleeting rush of adrenalin, a sensation of his heart beating in his throat for a few seconds, a sudden pang that would never outlast the immediate cause that gave rise to it. This new feeling was a quiet, low, nagging anxiety that would not leave him for days at a time, regardless of what he was doing. He could be eating his lamb chops in a restaurant or even watching his favourite actor, Louis de Funes, in a movie – Avner must have seen every film the French comedian had ever made – and the feeling would still be there. Sometimes it was like a dull pain, sometimes like a solid lump. Fear.

At first Avner actually thought it might be something he ate.

When he recognized it as fear, and he soon did, he became resentful and ashamed. For a while he was mortified at the thought that the others, Carl, Steve, Hans or Robert, might recognize it in him, and as far as Avner was concerned that would have been worse than anything. To counteract it he found himself saying, 'Guys, I'm scared', and 'Guys, I'm

251

worried', at every turn. This, of course, was braggadocio army-style, in the only form permissible, proclaiming courage by protesting the opposite too much. But he must have overdone it, because one day Carl said to him, very quietly, when they were alone:

'I know. I'm pretty worried myself.'

He spoke in a tone that caused Avner to stop pretending.

'Oh shit,' he said. 'You too? I wonder why.'

But Carl only shook his head. They never talked about it again.

Soon afterwards, the answer came to Avner in a flash. At the time, he was flying back from New York where he had just spent a week with Shoshana, which might have had something to do with the timing of his discovery. Not directly, but in a roundabout way.

Their reunion was not entirely happy. Shoshana had settled during the first week of April into the apartment in Brooklyn that Avner had found for her. While Avner was still in Beirut, she had moved in with the baby, Geula, and Charlie the dog. Alone. Without ever having lived outside Israel before. Without having any idea where Avner might be or how soon he might turn up in America. When he did arrive, about three weeks later, Shoshana clung to his neck with such desperate force that she actually caused him physical pain. If Avner had ever thought that the way they were compelled to live made no difference to Shoshana, her embrace alone would have been enough to change his mind.

They spent the first two days in bed. The third morning Avner woke up from a dream that he was being watched. He opened his eyes, and saw Shoshana sitting on the bed, looking at his face.

'What?' Avner asked sleepily.

'I don't know,' she replied. Her tone was serious. 'I mean, your hair isn't getting grey or anything, but . . . I don't know. You look about ten years older.'

Hearing this, he felt the fear that had almost disappeared during those two days hit him in the stomach like a fist. He said nothing but later, shaving, he kept examining his face in the mirror. Shoshana was right. He had aged years in the last seven months. He looked like a man in his mid-thirties, and he was only twenty-six.

'Well,' he said to his mirror image, talking out loud, which was hardly his habit, 'it looks like you can fool your brain more easily than you can your body.'

'Pardon me?' asked Shoshana, outside the bathroom.

'Nothing.'

He spent the rest of the week driving Shoshana around New York in a rented car, so that she could see a little of the city and not feel so strange. Until his arrival, she had gone no further than the corner store for groceries. He also introduced her to a couple of acquaintances. Shoshana knew no one, and she did not make friends easily. As usual, she did not complain, but as he watched her nursing the baby one afternoon in the somewhat dark, one-bedroom apartment, there was something so lonely and vulnerable about her that it made Avner feel unbelievably guilty. 'It's not going to be for long,' he said to her. 'I promise.'

She looked at him and smiled. Which made it infinitely worse. But there was not a lot he could do about it. At least she seemed to take great delight in Geula who, as far as Avner was concerned, was still ugly, though slightly improving with age.

Then, flying back to Europe, it came to him. The reason for his fear. He, Carl, and maybe the others as well. Why it was affecting them now, after seven months, after five successful assassinations, not counting Beirut. The reason was very logical, very simple.

Having done it, they were beginning to realize how little trouble it was to set up a hit. How easy it was for a few people, with some money and a little determination, to find and kill a man. With impunity. How a group of terrorists could have it all their own way. Not forever – never forever – but for a short while. Just long enough to eliminate four or five human beings.

And if it was so easy for them, it would be equally easy for others. If they could kill with such little trouble, they could be killed with just as little. If they could buy information about the *mechablim*, why should the *mechablim*, who had at least as much money at their disposal – and fewer scruples – not find out about *them*? Both sides had to leave traces in order to do their jobs. Both sides had to make contacts with certain people, one or other of whom might turn out to be an informer. And one informer would be enough. Avner's team could see a gun pointed at them on a street corner at any time; Avner's team could switch off the light at night and have their beds launched into the ceiling by an explosion.

Without any doubt, someone would by now be out there, gunning for Avner and his partners. It made good sense for them to be afraid.

It did not help matters that just then three incidents occurred which, though totally insignificant, shook the partners' nerves a little more each time. One night in Frankfurt the five of them decided to have dinner in a restaurant together. (In Frankfurt, they usually took their meals at the apartment of one or the other, taking turns shopping and cooking.) They were driving back in one car when Avner, who was at the wheel, decided to take a short cut through a construction site. Suddenly they were blinded by floodlights and loud hailers ordered them to stop. The next second they were surrounded by Frankfurt's police – conducting, of all things, a drug raid. Apparently some dealers were expected to make a drop at the construction site, and the team got caught in the police stakeout. Though they were released within minutes with profuse apologies – their papers were in order, they were not inebriated, and they had nothing incriminating in the car – the few seconds while they were required to stand at gunpoint, spreadeagled, with their hands on top of Avner's Opel sedan, seemed like the end to all five of them. They were absolutely convinced that they had been apprehended by German security. In fact, it was the first – and the last – time during the mission that they had any encounter with Western authorities.

The other two incidents involved only Avner and Carl. They occurred on consecutive Sundays in their Frankfurt safe house, both around 10 am, just as they were sitting over the remnants of their breakfast. In the first incident, there was a knock on the door – unusual, since visitors were supposed to ring the bell from the lobby – and, tiptoeing to the spy-hole, Avner could see two well-dressed strangers waiting in the hallway. With Carl covering him from the bedroom doorway, Avner turned the key in the lock, resting the ball of his foot against the lower part of the door.

The strangers turned out to be postal inspectors, investigating some theft from the mail. Apparently the concierge had let them into the building, where they were going from door to door asking the tenants if any of them had any letters missing. 'What a dangerous job,' said Carl wryly, after putting his Beretta away.

The incident on the following Sunday was much more sudden and violent. While Avner and Carl were reading their papers, their second-storey window fell in with a tremendous crash and an object flew into the room. They hit the floor immediately, covering their heads with their arms, waiting for the grenade to explode. After a few seconds they raised their heads cautiously. There was glass all over the floor but they couldn't see the missile that had come through the window.

Avner crawled to the outside wall, stood up with his back against it, and slowly manoeuvred himself into position to take a look through the shattered glass. What he saw was a little black boy, no doubt from the American compound across the street, looking up at their window. He had a baseball bat in his hand. 'Sorry, Mister,' he yelled in English when he noticed Avner, 'it was an accident. Could I have my ball, please?'

For two nights after that, Avner had the greatest difficulty falling asleep.

At the same time, Avner's own character was such that all the things that might deter others – fear, opposition, difficulties, disapproval – would only serve to spur him on. Without knowing it, without ever dreaming of analysing it in any way, he belonged to that very small minority of human beings who are fuelled by adversity. It was almost as if, because of some quirk of nature, the wiring in his brain had been reversed. He would function as a car might if some prankster switched around the accelerator and the brake. In a sense, being afraid would probably be the last thing to stop him.

And in spite of the many ways in which his partners might have been different from Avner – or from each other – this was clearly the one trait they shared.

Perhaps the Mossad psychologists did know something about their trade. They had selected five people who would instinctively try to rid themselves of whatever terrified them, not by keeping their heads down, but by attacking it. An unteachable habit of mind that would probably be as natural to a few people as it would be alien to most.

In May, out of the original eleven, they had four targets left. They could pick up no leads on the whereabouts of Ali Hassan Salameh. Abu Daoud, Number two on their list, was temporarily in a Jordanian jail. Number eleven, Dr Wadi Haddad, the military leader of the Popular Front for the Liberation of Palestine, seemed careful never to emerge from the Middle Eastern and East European countries that were out-of-bounds for the team.

This left Number five, a colourful, attractive Algerian by the name of Mohammed Boudia. He was well known to the French authorities, having been jailed in 1959 for sabotaging gasoline depôts on behalf of the Algerian Liberation Front. In a sense Boudia was a soft target, because he did not flaunt his links with Palestinian terrorism, and in 1973 only the Mossad and perhaps one or two other intelligence services suspected that his organization, the *Parisienne Orientale*, was a cover for the Popular Front. A director of the Algerian National Theatre after independence, Boudia was active in theatrical circles and in fashionable left-wing Paris society, producing shows with political overtones at the Théâtre de l'Ouest Parisien in the Boulogne-Billancourt, some of which were quite successful. Only a fraction of the people who knew him in Paris were aware of his role in terrorist activities, and even fewer were actually involved in them with him. The latter included some women with whom the handsome Algerian was quite popular.

At the same time, unlike his predecessor – and, according to some sources, subordinate – Dr Hamshari, Boudia did not rely solely on his cover to protect himself. He was known to avoid any set routine, almost never showing up at the same place at the same time twice, and he preferred to spend his nights in the various apartments of his several different girlfriends – though, as Steve was moved to remark, this last preference may have had nothing to do with security. He was also often accompanied by a bodyguard when he appeared in public.

Because he travelled a lot, the timing and length of his stays in Paris were difficult to pin down. According to some reports, he ought to have been at the PLO headquarters in Beirut at the same time as the commando raid, but either this information had been erroneous or Boudia had managed to escape. Other sources had him in Madrid on the day of the Mossad agent Baruch Cohen's death in January, 1973. At least one person suspected of trying to find out about Boudia or his organization – the unlucky Syrian journalist Hani Kuda, who may or may not have been working for the Mossad – had met a violent death.[1]

Throughout the month of May, Avner and his partners had been trying, without success, to track down the elusive terrorist leader. In Paris *Le Group* had no information either, and Avner decided to try Tony again in Rome. (One of Boudia's operations involved sabotaging the Trans-Alpine Oil Pipeline in Trieste, Italy, injuring eighteen people and causing millions of dollars of damage. Boudia was said to have carried out this coup personally, accompanied by two of his female friends, a Frenchwoman and a Rhodesian girl. According to Louis, Boudia's supplier for explosives was the same Greek who provided the fire bombs for Muchassi's assassination in Athens.) In any case, because of Boudia's Italian connections, Avner thought Tony's branch of *Le Group* might know more about him than Louis' people in Paris.

But Tony couldn't help. After a few days in Rome, Avner decided to call Louis again.

'Any news?' he asked the Frenchman he had by now begun to think of as his friend.

'No,' Louis replied, 'but why don't you come back here anyway? I've got someone who'd like to meet you.'

'How soon?' asked Avner.

'By the weekend,' Louis replied, 'if it's convenient.'

It was only Wednesday. Avner decided to rent a car and drive back to Paris. Though he loved flying, he also enjoyed driving and it was now his habit to vary his routine. Besides, it would rest his mind to drive for a couple of days. The route along the Italian and French Riviera was beautiful, especially in May, and if he drove through Switzerland he could drop in at the bank in Geneva. He could take a look at his personal bank account and see how much it had grown in the interval. Though money as such meant little to him, in the last months Avner's thoughts had increasingly turned to the things money could buy, especially for Shoshana. He began to indulge in fantasies – in the time-honoured fashion of all guilty husbands – about the things he would get for her. In Paris, for instance, he'd spend hours examining a model kitchen displayed in the windows of *La Boutique Danoise* near the avenue Hoche. They were quite something, that tall fridge with its icemaker and that self-cleaning oven. Shoshana would not have to be ashamed of such a kitchen, even in America.

On the long drive he tried not to think about the mission at all. He mused, instead, about his travels, about all the countries he had seen in the last few years. Just comparing the highways of Italy and France told a lot about the two nations. The French would embrace their mountains with fine networks of winding roads, while the Italians would bore and bull their way through them. With a brutal system of tunnels. Avner counted about fifty of them along the autostrada between Genoa and the French border.

There was also a difference, Avner thought, between the ways in which the various nationalities fitted their own cities, their landscapes, their architecture. For instance, French people seemed to belong in Paris, but Italians did not look as though they belonged in Rome. Not that Avner had anything against Italians – on the contrary – but he was struck by the contrast between those magnificent buildings and the way the people in the streets moved and behaved. It reminded him of a book about some place in India that he had read as a child, in which the ruins of a beautiful city built in the jungle by an earlier civilization were now inhabited by a race of monkeys. Only in that book the monkeys didn't ride motor scooters.

And the Jews? Well, now, there was a question. Of course, it was only Avner's private opinion – and unrelated to his love for Israel, or his feelings of patriotism – but from childhood, he had never been able even to pretend to feel at home in that Middle Eastern landscape. And for Avner, Jews, whether they were Yekkes or Galicianers, just didn't seem to fit it. Whether they realized it or not. The only ones who did fit came from the Arab countries, like Morocco or the Yemen. At least in Avner's view. This had nothing to do with ancient history, or with what the Jews of Europe had built and accomplished in Israel, which was stupendous; nor did it give the Arabs any right to try and push them into the sea. Over Avner's dead body would anybody push Jews anywhere. But he'd still say that in some strange way, they didn't fit the landscape. This was his opinion, and as a *sabra* he was entitled to it.

But it probably made little difference where the Jews ended up once the Cossacks and the Nazis and the rest had chased them out of Europe. Europe, where they may have fitted, but couldn't live without being massacred once or twice in every century; and the last time very nearly for good. So if Europeans were now unhappy about Israelis and Arabs turning their great cities into battlegrounds, that was unfortunate. They should have worried about it earlier.

And with this thought in his mind Avner found himself glaring defiantly at the hapless French official looking at his passport at the border.

Arriving in Paris, he called Louis.

'I'll pick you up tomorrow morning at nine,' the Frenchman said. 'Dress for the country. We're going to meet Papa.'

Avner was excited, but not altogether surprised. Considering the amount of money they had spent on *Le Group* in the last six months or so, it stood to reason that the Old Man himself might become curious. Though the various left- and right-wing terrorists and other clandestine groups which might have been included in Papa's earlier clientèle were by no means poor – the anti-Gaullist OAS fighting against Algerian independence had some extremely wealthy patrons, for instance, while hundreds of thousands of Palestinians working in oil-rich Arab countries were compelled to 'donate' 5 to 10 per cent of their earnings to the PLO – it was likely that no single group had spent more money for Papa's services within the space of a few months than Avner's team. Clearly, the old *maquis*-turned-privateer wanted to take a closer look.

For his part, Avner was most certainly interested.

The house in the country was somewhere south of Paris. It took them about two hours to reach it, though it may have been only an hour's driving time away. Once the black Citroën was on the highway Louis offered a pair of blind man's spectacles to Avner, saying, 'You don't mind slipping these on, do you?' The dark glasses cut off Avner's vision completely. Maybe Cautious Carl would have refused to wear them, but Avner felt that once he got into a car alone with Louis he could drive him into an ambush anyway. Avner's sixth sense, which he had come to trust implicitly, registered no danger.

Once the Citroën's feathery suspension began to sway on

some secondary roads, Louis told Avner to take off his glasses. The peaceful, hazy French countryside, rimmed by some blue mountains in the far distance, could have been anywhere. No one guarded the gates in front of the driveway leading up to the large, rambling country house. As they were getting out of the car, a shaggy sheepdog with an extremely friendly disposition jumped up to plant a slobbering lick across Louis' face, then repeated the performance with Avner.

Papa greeted them on the porch. He wore slippers. There was a dark blue sweater over his collarless shirt. (On a later occasion, in Paris, Avner would see him in an old-fashioned, black three-piece suit.) A man in his early sixties, Papa had iron-grey hair and a prominent nose. The grip of his large, freckled hand was firm. There was something in him that reminded Avner not only of his own father, but of Dave, the American ex-Marine firearms instructor, though they did not look at all alike. Perhaps it was their evident faith in cunning and force, which Avner could sense.

Possibly it was also the way Papa spoke. His English, like Dave's Hebrew, was badly fractured. Avner, expressing his regret over having no French, offered German, but the old man refused.

'*Mais non, monsieur, mais non.* I talk English. *Pourquoi pas?* I practise. Soon, the whole world talk English, *hein?*'

Oh well, thought Avner. At least Papa was not secretive about what was bothering him.

But Papa's dislike of the English was only an outer layer. There were many more layers and Avner could never make up his mind – then, or during a subsequent visit – what they might be. Papa seemed not to dislike individual people, except perhaps politicians. Whenever the conversation turned to a given person, Papa was likely to nod approvingly and say: 'Him I know, he's a fine man.' But groups or governments, forget it. They were all *merde* for Papa.

He introduced Avner to his wife, presumably Louis' mother, though Avner saw no sign of affection between the two. She looked older than Papa; in fact she was probably a few years younger. Walking quietly in and out of the room, she served them refreshments but took no part in the conversation and did not sit with them. The only person to stay in the room with Avner and Papa, in addition to Louis, was an elderly uncle. He said very little and spoke only in French. Soon Avner discovered an amazing thing about him, though. Apparently he was being used by Papa and Louis as a living computer, coming up with dates and figures in an expressionless monotone whenever they asked him. Avner decided to test him and asked Louis about the sum of money they still owed their Greek contact for some surveillance work. Louis turned to his uncle and translated the question.

The older man came up with what Avner believed was the right figure without hesitation.

It was certainly a safer method than keeping records. Avner was impressed. He wondered, though, what *Le Group* might do after the uncle, who looked to be in his seventies, passed on.

During the entire conversation, Papa only once asked Avner a point-blank question.

'You work for Israel, no?'

Avner repeated what he had already told Louis about seeking information on Palestinian terrorists. 'I used to work for the Mossad,' he added, 'but I don't any more.' This, technically speaking, was the truth. 'My partners and I now work for a private Jewish organization in America.'

Though this was a lie, it was not implausible and it fitted Papa's view of the world. It seemed to be the old Frenchman's opinion, as far as Avner could gather, that everything that actually worked in international sabotage or intelligence-gathering operations had some private interests behind it. God alone knew how Papa arrived at this conclusion – which was very much like the views expressed by his Quebec-born organizer, Kathy – but maybe it was a matter of judging everything by his own example.

Avner totally disagreed with it. No doubt, there were

some strongmen, oil sheiks, wealthy neo-Nazis, or the odd romantic-revolutionary playboy here and there who would fund or organize a terrorist group or terrorist action. Like the rich Italian publisher-businessman Giangiacomo Feltrinelli, who had managed to blow himself up near Milan about a year earlier, in the spring of 1972, trying to sabotage some industrial installations while wearing a Castro jacket. But Avner would have said that these quirky souls were only a drop in the bucket of international terror or counter-terror, no more significant than the occasional deranged individual who might go out and try to assassinate a national leader or personality entirely on his own. There might be some spontaneous groups of student revolutionaries or nationalists emerging briefly in one place or another, with no backing of any kind. But the major groups would all be sponsored, as far as Avner was concerned, by a state or a group of states. Mainly Communist states, with their ties going back ultimately to the Soviet Union or, less frequently, to China. Even individuals like Feltrinelli would somehow end up being sponsored by them, if not with money then with training, documents or weapons.[2]

But this evidently was not Papa's view. It intrigued Avner that a streetwise Frenchman, who knew so much about the nuts and bolts of clandestine movements in Europe, would seem to reach the same conclusions as the writers of cartoon strips, Hollywood movies or popular fiction, who had no first-hand knowledge of the underground whatsoever. Why would Papa think that it was all done by some mysterious individuals – businessmen or old aristocrats or whatever – plotting in their Swiss castles to take over the world? Because Papa did appear to believe something of the sort, if he believed anything. His knowing smile would suggest the same thing as Kathy's favourite expression: that all other explanations were for donkeys.

In which case, Avner thought, he and his partners were donkeys themselves. But if Papa liked the idea of a private Jewish group in America, Avner was not going to quarrel with it. And in the final analysis, who could tell anyway? Avner certainly couldn't. While Avner was not impressed with Papa's overview of the world, he was impressed with just about everything else about him. The old resistance fighter clearly knew his business. His comments were shrewd on all practical questions and, even more important, he seemed to have a certain presence. Avner would not have wished to cross him, but he came away from the meeting with the feeling that as long as he had Papa on his side he would be safe.

This was reinforced by the gesture the old man made when he walked them to the car. As Avner reached for the dark spectacles he had left on the dashboard, Papa took them out of his hand. 'Eh, *merde!*' he said, and handed the glasses to his son, who laughed and put them in his pocket.

On the way back he remarked to Avner, 'Well, it looks like you found favour with the old man.'

Avner smiled and muttered something about being glad. What he felt like saying was 'Good, then I might live a little longer,' but he did not want to test *Le Group*'s sense of humour.

The truth was that, having become involved with *Le Group*, Avner would always have the uneasy feeling that he and his partners had got a tiger by the tail. For the remainder of the mission he continued having not so much a love-hate as a trust-fear relationship with Papa and his sons. It is largely speculation – Avner not having learned much more at this or at his one subsequent meeting with Papa – whether *Le Group* was motivated by any discernible political impulses at all, or sold information and support for mercenary reasons alone. It is similarly hard to say whether their clients included the PLO, though Avner had no doubt they included the Baader-Meinhof Red Army Faction, for Andreas to have known Louis. It is possible that most of their political clients were anti-Gaullist conspirators and other adherents of 'black' – that is, right-wing – terror. This would explain Papa's evident belief in powerful private interests and old aristocratic families as the moving force behind international intrigues; his own experiences in this particular sphere would bear this out. It would also explain his dislike of the British, who shook the established world order by giving up their empire without a fight, yet retained the primacy of Anglo-Saxon institutions and spirit in the world by passing them on to the brash, rich and wholly unpredictable Americans. If Papa shared any of the politics of his anti-Gaullist clients, he would have had some of these views.

As a rule, however, the allegiances of privateers like *Le Group* are not ideological but financial, and often personal. In the abstract they may sell out a terrorist to a counter-terrorist or a Palestinian to an Israeli as easily as the other way around, but they may protect an individual in either camp because he's good business or because they like him. Avner's sixth sense suggested that as long as Papa liked and trusted him – or liked and trusted their business relationship – everything would be all right. And in terms of information and services *Le Group* was worth its weight in gold – which, as Hans put it, was exactly what Papa and Louis charged. But they were good: much better, far more reliable, than any of their regular Mossad contacts and Arab informers. Whether or not Avner's team could have tracked down any of the *mechablim* without them, the fact was that, up to the summer of 1973, they hadn't. Apart from Nasser, Adwan, and Najjer in Beirut, the Mossad's own sources came up only with Hamshari's address – included in the material Ephraim provided at the start of the mission – and the fact that Zwaiter could be found somewhere in Rome. The rest came from *Le Group*.

In fact, Carl dubbed Louis the *Deus ex machina*, which Avner could never remember and so changed to 'Moishe the machine'. He'd say: 'I'm calling Moishe the machine' whenever he was about to ring Louis.

A week later Louis reported that Mohammed Boudia was in Paris. The same evening Robert took a flight to Brussels.

265

Exactly a week after that, at around 10.25 am, Steve parked one of Papa's vans across the road from a small café called L'Étoile d'Or on the corner of rue Jussieu and rue des Fossés Saint-Bernard on the Left Bank. It was a Thursday, 28 June.

Boudia had been extremely difficult to pin down. Unlike any of their previous targets, he might spend the night anywhere and it was impossible to predict where he would turn up during the day. Or at what time. The only solution was to keep him under constant surveillance, and whenever they happened to find him alone, day or night, if the time, place, and other circumstances seemed favourable, do the assassination at a moment's notice.

Provided that the wary and experienced Algerian did not notice he was being followed and give them the slip.

To minimize that risk, Avner authorized Louis to do the surveillance on a very large scale, employing as many different people as he had available. Everything else being equal, one of the best ways to ensure that a target did not realize he was being followed was to avoid using the same people or vehicles around him twice. Within certain limits, it was just a question of money. In Paris *Le Group* had a dozen or more trained operatives at its disposal.

Since Boudia was often driving, Avner and Carl decided to have Robert prepare a car bomb, without excluding other possibilities. Shooting was always a standby method of assassination – it required the least in terms of preparation – but it was also the most difficult to get away from, and it carried with it none of the 'cleverness' Ephraim had talked about. Not to mince words, it involved less terror. Avner also disliked shooting because of the emotional burden for the team. Though always unspoken, it was a factor. Plainly put, pushing a button at a distance was easier than facing a man from two feet away and firing a series of bullets into his body.

The bomb Robert and his Belgian contact prepared was essentially the same type as the one used in the assassination of al-Chir, but smaller and somewhat simpler. Instead of six little bombs it used a single explosive unit of the fragmentation type. The method of detonation was the same. The bomb would be placed under the car seat and armed by pressure, after which the explosion would be set off by a radio signal. Using pressure alone would have been unsafe as it could injure passers-by or whoever might get into the car with Boudia; a purely radio-controlled device could be accidentally exploded by a stray signal while being transported or placed in Boudia's car.

At one point, while working out the arrangements, Steve suddenly said: 'You know, we're crazy. This is war, isn't it? Why am I sitting here puzzling over escape routes? Why is Robert messing about with his radio? You know what this guy Boudia would do if he wanted to kill any of us? I'll tell you. Eight o'clock in the evening he'd wire a bomb to our car ignition, or have one of his girlfriends do it, and by eleven he'd be sitting drinking tea in Algiers. He wouldn't care who blew up with us the next morning when we started the bloody engine. *C'est la* fucking *guerre*, he'd say.

'And what are we doing? Trying to figure how to park a van to get a clear line of sight. Making sure we're no more than a hundred feet away when he blows. I tell you, we're nuts. In the end, that's why *they*'re going to win.'

'Did you finish?' Carl asked after a little pause. 'You sure? Yes? Then please get back to what you've been doing.'

Boudia's current favourite was a stenographer who lived in rue Boinod in the 18th *arrondissement*. Though the Renault 16 the Algerian had been using remained parked outside his girlfriend's place all night on Wednesday the 27th, Avner was afraid that in the morning he would give the girl a lift and so did not want to risk planting the bomb. In fact, the girl left the apartment alone, almost an hour and a half after Boudia who was gone from the house by 6 am.

Interestingly enough, Boudia drove his Renault to within a block of where his girlfriend would later go to work in the 5th *arrondissement* on the Left Bank. It was a long drive from the rue Boinod to the rue des Fossés Saint-Bernard, at the foot of the boulevard Saint-Germain, and it took Boudia nearly three-quarters of an hour even though he had started out before the morning rush. The time was approximately 6.45 am when he backed his car into one of the angle-parking spots just outside the modern Pierre et Marie Curie building of the University of Paris.

Boudia got out and locked his car. One person from *Le Group*'s surveillance team followed him on foot. The other drove the car in which they had been tailing Boudia's Renault to the nearest telephone. Apparently Boudia was on his way to another girlfriend's home about a block away.

Within half an hour Steve and Robert pulled up in a van and double-parked in front of the Algerian's car. They wore repairmen's overalls. Although there were several stores on the opposite side of the rue des Fossés Saint-Bernard, pedestrian traffic was light at this hour in the morning, and in any case, the tall van standing in front of the car would hide it from the casual glances of passers-by. It was impossible to tell how soon Boudia might return, but he would be preceded by Papa's man, who had been following him on foot, and this would give Steve and Robert enough time to get away.

The type of bomb they were using would take almost no time to place under the driver's seat. It was a self-contained unit, like a small parcel, with no timer to set and no wires to connect. Opening the Renault's door took Steve less than thirty seconds, and Robert was finished in under a minute. Then Steve took another few seconds to lock the door again.

The explosive device was in place. It was not yet 8 am. Steve and Robert got back into the van, and drove it to the corner of rue Jussieu and rue des Fossés Saint-Bernard, where Avner and Hans had in the meantime managed to commandeer two parking places with one car. Now they pulled ahead, and allowed the van to ease in next to the kerb behind them.

Carl was somewhere in the neighbourhood on his own.

Nearly three hours passed. It was 10.45. No sign of Papa's man or Boudia. Then a large truck double-parked in the exact spot where Steve and Robert had stopped the van earlier, right in front of the booby-trapped Renault, blocking their line of sight. There was nothing they could do about it – though Avner considered walking down the street and asking the truck driver under some pretext to pull ten yards ahead. If Boudia got into the car right then, they might not even notice him until he pulled out from the parking space. And following his car, then setting off the explosion at another spot, would be very risky. It would make matters much simpler if the truck just moved.

A few minutes later it did.

But at almost the same time, a boy and a girl – university students judging by the books they were carrying – decided to have a conversation next to the Renault. The girl was actually leaning against the rear fender. They would move, of course, if Boudia got into the car, but perhaps not far enough. A moment earlier Avner was hoping that the Algerian would show up quickly, and now he was hoping he would delay until the students had finished their conversation. 'Come on, baby,' he tried suggesting to the girl telepathically, 'whatever he wants, say yes. Just move your ass.' It worked, because the students began walking away.

Eleven o'clock.

Papa's man came sauntering down the street.

Avner looked at Robert sitting next to Steve in the van, just to make sure he had seen the man. Robert nodded. Avner started up the engine in his car, knowing that Steve would follow suit.

Boudia was unlocking the Renault. He got in and slammed the door. He must have barely had time to turn over the engine. Avner did not even think he'd had enough time to insert the key in the ignition, but he must have, because the car started pulling out.

The explosion blew open the door of the Renault. It buckled the roof. In the sense of being both contained and deadly, it was Robert's most perfect bomb to date. It would probably not have injured anyone ten feet away from the car.

It was also unlikely that anyone inside the car could have survived it.

It also made a very loud bang. Within seconds, the street was filled with people. Reportedly Boudia's girlfriend, working in her nearby office, heard the explosion, although she did not know what it was. The 41-year-old Algerian was killed instantly. Knowing his background – and since the Pierre et Marie Curie building next to which the explosion occurred had its share of left-wing students working in chemical laboratories – the Paris papers speculated next day that Boudia could have been a victim of explosives he had just picked up there. As the car did not seem to be wired, this was also the initial theory of the police.[3]

Avner and his partners did not leave Paris until the first week in July. They left, as usual, one by one. Though the pressure in the pit of his stomach had not eased, Avner felt satisfied. Even Cautious Carl conceded that the mission was going well. In nine months they had taken revenge on nine terrorist leaders. They had three left on the list. If they killed two more they would even the score for the eleven Israelis at Munich – an eye for an eye.

What neither Avner nor Carl – nor Robert, who was very proud of his handiwork – had any way of knowing was that with the assassination of Mohammed Boudia, they had made room at the top of the Palestinian terrorist network in Europe. They had cleared the way for a high-level appointment. They had opened the door for possibly the most notorious terrorist of the terrorist decade. Within weeks another man would take the slain Algerian's place, renaming the *Parisienne Orientale* the Boudia-Commando. He was a pudgy Venezuelan christened Ilich Ramirez Sanchez at birth.

Soon to become better known as Carlos the Jackal.

Chapter 12

~~~~~~~~

THE YOM KIPPUR WAR

IN THE AFTERNOON of 6 October, 1973, Avner was flying TWA from Frankfurt to New York. Since 2 pm that day, Tel Aviv time, Israel had again been engaged in a shooting war with Syria and Egypt.

In the twelve months during which Avner and his team had been trying to find and kill eleven terrorist leaders in Europe, diplomatic and military developments had been taking place in the Middle East that would render the success or failure of their mission largely academic. In the early afternoon of the Jewish high holiday of the Day of Atonement, Arab preparations culminated in a massive attack against Israel on two fronts. In the south it was the Egyptian Second and Third Armies, comprising five divisions, launching the assault against occupied Sinai across the Suez canal. In the north it was five divisions of the Syrian Army moving against the so-called Purple Line – the cease-fire line at the end of the Six Day War – extending from Mount Hermon to the junction of Ruqqad Stream and the Yarmuk River near the Jordanian border. The two-pronged Arab attack threw the rough equivalent of NATO's standing forces in Europe against the defending Jewish armies. It was clear from the outset that, should the Yom Kippur War end in an Arab military victory, it would almost certainly mean the destruction of the State of Israel and – barring swift interference by the great powers – a possible massacre of the Jewish population on a scale to rival that of World War II.

Under the circumstances, Avner saw no point in continuing to sit in Frankfurt or Geneva, trying to monitor leads on Salameh or Dr Haddad. In fact, he would have found it emotionally impossible. The outbreak of the war caught the team almost as unprepared as it did the rest of Israel – almost, but not quite, since rumours of Egyptian troop movements and preparations had been reaching them (as they did other Mossad agents) since the spring of 1973 from their regular informers. Early in May they even left a message about it for Ephraim in Geneva, as both Avner and Carl agreed that they should, though strictly speaking it was not part of their assignment. But, as became evident after the Yom Kippur War, intelligence data from far more important sources than Avner's team had been reaching Jerusalem regularly during the year of Arab preparation.

All of which was water under the bridge by the afternoon of 6 October. Nor was there time to go and wait in Geneva for instructions. The situation called for a decision, which Avner made for the team as a matter of course. 'I'm joining my unit,' he said. 'I want Carl and Hans to stay in Europe and mind the store. Steve and Robert are free to make their own decisions. Any questions?'

As expected, the only one to argue was Hans, who felt that Carl alone could look after everything, but Avner was adamant about not leaving Carl on his own. He believed this would have amounted to aborting the mission, which none of them was prepared to do; and using this argument it was not even necessary for him to pull rank on Hans in the end. For security, Steve and Robert decided to reach Israel via South Africa. Avner opted for New York.

In the circumstances, Avner and his partners would probably have interrupted their hunt for the two remaining terrorist leaders even if they had been hot on their trail. Since the assassination of Boudia in June they had not had as much as a good rumour about Ali Hassan Salameh, while all reports had Wadi Haddad holed up in Aden, in South Yemen, for good. And even that was not all.

The truth was that after June Avner – and Carl, too, it

272

seemed to him – began to have second thoughts about the entire mission. Not just the mission, but the whole philosophy behind it. They never discussed it, but Avner couldn't help thinking about it, and his sixth sense told him that some of the others had been thinking about it as well – perhaps all the others, except Steve. The trouble was, as Avner fully realized, that thinking about such things was not only heresy, it was dangerous. Very dangerous. Their mission was something that people with doubts should never attempt to carry out.

Yet not to doubt was becoming increasingly difficult. It was not a question of remorse – at least, not in the ordinary sense of the word. Avner had no feelings of remorse for the *mechablim*, and he thought Carl and the others felt the same way. Speaking for himself, while he did not enjoy killing, he would have been willing to kill each and every one of the terrorists all over again. That wasn't the question. It was much more a feeling of futility.

In one way, of course, assassinating the *fedayeen* leaders was, and was meant to be, pure vengeance. A bomb for Yossef Gutfreund, another for Moshe Weinberger. A dozen bullets for the lost leg of Hannah Marron. As Golda Meir herself had put it in the *Knesset*, while the Government could not assure Israelis that they could put an end to terrorism, they would assuredly cut off a hand for every hand that hurt them.[1] They would – for the first time in millennia – make slaughtering Jewish men, women and children an expensive proposition. Avner saw nothing wrong with that. If anything, he continued to be proud of being one of the swords that cut off the hands of the enemies of Israel.

But, beyond vengeance, their mission was supposed to weaken and diminish anti-Israeli terror in the world. Not stop it altogether – that would have been unrealistic – but at least slow it down. Chopping off the heads of Ephraim's monster, as they had been doing, ought to have had some effect on the monster itself.

If Ephraim was right.

But was Ephraim right? This was the real question – and the answer to it seemed to be no. The monster was growing new heads, almost as if having them chopped off had stimulated new growth. Since their mission had started, the *mechablim* had assassinated Baruch Cohen in Madrid, had sent out a rash of letter bombs, some of them finding their targets, and had occupied the Israeli Embassy in Bangkok. In March they killed an Israeli businessman in Cyprus; in April an Italian employee of *El Al* in Rome. The very day of the commando raid in Beirut, the Palestinians had come within minutes of wiping out the Israeli Ambassador and his family in Cyprus, and were stopped just in time by a sky marshal from blowing up an *El Al* jet. Three days after Boudia's death they had shot and killed – in retaliation for Boudia, as a Voice of Palestine broadcast had claimed – Yosef Alon, Israel's military attaché, in Washington DC.[2] About three weeks later a combined group from the Popular Front and the Japanese Red Army hijacked a Japan Air Lines 747 flying to Amsterdam. Although their leader, a woman, managed to blow herself up *en route* with a hand grenade, the terrorists forced the plane to fly around the Middle East for four days, after which they destroyed it at Benghazi, though they did release the passengers first. On 5 August two killers from the National Arab Youth for the Liberation of Palestine attacked a TWA plane in Athens, just as it had landed on a flight from Tel Aviv. The toll: five passengers dead and fifty-five wounded. A month later, five Black September terrorists in Rome attempted to set up two Soviet SAM 7 ground-to-air heat-seeking missiles to shoot down an *El Al* jetliner. And just a week before, on 28 September, two *fedayeen* from *Saiqua*, the Syrian-backed terrorist faction, had hijacked a train in Austria filled with Russian Jewish refugees, extracting a promise from Austrian Chancellor Bruno Kreisky to shut down the Schönau Castle transient camp for Jewish emigrants to Israel in return for the hostages' release. This action, Avner was convinced, was part of a Syrian operation to distract the attention of the Israeli Government from the impending Arab attack, and in a limited way it might have been successful.

Golda Meir was so outraged by Chancellor Kreisky's spinelessness that, almost on the eve of the war, and against the advice of some people in her cabinet, she flew to Vienna in a futile attempt to change the Austrian leader's mind. The terrorists chose the location of their operation very smartly since Kreisky, a socialist and, incidentally, himself a Jew, was, on his record, the most likely of all European leaders to prostrate himself before a threat.

These were only the highlights of that year's terror: there had been many other smaller or less successful incidents. On reflection, it would have been difficult to say whether the team's operation had made the slightest difference to the terrorist threat – though, as Avner had to admit, it would have been impossible to tell what the same period might have brought with it if the nine *mechablim* had not been eliminated. Assuming the Arabs had not been totally hopeless at their jobs – and that was a fair assumption to make about people like Najjer, Adwan, Boudia and Hamshari – they would probably have organized some acts of terror in that time, had they not been taken out of action. But the bottom line was still the same.

Ephraim's monster was alive and well. Growing one new head after another. Sometimes deadlier than the one it replaced, as in the case of Carlos.[3]

There was an additional factor contributing to Avner's disillusionment. The events of the summer of 1973 had made it absolutely clear. It was something they had always suspected – in fact, Carl had asked Ephraim about it right after their first briefing – but they had not known it for certain until June.

Theirs was not the only team.

In June, 1973, a car bomb killed two Arab terrorists in Rome.[4] As it happened, Avner and the others did not even know about it until they received a rather puzzled query from Tony, wondering whether Avner had found anything amiss with his services since they had not been required on this occasion. It seemed that even Tony – well informed as he usually was – attributed the assassination to Avner's team, who had nothing to do with it. There was a possibility that the two Arabs were, in fact, killed by a rival terrorist group, but both Avner and Carl doubted it. Hearing the news they had glanced at each other, Avner raising his shoulders, and Carl scowling.

A dreadful fiasco that occurred on 21 July left no doubt about it whatsoever. On that day, in the small Norwegian resort town of Lillehammer, an Israeli hit team shot and killed an Arab whom they believed to be Ali Hassan Salameh. Several members of that team were immediately captured by the Norwegian police. That was bad enough in itself but, in addition, their victim was not Salameh. He was a Moroccan waiter by the name of Ahmed Bouchiki, pumped full of bullets as he was strolling peacefully with his pregnant Norwegian wife. A young Arab who, in all likelihood, had no connection with terrorism at all. A completely innocent bystander.[5]

Avner and his partners were shocked by the news when they heard about it, and for three different reasons. First, by killing the wrong man *and* being captured their colleagues in Norway had committed at one stroke two of the worst sins agents could possibly commit. Both were disastrous mistakes by any standards, but Avner and his team were imbued with an additional sense of taboo about them. These were the two errors they were trained above everything else never to make.

The second reason for their shock was that what happened in Lillehammer brought home to them for the first time how easy it was to bungle something really badly. Reading the papers, they felt like rookie racing-car drivers witnessing their first crash. If it could happen to those fellows – who were no doubt trained and selected just as carefully as Avner and his partners had been – it could happen to them. It wasn't a question of spending some years in a Norwegian jail – that was, comparatively speaking, nothing – but going to use Carl's expression, from hero to bum in the space of ten minutes. That would be truly awful.

Then, there was the third reason.

Other teams. On the face of it, there was no reason why there shouldn't be other teams. They didn't have a monopoly on the *mechablim*. No one had promised them an exclusive hunting licence. Ephraim certainly hadn't: he had simply told Carl that he couldn't answer that question when Carl had asked him. This was war; not a safari, with special privileges for General Zvi Zamir's guests to bag their own quota of monsters. If Avner had stayed in the army, he'd be fighting the enemy shoulder-to-shoulder with other units, and he wouldn't dream of objecting if the neighbouring unit started firing on the same target; on the contrary, he'd be grateful.

Yet there was something about their operation, something so special, that they were profoundly disturbed by the thought of other teams doing the same thing. Who could tell why? They couldn't quite put it into words. They were probably wrong about it anyway. But, after hearing about Lillehammer, Avner couldn't help wondering how many other people might have been brought to Golda Meir's apartment. How many other people might have had the Prime Minister put her arm around them, telling them to remember this moment, telling them that they were now part of Jewish history. How many other Yekke potzes might be running around the world, remembering her voice, her handshake, and then going out risking their lives believing that they were doing something extraordinary when in fact they were just foot soldiers like the rest, like any schmuck sweating it out in a tank on the Golan Heights.

But they *were* soldiers. Wasn't it rather shameful even to worry about something like that? Hans spoke for all of them when he said, after a little silence: 'Come on, you guys. Remember, we're not movie stars.'

True, but . . .

Why did the Galicianers have to give that team in Norway the same targets? Weren't there enough terrorists around? Did they have to send them after *Salameh*? Perhaps they gave every team the same list! Was it possible – Avner actually felt a sharp pang when this thought flashed across his mind – that back in Tel Aviv they didn't even *know* which team got rid of which terrorist leader? 'I'll read about it in the paper,' Ephraim had said. Was it possible that, even now, some other team was being credited with *their* work in Rome, in Paris, in Nicosia?

No, that couldn't be; after all, they had met Ephraim in Geneva before the Beirut raid. They had told him at the time what they had done to date, so he knew. But it probably made no difference to him. *That* was the problem.

But why should it make a difference to Ephraim? And wasn't the problem of Avner's own making?

When he ought simply to be a good soldier, wasn't all of this *Angst* just an excuse to help him feel 'disillusioned' because he was becoming afraid? Wasn't that the simple, dreadful truth? All these thoughts in his mind about futility, about it not making any difference, about not getting enough credit, about having to share the glory, all were just to cover up the pressure in the pit of his stomach. He was just looking for reasons so he wouldn't have to admit to himself that he was afraid. Wasn't that at the bottom of it: a coward trying to rationalize his fear?

The very idea made Avner shudder. Yet, it could have been the truth. In which case going to war was the best thing. Just going and joining his unit, where everything would become much simpler. A soldier like the rest, now that the country needed ordinary soldiers more than anything else. Open battle, with guns firing face-to-face. Being the first to scale a hill, being the first to lob a hand grenade into an enemy bunker. Action. Going into action, he could show himself that he was not afraid. Going into action would cure everything that was wrong with his stomach.

In New York people were in a turmoil. The news was that the war in Israel was going very badly, and literally thousands of people – Israeli immigrants, American Jews and even non-Jewish Americans – were trying to catch flights to Tel Aviv to lend a hand in the battle. It was a serious problem, in that people who would not have been much use in the fight were – out of the best of intentions – taking up space needed for others who could really help. Officials at the airport were trying to sort out the chaos as best they could, but it was difficult. The news that the Egyptian armies were crossing the Suez canal, establishing bridgeheads, and in some spots had managed to penetrate to 'Lexicon' – the main north-south road running along the canal on the Israeli-occupied side – underlined the urgency of the situation.

Avner decided to play no games, and travel on his own Israeli passport as a reserve major in an elite unit. This would assure him of a seat on the next *El Al* flight going, and he could sort out the repercussions afterwards. In fact, he didn't think there would be any. Unlike his last visit to Tel Aviv at the time Geula was born, this was clearly the kind of emergency where he would not be blamed for going back to Israel without specific orders. The country was so small, the space between victory and defeat in terms of modern warfare so narrow, that it created an unspoken understanding about what every Israeli should do immediately and on his own in wartime. Even if later he should be reprimanded for going back, Avner could count on being forgiven for it.

He did not even leave the airport, but called Shoshana to come and meet him there. She brought Geula who, at ten months, was beginning to look not only like a small human being but like a girl. It was the first time that Avner could actually feel anything for her other than distant curiosity. This was his daughter! He kissed her, kissed Shoshana, and asked her to try to reach one of his friends in Tel Aviv by phone – lines to Israel were almost impossible to get – asking him to bring a car to the airport. The headquarters of his unit was just south of Haifa, a little over an hour's drive from where he would be landing at Lod. Like many Israelis, Avner was planning to drive to war in his private car.

As it happened, it was his idea of driving to the war that landed Avner in trouble. The plane arrived at Lod after an uneventful flight, and Avner's friend was waiting for him with the car. Avner embraced his friend, took the keys, threw his suitcase into the back seat, and a few minutes later was driving along the highway towards Haifa. Within a mile he was flagged down by a pretty but unsmiling girl in a police uniform.

'What's the matter?' Avner asked, puzzled. He hadn't even been speeding.

'Don't you know what day of the week it is?' asked the *sabra*.

For a second Avner had no idea what she could possibly be talking about. Then he remembered. Of course! In the urgency of getting Avner a car, both he and his friend had forgotten something. The gasoline shortage in Israel resulted in a sticker system, where cars with a certain sticker could be driven only on alternate days on public roads. Avner's car had the wrong sticker for that particular Sunday.

In wartime Israel, it was regarded as a serious offence. There was no use protesting. The policewoman had him follow her to the traffic magistrate's courtroom immediately. There, sitting behind a desk in all his official splendour, was an elderly Galicianer with a neatly trimmed white moustache.

Avner excused himself as best he could. He explained that he had been abroad and, as a reserve officer, had just been trying to drive quickly to his unit so as to join the war. He was sorry about his infraction but, since he had been out of the country, it had not even occurred to him, and so forth. Could he now please be on his way?

The magistrate seemed sympathetic. 'Go, go join your unit,' he said. 'Under the circumstances, I'll let you off with a fine.' He fixed the amount at 200 Israeli pounds, which wasn't much. But Avner had hardly any Israeli currency on him.

'Could you please give me some time to pay?' he asked.
The Galicianer looked at him.

'Now you want time?' he asked. 'You must be crazy.
You're going to the war, aren't you? If you get killed, who's
going to pay the fine?'

Avner heaved a deep sigh. Oh well, he thought. It was
nice to be home.

A tragic day for Israel was a day of jubilation for patriots of
the Arab world. For a quarter of a century, since the establishment of the Israeli State, the Arab forces had hardly won
a battle, let alone a war. The Egyptian army's successful
crossing of the Suez canal on 6–7 October, 1973, became a
matter of celebrating not merely a military victory but, in
effect, the recovery of lost honour. Even manhood. Not just
as a fanciful metaphor, but as a matter of deep and genuine
feeling. For instance, in a poem published a year after the
Yom Kippur War, the Syrian bard Nizar Qabbani described
the act of making love after hearing the news that the Arab
warriors had crossed the canal:

> Did you notice
> How I overflowed all my banks
> How I covered you like the waters of rivers
> Did you notice how I abandoned myself to you
> As though I was seeing you for the first time.
> Did you notice how we fused together
> How we panted, how we sweated
> How we became ashes, how we were resuscitated
> As though we were making love
> For the first time.

Poetry, infinitely more important in twentieth-century
Arab culture than in the West as a gauge – as well as a guide –
for political thought and action, was registering and, to a
considerable extent, helping to create the shock waves of
militant nationalism that were spreading across the Arab
world. Though Nizar Qabbani's new-found potency must
have been short-lived – by 14 October the Israeli forces had

stemmed, and by the 16th they had begun to turn the tide of the Egyptian attack in the Sinai – the emotions underlying his poem would not have been affected by Major-General Ariel Sharon's division recrossing the Suez canal. Israel's sword, slicing through the soft tissue that connected the Egyptian Second and Third Armies, may have cut the attacking forces in half, but had probably caused little injury to the spirit of Arab resistance. This spirit, thriving on failure no less than on success, was widely recognized in Israel. During the first disastrous days of the Yom Kippur War, for instance, it gave rise to the popular speculation that the Americans were not pressing for a cease-fire because Secretary of State Henry Kissinger believed the Arabs needed a sound military victory to regain their self-respect and come to the conference table in a more conciliatory mood.

In a curious way Arab feelings reflected – just as Chinese or Russian feelings about the Japanese did earlier in the century – the special humiliation of a Goliath beaten by David. While much has been written about the suffering of the weak at the hands of the strong, the extra psychological damage the strong suffer when repeatedly defeated by weaker forces is seldom remarked upon, though it is known to give rise to unusual fury. It could certainly turn a patriot, in Nizar Qabbani's words:

> From a poet of love and longing
> To one who writes with a knife.

Many other intellectuals progressed from calling for armed struggle to taking part in it, and Tawfiq Zayyad had no compunction about naming the land of enlightenment and human rights that served as his example:

> My friends in the fertile sugar fields
> My friends in the oil refineries of proud Cuba
> From my village, my precious home
> I send you greetings:
> My friends who have filled the world with the fragrance of struggle
> Keep up the pressure on the imperialists

Press on – the wings of the eagle are stronger
Than the hurricanes
The imperialists do not understand
The language of humility and tears
They only understand the people surge
To the arena of struggle.[6]

Such poems made it evident that many intellectuals of the Palestinian resistance had resolved by the late 1960s to make common cause with international Communism. In some cases this might have resulted from genuine conviction; in others, from a sense of expediency. No doubt, just as the Soviet Union was not above using Arab nationalism for its own purposes, there were Palestinians who would have been perfectly prepared to use the Soviets for furthering their own national goals without any deep commitment to Communist ideals, and none at all to the foreign policy interests of the Soviet Union. What mattered to them was what they saw as the liberation of Palestine, and by 1968 a pact with the devil, to most *fedayeen*, would not have seemed too high a price to pay for it.

In this sense 'a pact with the devil' entailed much more than an alliance with Soviet interests. In their progress from national resistance to international terror, some Palestinians – like many others, including such Zionist factions as the Irgun before them – had come to believe that the end invariably justified the means, and that no act of indiscriminate brutality against non-combatants and civilians could give rise to moral objections as long as it was thought to serve the establishment of a national state.[7] So it was that the *fedayeen* crossed the line between freedom fighting and terrorism. But it was their methods, not their cause or even their ultimate goals, that removed the moral ground from under their feet – however much it may have helped them to publicize their struggle.

A struggle that was complicated further by the outcome of the Yom Kippur War. Ultimately another military victory for Israel, it also revealed for the first time that the Jewish nation-state was not invincible. This may have been less of a surprise to the Israelis themselves than to their enemies. In any case, it presented an ideological and tactical dilemma for the Palestinians. It was not so much a new rift as the deepening of an earlier one between the two great factions of the 'armed struggle', represented by Yasser Arafat's Al Fatah on one side and George Habash's Popular Front on the other.

Though both sides believed in the destruction of the Israeli State as the struggle's ultimate aim – and also in some form of Arab-style socialism for the entire Middle East – Arafat and Habash never saw eye to eye on questions of emphasis, tactics and priorities. For Dr Habash, who is a militant Marxist-Leninist first and an Arab nationalist second, the Palestinian struggle is only one arena in a larger campaign for pan-Arab Marxist rule and against 'imperialism'. For Arafat, a Palestinian patriot before anything else, the first priority is 'the liberation of Palestine', to be followed later by what he would refer to as 'the liberation of man', meaning some kind of Arab socialism.

Both embrace violence, even terrorist violence, but while Arafat has favoured the 'palestinization' of guerrilla operations – meaning Palestinian *fedayeen* conducting armed raids inside Israel and Israeli-occupied territories only – Dr Habash supports international attacks, often in collaboration with other terrorist groups. It was for this reason that Black September, Al Fatah's 'dirty tricks' squad of international terrorists, was not officially acknowledged by Arafat – though inside the PLO its existence was never a secret. This enabled Arafat to maintain a façade of relative moderation to the outside world.

In one sense, it was more than just a façade. After the Yom Kippur War, negotiating the establishment of a Palestinian state at a conference table in Geneva became at least a remote possibility. Since Israel was not likely to negotiate itself out of existence, the PLO would have to moderate its stand if it hoped to participate. Without going as far as acknowledging Israel's right to exist, Arafat believed that, if only for strategy, the PLO should refrain from calling for its unconditional destruction.

Dr Habash and the Popular Front rejected this approach. For them, the Zionist-imperialist state had no right to exist. And so the Rejection Front was born, supported by the Rejection States, such as Syria, Iraq, South Yemen and Libya. The many smaller factions inside the PLO chose their own sides with Fatah or the Rejection Front, though the overall leadership was retained by Arafat.

Israel, for its part, viewed Arafat with great ambivalence. Officially it did not recognize the PLO, even in its moderate guise, any more than the PLO recognized Israel. But some Israelis believed that a negotiated settlement would perhaps be possible with a Palestinian leader of Arafat's type. Others were convinced that the Fatah chief was no more 'moderate' than the most outspoken of the *mechablim*. And although Avner and his partners rarely talked politics, on this issue even they were divided. Steve, Robert and Hans would not give Arafat the time of day, but Carl did not take quite so pessimistic a view. Avner was in the middle. But what he was sure of was that Salameh, Arafat's Black September strategist, must be assassinated.

Known as 'Abu Hassan' in the Palestinian resistance, Salameh was wealthy and had been educated at the Sorbonne. Unlike Yasser Arafat to whom he was distantly related, Salameh was described as 'wildly handsome and irresistible to women'.[8] He was an upper-class Palestinian whose father, Sheikh Salameh, had been an active fighter in the Arab resistance long before the creation of Israel. The elder Salameh had conducted raids on Jewish settlements in Palestine before Ali Hassan was born and was finally killed by a *Haganah* bomb in 1948.[9]

As his father's son, Salameh came to the 'armed struggle' naturally. Because of his social background, however, he was less drawn to the Marxist factions within the Palestinian

285

movement than other terrorist leaders. This did not mean that he would not cooperate with them to further the Palestinian cause. One of his closest collaborators in Paris, for instance, was the Marxist Mohammed Boudia, who had reportedly been a member of the Communist Party since the 1950s. But Salameh would also collaborate with people on the extreme right, such as François Arnaud, founder of the neo-Nazis in Switzerland, who had reportedly handled financial matters for the Palestinians in Europe as he had for the Nazis during the war.[10]

For some reason Avner and his partners had become more obsessed with 'getting' Salameh than with the assassination of any other terrorist leader. Not only was he Number one on their list, but he was generally regarded in Israel as the man responsible for the murder of the Olympic athletes in Munich. Though no one could be certain that the idea of attacking the Israeli team in the Olympic village had originated with Salameh, the Mossad believed it had ample evidence that he had been in charge of the planning and coordination. He had thus become the symbol of the *mechublim*. In counter-terrorism, as in terrorism itself, military objectives often took second place to symbolic acts. In a sense, assassinating Salameh became the equivalent of capturing the enemy's flag.

It was this obsession that helped explain the Mossad's fiasco at Lillehammer, an operation which otherwise seemed so very unprofessional. For an unusually large number of agents to descend on a remote, tiny resort town where strangers would automatically attract a great deal of attention, in which there was no place to hide, and from which escape was impossible except via two long, easily controlled autoroutes, was to invite capture even if no error had been made about the target. And while some aspects of the operation that would flabbergast outsiders later – such as two agents being arrested while returning a leased car at Oslo airport to save a day's rent – surprised Avner somewhat less (he being familiar with the grandfather of all Galicianers auditing expenses in the bowels of the Mossad), there was no question that the operation was recklessly mounted. This could only be explained – if not excused – by the obsession of the Mossad with eliminating the man who had become, for Israel, the personification of international terror.

Though sharing the obsession, Avner resolved that he and his partners would never share the recklessness. They would not make similar mistakes.

As events turned out, they very nearly did.

Chapter 13

ALI HASSAN SALAMEH

It took the Mossad – evidently having more important things to worry about – until 22 October to discover the unauthorized presence of Avner, Steve and Robert in Israel. They rejoined their units on arrival, just like any officers coming back to Israel from abroad. Their commanders had no idea what they had been doing since leaving the active list and, in the middle of the war, would have been unlikely to inquire. In Avner's unit, by the time he had reached the base, even the cooks had been sent to the front. He was immediately given his operational assignment, and saw action at the northern front against the Syrians and in the Sinai against the Egyptian Third Army. Once again, he was lucky enough to escape without a scratch, as were Steve and Robert in their respective units.

The computers did not catch up with them until the hostilities had all but come to an end. In the north, Mount Hermon had been recaptured, and General Sharon's division had already surrounded the Egyptians in the south. It was in the southern sector, on the west bank of the Suez canal, that an officer in a jeep grabbed Avner and shoved him into a helicopter with instructions to report to Mossad headquarters in Tel Aviv.

On the way he wondered if Steve and Robert would already be there waiting for him, but they weren't. Ephraim was.

'Are you guys all crazy?' he said when Avner was led into his office. 'You think you're such heroes we can't win the

war without you? I should have you all court-martialled!'
Despite Ephraim's words, Avner could tell from the tone of
his voice that, as he had expected, there would be no real
repercussions.

'I want you to get out of Israel today,' Ephraim continued. 'Go back to Europe and finish what you're doing. If
we need you back here, we'll call you. Unless you're ordered
to come back, I don't want any of you to show up in Israel
again. Do I make myself clear?'

Though Avner supposed Ephraim had every right to talk
to him in this tone, there was something in his voice that
rubbed him the wrong way. They had come back because the
country was in mortal danger, as had thousands of other
Israelis and Jews. It was also true that they had thereby
violated operational procedure. But hell! It seemed to Avner
that whenever he risked his life for Israel, whenever he did
something above and beyond the call of duty, there would be
some Galicianer facing him down and chewing him out. Or
giving him a fine, like the magistrate in Tel Aviv on the very
night of his arrival. Was there to be no end to it?

The one thing Avner couldn't do, whenever he felt that
way, was to keep his mouth shut.

'Let me tell you something,' he said to Ephraim. 'I don't
even work for you guys. Remember? You don't order me to
do anything!'

But his outburst only made Ephraim laugh. 'Oh, get out
of here,' he said, 'before I throw something at you. Get
out . . . or rather wait a minute. You reminded me. I want
you to sign this.'

Avner picked up the long, closely typed piece of paper.
'What is this?' he asked.

'Well, read it,' Ephraim said. 'You can read, can't
you?'

Avner started looking at the paper, but at that moment,
he just couldn't be bothered trying to take it all in. He picked
up a pen from Ephraim's desk and signed it. It was probably
another dental plan or something.

Being in Tel Aviv, Avner used the opportunity to see his parents before going to the airport. His mother first, then his father. Neither of the visits turned out too well.

His mother, as usual, after a perfunctory personal remark or two – Thank God, at least you're all right – immediately turned the conversation to Israel and the treachery of the world in allowing the war to happen. It seemed to Avner that, once again, his mother was far more concerned with the fate of Israel than with *his* fate; and that the hardships assailing the country affected her much more deeply than any hardships Avner might have experienced in fighting for it. It was Israel this and Israel that – and she also kept expressing her hope that by the time Avner's kid brother Ber reached military age in a couple of years, there would be peace.

Avner reflected, perhaps unjustly, that as always Mother was concerned with peace for the sake of Ber, and seemed not to care that *he* might be killed going to war for it in the meantime. Nothing about Avner appeared to interest her. While he couldn't have told her what he was doing in Europe – she must have surmised that he was doing 'something for the Government' – it hurt him that she didn't even ask. Not even in a general way. She did ask about Geula and Shoshana, but other than that it was Ber and Israel. It seemed to Avner that nothing had changed since Mother had sent him to the kibbutz.

The visit with his father turned out badly for different reasons.

Father had become even older, sicker, and more broken. At the same time the two of them were so similar – not in looks, but in the way their minds and emotions worked – that seeing his father, Avner felt as if he were looking into a mirror twenty or thirty years hence. It was uncanny. Father must have felt it too, because he kept repeating things like: 'Just wait, in a few more years you'll be sitting here, waiting for *them* to call. They've squeezed you dry, they've locked away the rubies a long time ago, but you'll still be waiting. Even though you'll know better by then. You don't believe me, but you'll see.' The trouble was, Avner was beginning to believe his father.

He could hardly wait to get to the airport. Without even giving Steve and Robert a chance to catch up with him, he flew back to Europe.

But November passed in Europe, then December, without anything happening, though the period of nothing happening was filled with activity. In fact, as Carl remarked, they had never worked more to less effect during the mission. Almost every day one of them would pick up a new rumour about one or another of their targets. Salameh, especially, was forever reported to be turning up in Paris one day, in Spain or in Scandinavia the next.

Rumours were also rife about Abu Daoud, their Number two target, the only one who had been completely out of the picture from February to September that year. Abu Daoud had spent those seven months in a Jordanian prison, following an unsuccessful operation to kidnap some members of King Hussein's cabinet. He was captured in Jordan on 13 February and made a public confession on television, revealing the link between Al Fatah and Black September for the first time (no particular news to the Mossad). Two days later, along with his entire group of Black September comrades, he was sentenced to death. However, King Hussein commuted the death sentences, and in September, 1973, less than three weeks before the Yom Kippur invasion of the Sinai and the Golan Heights, Abu Daoud (along with nearly a thousand *fedayeen* the King's troops had captured over the years) were released from Jordanian detention. Since that time, if the informers were to be believed, he had been sighted in every European capital.

The team's failure to get a real lead on Salameh was starting to get on their nerves. Avner could sense it. They were still fine; they could still act with perfect efficiency. But every day they were all getting closer to the edge. They had been on the mission for over a year, and it was taking its toll. Fighting with his army unit had been a relief, as Avner had expected it would be, but now the knot was back in his stomach.

Harder than before.

As for the others, whether they would own up to it or not, Avner had little doubt that they were feeling the pressure. Hans was spending more and more time with his antique-furniture business, maybe pretending to himself that this was his main reason for being in Frankfurt, as Steve had remarked rather sharply on one occasion. He was even turning a profit. Robert, closeted in his bedroom, was building an elaborate toy; he had been working on it every spare moment for weeks. Avner once caught a glimpse of it, and it seemed to be a giant Ferris wheel made entirely of toothpicks.

Carl seemed the strangest of all. He didn't really do anything out of the ordinary. He'd be sitting on the couch, reading, sucking on his cold pipe, as had always been his habit. But these days he'd look up once in a while and ask the strangest questions. Once he turned to Avner and said:

'Do you believe in the transmigration of the soul?'

'Pardon me?' replied Avner, startled.

Carl didn't repeat the question. He shook his head, and went back to his book. Avner remembered the occasion mainly because it was Carl's turn to cook dinner – a traumatic event at the best of times. Versatile as Carl was, he did not include the culinary arts among his skills. Avner, in his role as 'Mother Imp', always concerned about everyone getting enough good, wholesome food, would invariably offer to take Carl's turn without telling the others, but the resident philosopher of the team wouldn't hear of it. 'When it's my turn, it's my turn,' he'd say. 'What's wrong with my chicken casserole?'

What was wrong with it on this occasion was that Carl, preoccupied with the transmigration of the soul, served it without noticing that he had forgotten to turn on the oven.

On 7 January, 1974, some solid-sounding information finally reached the team. It came from Papa and concerned both

Ali Hassan Salameh and Abu Daoud. The two of them were supposed to be meeting in the little Swiss town of Sargans, near the border of Lichtenstein. Inside a Catholic church.

'Damn,' said Carl, looking at the map. 'A little town, with three Alpine roads, in mid-winter. It's Lillehammer all over again, only worse.'

'Not necessarily,' said Avner. 'It's a border town, so after the hit everybody would expect us to cross into Lichtenstein and then straight into Austria. They'd have a whole reception committee at Feldkirch. But we could simply drive back to Zürich. 'Better still, put some skis on the cars and whip straight down to St Moritz. Or Davos, it's even closer. Mingle with the ski crowd. Let's book rooms for five German businessmen at Davos right now.'

'It's still only three roads,' Carl replied, shaking his head.

As it turned out, it was to be fewer roads than three. The day after Avner and Carl had driven around Sargans – only the two of them because, remembering Lillehammer, they did not wish to appear in the little Swiss town in force – word came from Louis again. A slight correction. The terrorist leaders were meeting inside a church in a little Swiss town, but not Sargans. They were to meet near a neighbouring town on the other side of the Alpine lake of Walensee, a few miles closer to Zürich. The town was perhaps a bit larger than Sargans in terms of population, but even further off the beaten track. It was called Glarus, with only one highway – the A17 – running through it: north to Zürich and south, bearing west, through Altdorf and around the magnificent Vierwaldstättersee to the city of Luzern.

Glarus. In the heart of Switzerland, where the forty-seventh northern parallel crosses the ninth eastern longitude. In an area of mixed broadleaf deciduous and needleleaf evergreen trees, watered by an annual precipitation of forty to sixty inches. In January, that meant a great deal of snow.

Salameh and Abu Daoud were supposed to meet inside the church on Saturday, 12 January. Avner, Steve and Hans, driving in two cars, scouted the town on Friday, the 11th. They left Robert and Carl in their safe houses in Zürich.

Robert chose this time to come down with a particularly nasty case of stomach flu. He couldn't keep his food down and was plainly feeling as sick as a dog. Avner considered leaving him behind altogether unless he had improved by Saturday, though Robert wouldn't hear of it. They struck a compromise by agreeing that he, rather than Steve, would be driver of the backup getaway car. Steve and Hans would participate with Avner in the actual hit. The arrangement was not ideal because Steve was a better driver than Robert, and the roads in the region were unusually treacherous. In the circumstances, however, it seemed to be the only choice.

Friday was clear and cold. The church was near the edge of town, its main doors opening on a square built around a little fountain. In the back was a graveyard. A few steps led from the square to the large double doors, with a smaller door cut in one wing which, unlike the main doors, seemed never to be locked. Inside, the long, narrow nave led straight up to the altar. Avner, who knew nothing about churches – or about synagogues for that matter – either as edifices or as places of worship, was setting foot in one for the first time. He was intrigued by the refracted light coming through the stained-glass windows.

To the right of the entrance there was a door, leading from the nave of the church into a fairly large room that seemed like a combined library and reception area. A large wooden table in the middle of the room was covered with books and religious tracts. The walls were lined with more books. Another door, at the back of the room, opened to a staircase. Going up, it led to a gallery and the organ. Going down, it led to various other rooms in the church's basement.

This, according to Hans, was the only place for a meeting. The sacristy in the back of the church would have been insufficient, and there seemed to be no rectory attached to the main building, only some sheds. The priest lived either in a nearby house or in some kind of apartment in the church basement. For that reason Hans thought it would be unsafe to look into all the rooms opening from the bottom of the staircase. They could burst through them in a few seconds the next day. In and out. Surprise. The *mechablim* would be trapped. With one of the team covering the top of the staircase, there would be nowhere for them to go.

In retrospect, it may not have been the most carefully devised plan, but it was certainly audacious. And it would be unexpected. Besides, time was pressing. They had been on Salameh's tail for over a year – who could tell how long it would be before they'd get another chance?

There was no question about spending the night in town; it had a few guest-house-type hotels, but nothing else. Five men booking in the night before, then leaving on the day of the assassination, would have attracted the most unwelcome attention. There might not even be five rooms available, and Zürich was only forty-five miles away. The way to Luzern was about double that distance, and then another forty miles or so back to Zürich, but Avner decided to explore that route as well for an alternate escape after they had finished at the church. It might be necessary for them to split their forces after the hit, one car driving to Luzern and the other to Zürich. In the evening Avner called Louis to arrange for an extra safe house in Luzern in case they needed one.

The next day, Saturday the 17th, was somewhat milder. The sky was overcast, with an occasional light flurry. The main highway from Zürich was bare, but the road leading to Glarus had patches of snow.

Avner, Steve, Robert and Hans were driving in one car, with Carl following in another. They were each armed with a Beretta from the very first cache of arms Avner had purchased from Andreas' Swiss dealer, Lenzlinger. Avner had left the arms in Switzerland at the time, along with the passports, and it was Hans' suggestion that they might as well use the guns now.

Avner and Steve also decided to carry a smoke bomb each. The small canisters – commercially available – fitted into their car-coat pockets, though not very comfortably. But, as Carl agreed with Avner, for an attack on a basement room they were the best. People couldn't jump out of windows, and if they elected to stay inside the room they would become defenceless within thirty seconds. They would probably not stay inside, though. They would start coming out of the door one by one. Easy targets. A smoke bomb could also cover a hasty retreat up a staircase better than anything else. Unlike a hand grenade, it would make no noise; it would alert no one. Before anyone discovered what had happened at the church, the team could be halfway to Luzern.

Maybe. 'Lloyd's would never insure it,' was how Robert put it when he heard about the plan.

Avner had his doubts, too, but neither he nor Carl could come up with anything better than an attack inside the church. Salameh and Abu Daoud would not travel with an army to a little Swiss town for a surreptitious meeting. At most, they'd have two or three bodyguards. Taking four or five unsuspecting people inside a building was one thing; trying to ambush them on the open road was quite another. To attempt the latter, Avner and his four men would have to split two ways to set up two roadblocks to cover both exits from Glarus, rendering half of their own forces useless. They would have to try to get away in what by then could be a badly damaged car from an assassination in the open that would be detected in less than ten minutes. The main road to Glarus was not at all deserted. Besides, if Salameh decided to spend the night in town, what would they do? Freeze on the highway waiting for him?

No. The church was the better plan.

It was even possible – though they couldn't count on it – that an attack inside the church, successful or not, would not be reported to the Swiss authorities. Over the years churchmen of all denominations have been enlisted by extremists of both the left and the right to give them shelter and support in their 'struggles of conscience', but frequently without the knowledge or approval of the church's upper hierarchy. While the higher echelons might sometimes participate *themselves* (the Patriarch of the Orthodox Church would soon be arrested smuggling weapons for the PLO from Lebanon to Jerusalem), more frequently the assistance would come from an individual priest whose mind and conscience had been influenced by some terrorist cause. For some obscure psychological reason a minority of the religious were highly susceptible to nationalist, Fascist or Marxist extremism.[1] If Salameh was using the church of such a renegade priest, the priest would have every reason to hush up whatever might happen inside. If the attempt should be unsuccessful, the *mechablim* themselves would not wish the Swiss police to know about it, at least not until they had got safely out of Switzerland.

By the time they pulled up in front of the church, stopping the cars on both sides of the square, it was already getting dark. Avner, Steve and Hans got out of their car and Robert slid behind the wheel. He kept the engine running, as did Carl whose car was parked about a hundred yards away.

Hans entered the church alone. Avner and Steve stayed outside, like ordinary tourists using the last of daylight to take snapshots. According to the schedule of services hung on the main door, the last of the worshippers would soon be leaving, though the little door would not be locked. Then, except for the terrorists, the church would be empty.

Presumably.

So far, their timing seemed to be accurate. In less than twenty minutes a mixed group of worshippers and tourists – fewer than thirty people in all – came strolling out of the church. Followed by Hans. He was the last person to leave. He nodded pleasantly to the attendant who was locking up the main doors, then ambled over to Avner and Steve.

'Saw two Arabs,' he said curtly. 'Young, wearing black sweaters. Probably bodyguards, but unarmed as far as I could see. They were walking up the aisle, then went into the room on the right. One of them was carrying a tray covered with a white cloth.'

'Are you sure they were Arabs?' asked Avner, though Hans would have been highly unlikely to make a mistake about that.

Hans shrugged. 'Well, they were talking Arabic,' he said. 'Pretty loud, too, as if they owned the place.'

'Let's go,' said Avner, handing the camera to Robert through the open car window.

He walked briskly up the few steps leading to the church door, with Steve following right at his heels. Hans was walking after them at a leisurely pace. The plan called for Avner and Steve to carry out the attack, with Hans stationing himself just inside the main door to prevent other people from entering and to cover the escape. He was not expected to use his Beretta unless it was necessary.

Inside the church it was almost completely dark. It would have been difficult to walk quietly on the echoing stone floor and Avner did not even try. The door to the room on the right of the nave was only ten steps away. Avner and Steve covered the distance in less than four seconds, taking out their guns together and pulling back the slides. By the time Avner kicked in the door the guns were in firing position.

The Arabs in the room looked up.

There were three of them, not two, sitting at the large table, eating. The tray Hans had seen was on the table too, with glasses of milk, cheese, hard rolls and fruit.

The books and religious tracts had been shoved to one side. The only other thing on the table was a Kalashnikov.

And in front of the Arab closest to the door, on the table, sticking out from under the white tablecloth, the butt of a pistol. A Tokarev, unmistakably, with a little hook like a paperclip at the end of the magazine. Probably the 9 mm Tokagypt model, popular in Arab countries. And the next thing Avner saw, while his eyes were still on the gun, was a hand sliding over the grip. The young Arab was going for it.

Steve must have seen it, too, because he was already firing. Twice, then twice again. Avner, whose gun had been trained on the other young man at the opposite side of the

298

table, fired a split second later. The truth was he had no idea what that man was doing at the exact moment when he pulled the trigger because his attention was still focussed on Steve's target, who had been going for his gun. But the way the confrontation developed it would have been impossible for him not to fire. The second Arab was slightly to his right. If he, too, decided to go for a weapon, by the time Avner had turned his head to check it could have been too late. The risk was too great. The reflex too automatic. Avner fired twice, and the second Arab was slumping over, sliding between the table and the chair.

Perhaps the third Arab would not have had to be shot if there had been a little more time.

This young man, sitting closest to the Kalashnikov, had jumped up the minute Avner and Steve burst through the door. But then he had raised his hands. Way over his head. Both Avner and Steve had seen him do it, which was why they turned their attention immediately to the other two.

However, seeing his comrades being shot, the third Arab must have concluded that he'd be killed too, no matter what he did. That was one possibility. The other possibility was that he became confused. The third, that he became enraged. He might even have thought that, after the rapid firing, Avner and Steve would have no more ammunition left. Whatever his reasons, he suddenly lowered his hands and jumped towards the Kalashnikov.

Avner and Steve both fired at him. Twice. He had been standing and the four bullets, grouped closer together, hit him in the stomach. He doubled over and continued squirming on the floor. The other two were already silent. Ten seconds might have elapsed since Avner and Steve had entered the room.

They had killed or severely wounded three Arabs who were not on their list.

Though that thought did flash through Avner's mind, there was no time to worry about it now. He slammed a fresh clip in his Beretta and, motioning to Steve to cover him, tried the door leading to the stairwell. It was open. He glanced up in the direction of the gallery, not expecting to see anyone. Then he ran down one flight towards the basement. Steve remained at the top of the stairwell, covering Avner, but also casting an occasional glance at the bodies of the three Arabs in the room. Though they had each been shot at least twice, it was impossible to tell if they had all been put out of action for good.

Avner kicked in the door at the bottom of the landing. He expected it to be locked, but it wasn't. It wasn't even closed properly. As the door was whipping open, he was ready to see the face of Salameh and, perhaps, Abu Daoud. Two faces he had carefully committed to memory. Or the room might be empty. In that case, he would run further along the hallway where there were two more doors. What he did not expect was what he did see.

Three priests.

Three ordinary priests sitting at a table, wearing their dog-collars. Three astounded priests, looking at Avner bursting through the door with a gun in his hand. Not Salameh or Abu Daoud disguised as priests. Three regular Swiss priests, two younger ones and one older, with white hair and a ruddy face, staring at him as if he were mad.

Three frightened priests. Avner was certain that they must have heard something of the gunshots and the sound of falling bodies overhead.

Of course, the terrorist leaders could be in one of the two rooms further along the hallway. That was possible. But he would have to do something about these three men before he could pursue others.

Shooting them was unthinkable.

Should he call Steve down to guard them? No. That would mean that the priests would see him, too, and it was bad enough that they had seen Avner. It would also mean splitting his attacking force by another 50 per cent. Later Avner would recall that the thought occurred to him at that moment in precisely these military terms. A command deci-

300

sion would have to be made. Avner could not go after two terrorist leaders alone, with Steve out of action guarding three prisoners, and Hans standing uselessly at the church door. But what would happen if the priests decided to push him aside and start walking out through the door? He couldn't hold them back alone, and neither could Steve, without using a gun. Yet a gun could not be used under any circumstances. *Israeli Agents Shooting Priests in Swiss Church* – it could do more damage to the country in one minute than the *mechablim* had done in five years.

Avner started backing away, describing a threatening circle with the barrel of his gun.

The command decision was to abort.

He could see that the priests would be too frozen in astonishment and fear to make any kind of move for another few seconds. Maybe longer. It would give him and the others enough time to get away.

He backed out of the room, slamming the door behind him with his left hand. He ran to the stairwell – calling to Steve so he should not fire by mistake – then ran up the stairs, motioning his partner to follow him. Steve was staring at him but asked no questions. The three Arabs were lying in the room in puddles of blood and milk. One was obviously still alive as he was moaning, and Avner could not be certain about the other two. Hans was crouching behind a pillar in the vestibule, holding his gun in his hand.

'What happened?'

'Nothing,' Avner replied, putting his own gun away. 'Nobody there, only three *galachim*.' For some reason he used the Yiddish word for Gentile priests, though he hardly ever spoke Yiddish. 'Let's get the hell out of here.'

In a couple of seconds they were at the cars. It was still not completely dark. They couldn't have spent more than seven or eight minutes inside the church. 'Luzern,' Avner said to Robert, pointing west. His sixth sense suggested that they should not go back to Zürich. He opened the door for Hans and Steve, then waited for Carl to pull up in the second car.

301

They drove along the snowy mountain serpentine at a moderate speed. Avner was tempted to have them chuck the guns out of the car along with the smoke bombs, but then he changed his mind. Should they run into a roadblock within the next forty minutes it could only mean that the priests had alerted the police, and they could identify him anyway. The smart thing was for him to carry all the weapons in one car and let Carl drive with the others. Then there would be nothing to tie his partners to the shooting in the church. There was no point in all of them getting caught.

As they were stopping at the roadside for a few seconds to make the transfer, Robert said, 'Well, we did a Lillehammer, didn't we?'

'What do you mean, a Lillehammer?' said Steve, outraged. 'We didn't shoot any waiters. We shot three terrorists with Kalashnikovs! You think those guys go to Swiss churches for lunch?'

'Okay, later,' said Carl. 'For now, let's just keep driving.'

Avner decided to say he had come from Lake Como just across the Italian border if he was stopped. He knew the place well enough to describe it, and the German passport with which he was travelling would not necessarily have been stamped at the border. Unless they searched his car and found the guns, a casual 'Lake Como' might have done the trick.

But there were no roadblocks on the road to Luzern.

In Luzern they settled into the safe house. Avner called a local number from a phone booth nearby for a man to come and collect the weapons. Then he called Papa's contact in Zürich.

'They were not in there,' he said to the person who came on the line.

'Yes, they were,' the person replied.

That was pretty much the end of the conversation; there was nothing else to say. Who could tell if Salameh and Abu Daoud had been in Glarus or not? It was certain that, after what had happened in the church, they wouldn't be staying there for long. Steve was right about one thing, without any doubt: three armed Arabs in black sweaters weren't there just for lunch.

'And there's another reason why this wasn't like Lillehammer,' Avner said to Robert back at the safe house.

'Why?'

'We haven't fucking been caught,' Avner said, 'have we?'[2]

Chapter 14

LONDON

THE MONTH OF MAY, 1974, found Avner, Carl and Hans in London.

It was only Avner's second visit to the British capital since the months he had spent there during his field training as an agent. His personal network of informers was mainly in Germany – except for Papa's people, of course – as Hans' was in Paris and Carl's in Rome. London and Amsterdam were Robert's beat, and Steve's. At the same time the partners had always been flexible about meeting one another's contacts. Whenever a good rumour cropped up they'd send whoever happened to be available to track it down. There were only five of them, after all. Though informers – all informers, not only Arabs – felt more comfortable dealing with their regular contact, they'd generally sell information to the others if they were satisfied that it was safe for them to do so.

Now the information came from London, but Robert was busy in Belgium and Steve happened to be on one of his infrequent three-day leaves with his parents in South Africa. That left Avner, Carl and Hans to check out the rumour that Ali Hassan Salameh, who was known to have an ophthalmological condition of some kind, would be arriving in London towards the end of May for a consultation with an eye specialist.

When they arrived on 9 May, a Thursday, Hans went to a safe house. Avner and Carl checked into the Europa Hotel on the corner of Duke Street and Grosvenor Square. At that point they were not planning to do the hit. They merely wanted to talk to the informer and make some preliminary studies of the scene. Where would Salameh be staying? Where was the eye doctor's office? Was another rumour, according to which Salameh would be meeting with some of *his* contacts in some appliance store in the heart of London, true? If so, what was the exact location? Haunted by the spectre of Glarus, Avner wanted to be sure.

Glarus may not have been another Lillehammer, but it was a fiasco all the same, their first total failure. Not only did Salameh and Abu Daoud escape – if they had been there in the first place – but Avner and Steve shot and perhaps killed three other people. Maybe not 'innocent bystanders' in the strict sense – Israeli commandos seldom experienced great pangs of conscience about firing at Arabs armed with Tokarevs and Kalashnikovs – but nevertheless people who were not on their list. It was wrong. It was a mistake. Beyond any argument, it was the kind of blunder it had been a matter of pride for them never to make.

What happened in Lillehammer, and to a lesser extent in Glarus, underlined the validity of the reservations many people had about counter-terrorist operations of any kind. Those Israelis who maintained that it was vain to suggest that a mistake would never be made were proven to be absolutely right. This, after all, used to be Golda Meir's own position. 'How can you possibly be sure,' she had reportedly countered whenever the subject came up, 'that innocent people won't be hurt?'[1] The answer was that you simply couldn't.

But it was also true – and this might have been the argument that swayed the Prime Minister in the end – that of all possible measures involving the use of force, selective operations of counter-terror were likely to claim the fewest innocent victims.

'Hell, we got nine of them,' Steve would say, whenever the subject of Glarus came up. 'Nine leaders. How many civilians would the air force have vaporized before they got nine top terrorists?'

It was true enough.

However, this argument did not take into account a psycho-political factor that played as great a role in counter-terrorism as it did in terrorism itself. The Glarus incident didn't make the news – it must have been hushed up – but one innocent bystander shot at point-blank range in a Western city could do the image of Israel more damage than ten ground-to-air missiles causing dozens of civilian casualties during a Middle East skirmish.

'Bomber pilots can be indiscriminate,' was how Carl put it. 'The artillery can be indiscriminate. They can even make mistakes. We can't.'

Avner and Hans could see this argument, but it would only exasperate Steve or Robert. 'For heaven's sake,' Robert would say, 'whenever the *mechablim* blow up a busful of Jewish kids, they gloat. They machine-gun some pregnant Jewish women, they're proud of it. They don't do it by mistake: they go for women and children on purpose. On purpose, for heaven's sake! What are we all blathering about?'

This was also true. On 17 December, just a few weeks before the team's attempt at Glarus, a group of Palestinian terrorists fire-bombed a Pan Am airliner at Rome, burning thirty-two passengers to death and injuring another forty. Then, on 11 April, in the northern Israeli town of Qiryat Shemona, the *fedayeen* attacked a residential building, killing eighteen people and wounding sixteen, many of them women and children. That very month, May 1974, twenty-two children would lose their lives when terrorists from the Democratic Popular Front took them hostage in the northern Galilee town of Maalot. For the terrorists, killing noncombatants was not an error. It was the very aim of most of their operations.

'So?' Carl would reply to such arguments. 'That's the difference. Does it bother you that there's a difference between the *mechablim* and us? It doesn't bother me.'

Carl seemed more deeply affected by the blunder at Glarus than any of them. He wouldn't sit and mope, but he would be even more thoughtful, sucking on his pipe longer than usual before commenting on a plan. Cautious Carl had become doubly cautious since the Swiss incident. Avner, for his part, agreed with him. He had little patience with abstract arguments, but he could feel that Carl was right. 'Guys, let's not talk more philosophy, okay?' he would say at the end of a discussion. 'If we knew about philosophy, we'd be teaching at the university in Jerusalem for double the money. Let's just talk operations. That's our job.'

There was no opportunity for talk in London, anyway. Avner wanted to accomplish as much as possible in three or four days, then fly back to Frankfurt to meet with Robert and Steve. If they found out that Salameh was arriving at the end of May, and circumstances seemed to warrant an attack with explosives, Robert would have to go back to Belgium immediately to prepare. There wasn't much time.

The arrangement was for them to meet the informer in the lobby of the Grosvenor House Hotel in Park Lane. There was no time set for the meeting; one or another of the three would sit in the lobby for an hour or two, and would then be relieved by somebody else. If the informer came, whoever was sitting in the lobby would make eye contact with him, then phone the others before walking at a leisurely pace to Brook Gate in Hyde Park. There he would meet with the informer who would walk there on his own. The other two would cover the meeting without approaching them, just to make sure that the informer was not being followed and there was no likelihood of an ambush. This was normal procedure. According to what Avner had heard at the time, the Mossad agent Baruch Cohen may have died in Madrid because the procedure was not followed for some reason when he was meeting one of his informers.

The meeting was to be on the 9th, 10th or 11th, some time between 10 am and 4 pm. Such loose arrangements were not at all unusual, though they were a pain in the neck. Avner was beginning to find the constant sitting around and 'eye-balling' that the work could entail increasingly tedious. He had loved it at first, finding it romantic and exciting, but now it was becoming a bother. Perhaps he was just too tense – or getting older.

The informer did not show up the first day.

The second day, a Friday, after Avner had been relieved by Hans and was walking back to his own hotel, he suddenly had the feeling that he was being followed. He had come out of the back door of Grosvenor House, walked straight along Reeves Mews, then turned left onto South Audley Street for the brief jog to the United States Embassy. He was about to cut diagonally across Grosvenor Square when he began to sense another person walking behind him. This was hardly unusual in London, but Avner could feel the eyes of this person resting on the back of his neck. It was a prickly, physical sensation, and at first he actually tried to brush it away with his fingers; a second later, he realized what it must be.

Avner had always taken his sixth sense very seriously. As a rule, it gave him no false alarms. When it warned him, there was danger. Once, while still an ordinary agent, carrying some money for informers, he had left a safe house in Munich in the middle of the night for no tangible reason. He had just come in, planning to go to bed, when suddenly his sixth sense told him to pack his bags immediately and walk out. He did so and had hardly turned the corner when he saw German police cars pulling up in front of the house. They were raiding the place.

Avner never imagined that there was anything mysterious about his sixth sense; he simply thought that he was unusually sensitive to small signals. Others might not perceive them, but he could pick up signs, almost subconsciously, then have his brain decode them in some fashion. In Munich, for instance, it might have been the way the woman who ran the safe house looked at him when he came in. If she had been expecting the raid, there could have been something in her glance that a few seconds later triggered an alarm in Avner's mind without his knowing exactly why.

Now he did not turn around. Instead of cutting across the

park – a walk of less than five minutes to the Europa Hotel – he continued along North Audley Street. He had no doubt that he was still being followed, but though he tried to catch a glimpse of the person tailing him in the windows of stores and the windshields of passing cars, he couldn't. He did not think that he would be attacked in broad daylight. Not at the corner of North Audley and Oxford Streets. But one could never tell. Avner wished he were armed and hoped that whoever was following him would assume he was.

Unless he was being tailed by British counter-intelligence. It was a possibility. In which case, if their informer did not show up that day, it would be wiser for them to get out of England the next morning. Robert could always pick up the trail when he came back from Belgium.

Avner turned right onto Oxford Street and started walking towards Oxford Circus. If there was someone still behind him by the time he got to the Bond Street Underground, he would duck in and eventually make his way by tube to Finsbury Park. They used to have a safe house in Crouch End. He would shake off whoever was following him sooner or later.

However, before he got even as far as Duke Street, the prickly sensation was gone. It vanished as suddenly as it had come. Still, as a precaution, he did not go back to the Europa but went into a restaurant where he could sit by the window. He ordered a cup of tea and continued watching the shoppers on Oxford Street for nearly an hour. Nothing. As far as he could tell, nothing.

It was strange. He had not yet done anything to lose whoever had been following him when the surveillance was abandoned. Though he could have been mistaken about someone following him in the first place, Avner didn't think so.

Whatever it was, there was something wrong.

The informer did not show up again, and Avner went for an early dinner with Hans and Carl to a little curry place that Carl had discovered in Marylebone Lane. Avner was not keen on curry but Carl had lately become very fond of Indian and Pakistani dishes. Perhaps it had something to do with the transmigration of the soul.

Though that particular subject did not come up during dinner, some related subjects of a similarly mystical nature did. Carl seemed to be in a strange mood, and it even affected Hans. For instance, when Avner reported his feeling that he had been followed by someone earlier in the afternoon, within seconds the conversation slipped somehow into a discussion of 'feelings'. It was almost frivolous. Without meaning to dismiss the practical implication of Avner's experience, Hans, and especially Carl, turned it into part of some larger concern that seemed to preoccupy them that evening. Something transcendental.

'Feeling can be very powerful,' said Carl. 'Take levitation, for instance. Do you believe I could levitate if I really concentrated on it mentally?'

'I have no idea, Carl,' Avner replied somewhat impatiently. 'You should try it sometime. It might be fun. What about doing it after the mission is over?'

Carl laughed, and Hans said: 'Maybe you had Carlos walking behind you this afternoon. Maybe he was nipping over to London to visit his mother.' The suggestion was not altogether ridiculous, because the woman, Mrs Sanchez, was known to own a boutique in one of London's elegant shopping streets nearby. Though Carlos was most unlikely to visit her there at this stage of his career, he *had* certainly appeared in London in person, only a little over four months earlier, to carry out two terrorist attacks: in December, the attempt on Sir Edward Sieff, president of Marks & Spencer, and a leading British Zionist; in January, a bomb attack on the Israeli Bank Hapoalim in London in which a woman was injured.

'Look,' said Avner, 'Carlos or not, I don't like it here. We've been hanging around that hotel for two days now. Our guy hasn't shown, but somebody could have picked us up. I suggest we get out of here tomorrow morning. In a few days we can send Robert and Steve over to try again.'

Avner was right; if they had been spotted by then, they would have been foolish to persist. It might even endanger the informer. It was better to have some new people try to make the contact a few days later. Carl and Hans didn't argue the point, but Hans said: 'Look, I stay at a safe house and I know I haven't been followed by anybody. We were supposed to meet the guy on the 9th, 10th, *or* the 11th. That's tomorrow. Why don't you and Carl leave in the morning, and I'll stay until the afternoon.'

'To meet him alone?' Avner shook his head. 'Too dangerous.'

'Trust me,' said Hans. 'I'll be careful. We don't have too much time.'

Avner agreed, though reluctantly.

Carl and Avner shared a corner suite at the Europa Hotel: two separate rooms with only a small foyer in common. From the corridor a double-winged door opened into the foyer. Facing it, another lockable door opened into Avner's room, while on the left a third door opened into Carl's. The rooms were connected only through the foyer.

In 1974 the Europa Hotel had not yet received the facelift that would transform its Etruscan Bar. At that time the lounge's couches and armchairs were covered with dark leatherette, and a large painting depicting *The Rape of Europa* hung on the wall. Carl, who was not much of a drinker, did like having a quiet glass of beer in the evening, and would sometimes sit for fifteen or twenty minutes at the bar there before going to bed.

After dinner that evening, Avner left Carl and Hans at the restaurant to go and look for some souvenirs for Shoshana. He got back to the hotel around 10 pm. Before going up to his room, he had a look in the Etruscan Bar to see if Carl was there. Actually, after his curry, Avner rather felt like a glass of beer himself.

Carl was not at the bar but there were some empty stools on either side of a slim, blonde woman. A young woman – perhaps in her early thirties – with straight, shoulder-length hair and calm blue eyes. A striking woman, very much Avner's type.

Avner sat on the stool beside her and ordered a glass of beer.

The first thing that struck him, even before he began talking with her, was that she put her handbag on the other side of the counter after Avner sat down beside her, then turned away slightly when she reached into it for a package of cigarettes. It was not a suspicious gesture at all, only something that Avner happened to register in the back of his mind.

The second thing that struck him was her perfume. It was a curious, musky smell. Pleasant enough, but quite unusual.

Their conversation was the noncommittal small talk of strangers sitting at any bar. Avner opened it with some remark about the type of glass in which the bartender chose to serve the beer. The blonde girl laughed softly, and made some vaguely humorous rejoinder of her own. She spoke English with a slight accent that might have been German or Scandinavian. She offered Avner a cigarette which he declined. She was not at all aggressive, but seemed quite eager to talk. For a few minutes they chatted about women's fashion. Avner had no great interest in the subject, but he had discovered some time ago that it was an easy way to keep a conversation going with most women.

And he wanted to keep the conversation going. She had creamy skin, with just a hint of freckles around her nose. She wore her green silk blouse with two of the top buttons undone, still high enough to show no cleavage, but as she was turning slightly on the bar stool, the line of her small breasts seemed firm and shapely. A pretty blonde girl. There was no point in denying it. Avner would have been delighted to take her to bed. Shoshana was far away, and at that moment he could even persuade himself that he was feeling lonely.

Perhaps he would have asked her to come up to his room if she hadn't suggested it first.

'It's so nice talking to you,' she said. 'Why don't we go up to your room and have another drink?'

312

Avner was quite certain that she was not a callgirl. He could always recognize a hooker from a hundred yards, upwind, even if she was very high-class; and prostitutes never interested him. He had started talking to this girl precisely because he could see she wasn't a hooker. Of course, she could have been one of those modern, outspoken Scandinavian girls Avner had heard about more often than he had met. It was a possibility. But there were other possibilities. Avner was still feeling a little edgy because of his earlier suspicion that he was being followed.

'Wouldn't that be nice?' he said to her. 'But I can't. Got a very early day tomorrow. Believe me, I'm sorrier than you are.'

He *was* sorry. He felt like a bit of a fool as he stood up, putting some money on the counter. The blonde girl made no attempt to change his mind, only shrugged and smiled. Avner carried the smell of her perfume in his nostrils all the way to the elevator.

Just as he was about to push the call button, the doors opened and Carl stepped out. 'Going up already?' he asked Avner. 'I was just going to the bar for a drink.'

'I may see you later,' Avner said, holding the door open. 'I want to write a couple of postcards.' He stepped inside, allowing the doors to slide shut.

Avner spent perhaps half an hour in his room, writing a postcard to Shoshana, then, as a matter of habit, packing his bag so that he would not have to bother with it in the morning. He turned on his television set and looked at it for a few minutes, but he felt too restless to settle down. Then he decided to go downstairs again to mail Shoshana's postcard. There was really no hurry about it, but perhaps he wanted to atone for thinking about the blonde girl at the bar. Besides, they were checking out in the morning and he might forget. He liked mailing a postcard to Shoshana from every city where he found himself. In a way, it was still a matter of pride to him that he could travel so much: a chicken nail-clipping kibbutznik from the Wilderness of Judah sending postcards from all the great capitals of the world.

313

Avner preferred not to hand his mail to the clerk at the reception desk, so he walked across the street to where he remembered seeing a post box. It was a pleasant night, and after dropping the postcard through the slot, he stood on the corner for a few seconds, looking at the dark trees in the square, filling his lungs with air. Then he crossed the street back to the hotel. He walked through the lobby and, on an impulse, ran up the few steps to look into the Etruscan Bar. Carl might still be there.

But he wasn't sitting at the bar, where he would normally sit, or at any of the tables.

The blonde girl wasn't there, either.

Avner walked back to the elevator. The minute he stepped inside, he could smell the musky aroma of the blonde girl's perfume. Oh well. She must have gone up to her own room; she could easily be a registered guest in the hotel. In fact, she might be staying on the same floor, Avner thought, since he could still smell her perfume in the hallway that led to their corner suite.

When he opened the door leading from the corridor to the small foyer he shared with Carl, the musky smell hit him with full force. It was stronger than in the elevator. It was unmistakable.

It could mean only one thing.

Carl had brought the girl up with him to his room. He must have. Probably just a few minutes ago, while Avner was posting the card.

Avner stopped in the foyer and listened, but all he could hear was the faint sound of his own television set which he hadn't switched off. For a second he thought he also heard a woman laughing in Carl's room, but he couldn't be sure. Well, it made no difference anyway. If Carl invited the blonde girl, he invited her. He had every right to, as far as Avner was concerned. It was certainly none of his business.

Avner unlocked his own door and went inside.

Imagine, Carl inviting the blonde girl. Cautious Carl. Carl, the perfect husband; Carl, who'd buy even more souvenirs for his wife and little daughter than Avner would for Shoshana. Carl, who was over forty, who seemed never to look at a girl, who'd do nothing in his free time but read his books and smoke his pipe. If it had been Steve, or Robert, or Avner himself, it would not have been surprising. For some men it was a torture to do without women.

But Carl?

And what about the blonde girl, about whom Avner had such ambiguous feelings? The girl who was no prostitute but had still asked to have a drink with Avner less than an hour before she had gone upstairs with Carl – who had been in a strange, vulnerable mood all day. True, Carl had a sixth sense every bit as acute as Avner's, but his guard might be down tonight. Perhaps, Avner thought, he should interfere after all. He *was* the leader.

It was as easy as picking up the bedside telephone and dialling Carl's room. 'Hi, Carl? Get her out of there. We're leaving early in the morning. Sorry, but it's an order.' That was all.

Except, Avner didn't do it.

He couldn't bring himself to do it. Carl would have obeyed, but maybe with very poor grace. Perhaps he would have thought that Avner was jealous, or that his nerves were played out. There were never any firm rules about women, about sex. Don't do it was the obvious advice, but everyone knew that it wouldn't always be followed. Human beings had certain needs; some people even said it would be too dangerous for agents to suppress their needs altogether. It would only distract them to the point of uselessness.

Besides, what was the harm?

Avner undressed and watched television for a while. He could hear nothing from the other room through the connecting wall. When he switched off the television, he could still hear nothing. Eventually he turned off the light and went to sleep. He slept as soundly as usual.

He opened his eyes around 7.30 am. It was time to shower and dress. His bag was already packed, and he just shoved in his toothbrush and shaving kit before zipping it up. He generally preferred having breakfast in the restaurant to room service, and before leaving he rapped on Carl's door in case he wanted to join him. There was no answer. In the foyer, Avner could still smell a faint trace of the blonde girl's musky perfume.

After breakfast he came upstairs again. He had lingered over his coffee, expecting Carl to come down, but he hadn't. It was getting late. Whether the girl was still in his room or not, it was time for Carl to get a move on. Avner started knocking on the door with some authority.

There was no answer.

Avner fought to keep calm. There was clearly something the matter. Carl was not a late riser under any circumstances, and he would never miss a plane for sleeping in. None of them would. Avner took a deep breath, and closed the double doors between the foyer and the hallway. Bending down, he inserted a credit card between the tongue of the lock and the frame of Carl's door. It would not have been enough if the door had been locked from the inside.

The door was not locked.

Avner walked in. Carl was lying on his back on the bed under the covers. His eyes were closed. When Avner pulled back the blanket he could immediately see the little star-shaped mark of a bullet fired at close range. There was some dried blood and a ring of black powder burn around the wound. Carl had been shot through the chest and he was quite dead.

Chapter 15

HOORN

AVNER LOOKED AT his partner's body for a few seconds, then replaced the blanket. The things he did next were totally automatic. He made a quick search of the small apartment without expecting to find anything or anyone. He checked that the blinds and curtains were drawn. He took Carl's room key from the dresser and the 'Do Not Disturb' sign from the doorknob. He left the room, double-locking the door from the outside. Then he closed the second door leading from the foyer to the hallway and hung the sign outside. It was still only 9 am. The sign would keep the chambermaids away for at least another couple of hours.

He left the hotel through the baggage room without passing the front desk. From the nearest public phone he dialled two numbers. The first was Hans' safe house. 'Sorry, Hans,' he said when his partner came on the line. 'The movie's off tonight. I'll talk to you later.' He rang off immediately. This was a prearranged message of extreme peril, and Avner knew that after receiving it Hans would leave the country as soon as he could and make his way back to Frankfurt.

The second number he dialled was Louis' in Paris.

Luckily the Frenchman was in. 'I have only enough change for three minutes,' Avner said, 'so I wonder if you could call me back. One of my partners is dead.' He gave Louis the number of the phone booth, then waited. The phone rang in fifteen minutes.

It was Papa himself.

'You go back and wait,' the old man said after Avner explained to him what happened. 'You pack heveryt'ing. Your bag, 'is bag. You wait. My man, he come, he knock t'ree time. You don't do nothing, *tu piges*?'

'I understand,' said Avner. 'Thanks.'

He went back to the hotel, slipping in through the side door again. He re-entered the suite, leaving the 'Do Not Disturb' sign hanging on the doorknob. He looked around to make sure no one had come into the rooms since he'd left. Then, slowly, methodically, emptying his mind of all other thoughts, he packed Carl's belongings. He carried the bags over to his room, and placed them alongside his own suit-cases.

He went back to Carl's room, locked the door from the inside, and sat next to the bed looking at his friend. On an impulse, he pulled back the covers again and forced his eyes to run over Carl's naked body. A good-looking guy. Over forty, but trim, shapely, without an ounce of extra flesh. He used to carry himself with a hint of a stoop, but that was not visible now.

What could have happened? Had he already screwed her ('made love' simply wasn't the right expression under the circumstances) when he got shot? Avner couldn't bring himself to examine Carl's genitals more closely and, in any case, he wasn't sure if he could tell. He did look at his hands, his fingernails. Carl wasn't armed, but he would probably have put up a hell of a struggle if he had been aware of an impending attack. He was quick and fully trained in unarmed combat.

All of which would not have mattered if he had been caught off guard or shot in his sleep. His hands seemed to be unmarked. No defensive wounds or scratches. No hair or fibre in his fingers.

Why was he killed? Was it the blonde woman who shot him? Avner had no doubt that she had been in Carl's room at one point; he could still smell her musky scent. But Carl could have been killed by someone else after she left.

Did she go to his room in order to kill him or set him up to be killed? Or did she simply want to get laid? But Carl was cautious and observant – did he notice something about her that she did not want anyone to know? Could he, for instance, have gone through her handbag while she was in the bathroom – and could she have seen him do it? If Carl had come upon something suspicious – a gun, an odd passport – he might not have said anything to her. He might have pretended to have seen nothing. She, playing it equally smart, could also have pretended that she hadn't noticed him noticing – and then bang! While he was lying in bed with the lights out. It would have taken her a split second.

Pure speculation. Who could tell?

And what if Avner had taken the blonde girl up to his room? Would he be lying on his bed now, like Carl, with a bullet hole in his chest?

It was more than possible.

But why would Carl – Carl, of all people – do something like this? Cautious Carl – and also Carl the Radar, Steve's nickname for him because he could look up from his book and say, 'Guys, somebody's going to ring the doorbell,' and sure enough, a minute later somebody would. Carl, who had an absolute rule about never taking anyone to a safe house or hotel room while on the mission. Once when Robert ran into an old friend in the street and took him to his apartment in Frankfurt, Carl was so furious on hearing about it that he wouldn't talk to Robert for a week. Avner defended Robert at the time because he thought that, under the circumstances, it would have been more suspicious for Robert not to ask his old, close friend to drop by. But Carl was adamant about his rule, and he was probably right.

Yet it was Carl who had fallen into a honey trap – the oldest, cheapest trick of all.

Did he perhaps know the blonde woman? Carl had a large number of contacts, more than any of the others, since he had been in the field longer. Was the blonde girl someone he knew and trusted?

What did he really know about Carl, Avner started wondering, looking at his partner's features, once so familiar, and now set in the closed, tight, secretive mould of the newly dead. Probably more than he knew about the others, because they had roomed together and shared the burden of the planning, the leadership. But even so, Avner didn't know much. Carl had been born in Hamburg, as Avner recalled it, and sent to Israel by his parents in the late 1930s when he was a boy of six or seven. Grew up with an aunt and uncle in Nahariya. Went to some kind of agricultural school, and then joined the army. Stayed on as an instructor until he was picked up by the Mossad. Played the violin. Read a lot of books. Divorced one wife, a gentile woman from Germany, Avner remembered Carl telling him, who hated the Nazis and emigrated to Israel after the war, but eventually suffered a nervous breakdown and had to be hospitalized. Then he married a Czech girl who already had a daughter from a previous marriage. Avner knew that Carl doted on his adopted daughter because, whenever he had the time, he would write her long fairy tales illustrated with spindly drawings. At least once a month, he'd mail her a fairy tale to Rome where she lived with her mother.

That was all Avner knew. Except that now Carl lay dead on the bed in a London hotel room.

For a second Avner became so furious with him that his fists closed involuntarily. He would have liked to shake him, scream at him, punch him in the face. Poor bloody upright cautious courageous Carl. Carl the Radar. Carl the Gullible. Carl, who was wondering if he could levitate.

Carl, who after the Zwaiter hit, when the rest of them were slapping each other's backs in the safe house in Latina, said to them: 'Guys, I wouldn't be jumping up and down. We just killed a man. There's nothing to celebrate.'

None of them would have come up with a statement like that except Carl. And none of them would have accepted it from anybody but Carl. He had the right to say it. Carl had the right to say anything.

Now Carl was dead. But the mission would continue. And whoever had killed Carl would pay.

Papa's man – Papa's men, really, three of them – arrived half an hour later. They knocked on the door three times and Avner let them in. They spoke English to Avner, but Italian to each other. They had with them a large baggage trolley and a dark plastic body bag.

'You can leave now,' their leader said to Avner. 'Give me both keys, his room and yours. Don't check out and don't bother with your luggage.' He gave Avner an address in London. 'Wait for us at that place. We'll check you out and deliver the suitcases to you by tonight.'

The oldest Italian was dressed in a dark suit, and spoke in the sombre tones of an undertaker. Maybe that was his regular occupation. Avner remembered what Papa had said at one of their meetings: 'Why would you dig a grave? I'll send you a gravedigger. For a small fee, *n'est-ce pas?*' Who could tell where Carl's body would end up? But it was the only way. The British authorities couldn't be involved: it would mean the end of the mission. Worse, it might compromise Israel in the most awkward fashion.

'There may be an ejected shell somewhere,' said Avner. 'And some blood on the bedsheets.'

'Don't worry,' Papa's man answered. 'We'll take care of everything.'

Avner had little doubt that they would. By bribes or by stealth, or by a combination of both. Money talked in London too, and some hotel employees could surely be persuaded to be discreet. By tomorrow the corner suite would be spotless, ready for the next guests.

Nothing, on the other hand, would resurrect Carl.

Meeting his partners in Frankfurt, three days later, Avner was convinced they would blame him for Carl's death. He was certainly blaming himself. After all, he had noticed that Carl was in a vulnerable mood; and he had had some misgivings about the girl. Otherwise he might have taken her up to his own room. Wasn't it his duty to warn Carl, and not worry about what Carl might think of him? He wasn't in a popularity contest. Being the leader of a mission meant having the courage to make decisions his team might dislike. A different kind of courage from facing gunfire, but courage all the same. Avner didn't have it, so Carl's death was his fault.

But his partners did not seem to think of it this way.

They were shocked, saddened and angry, though each in a different way. Hans muttered something about those taking up the sword dying by the sword, but Steve turned on him in fury:

'I don't want to hear that sanctimonious shit,' he yelled. 'What sword did the children of Qiryat Shemona take up? Most of the people killed by the *mechablim* never had a gun in their hands. You know that as well as I do.' Then, calming down a little, he said: 'Poor Carl should have screwed around a little more often. Then he wouldn't have fallen for the first goddamn slut who batted an eye at him.'

'Are you sure,' Robert asked Avner, 'that she shot him? Or set him up?'

'I think so,' Avner replied, 'but no, I'm not sure. I'll be sure the minute I find out who she is and what she does for a living.'

'What about the mission?' Hans asked. 'Is it suspended?'

It was the most important question. Avner considered it carefully.

'Not as far as I'm concerned,' he replied finally. 'We report Carl's death, of course. If they want us to stop, they can let us know. We don't even ask the question. Unless and until we hear from them, we continue. 'But in the meantime, I also find out about the girl. Agreed?'

They nodded, understanding, without Avner having spelled it out that 'finding out about the girl' would not be reported to Tel Aviv. In a sense, it was a private matter. It had nothing to do with the mission.

The next day all four of them flew to Geneva. Avner left a message for Ephraim in one safe-deposit box, then, for the first time using his own salary account, he withdrew ten thousand dollars in cash. The others took the same amounts from their own private accounts. Though they naturally couldn't touch Carl's account, Ephraim would make sure that his widow received the money in it in due course. In the meantime they wanted to give her forty thousand dollars of their own money, along with Carl's personal belongings. The same evening Hans and Steve flew to Rome to see her. While it had crossed Avner's mind that, as leader, he ought to break the news to her himself, he decided against it. If such things could be handled at all, Hans would handle them better.

Avner flew to Paris.

He started out by meeting Louis and settling the London expenses. Then he gave him a description of the blonde woman. In less than a week Louis contacted him, saying that he had four photographs for Avner to view. They were ordinary black-and-white prints, one evidently taken with the subject's knowledge, the other three looking more like long-lens photos taken by a surveillance camera. Avner put one of the surveillance photos aside at once: it was obviously not the woman. He examined the other three very carefully.

The women in all three pictures fitted the description he had given to Louis in a general sort of way. The fact that the photographs were monochrome did not matter much, because the most transitory thing about many women is the hair colour or, in an age of contact lenses, even the eye colour. Avner wished pictures had an olfactory dimension: he knew he would recognize that perfume again. As it was, it took him some minutes to point to one of the pictures. It was a photograph of a young woman walking out of a drugstore in Paris.

'This one,' he said to Louis. 'Who is this girl?'

'I'm glad you picked her,' said the Frenchman, instead of replying directly to Avner's question.

'Why?'

'One of the others has been in a Swiss jail for the last six months,' said Louis, 'and the third one is dead. The name of this one in the drugstore is Jeanette. She's a Dutch girl.'

'What is she? What does she do?'

'She kills people,' replied Louis, 'if you pay her enough.'

The information was not surprising. Though most trigger-men of international terror were male, there were also dozens of women among them. In addition, that is, to the many dozens who participated in terror – or ordinary violent crime – in an auxiliary way. Some female terrorists, like Leila Khaled, Rima Aissa Tannous, Thérèse Halesh, the German Ulrike Meinhof and Gabriele Kröcher Tiedemann, or the American Bernardine Dohrn and Kathy Boudin became quite notorious. They did not merely run safe houses, conduct surveillance, or drive people from one point to another. Several women planted explosives, used guns, hijacked planes, or acted as commanders in the world of international terror. Some did it as a matter of course, others, in an attempt to prove that women were as 'good' as men – apparently oblivious to the fact that their acts merely proved women to be equally unthinking and cruel.

Avner had certainly been trained not to underestimate female terrorists, quite independently of what happened to Carl. The Mossad always regarded women as not only equal but possibly superior to men in organizational ability, deception, dedication to a cause, and in having ruthlessly single-track minds. The only areas where they might have been slightly inferior were mechanical efficiency and predictability under fire. They were a little more likely to miss, to blow themselves up with their own hand grenades, or to surrender in hopeless situations – though this last only indicated that women had a healthier sense of self-preservation than men. Under certain circumstances, this quality could only make them that much more dangerous.[1]

'Who hires her?' asked Avner.

Louis shrugged.

'Whoever can meet her price, I guess,' he said. 'I understand a lot of people have used her in South America.'

'Where is she now? Can you find her?'

'Between jobs, she lives in a little coastal town in Holland,' Louis replied. 'The place is called Hoorn. It's about thirty kilometres from Amsterdam.'

Avner nodded. He knew where Hoorn was. 'Does she live in a house, an apartment?' he asked.

'On a houseboat, believe it or not.' Louis laughed. 'I'm not sure if she's a lesbian or goes both ways, but she lives there with a girl. At least, when she's there. But she's not there now.'

'Can you find out when she will be there,' said Avner, 'on a business basis, of course?'

'I'll certainly try,' Louis replied, 'and if I can, I'll let you know. And, except for expenses, it'll be on the house.'

'I appreciate that,' Avner said. 'Contact me when you hear something.'

With that, he flew back to Frankfurt. The others were already there. Breaking the news to Carl's widow had been a traumatic experience for both Hans and Steve, and they just shrugged when Avner asked them about it. 'What did she *say*?' Hans asked, repeating Avner's question. 'Did she take it *hard*? Well, how did you expect her to take it?'

'More important,' said Steve, 'how soon can we find the cunt that killed him?'

'Easy,' Avner said. 'We'll talk about that right now, but let's just take it easy.'

He repeated Louis' information, then he said: 'Let's assume first that I didn't make a mistake when I identified the photograph . . .'

'Well, did you?' interrupted Hans.

'No, I didn't,' replied Avner without hesitation, 'but none of you have any way of knowing that for certain. Okay. Let's say she is the woman who went up to Carl's room. Let's also say that Louis' information is correct. Let's say she's a hit woman, under contract to the PLO. They pick us up as we're hanging around Grosvenor House in London, and send for her to waste one of us. She does. Okay, we find her in Hoorn. What do we do?'

'Kill her,' said Steve promptly. 'Is there any doubt about it?'

'I see what Avner is getting at,' Robert said. 'We're dealing with two unknown quantities. One, what if Avner is wrong, and two, what if Louis is wrong? It's not like the *mechablim*. With her, we have no other data to check the information against. What if . . . oh, I don't know, what if she was a hooker who shot Carl because he wouldn't pay her?'

'Bullshit,' said Steve. 'It's Carl you're talking about. Do you think he would have jeopardized the mission to argue with a hooker? He would have paid her triple, anything, just to get rid of her. It just won't wash.'

Steve was quite right in that. But. 'What if there was no argument?' Hans asked. 'She was a hooker and simply shot him to get his wallet.'

'Yes, except there was nothing missing,' Avner said. 'His wallet was right there in his jacket pocket. It had more than a hundred pounds in it, cash.'

'You see?' said Steve. 'Anyway, what's the difference? If she shot him for his wallet, we let her get away with it?'

'There is a difference,' Robert said. 'We're on a mission. We don't take time off hunting whores like Jack the Ripper. The point is, though, she wasn't a hooker. If she had shot Carl for his money, Avner is right, she would have robbed him.

'But what if she was just some woman out to get laid? She got laid, she said goodbye. Carl was shot by an entirely different person. What if that's what happened?'

'Carl was shot by a different person,' Avner asked, 'while lying in the bed naked? Carl never even slept naked. I roomed with him. I know.

'Besides, isn't it too much of a coincidence? Carl getting killed by an entirely different person *after* screwing a woman

Louis identifies as a hired gun? Who first tries to pick me up? After I'm being followed in the street in London? Sorry, I don't buy that.

'If she didn't shoot him herself, at least she set him up for somebody who did.'

'Right,' said Robert, 'except we're back where we started from. *If* Louis is right about who she is, I don't think there's much doubt. She killed Carl – alone or with somebody else, it doesn't matter. If he's right. And, of course, if Avner is right about the woman in the photograph being the same girl.'

Hans turned to Avner. 'Well,' he said, 'are you sure about the picture?'

'Yes,' said Avner.

'And are you sure about Louis?'

'I'm prepared to take his word,' Avner replied. 'Are you?'

They looked at one another. So far, Louis had never given them mistaken information. Even in Glarus, whether or not Salameh and Abu Daoud attended a meeting together, there *were* three armed Arabs in the church.

Checking with Ephraim would have been pointless. The Mossad would never give them permission to kill anybody in Holland, whether that person had murdered their partner or not. Checking would only put them in a position where they would have to contravene a direct order. Steve stood up. 'Guys, guys,' he said, 'what are we waiting for?'

They waited, as it turned out, only for Louis to tell them that the blonde woman was arriving back in Holland. That information was not quick in coming – but they did not abandon the mission while waiting. During the summer there were several false alarms – both about the girl *and* about Salameh and Abu Daoud – but it was only around the middle of August that Louis had the definite word. 'Jeanette' would be arriving in Hoorn sometime within the next seven or eight days.

The same evening Robert left for Belgium again.

This time he did not go to design some new type of bomb.

There were several factors militating against the use of explosives in Hoorn, one of which was that putting a bomb in the blonde woman's houseboat would not give them enough satisfaction. They wanted to see her die.

The truth was, they all felt a special hatred for her, quite unlike the somewhat impersonal feelings they had about their other targets, including Ali Hassan Salameh. Avner never attempted to put it into words until much later, but he had no trouble sensing the difference. Much as killing the *mechablim* was a matter of retaliation – pure revenge, really, revenge for the eleven Israelis in Munich – it was still devoid of personal animosity. It was as if they could somehow understand something about the terrorists on their list, perhaps even respect them, in the way hunters respect a cunning, determined quarry. But not the blonde woman.

She had killed one of their personal friends – a brother, a comrade in arms – which was much more than the abstraction of an 'enemy' assassinating their compatriots. But even that wasn't everything. Avner doubted if they would have hated an ordinary Palestinian terrorist shooting Carl in the street nearly as much. The point about the blonde woman was that she had murdered by betrayal, depriving Carl even of the dignity of dying at the hand of a worthy adversary. A female, using a biological weapon, exploiting a moment of male weakness, loneliness, to deprive him of his life. A shelter turning into a trap. It had the effect of totally reversing in their minds all the customary masculine compunctions about harming women. On the contrary. Because of what she had done, they had fewer inhibitions about killing her than they would have had about killing a man. They were ready to tear out her heart.

Robert's plan was to convert a section of tubular bicycle frame into a single-shot gun firing a .22 bullet. It was summer – a rather hot summer, in fact – and the Dutch coastal town was filled with bicycling young men and women. Using this device, they wouldn't have to smuggle guns across the bor-

328

der. And Robert's Belgian friend could make the simple zip gun-type weapons for a fraction of what it would cost to buy four Berettas from Papa's Dutch contacts. They could ride up to the houseboat wearing T-shirts and shorts, without arousing the slightest suspicion. After the hit they could snap the tubes into place and ride up to a van parked maybe half a mile away. No weapons on anyone. It would never occur to anybody to examine their bicycle frames. It was a foolproof plan.

'Are these things going to be accurate enough?' Avner asked.

'From four or five feet?' said Robert. 'I guarantee it.'

'Who cares, anyway?' Steve added. 'Let me within four feet of her, and I'll break her neck. Just let's go do it.'

The 21st August was a warm summer Wednesday, with crowds of vacationing students strolling and bicycling on the boardwalk. The team had been keeping the houseboat under surveillance for two days before 'Jeanette' arrived. When she pulled up in a taxi, some distance from the boat, Avner recognized her at once. 'That's the one,' he said to Steve. 'She'll go on board. Just wait and see.'

She did. Dressed in a light-coloured skirt and blouse. Carrying a small overnight case. Looking strikingly pretty.

The problem was that her girlfriend – a very fair-skinned girl of about twenty, with closely-cropped brown hair, whom they had observed coming and going in the past two days, invariably wearing blue jeans, with a red knapsack on her shoulder – was also on board. She might eventually leave, if only to ride her bicycle into town on some errand. Or she might stay on the houseboat. Since it was only 3 pm, they decided to wait.

The girl with the red knapsack did not leave until nearly 9 pm. The sun was already setting, though it was not yet dark. Avner decided that the best thing was to make an immediate move. They could not know whether the younger girl would stay away for only twenty minutes or all night. Over the past two days they had observed no pattern to her movements, but she was getting on her bicycle, so there was a good chance that she would give them at least twenty minutes. They needed no more.

Robert was waiting in a van parked less than half a mile from the houseboat's mooring. Two Dutch contacts from *Le Group*, also in a van, were parked about fifty yards away. Their job was disposal. Avner did not want the woman's body to be found if this could be avoided. If she simply disappeared, with her unpredictable timetable it could be weeks or months before she would be missed by anyone. In that time, with luck, they might even finish the mission. The partners preferred it this way because of the Mossad. If Ephraim got wind of their private vendetta in Hoorn before the mission was finished, he might respond in a number of ways, none of them pleasant. He might even decide that the team was out of control and cancel everything.

Avner had an answer ready in case Ephraim found out about the action. 'We had to do it,' he would say, 'for security. She had seen me in London with Carl. She might even have seen Hans. She could identify us.' At best, it was a half truth.

Now, holding the short section of metal tubing fitted with a crude trigger, Avner stepped onto the wooden gangway leading to the boat. It was a few minutes after 9 pm. Steve, armed with a similar weapon, was immediately behind him. Hans remained on the bridge, leaning against the railing. The agreement was that he would not come on board unless Avner and Steve needed assistance.

The women kept a small pet cat on board and it set up an unbelievably loud protest the minute it saw Avner approach the cabin. It sat on the railing of the boat, swishing its tail and miaowing, in spite of Steve's best efforts to calm it down. The air was still very hot and humid. The door to the cabin was half open, and Avner was sure the blonde woman, who was sitting at a small writing desk, dressed in a blue house-coat, her back to the door, would soon be alerted by the wailing of her cat. But she must have been used to it. She did

330

not look up at all until Avner pushed open the door.

She was wearing the same perfume. The smell in the cabin was unmistakable. If Avner had had any lingering doubts about her identity, they disappeared in that second. She was the woman in Carl's room.

She turned her head and looked up at Avner without any fear in her eyes. He was standing in the doorway with the red disc of the setting sun right behind him, and she might have been unable to see him clearly. However, Avner could see her right hand move towards the drawer of her desk.

'If I were you, I wouldn't,' he said to her in English, stepping closer.

Steve came into the cabin, followed by the cat. It immediately jumped onto the desk, still miaowing wildly. It was an eerie sound, setting their nerves on edge, though they tried to pay no attention to it.

'Well, and who are you?' the woman said, looking from Avner to Steve. Avner could see her right hand again edging closer to the drawer in her desk, while her left hand was going up to her breast, spreading her blue robe wider, starting to expose her cleavage. It was hard to tell whether the gesture was conscious or involuntary. In any case, it was the wrong defence under the circumstances. Both Avner and Steve noticed it and it only made them cold with fury.

'Watch it, she has a weapon,' Steve said in Hebrew, and Avner nodded, without taking his eyes off her right hand.

'I know,' he replied. Then, speaking in English, he said to her: 'Do you remember London?'

Avner could see her eyes go to the bicycle tube in his hand. She obviously didn't realize what it was, but might have thought they were planning to bludgeon her with it. Her lips curled in a defiant, disdainful smirk. Abandoning all pretence, she tugged at the desk drawer.

Avner pulled the trigger. So did Steve. Almost at the same time.

The cat jumped straight up in the air.

The blonde woman was still sitting in her chair, bending

slowly forward. She was gasping for breath. She raised her head once more, and there was blood trickling from the corner of her mouth.

The zip guns were single-shot weapons. Avner reached into his pocket for another bullet.

Before he could reload, the woman had slumped to the floor. Behind them, the door was flung open and Hans strode in, walking much as Avner had seen him walk in Athens when he had thrown the fire bombs into Muchassi's room. 'Let me get at the bitch,' Hans said, pushing them to one side. He bent down and fired his zip gun into the back of her head. By that time she was probably already dead.

'Come on, Hans.' Avner motioned Steve to help him pull their partner away from the woman's body. Hans looked ready to tear at the corpse with his fingers. He followed Avner and Steve back to the shore, still cursing her under his breath.

Outside it was almost completely dark. Avner signalled to Papa's men to back the van up to the gangplank and remove the body from the boat. There was time. Avner had glanced at his watch going in, and now saw that they had spent exactly three minutes and thirty seconds inside. The girl with the red knapsack was unlikely to be back for at least another fifteen minutes.

They snapped the metal tubes into place, mounted their bicycles, and rode back to where Robert was waiting in the van. 'We got the bitch,' Hans informed him while they were loading the bicycles in the back.

Avner could understand Hans. It wasn't just a matter of avenging Carl. Avner had by then shot two people at close range, Wael Zwaiter and Basil al-Kubaisi. He had found shooting them much harder than shooting this woman. In the little time the two terrorist leaders had between noticing Avner and being shot, they had both pleaded for their lives. They kept saying 'No, no,' in Arabic and English. Avner had shot them, but they had made it impossible for him at that moment to think of them as enemies. They were only human beings in the extreme, last, vulnerable moment of their lives.

This woman was different. She didn't plead. She kept looking at him with cold hatred in her eyes. Her face reflected nothing but disdain and defiance. If she had deliberately tried, she could not have made it easier for Avner to kill her.

Chapter 16

TARIFA

On 14 September, about three weeks after the Dutch woman's death, Robert's life came to an end in a farmer's field near the little Belgian town of Battice.

Robert did what he had always said the terrorists were doing with boring regularity. He blew himself up with one of his own bombs.

The details were scanty. Robert had driven the van to Belgium to return the bicycles the day after the Hoorn episode. He was to stay there to help his friend with some new weapons they were designing. Avner had no idea what kind of weapons they were supposed to be, and wasn't particularly interested at the time. Robert had explained something to Steve – who was more intrigued than Avner by lethal gadgetry – about a new type of chemical he was hoping to experiment with. Apparently it had worked only too well.

Robert would check in by telephoning Frankfurt every day. Avner had no way of contacting him in Belgium. The agreement was that Robert would phone between six and seven – or ten and eleven, if there was no answer earlier – to see if he was needed there. The rest of the team had gone into high gear, running down every possible lead on the three remaining terrorists on their list. After Hoorn they had all agreed that the mission should be brought to a conclusion as speedily as possible.

Following their report on Carl's death, they had received no new instructions from Tel Aviv; the only word was a terse 'message acknowledged' in the Geneva safe deposit. Still,

Avner and his partners were certain the Mossad would terminate the mission unless they produced some more results by the end of the year. The fact was that since the assassination of Mohammed Boudia on 28 June, 1973 – well over a year before – there had been no successful operations of Israeli counter-terror. Only disasters like Lillehammer, fiascos like Glarus, and tragic losses like that of Carl. Unless they succeeded in tracking down Ali Hassan Salameh, Abu Daoud, or Dr Haddad quite soon, it was unlikely that they would be allowed to continue.

Yet being recalled before finishing – even though no one would blame them – meant failure. They all agreed on that: they didn't even have to discuss it. Being forced to leave a job undone, especially going back without getting Salameh, was for all of them the equivalent of a defeat. It was not in the Israeli tradition. Death, or even disobeying a direct order to retreat, would have been preferable – though to disobey would have been difficult if the Mossad froze the mission's account. (They did talk about this possibility, and Hans suggested that for a while they could use the money in their own personal Swiss accounts if their operational funds should ever be cut off.) Later Avner would admit that, at least in this sense, they were every bit as fanatical as the *mechablim*.

This sense of hurry was one of the reasons Robert wanted to experiment with his new chemical, while Avner was holding the fort in Frankfurt and the other two partners were checking out informers elsewhere in Europe. On 13 September Avner had spoken with Robert on the telephone at the usual time. 'I'll be finished here in two or three days,' he had said.

'That's okay. There's nothing new here,' Avner replied before hanging up.

The following day, when the phone didn't ring between six and seven, Avner wasn't particularly worried. The two different check-in times they had set up gave both of them some flexibility. Indeed, the phone rang in Avner's Frankfurt safe house at five past ten.

It was Louis.

'I'm sorry,' the Frenchman said. 'I've got some bad news.'

'Is it Robert?' Avner asked. It wasn't a premonition; he simply knew that *Le Group* was aware of Robert's Belgian connection. Ever since the al-Chir hit in Cyprus they had been using Papa's couriers to smuggle explosives for them from Belgium.

'There's been an accident,' Louis said. 'It's nobody's fault and there's nothing you can do.'

Avner's throat went dry.

'I see,' he said.

'We can look after everything if you want us to. You know, like in London. It's probably the simplest.'

'Yes,' Avner had some difficulty getting his words out. 'Yes. The simplest. Go ahead. Yes . . . Thanks for calling me.'

'Listen,' said Louis, 'these things happen.'

'Oh yes,' Avner replied. His voice was completely flat. 'They do happen, don't they?'

There was a little silence.

'Well,' Louis said finally, 'call me if there's anything else I can do.'

There was nothing more to say. Avner put the receiver back, stared at it for a few seconds, then drove over to the safe house Robert had shared with Steve. Avner let himself in with a spare key, and started packing what he knew to be Robert's belongings in a suitcase. The place was in an unbelievable chaos – Steve was very untidy and Robert had never cared one way or another – but Avner had no trouble separating Robert's things on the floor and behind the sofa from Steve's. His memory, poor for names or numbers, was excellent when it came to physical details. Robert's ties and socks were totally unlike Steve's, and there was no question who the books and toys belonged to. When he finished packing, the suitcase wasn't even full. Robert must have taken most of his clothes with him to Belgium.

In an envelope there were some letters from Robert's wife written to an address in England. There were also a couple of pictures. Avner tucked the envelope behind the clothes before closing the suitcase. It crossed his mind that Robert's bag had probably never been packed as neatly in his lifetime as it was now.

The only thing he didn't know what to do with was the giant Ferris wheel built of toothpicks. It was the last toy Robert had put together; he had been working on it for months. It was standing in the middle of the heavy working table in Robert's bedroom, measuring almost three feet across, a fragile yet intricately elaborate structure. Avner touched the wheel tentatively with his forefinger, and it immediately began to spin, whirling six little gondolas round and round its delicate axis. Without thinking, Avner started spinning the wheel faster until all of its separate components became one continuous blur. Finally, when it was going as fast as Avner thought it could go, he let go of it. Turning his back on the spinning Ferris wheel, he looked around the room once more to check if he had left anything behind, but could see nothing. The pillows lay crumpled on the unmade bed just as Robert must have left them when he last got out of it. At this moment he heard a sudden noise, like the swish and flutter of a bird's wings flying across the room, and he turned around.

The Ferris wheel was gone. There was only a large heap of toothpicks spilling from the table to the floor.

Avner picked up the suitcase and took it down to his car, then drove to the bus station and put it into a locker.

Hans and Steve arrived back in Frankfurt a day later.

The three partners went for a walk around the large city park near the safe house where Hans was living alone. They strolled there for nearly three hours, trying to decide what to do. Avner noted with a detached, almost clinical interest that the old, painful pressure in the pit of his stomach was now completely gone. What he felt was cold rage, coupled with an absolutely rigid, blinkered determination to finish the job. At

337

the very least, get Salameh. If they didn't, Carl and Robert had died for nothing.

Hans and Steve agreed with him.

'We have to go to Geneva and leave a note about Robert,' Avner said, 'but we don't wait for an answer. We simply go on.'

'Someone will have to tell Robert's wife,' said Hans. 'I'd just as soon not do the *chevrat kadisha* this time.'

This was a reference to Israel's state-owned funeral company. When Hans and Steve went to see Carl's widow in Rome, they had referred to themselves as the *chevrat kadisha* squad. Hans was quite traumatized by the experience even though Carl's widow had behaved with much dignity. This time it was likely to be worse: Robert's wife, a very good-looking French-Jewish woman, nicknamed Pepe, whom Avner had met once before, was reputed to be a somewhat temperamental lady. In fact, she was a bit of a princess. Unlike the others, whose wives were content to wait until their husbands contacted them, Robert was obliged not only to give Pepe an address in England to which she could write (forcing him to go there periodically to collect her letters) but even to give her phone numbers and times when she could call him. Though Robert was delighted to hear from her, it still meant arranging his schedule so as to make himself available to her demands. On a mission this was often very difficult. Though Pepe was by all accounts a loyal and loving woman, her personality made her only marginally suitable to be an agent's wife.[1] She was, in fact, a somewhat distracting influence on Robert and therefore, by extension, on the team.

They had two children. When Robert had the family brought out of Israel at the start of the mission, he first settled them in Brussels. He knew that he would have to travel to Belgium quite frequently, so having Pepe and the children there seemed to make sense. They could spend at least a few hours together every time he had to pass through Brussels on business. However, these short visits didn't work out. They only upset and preoccupied both Robert and Pepe, so finally Robert shipped his family off to Washington DC, for the duration. Pepe had a favourite uncle living there – a diplomat attached to a European embassy – who was glad to have her and the children to stay at his home.

Avner could understand why Hans wouldn't want to go and break the news to her.

'We'll go to Geneva first,' Avner said. 'After that, I'll fly to Washington myself. If Steve wants to come with me, okay. When we come back, we do it. We get the *mechablim*. Come hell or high water. No big plans, no explosives, nothing. There are only three of us left, but that's all right, because we'll do it in a different way. Hans, while we're gone, get in touch with Louis. Tell him to get hold of three Uzis.'

'Atta boy, chum,' said Steve.

There *was* another way of setting up a hit. It was infinitely more dangerous than the carefully plotted and elaborately planned methods they had been using until now. It did not offer the team nearly as good a chance of getting away. If not exactly suicidal, it was a fairly desperate method. But it was possible.

Frontal assault. Relying on little more than surprise and firepower.

Instead of shadowing a target until everything was known about his schedule and habits; instead of planning a careful escape; instead of physically removing themselves from the scene of the assassination through the use of explosives, it was possible to proceed on the basis of only two pieces of information. Namely when and where. The location and time of the target. Nothing else.

If they could find out, for example, that Salameh was at a given place at a given time, it was just possible for three determined men armed with submachine guns to kill him. With no reference to the nature of the place where he was or of the forces he might be surrounded by, and with even less reference to the team's chances of escaping afterwards. Possibly even without reference to the lives of bystanders, or the risk of the discovery that the assassination was the work of an Israeli commando group. It was simply another way. It was possible, if the killers had little or no regard for the consequences, to assassinate anybody. All they had to do was get within sixty or seventy yards of the target.

A team of only three people would almost be forced to consider doing a hit in such a kamikaze fashion.

'Of course, I'm not saying that this is our first choice,' Avner added. 'We're only three, but we do have support from Louis and his people. We might get lucky; we'll certainly continue looking for smarter ways. All I'm saying is, we don't exclude anything. As a last resort, we go for any good chance. We don't stick with zero risk.

'Do you agree?'

'I agree,' Steve replied promptly. Then he turned to Hans.

'Well,' Hans said, 'frankly, this is not a command decision. Strictly speaking, I don't think we have a right to do this. What Avner is suggesting is changing objectives for the mission, or at least reversing priorities. For this kind of thing we should go back to headquarters.

'But,' Hans continued after a pause, 'in fact, I agree. I just want us to be clear about what we're doing.'

Without any doubt, Hans was right. They *were* reversing priorities. Except, like Avner and Steve, Hans also had little capacity for giving up. He had given a clear enough indication of that with Muchassi in Athens. Like the others, for Hans the idea of letting go was completely alien. That might have been an inevitable problem in launching missions of this kind. People single-minded enough to embark on them in the first place might be too single-minded to stop at sensible or politically expedient limits. They would also exert psychological pressure on each other to continue no matter what. As Avner put it later to Steve: 'I wasn't worried about Hans. If we said yes, there was no way he'd disagree.'

But Hans also raised another point.

'You were talking about support from Louis and his

people,' he said. 'I think we should talk about something else, too. It's been on my mind ever since London.

'Except for the five of us, who knew that we were going to London? Only Louis. Who knew about Robert in Belgium? Louis again.

'Now Carl is dead and so is Robert. What if Papa double-crossed us? He's selling the *mechablim* to us; why shouldn't he sell us to the *mechablim*? Have you ever thought about that?'

In fact, Avner had thought about it. He had thought about it long and hard; he had thought about it throughout the summer. On the one hand, it would have made sense for people like Papa, Louis, Tony – not to mention Andreas – to betray them. If what Louis said about *Le Group*'s ideas was true, they would only delight in all sides destroying one another. The sooner the better for Louis' *tabula rasa*, the clean slate that was required before the new and better world, whatever it might be, could be built. It would also make sense economically. After all, Papa could make money from the *mechablim* for the setting up of Carl, then from Avner for disposing of his body. Then, more money for finding the Dutch hit woman and for disposing of her body. Then maybe money from the Arabs again for setting up Robert to be killed – accidentally or otherwise. More money still for disposing of his body for Avner, and so on.

It was possible. Played cleverly, it might even enable Papa to have all sides think of him as a friend, each giving him freely the information that he could then sell to the opposing side. It could be a safe, never-ending source of income.

In the end Avner dismissed the possibility simply because he did not believe it.

'Papa could have sold us out long ago,' he said. 'When we were all together. Why didn't he sell us out in Cyprus?'

'Maybe no one offered to buy,' Hans said. 'Or maybe he didn't want to kill the hen that was about to lay a golden egg.'

'Is that what you believe?' Avner asked.

'I don't know what to believe,' Hans replied. 'I'm just

wondering if we're not trusting his people too much. After all, they're just a bunch of mercenaries. Without them, or groups like them, the terrorists couldn't even operate. They don't just work for us. They work for half the Red Armies in Europe. For all we know, they work for the Mafia.'

It was true. Avner could only shrug.

'It's even possible,' Hans continued, 'that they're set up and financed by the Russians. Have you ever thought of that? The KGB could plant a private group like that to support the terrorists. It wouldn't be such a stupid idea. Maybe they themselves don't even know who's really behind them, or maybe only Papa knows. What about that?'

Now Hans was going too far. In fact, Avner thought, he was beginning to sound a little like Papa. Suddenly he recognized what it must be: the onset of agent's paranoia, the effect of having been underground for too long. It could cause weary field agents to suspect conspiracies at every turn. Though it was not totally divorced from reality like clinical paranoia, it exaggerated sensible fears and suspicions out of all proportion, or attached them to the wrong targets. Papa may have suffered from a form of it himself.[2]

'Yes, there could be a leak through Papa, or through someone in his group,' Avner said to Hans, 'and there could be a leak through one of our own informers. We have an Ahmed or a Yasir in every second city, and sometimes they also know where to find us. One of them certainly knew we would be in London at the time that Carl was killed. But yes, it could be Papa. To make more money, to be everybody's friend, to cover his own ass, who knows? But the point is, Papa also delivers. We didn't ask any of these questions while he kept turning up one *mechabel* after the other.

'So maybe that's included in the price. He gives to us, he gives to other people. It's possible. So, would you say, stop taking from him? I'd say no. Let's keep taking whatever he has to give. Just keep a sharper lookout, that's all. Be even more careful. If he wants to sell us, he has to give us first. Yeah, it's a risk. Isn't it worth it?'

Hans thought about this. 'A hell of a risk,' he said finally. 'Is that what you believe?'

'No,' Avner replied firmly. 'It isn't what I believe. Maybe I'm crazy, but I trust Papa. I trust Louis and Tony. But I couldn't prove it. You're right to bring up the question. It's smart to be suspicious. But what's our option? Dropping them because we're suspicious means dropping our best source. For information, for support, for everything. How many terrorists would we have got without them?

'Why not assume that they may be selling us out. Fine. Then just keep using them, but double every precaution. Mislead them a little. Change every move at the last minute. Isn't that the smartest way?'

Hans started to laugh. 'You're crazy, you know,' he said to Avner. 'I mean, we're all crazy, but you may be the craziest of us all.'

'He's right, though,' Steve said. 'That's the way to do it.'

So it was settled. The bottom line in Avner's own mind, though, was that he did trust *Le Group*. If he really hadn't trusted them, he probably would have broken off contact with them in spite of what he said to Hans. He was *not* that crazy. He was only relying on his sixth sense.

Perhaps mistakenly.[3]

Washington turned out to be even more difficult than Avner had anticipated. Pepe was hysterical. For some reason she focussed on Steve, started beating his chest with her fists, screaming at him that he had killed Robert. Steve just kept backing away from her with his eyes on the floor until Avner grabbed Pepe from behind and held her in his arms. Then she started crying. Her uncle had at least had the good sense to take the children out of the house before Steve and Avner arrived.

They had taken money from their own personal accounts for Pepe, just as they had contributed to Carl's widow, though this time they gave only five thousand each, making a total of fifteen thousand dollars. They all felt a little ashamed about what they regarded as their lack of generosity but – though they didn't really talk about it – they were obviously beginning to think about their own families. If they were picked off one by one, yet wanted to contribute forty thousand dollars to each widow, the last to survive would literally have no money left for his own wife and children. Though the family would get a regular pension, it wouldn't be much.

Avner stopped in New York for a couple of days before flying back to Europe. After a year and a half, Shoshana was getting used to living there. She had even blossomed, Avner thought, and was obviously proud of the way she had conquered – entirely on her own – this strange, frightening metropolis, so different from the Israeli cities she had known. As for Geula, she had grown from the ugliest baby into the most beautiful toddler. Then there was Charlie, who became so excited at the sight of Avner that he leaped up and bit his master on the nose. Then was so ashamed that he couldn't be coaxed out from behind the couch for hours.

It crossed Avner's mind that it would be wonderful to chuck everything, forget the mission, Europe, the *mechablim*, maybe even Israel. To write a letter of resignation, drop it in a postbox, then settle down in Brooklyn with Shoshana, the baby and the dog to a perfectly peaceful and maybe prosperous American life. Why not? He had fought in two wars, and helped eliminate nine top terrorists at considerable risk to himself. What more could any country expect of a man? Maybe even his mother would agree that he had by now done his duty by Israel.

But the next day he was at Kennedy Airport, catching a TWA flight to Frankfurt. As usual, he would not let Shoshana go to see him off. 'I can't promise you,' he said to her as he was leaving, 'but maybe the next time I come it will be for good.'

This was during the last week of September, two years almost to the day from the time they had started out on the mission in 1972. Avner felt that in that period he had grown from a boy of twenty-five into a middle-aged man of twenty-seven. Unless they finished the mission soon, he wondered if he would become an *old* man of twenty-eight. It had been known to happen to agents, though Avner had never believed it until now.

Since Carl's death, Avner had begun to find it increasingly difficult to sleep in his own bed at night. This had never been a problem before but was now especially true when he was alone in his Frankfurt safe house or travelling and spending the night in hotel rooms. Lying on his bed, he simply couldn't fall asleep. After a while he solved the problem by sleeping in the closet. He'd put his pillows and blankets on the floor, close the door from the inside, and go to sleep. From a safety standpoint it made sense: a bed could be rigged with explosives, and intruders at night would look for him in the bed first – by which time Avner, a very light sleeper, would be likely to waken and deal with them. Though he could justify sleeping in the closet in these terms, the bottom line was clearly his nerves. His partners would see it this way, too, no matter how much good sense it made. As a result, Avner continued sleeping in the closet whenever he was alone, but said nothing to the others about it.

By the time Avner and Steve arrived back in Frankfurt, Hans had checked the safe-deposit box in Geneva. There was a message in it from Ephraim. It acknowledged the team's message about Robert's death, then continued with a single line of instruction:

Terminate immediately.

However, the assets in the operational account were not frozen or withdrawn. Hans knew, because it was the first thing he checked after reading Ephraim's message. This was not surprising; Ephraim would expect them to wind down their affairs cautiously, settle outstanding debts to informers, and so forth. Though there would probably be no more money deposited in the account – unless they requested additional funds, giving their reasons – there would be a period of grace during which they would still have disposition of over a quarter of a million dollars. To be on the safe side, Hans had immediately transferred most of it to the other accounts Carl had opened for the team in several European capitals at the start of the mission.

'What did you do with Ephraim's message?' Avner asked Hans.

'I left it in the safe,' Hans replied.

This was a minor precaution; as long as the message was still in the safe, the Mossad might conclude that the team had simply not yet picked it up. There were not set periods for them to check for messages in Geneva and no alternate ways to be contacted by headquarters. If Ephraim really started checking, he would discover soon enough that they had looked into the box: a dated log sheet had to be signed each time they had opened; but leaving the message there just might gain them some time.

And time was important, because Avner and his partners were firmly resolved not to obey the Mossad's order to terminate the mission. At least, not immediately. Not until their money had run out. Not until they had had the chance to hit the remaining terrorists on their list.

They did not think of their disobedience as mere vanity, insubordination or fanaticism. In their own minds they justified it by calling it a valid field decision. By the end of 1973, they could see the disarray into which the forces of terror had been thrown by the elimination of nine of their top leaders. They could see it at first hand by the very difficulty of getting any information from their regular Arab sources. Their losses had to force the remaining leaders to abandon their Middle East or East European hiding places and come to Europe to reorganize their networks.[4] Sooner or later, within weeks or at most a few months, Salameh, Abu Daoud or Dr Haddad would come to Europe in person. The team, being in the field, could see this more clearly than anyone at headquarters back in Tel Aviv. It was a valid part of the Israeli tradition for a field commander not to break off an attack or abandon a pursuit if he could see that the enemy's ranks were

346

breaking. It was his duty not to obey blindly headquarters' command if he could plainly see that it was issued in ignorance of local conditions.

This, generally speaking, was true. Whether or not it was true in this particular instance was a different question. At any rate, Avner and his partners had no difficulty convincing themselves that it was.

'Let's say,' was the way in which Avner put it, 'that we had a perfect operation set up for tonight. Would we abort it just because of Ephraim's note?'

It was a good argument. But at the time they had no operation, perfect or imperfect, set up for any night.

During the month of October they continued tracking down leads from local informers. The rumours were constant about impending top-level meetings involving Ali Hassan Salameh, Abu Daoud, or both. On two occasions – once in Milan and once in West Berlin – Avner and Steve, with Hans acting as a backup, had staked out apartment buildings to which the terrorist leaders were supposed to come. On both occasions they had submachine guns in the trunk of their car, ready to do a frontal attack on sighting any of their targets. On both occasions they did see Arabs entering and leaving the buildings, but – remembering Glarus – they made no move. Nor would they do so without actually seeing Salameh, Abu Daoud, or Dr Haddad, without making a positive identification.

Which they were unable to do in either Milan or West Berlin.

Then, early in November, the word came through Louis that Ali Hassan Salameh was supposed to arrive in the small Spanish town of Tarifa, on the Atlantic coast between Gibraltar and the Portuguese border.

Allegedly from Algiers.

The three partners flew to Madrid, arriving on 8 November. They examined the weapons that Papa's contact there had got for them: three .22 Berettas, and three Uzi submachine guns (of the European type, manufactured under

347

licence from Israel, with a slightly larger magazine and longer barrel than the original weapon) then drove south to the coast in their rented car. As a precaution, they did not take their guns along with them but had Papa's contact bring them to Tarifa in a small pick-up truck.

Tarifa, on the southernmost tip of Andalucía, only eight miles across the Strait of Gibraltar from Morocco, lies geographically in Europe. However, it looks as much like an Arab town as any in North Africa. The character of its architecture is still completely Moorish, superimposed in places on earlier Roman amphitheatres and aqueducts.

Just outside the town, Avner and his partners checked into a hotel and waited for Papa's man to arrive. They needed him not only for the guns, but also to point out the particular villa where the Arab terrorists' meeting was supposed to take place. It was, apparently, a large, rather isolated house on the top of some low cliffs lining the beach. It belonged to a wealthy Spanish family who hardly ever used it. Their daughter, a political science student who had got involved with some Marxist revolutionaries at a French university, was apparently responsible for lending it to the Palestinians.

Avner's plan was to penetrate the grounds in a silent commando-type operation. The house would probably be guarded, but perhaps not too well. At any rate, a scouting party could find this out and whether any of the top *mechablim* were in the house or not. The team would attack only if they could confirm through direct observation that they were. If the house seemed too well guarded for any attack by three men to succeed, Avner did not rule out the possibility of contacting the Mossad through emergency channels for reinforcements or instructions. He meant to act very responsibly. There was to be no kamikaze attack, even if Salameh or Abu Daoud was inside the house. The team had resolved not to proceed unless there was a reasonable chance of success.

Papa's man arrived in Tarifa on 10 November. He delivered the weapons, then drove with the team to the foot of a gravel road, about a mile long, winding its way up the cliffs from the coastal highway. It was not a private road, but there were only three houses on it, surrounded by sizeable private grounds. Papa's man explained that the very last house, where the road ended in front of a large iron-grille gate, was the one in question. They couldn't miss it.

Avner, Steve and Hans drove halfway up the road around 10 pm the following night. The night of 11 November was damp and windy. The wind blew from the direction of the Strait of Gibraltar, the south-east, picking up dead leaves from the ground and swirling them in the air. The sound of footfalls would not be easily heard on such a night. The cresting moon was completely covered by clouds. The trees and bushes grew in thick, dark, gnarled shapes on both sides of the road. It was ideal terrain, and an ideal night for a reconnoitring party.

Steve stopped the car before reaching a bend in the road, about a quarter of a mile from the main gate. He made a three-point turn, leaving the vehicle parked facing the direction from which it had come, on the shoulder of the road, almost in a shallow ditch, where it was half hidden by the bend as well as by some roadside bushes. As a precaution, he disconnected the brake lights: if they were pursued, there was no point in giving themselves away every time the driver touched the brakes; then he followed Avner into the bushes on the seashore side of the road. Hans stayed by the car, armed with one of the Uzis.

Avner and Steve had left their submachine guns in the trunk. Their immediate purpose was to reconnoitre, not to attack. Should they see Salameh or Abu Daoud – and should they decide that it was feasible for the three of them to make an assault – there would be time enough to come back for the Uzis. Now, armed only with their small Berettas, they planned to penetrate the grounds of the house by skirting the main entrance and, making their way through the bushes, approach the building from behind. The villa backed onto the sea, so that following the line of the cliffs should take them to the back garden.

The bushes, though thick, were not impenetrable. Wearing dark pants and black sweaters, walking cautiously and stopping every now and then to look and listen, Avner and Steve took about twenty minutes to cover the distance. The house and its immediate surroundings were easy to see, as there was light coming from nearly every window. They could see no guards patrolling the garden. Knowing something about the Palestinians, Avner and Steve doubted that the guards would be stationed far from the house. Arabs, like Africans in general, are not nightfighters and tend to shun the dark. The guards, if there were any, would prefer to take up their posts as close to the brightly lit windows as possible. Depending on their training. Arab guerrillas with Russian or Cuban training would no doubt fight in the darkness as well as any other soldier. Like King Hussein's British-trained Jordanian troops.

Coming up to the corner of the house, Avner and Steve could hear voices talking in Arabic. The voices were not coming from inside the house but rather from a stone patio just outside the French windows leading to a swimming pool, which was empty except for dead leaves and a few fingers of brackish water collecting at the deep end. Flattening themselves against the wall just around the corner of the house, Avner and Steve couldn't see the speakers. However, they could make out some of the words.

'Why not tell him we need more money?' one man said. 'Are you afraid to say it?'

'We need a handful of fruit, that's all,' replied another voice.

There was no question about it. Whether any of the terrorist leaders were inside the house or not, the people on the patio were Arabs. Once again Papa's information was at least partially correct.

The next sound that came to their ears was the click of a glass door closing. They could not hear the voices any longer. Very cautiously, Avner peered around the corner.

Yes. The stone patio was empty.

Without looking to see if Steve was following him, he tiptoed in the direction of the French windows. He was confident that no one could see him standing on the dark patio from inside. On the other hand, he could easily see every person in the brightly lit room. There were seven or eight Arabs standing and talking next to a long table laden with fruit. Two of the Arabs were wearing their checkered *keffiyeh*s.

'*Mechablim*,' Avner heard Steve's voice whisper beside him. He nodded. Though he could see no weapons, they were probably terrorists. But *keffiyeh*s were not worn solely by the *fedayeen*. These Arabs, at least in theory, could have been perfectly legitimate visitors to Spain. Tourists, students or businessmen. The only way to be certain that they were terrorists was to recognize one of them. Salameh or Abu Daoud. Or Dr Haddad. Or George Habash or Ahmed Jibril. Or any of the others.

But Avner and Steve recognized no one in the room.

Of course, there were many other rooms in the villa. There could easily have been as many as a dozen other people in it. Also, according to Papa's man, the Arabs would not arrive all at once. Perhaps more were due within the next few days. Perhaps the meeting, if there was to be one, had not yet even begun, and the Arabs in the room were only some foot soldiers in the vanguard.

Avner and Steve were still standing on the patio, looking through the French windows, when they heard the unmistakable sound of bushes swaying and crackling behind them. Someone was making his way through the undergrowth. Someone unsuspecting, judging by the noise he was making, was coming along the path behind them.

They turned. With the lights behind them, they knew they would appear as silhouettes to anyone approaching from the garden. He would not make out their faces immediately. But he would soon realize that they did not belong there. Two Israeli agents, surrounded by presumably hostile Arabs in a remote Spanish garden. They could take no chances. Even as they turned, their knees were bending in a combat crouch. Their right hands were coming up with their Berettas, their left hands describing an arc in the air as they pulled back the slides.

They looked at the person who had stepped out from the bushes. A young Arab wearing his *keffiyeh*. Standing maybe ten feet away from them, looking uncomprehendingly at the guns in their hands. Even if he had noticed them from the bushes long before they had heard him, he was clearly not expecting them to be hostile. He had probably taken them for two of his comrades.

A young Arab. His right hand in front of his fly, as though he had just been buttoning up his pants. In his left hand a Kalashnikov.

He began raising it.

Avner and Steve fired together. Twice, and twice again. The November wind, swirling the dead leaves, swallowed up the pop-hiss of their guns. *Pffm-pffm*, *pffm-pffm*. *Pffm-pffm*, *pffm-pffm*. The Arab boy was trying to balance himself as they were stepping closer. Then he doubled over and fell to the ground sideways, squirming, trying to breathe. He did not drop his Kalashnikov as he fell. He was holding it in his left arm, looking up at Avner and Steve, cradling it closer to his body.

Inside the house no one seemed to hear or notice anything. People were still standing next to the long table, eating, talking, gesticulating. Avner could even hear the sound of laughter. Without putting his gun away he turned and started walking out of the garden. Not in the direction from which they had come, but the short way, toward the main gate. Steve followed him. They were walking quickly, turning around once in a while. No one was following them. Outside the gate they broke into a run. Downhill, with the damp November wind behind them. Pursued only by the dead leaves. Running faster and faster.

Running. Avner would always remember that. They ended their great, historic mission running down a winding gravel road in Spain like a couple of schoolboys who had done something irrevocable and were now trying to escape their punishment.

Chapter 17

~∞~

FRANKFURT

LIKE MANY OTHER ANDALUCIAN CITIES, Tarifa has a violent history. Though Avner did not know it, only a few hundred yards from where the young Arab guerrilla lay, a man who has gone down in history as Guzman the Good had sacrificed his nine-year-old son rather than give up the *alcazaba*, a Moorish fortress, its ruins still a minor tourist attraction, to its besiegers. At Niebla, 115 miles north-west along the Costa de la Luz, Arab military scientists had introduced gunpowder for the first time in the history of European warfare. In the period between the thirteenth century when these events occurred and Avner's own time, the nature of human conflict had changed little.

Historical comparisons, however, were the furthest thing from Avner's mind, or Steve's, as they ran breathlessly towards the spot where Hans was waiting beside the car. Steve drove maniacally and without lights, until Avner yelled at him to pull over. They were not being chased. There was no point in calling attention to themselves by turning the coastal highway into a racetrack. Calming down a little, Steve reconnected the brake lights. Hans had put his submachine gun back inside the trunk; however, they did not relinquish their .22s until they were safely back at their hotel.

Sitting in Avner's room they tried to collect themselves and assess the situation. They were not in any immediate danger. Since ordinary Arab tourists or businessmen were not likely to wander around with Kalashnikovs, the Arabs in the villa were undoubtedly terrorists. As such, they would

354

almost certainly not call in the police. Nor could they start a house-to-house search of the area for assailants they had not even seen. The only person who could give any kind of description of them, the Arab boy with the assault rifle, was probably dead. Even if the Arabs called the police, there was nothing to connect Avner and his partners with the attack. They were West German tourists, like thousands of others, with impeccable passports. Apart from the guns, the only thing that could possibly connect them to the shooting would be the impression of their tyre-treads on the gravel road.

Avner called Papa's man to come for them with another vehicle in the morning, collecting the guns at the same time. They would be, he thought, safe enough at the hotel for the night. The next day they could drive back to Madrid in a new car with no weapons and without having to worry about searches and roadblocks.

Which was what they did. It was a long drive and they sat in the car without saying much, Avner relieving Steve occasionally at the wheel. Avner knew they were all thinking about the same thing even when they were talking about something else. Had they acted wrongly? Could they have done anything else? Had they lost their heads? Should they have attempted to withdraw without shooting the Arab boy? Did they really kill him in self-defence?

Did they, in fact, kill him? Was he by now the fourth unknown Palestinian they had killed? Four people who, while not innocent bystanders like the waiter in Lillehammer, were nevertheless not on their list. Five people, counting Muchassi in Athens. Six, counting the KGB agent. Seven, counting the blonde girl in Hoorn.

Without getting Salameh, Abu Daoud, or Dr Haddad.

Was this the inevitable consequence of missions like this? Or were they doing something wrong? Was the job getting to them? Were they losing their nerve?

Had they, in the final analysis, failed?

Certainly since the assassination of Boudia, nearly a year and a half before, they had reached none of their targets. But they had killed four Arab foot soldiers and a Dutch woman – and lost Carl and Robert in the process. Two top agents in exchange for no military gain in the war against terror. This was failure. This was defeat. There was no other way of looking at it.

Worse, by now they were acting in defiance of plain orders. They were acting without authority. Running around Spanish gardens shooting Arabs. Like amateurs.

Like terrorists.

This was what Hans said just before they turned off the N4 autoroute at the outskirts of Madrid. 'You know,' he said, 'we did this just like the *mechablim*.'

Neither Avner nor Steve contradicted him.[1]

During the following week they left Madrid one by one and made their way back to Frankfurt. As with the shooting in Glarus, they could find no mention of what had happened in Tarifa in any of the papers. It was possible that they had missed the news items in Spain as well as in Switzerland, but it was more likely that the shootings were hushed up[2] The terrorists would certainly not wish to call attention to themselves as long as they could avoid it.

The fear of discovery was, therefore, minimal. After the first few days – certainly the minute they had got out of Spain – Avner and his partners did not have to worry about it at all.

They were worried about something entirely different. Something very difficult to put into words. 'Failure' or 'disgrace' did not quite express it. Nor did 'guilt' in the ordinary sense. It wasn't even a sense of futility.

They felt rejected by luck. Like all soldiers, they were not without a certain superstition. Also, there is an indignity attached to being betrayed by something which favoured one before: success, a woman, a winning streak, fortunes of war. It brings with it a sense of hurt and humiliation, a sudden questioning of every value and belief.

Avner experienced a little of this feeling after Carl's death, and even more after Tarifa. Steve experienced it to some extent. But now it hit Hans with full force.

He became introspective. Never very talkative, now he'd go for days without saying anything at all. He'd do his job methodically as before, but in such a withdrawn, detached manner, with such obvious misgivings, that Avner became seriously worried about him. At the same time he would not hear of quitting. The subject didn't really come up – they had all agreed that they wouldn't quit until their money ran out – but once when Avner asked him if he was feeling all right, Hans replied through gritted teeth:

'Look. There's no stopping now, so let's not talk about it. Let's just do it. There's nothing to talk about any more.'

So they didn't talk. They tried doing it. They tried doing it for seven more weeks.

Without the slightest success. Without even a lead worth spending any of their steadily diminishing resources on. Hans was especially adamant about being careful with their money, so that if a good operational possibility presented itself they would not be caught short. He was right, because it would have been the ultimate irony to find Salameh, only to discover at the last minute that they did not have the money left to go after him. But it never came to that.

They could simply make no contacts. Not through any of their regular informers, not through Louis or Tony. Not through Papa. If they had been after other terrorists, they might have succeeded: 1974 had been a very active year for the *mechablim* in Europe, especially for a group backed by Libya's Colonel Qaddafi, called National Arab Youth for the Liberation of Palestine. Led originally by a man named Ahmed al-Ghaffour and later by Abu Nidal, this group consisted of terrorists for whom Black September or the Popular Front was no longer extreme and militant enough (al-Ghaffour was eventually captured and probably executed by the forces of Black September leader Abu Iyad). In 1974 the National Arab Youth successfully attacked three airliners. On 8 October, they blew up one – a TWA jet *en route* from Tel Aviv to Athens – over the Aegean Sea with a loss of eighty-eight lives. Three weeks earlier, on 15 September, terrorists had thrown a hand grenade into Le Drugstore on the Champs Élysées in Paris, killing two people and wounding twelve, in a combined operation of the Popular Front and the Japanese Red Army. Led by Carlos the Jackal.

Carlos, for whom the team felt especially responsible; Carlos, for whom they had made room at the top by killing Boudia. But it made no difference. He was not on their list. Abu Nidal was not on their list. They could hardly contact Ephraim for a change of assignment when even their original assignment had been cancelled. There was to be no more unilateral action; they could not justify it. They could only try for the remaining terrorists on their list. Especially Ali Hassan Salameh.

Getting Salameh would have made all the difference.

But as far as they could tell, Salameh was not coming to Europe.

They spent Christmas and New Year's Eve in Frankfurt. The city was in a festive mood; Avner, Steve and Hans were not. Hans, in fact, was combining several moods that should have been mutually exclusive. He was dejected and introspective, but at the same time he was becoming increasingly paranoid and even combative. He started carrying a gun. Previously they had never gone around armed unless they were on an operation, but Hans' paranoia was contagious. Now, even Avner and Steve began carrying weapons just in case their partner's feeling that somebody was on their trail was accurate – perhaps as the result of a leak through Papa's organization, after all. Hans even believed that Tarifa could have been a trap, though Avner was convinced he was mistaken about that; a trap would have confronted them with crossfire, not one lone terrorist buttoning up his fly. But after the mysterious deaths of Carl and Robert such suspicions could not be dismissed. Maybe the terrorists in Tarifa *were* tipped off, but did not expect the Israelis until later. In fact, Avner had told Papa's man, as a normal precaution, that they would wait in Tarifa for some friends before taking any action.

In any case, they armed themselves in Frankfurt, despite the additional risk. And Avner noticed the heavy, black scuff marks at the bottom of Hans' door in his safe house: evidently he would not open it now without resting the ball of his foot against it. All agents were trained to do that, and it could make the difference between life and death in the case of an unexpected assault, but Hans had not been in the habit of doing it. None of them did it often. Like their 'soft' targets, they had until now mainly relied on their covers.

At the same time Hans would go for long walks, alone, late at night, in the immense park near his safe house. He had always been fond of walking, but in the past he would walk at relatively sane hours and in reasonable weather. Now he would walk for hours in the snow, in the bitter winds of December, as late as midnight, along the totally deserted pathways of Ostpark, north of Frankfurt's eastern railway station. He would even sit for an hour or two on a bench at his favourite secluded spot, next to an artificial pond, which was full of black mallards in the summer, but was now frozen over.

'The ducks have much more sense than you,' Steve said to Hans once, when he'd had to go to the duck pond to obtain some information.

'Well, I can't sit cooped up at home,' Hans had replied.

Avner could understand. Certainly at that stage of the mission he would not have wished to live on his own either. After Robert's death he had Steve move into the safe house he had previously shared with Carl, because even putting up with Steve's disorderly bachelor habits was preferable to living alone. But when he had suggested to Hans that they should look for a safe house where they could all stay together, Hans refused. 'Don't worry about me,' he'd said. 'I'm fine.'

Which simply wasn't true.

On the night of 6 January, 1975, Hans left his safe house sometime after 9 pm. It had to be after nine, because Avner had called him around that time on the telephone. They talked for a few seconds – they had nothing important to discuss – then hung up, with the understanding that they would check with each other later. This was routine. When Hans failed to call by midnight, Avner rang his number. There was no answer. There was still no answer at 1 am.

This was unusual. Hans would go for long late-night walks, but had never stayed out until past midnight. It was always possible that an informer would send him word, asking for a meeting unexpectedly, but in such cases they had made it a rule to alert each other. Especially lately. If he had gone to such a meeting, Hans would have phoned. He knew that Avner and Steve would be at their safe houses. Avner became worried.

'I want to take a drive over,' he said to Steve. 'I don't like it that he's still out.'

Steve shrugged. 'He's probably sitting on his goddamn bench by the duck pond,' he said, 'but let's go.'

The drive from the vicinity of Hügelstrasse in the Eschersheim district where their safe house was located to near Röderbergweg, where Hans lived, took them less than twenty minutes. Hans was not at his safe house. Avner let himself in with a spare key, but there was nothing out of order. Evidently Hans had gone out for some reason and had simply not come home yet.

It was a bitterly cold night, and nearly 2 am by that time. Even in his current mood Hans was unlikely to be strolling or sitting in the park, yet that was the only safe explanation. Anything else could only mean that there was something wrong.

'If he's at the duck pond,' Steve said, 'he'll need a good excuse for me not to break his nose.'

They knew the route Hans usually took to the park. He would walk a short distance along Röderbergweg, then take a rather picturesque terraced path called Lili-Schönemann-Steige (after a childhood friend of the poet Goethe) down to a four-lane road at the bottom of the ravine. Once he'd crossed Ostparkstrasse he'd be at Ostpark, which he'd usually enter a few hundred yards north-east from where he had crossed the road, along a well-marked path. After some twists and turns, this path would take him to the duck pond.

Avner and Steve were expecting to meet Hans sauntering back, but they didn't. The walk took them about fifteen minutes. The park was pitch-black, the entire area totally deserted. However, as they approached the artificial pond, there was enough reflection off the ice for them to make out the figure of a man sitting on the bench. It was, indeed, Hans.

But Steve did not break his nose. Hans had a perfect excuse. He was dead.

Seeing Hans dead in the park, Avner's first thought was not that he had been murdered. His first thought was that Hans had killed himself.

The bushes formed a little arbour by the pond. The shoreline was a few feet above the frozen lake, separated from it by a low stone wall and a wooden railing. The body was in a half-sitting posture, slumping forward against the railing, the head lolling sideways, the eyes open in an expressionless face. Hans' topcoat was unbuttoned. At first Avner could see no obvious wounds anywhere on his head or his body.

It was very dark. They had not thought of bringing a flashlight and did not have matches. 'Watch out,' Avner said to Steve under his breath. In spite of the intense cold, Hans' body was still not frozen. He had probably not been dead for more than an hour, maybe less. Whoever killed him might still be in the area.

Because he *had* been killed. The first thing Avner checked was Hans' gun. It was still tucked into his belt behind his hip. It had not been fired. He had not shot himself. Nor had he died of natural causes. Though Avner could still see no wound, he could feel a sticky, gummy substance, like half-dried pitch, as he was reaching for Hans' gun. It had to be blood from a wound on his body. A wound that was not self-inflicted.

'He was killed,' Avner said, handing Hans' gun to Steve.

For a few seconds neither of them spoke. They were stunned, but they were also frightened. The park was immense and silent; in all directions they could see only icy bushes and dark trees. It was a windless night. In the far distance they could hear the monotonous hum of the city, interrupted once in a while by the metallic clang of a shunting freight car in the railway yard. Steve clicked back the bolt on Hans' gun. 'You check his wallet,' he said to Avner. 'I'll keep a lookout.'

Ironically, it could have been a mugger. Frankfurt was not a particularly crime-ridden city, but it was a huge, industrial town, filled with guest workers from all over southern Europe. It had a tenderloin district; it had pimps, burglars, drug addicts, prostitutes, like any other metropolis. Ostpark was in a peaceful, middle-class neighbourhood, but no deserted park is completely safe late at night. There were probably a dozen or more robbery-murders in Frankfurt every year. Hans would not have appeared particularly hard to rob; a lone, middle-aged man sitting on a bench could look like a natural victim. Muggers might even mistake him for a drunk. And while Hans would probably have chosen not to defend himself for a few Deutschmarks, but would have handed over his wallet, even his watch, a nervous hold-up man might have shot him anyway. It was one possible explanation.

But Hans' watch was on his wrist. His wallet was in his pocket, intact.

Could Hans have been betrayed by an informer? It was unlikely that he would have made an appointment to meet anyone at that particular spot. Not only was the park deserted late at night and hardly a place for meeting informers, but it was also a very personal place for Hans, his private hideout for rest and contemplation, a place for him to be alone.

It was, incidentally, also a very difficult place in which to follow someone without being noticed. Hans would not have gone to the duck pond with anyone walking behind him late at night. Of course, people driving by on Ostparkstrasse could observe him entering the park, and, if they were familiar with his habits, might guess where to find him. But only Avner and Steve knew about the artificial pond. The park was very large, and Hans could have gone anywhere in it. Finding him accidentally would have been very difficult. Terrorist hit-men wandering around the park could freeze long before coming upon Hans in that secluded little arbour.

Yet, if he wasn't robbed, who else but terrorist hit-men could have killed him?

Avner removed Hans' wallet, which had a German driver's licence and some social security identification in it. He carried no other papers on him. Looking more closely, Avner thought that most of the coagulated blood was around the middle of Hans' chest where he could also feel a long tear in his sweater. It was impossible to be certain, but it looked like a *knife* wound, which made the thing even more mysterious. How could anyone have got close enough to Hans to stab him without his trying to pull his gun? He would have had to be truly unsuspecting – or a second person would have had to hold him at gunpoint. But even then it was unthinkable that Hans would have just sat there, waiting to be stabbed. Even as a reflex he would have raised his hands to ward off a knife, yet Avner could discover no slash marks or blood on his gloves or his sleeves. If he was stabbed, it looked almost as if he had been stabbed in his sleep.

Which was also unthinkable.

It crossed Avner's mind then that he knew nothing about Hans' sexual habits. He was married, but that didn't mean much. Although there was absolutely nothing about Hans that would have made Avner suspect homosexual tendencies – even the thought was slightly ludicrous – it was also true that Avner simply didn't know. While he doubted that Ostpark in January was a trysting place for homosexuals, again, he didn't *know*. If Hans had made an unwanted homosexual advance to someone, it might explain the circumstances of his death.

But it was such a far-fetched thought that Avner could not bring himself to mention it to Steve. Not then, not later. Steve would probably have taken a swing at him for even suggesting it.

'I'm going to make a phone call,' Avner said to Steve. 'Wait for me at the entrance to the park.'

The nearest phone booth on Ostparkstrasse was only a ten-minute walk away. Avner called Louis is Paris. 'It's a situation like in London,' he said to him. 'Let me tell you where I am.'

Louis listened in silence while Avner carefully explained to him the location where he would be waiting with Steve for Papa's men. The Frenchman asked for no other details and Avner offered none. Before ending the conversation, Louis asked: 'Is there anything else I can do?'

'Not for the time being, thanks,' Avner replied.

He didn't know it, but this was to be their last conversation. Avner would never talk to Louis again.

He waited with Steve at the main entrance to the park for the men who would remove Hans' body. They waited for nearly an hour and a half. Later Avner would recall in some amazement that they did not even feel the cold. It was a vigil spent in almost total silence. In fact, they exchanged words only twice. The first time was when Steve said:

'You called Papa. You don't think they had anything to do with it?'

'No, I don't,' Avner replied.

It was the truth. But even if he was wrong, Avner believed there was nothing else he could have done at this stage. If Hans' body was found, it could spark an investigation by the German authorities. Something they couldn't risk. If *Le Group* had had Hans killed, let them dispose of his body. They could do him no more harm.

When Steve spoke the second time, he said:

'For a long while I thought we were smart. But maybe we were only lucky.

'Then maybe we ran out of luck.'

There was nothing Avner could reply to that, so he said nothing. Steve's remark that night might have summed up the entire mission better than anything else.

Papa's men arrived shortly before 4 am with a public-works truck. It was the kind of vehicle that would attract no attention driving into a park. Avner and Steve guided the men to the duck pond and waited until they put Hans' body in a canvas bag, then into the back of the truck. The two men were both Germans, and probably worked in Frankfurt as ambulance attendants or undertakers. The whole procedure took no more than seven or eight minutes. Then they backed the truck out of the park along the narrow, twisting pathway.

For a few more minutes Avner could see the truck's headlights vanishing and reappearing through the black winter trees. Then he could see nothing. Hans was gone. The way Carl and Robert were gone. As if they had never existed.

Avner and Steve spent the following weeks trying to decide what to do. To be more precise, trying to postpone a decision by occupying themselves with routine matters. They closed down Hans' safe house and changed their own. Using a power of attorney Hans had given Avner earlier, they sold his antique-furniture business. They flew to Paris and paid Kathy what they owed *Le Group* – Louis was out of town – then drove to the small town in France where Hans' wife was living.

She was an Israeli woman, very different from Robert's wife. 'Is Hans with you?' she asked Avner when he telephoned her.

'Well – no.'

'I see,' she replied, after a moment's pause. She evidently understood. There was no need to tell her anything.

When they arrived at the house, she took the suitcase that contained Hans' personal belongings, and invited Avner and Steve into the living room. She offered them tea, and after a few minutes of polite conversation, asked them to tell her every detail they felt free to talk about. They could tell her very little. She wanted to know where Hans had been buried.

Avner looked at Steve. 'I'm sorry,' he said finally. 'I can't tell you. I . . . nobody knows.'

'I see,' she replied, still totally self-possessed. 'Will you excuse me for a minute?'

She went into another room and stayed there for about fifteen minutes. When she came back, her eyes were dry, though perhaps a little red. 'Please forgive me,' Hans's wife said. 'I know I should pull myself together. Would you like another cup of tea?'

When Avner tried to give her an envelope containing some money, she refused it. After a few more minutes they left the house, feeling not only wretched – they expected to feel wretched – but somehow ashamed and guilty. They felt as if everything had been their fault. Or worse, as if they had recklessly played with something and had broken it to pieces. Something that was of inestimable value to someone else.

Perhaps it was seeing Hans's widow that finally sealed their decision. They did not really talk about it, not in so many words, but each knew instinctively that the other had made up his mind. They closed one bank account after another, in Amsterdam, in Zürich, in Paris. They were bringing the mission to a close. There were only two of them left. There was no way they could continue.

Finally they flew to Geneva. They removed Ephraim's message – *Terminate immediately* – from the safe-deposit box where Hans had left it after Robert's death. There was by that time another message, saying: *Acknowledge soonest*.

Avner encoded a reply and put it back. It read: *Message acknowledged. Lost Hans*. He could think of nothing else to add.

Leaving the bank, Avner and Steve walked across the pont de la Machine where they had talked after their first Geneva meeting in September, 1972. 'You were right in one thing, anyway,' Avner said to Steve. 'The two of us are still alive.'

The mission was over.

PART IV

Coming in from the Cold

Chapter 18

------------·∾∾∾·------------

AMERICA

HANS HAD DIED IN JANUARY; by the time Avner and Steve had settled their affairs in the Geneva bank and were walking back to the Hotel du Midi it was the first afternoon of spring, 21 March, 1975. They still had a few things to wind up in Europe: there were safe houses to close, minor informers to be paid off. Both Avner and Steve had left their personal accounts in the Geneva bank intact, each noting that in spite of their payments to their comrades' widows they still had almost one hundred thousand dollars left. It was a somewhat bitter satisfaction, and they noted it with a shrug and perhaps a twinge of guilt. Still, they would be all right, at least in this sense. Though Avner had become used to spending large sums in the course of the mission, a hundred thousand dollars in his own account still seemed an astronomical amount to him. It crossed his mind for the first time that he was rich. He could buy the fantastic Scandinavian kitchen from the store on the avenue Hoche for Shoshana with ease. He could buy her *two* kitchens, if he wanted to.

Having made the decision to quit, they felt depressed and relieved at the same time. Though Black September seemed not to be active any longer, the Popular Front's Boudia-Commando, led by Carlos, was boldly (though unsuccessfully) attacking *El Al* planes with rocket launchers in Paris. The Baader-Meinhof gang was equally boldly, but more successfully, kidnapping industrialists in Germany and holding them to be ransomed by a compliant West German government. Reading the papers, Avner and Steve wondered if their mission, for which Carl, Robert and Hans had given their lives, had made even a dent in international terror. Ephraim's many-headed monster was not slowing down. And even where it appeared to be slowing, as with Black September, it was probably just as much due to a policy decision by Arafat's faction of the PLO after the Yom Kippur War. It was possible that some of the *mechablim* now saw the United Nations and the conference tables in Geneva as better staging areas from which to push the Jews into the sea.

Not that it mattered. What they did had to be done, as far as Avner and Steve were concerned. Israel could not allow her sons and daughters to be murdered with impunity. In the spring of 1975, even in their blackest mood in Geneva, Avner and Steve would have defended the mission unequivocally.

They shared out what mop-up work there was still to be done. Then they embraced awkwardly, a little ashamed of their own emotion, before each went his separate way.

Avner arrived in New York on 10 April, without having made up his mind about the future. In fact, he felt too drained even to think about it. Technically, he had not been employed by the Mossad since 1972, and now that his mission had been cancelled he felt that he owed no immediate duties to anyone. At one point he would obviously have to go back to Tel Aviv to be debriefed, but Avner couldn't have talked about the mission with anyone just yet. All he wanted to do was to spend a couple of weeks with Shoshana.

As it turned out, he stayed in New York for nearly a month. It was like a holiday, filled with the guilty pleasure of a child staying away from school. There was perhaps no reason for Avner to feel this way about it, but he did. He'd make love to Shoshana two or three times a day, he'd go for long walks with her, take her to restaurants, to the movies. He'd play with Geula. He'd try to teach Charlie to fetch the newspaper from the door.

Shoshana asked only one question, after Avner had been in New York for about three weeks. 'This time, when you go,' she asked, 'how long will you be away?'

'I didn't say anything about going,' Avner replied.

'No, but you will,' Shoshana said matter-of-factly. 'Any day now, you'll tell me you're going. What I want to know is, will you stay away for long?'

'You know something,' Avner said, 'maybe this time it will only be for a week or two. And after I come back, maybe we'll take a trip together. Rent a car and just drive – I don't know, all across America. Would you like that?'

Shoshana laughed. 'Where would we get the money for that?' she asked.

'I didn't tell you before,' Avner said, 'but we'll have a little money coming in now. A kind of a bonus. Don't worry, we can take a trip with no trouble.'

'Really?' Shoshana asked. 'Do you mean it? We've never had a holiday together.'

'I promise,' Avner said. 'You'll see. We'll have a holiday – just you, Geula, and me. And Charlie, of course.'

A few days after that conversation, Avner received a phone call from a Mossad agent in New York. 'Well, well,' the man said, when he heard Avner's voice, 'I might have guessed. Everybody's looking for you, and you're just sitting there as if you didn't have a care in the world.'

'Is there anything I should care about?' Avner asked.

'How should I know?' the man replied. 'You should know that better than I. All I know is that there are people waiting for you back home. Now that I've got you, I'll tell them that you'll be aboard the first flight tomorrow. They'll be glad to hear it.'

'You tell them whatever you want,' Avner replied, and put down the phone.

But he was at Kennedy Airport the following day, carrying a small suitcase. He still felt drained. The last thing he wanted to do was recount the entire chronology of the past two and a half years. But there was no point in delaying it. He

371

knew he had to submit to a debriefing sooner or later. It was routine. What really worried him was something else.

The debriefing would be only a prelude to a decision. A decision he would have to make. A decision he would not be able to delay any longer.

Ten hours later he stepped onto the sizzling runway at Lod Airport. The red disc of the setting Mediterranean sun was slipping fast into the sea. The heavy air filled Avner's lungs oppressively, like wet cotton. It was such a familiar feeling that it almost made him smile. It was like coming back to Israel from Frankfurt when he was a child.

Ephraim was waiting for him at the glass customs booth, accompanied by two men Avner didn't know. 'Well, well,' Ephraim said, putting his arms around him, 'it is really good to see you. Look, guys, this is Avner. I can't tell you how proud we are of you.

'Welcome. Welcome home.'

For a week in May, Avner was a hero.

The three-day debriefing in a private apartment, though intense, was friendly. Ephraim was lolling about the room, folding and unfolding himself, trying to arrange his loose limbs like an oversized string puppet. The other two men assumed a respectful, even deferential air, as far as two Israeli *sabras* could ever be said to be deferential. To Avner's amazement, the mission was being regarded as a great success.

It was a totally different mood from the one in which Ephraim had met Avner and Carl in Geneva before the Beirut raid. Or the mood at their meeting in Israel after the Yom Kippur War, a year and a half ago. Then Ephraim seemed like a lion tamer, all but holding a chair in front of him and cracking a whip as he spoke. Now, everything was fine. Who could say why?

Avner considered that the positive achievements of the mission had occurred in the beginning, certainly during the period before the war of 1973. It was then that they deserved a medal, if at all. It was then that he would have expected a

'Well done!' from Ephraim instead of sour remarks about the time it was taking them, the money it was costing, not to mention the chewing out they all received for coming back to fight in the war. Ever since that time the team had had only losses and near-misses. Complete or semi-disasters. Carl. Robert. Hans. The three Palestinian foot soldiers in Switzerland, and the one in Spain. Yet it was now that Ephraim was patting him on the shoulder.

Avner couldn't understand it. Maybe everyone was relieved that it was over. Maybe they had expected something worse, another Lillehammer. Perhaps Ephraim – who was, after all, just a bureaucrat, like any other – had received indications of approval from the higher echelons. Indications which he hadn't received before. In a bureaucracy – every intelligence agency is one – approval by the brass is finally all that matters. If such approval was communicated to Ephraim, he'd naturally begin wagging his tail.

He was certainly wagging his tail at Avner now, he and the other kibbutzniks. So that, in the course of those three days in that Mossad apartment, Avner became not only the little Dutch boy, but also Lieutenant-Colonel John Wayne of the United States Cavalry. A man the toughest kibbutznik would respect. Everything he had ever dreamed of as a child. All his fantasies from the kibbutz were becoming reality. He had, apparently, shown them what he could do. A real, genuine hero. For the first time in his life.

Ephraim took notes as Avner gave him a careful, detailed account, trying his best to omit nothing. Maybe they were also taping the conversation; Avner didn't know, and he didn't want to ask. But they seemed to be applauding the successes and minimizing the failures. Salameh – well, a pity, but you tried your best. Muchassi – it was a valid field decision, even though he was not on the list. The KGB man – we heard nothing. Maybe you missed him after all, but even if you didn't, what else could you do? The Russians would have their own reasons to keep quiet about it. The young terrorists in Switzerland and in Spain – we can't sit in judgment. They were *mechablim*. You only did what you thought you had to do. Carl, Robert and Hans: a tragedy, but what do you expect? You can't fight a war without losses. Yes, you should have quit when you were instructed, but we can understand why you didn't. We'll say no more about it.

The only thing Ephraim shook his head at was the killing of the woman in Hoorn. 'That was wrong,' he said. 'There you were simply disobeying orders. I don't care about your reasons. Whether she killed Carl or not – I'm not doubting that she did – shooting her was murder. We would never have permitted you to do it.'

'Well, you had nothing to do with it,' Avner said. 'We did it on our own. Consider that we were taking a leave of absence.'

'Don't be an idiot,' Ephraim replied sharply. 'Maybe in the movies.' It was the only time he struck a note of censure, but even then he did not persist. 'Anyway, what's done is done,' he said. 'We have no choice now. But remember, we don't joke about unauthorized action. Ordinarily it means dismissal.'

Avner said nothing. Dismissal from what, he thought. I'm not working for you anyway. But it was simpler to keep quiet.

The only aspect of the mission about which he gave Ephraim no detailed information was *Le Group*. He said nothing about Louis or Papa. It was always 'a contact in the terrorist network' or a code name he'd invent for Ephraim's benefit. 'Then we called Paul,' he'd say, or 'Then we called Haled.' It was not only because of his father's warning about always having a card up his sleeve, but because Avner continued to believe that giving any details to the Mossad would amount to breaking faith with Papa. It was his judgment – perhaps only his hope – that Papa had never broken faith with him. In spite of what had happened to Carl, Robert and Hans. Ultimately, Avner couldn't have told Ephraim too much anyway. All he really had were some phone numbers where he could contact or leave messages for *Le Group*. And perhaps the ability to find again a house somewhere in the

French countryside, which Papa may or may not have been using as his headquarters.

Ephraim didn't press him. All agents like to keep their personal informers to themselves. Partly for security, and partly because having contacts represents something of a cachet. It assures an agent that he will not be replaced by a computer.

After seventy-two hours Ephraim hugged Avner again and let him leave the apartment.

Avner had seen other agents who were regarded as heroes; agents with great reputations; agents to whom everyone deferred, though hardly anyone actually knew what they had done. Now, quite evidently, he had become such an agent himself. He could tell from the way people were clapping him on the back when he walked into headquarters after the debriefing to settle some outstanding administrative matters. In various offices, people he hardly knew kept pumping his hand as he surrendered chequebooks, documents, safe-deposit keys, and other paraphernalia from the mission. The Grandfather of the Galicianers grunted with approval as Avner handed him some accounts and several thousand dollars in cash which he still had on him from operational funds. At a brief meeting even the new *memune*, General Yiczak Hofi,[1] shook his hand, wearing an expression that came close to being a smile.

However, as Avner would later say to his father, nobody offered this time to drive him to the Prime Minister.

The grapevine must have reached even Father in retirement, though he was not aware of the details. 'I hear you did well,' he said when Avner walked into the garden. 'I hear they think you're the blue-eyed boy.'

'Yes,' Avner replied, 'that's what they think.'

His father looked up sharply. 'Don't you?' he asked.

Avner shook his head. 'I don't know,' he replied.

'It doesn't matter,' his father said, after a pause. 'Never mind what you think; never mind what you did. Today you're on top. Take. Take right now. Today they'll give you.

'Tomorrow, forget it. Tomorrow you'll be nothing.'

'I don't want anything they have,' Avner replied. 'There's nothing they can give me.'

His father pulled himself up in the chair. 'Listen to me,' he said. 'You didn't listen to me before, but listen to me now. What's done is done. It could have been worse, but you were lucky. Today you have a chance.

'But it's your only chance. It's only today. Tomorrow they'll be locking up the rubies. They won't even give you the time of day. You'll be sitting here waiting for a phone call, but that phone call will never come.'

'But what if I don't want their rubies?' Avner asked. 'What if I'm not interested in getting a phone call?'

His father looked at him, sighed deeply, then suddenly seemed to lose interest. 'You don't understand it,' he said, not so much to Avner, it seemed, as to himself. 'You'll just have to go through it, like everybody else. Then you'll understand it, but it'll be too late.'

Though his father would say nothing more, Avner thought he could piece together the reasons for his continuing bitterness. His new wife, Wilma, had died a year earlier. She had died after a fairly lengthy illness, due to a condition which, according to Avner's father, had developed while he was incarcerated as a spy for Israel. However, she was not an Israeli – she wasn't even Jewish – and therefore not entitled to medical insurance that would have provided free treatment. Father had to pay for her treatment himself. It was, apparently, very expensive and had cost him the better part of the compensation he had received after his celebrated mission. In spite of everything Father had done for the country, 'they' wouldn't contribute a penny.

Avner did not learn any of this from his father. As usual, apart from his vague, bitter, general remarks, he had told Avner nothing. It was Avner's mother who told him about it when he saw her. She had gone to Wilma's funeral. Apart from some kibbutzniks and Father, she was the only person present when they lowered Wilma's coffin into the ground. It was more than ironic, Avner thought. It was bizarre.

Mother understood Father's bitterness about 'them' but she did not share it. In this tiny, besieged country everybody was at risk; many families had lost fathers, mothers, sons and daughters in the wars; and if you had to give special recognition to everyone who had made special sacrifices, you'd be giving it to every other man and woman. What was the difference between 'ordinary' and 'extraordinary' service? You could lose your life just as easily driving a tank as doing a secret mission. Maybe more easily. If you made exceptions for everyone, the country would go bankrupt. 'You're an Israeli, you do your duty,' Avner's mother said. 'You don't expect a reward. The Jews have a country: that's your reward.'

'Well, Wilma wasn't an Israeli,' Avner said.

'She did what she had to do,' Mother said coldly. 'I did what *I* had to do. You think it was easy? What reward did I get? Mind you, I wasn't asking for any.'

'Mother, you're a saint,' said Avner unsympathetically.

'What do you mean, a saint? What kind of talk is that? Just because I don't agree with your father?'

'Well, Father certainly isn't a saint,' Avner said. 'That's the only thing wrong with him. You are, and that's the only thing wrong with you.'

But being flippant with his mother altered nothing. The truth was that in his own mind Avner still couldn't escape the feeling that his mother was *right*. She had the correct standards. The fact that Avner – or his father – couldn't live up to them was not Mother's fault.

Or, by extension, Israel's.

Avner returned to New York before the end of May. In his own mind he had made his decision by that time, but he said nothing about it to Ephraim at their last short meeting, just a few hours before Avner's flight was due to leave. 'Take some time off, rest, do whatever you want,' Ephraim said to him. 'We'll talk about your next assignment when you come back.'

'Okay,' Avner replied noncommittally. 'We'll talk.'

In fact, the person he wanted to talk to was not Ephraim but Shoshana. He did talk with her the first night he was back in New York. 'You have lived in America for two years now,' Avner said to her. 'Do you like it?'

'Yes,' said Shoshana. 'I like it.'

'Do you miss home?'

'Yes,' Shoshana replied. 'Don't you?'

'I miss it and I don't miss it,' Avner said. 'But I don't think I want to live in Israel any more. I want us to live – well, maybe in America. What do you think?'

'You mean, to emigrate? Live here for good?'

'Yes,' Avner replied, 'that's what I mean.'

Even as he said it, the enormity of it hit him, as it must have hit Shoshana. They were both Israelis. They were *sabras*. For them, emigrating didn't mean quite what it meant for a Swede or an Italian. Although changing countries, giving up one citizenship for another, might be a very big decision for anyone, for an Israeli it was a bigger decision still. It wasn't just saluting an additional flag, choosing to speak a different language, or electing to pay taxes to a different set of bureaucrats. For an Israeli, it meant returning to the Diaspora. It meant rejecting the Jewish homeland, the idea for which tens of thousands of Jews had died, and hundreds of thousands were still facing death every day. It almost meant deserting in the face of the enemy.

Yet, by the end of May, 1975, Avner had made up his mind to emigrate.

And only Shoshana could have changed his mind at that point.

'Does it mean we stop being Israelis?' she asked.

'No,' Avner shook his head. 'We are Israelis. How could we stop being what we are? If there is a war or anything, I take the first flight. Believe me.'

Shoshana shrugged. 'I know that,' she said, 'but that's not what I meant. We're talking about something else.'

She was right. Avner knew she was right. In a war a lot of

people would have taken the first flight, people who weren't even Israelis. Emigrating did mean something different. It had little to do with what a person would or would not do for Israel in an emergency.

'I know,' he said to her. 'I just don't want to go back there to live. I can't explain it. It has nothing to do with the country or . . . or the idea or anything.'

Shoshana looked at him. 'Has it got to do with your work?' she asked.

'Maybe.'

'I'm not asking you any questions,' Shoshana said. 'But if we decide, let's decide now.' She looked at their daughter who was asleep in her cot. 'Before Geula even goes to kindergarten. I don't want her to grow up in two places. At least let her be one thing or another.'

It was when Shoshana said this that Avner realized how hard the decision must be for her.

'We don't have to stay,' he said to her. 'I mean it. If you want us to go back, we go back.'

'No,' Shoshana said. 'I think it's better if we stay.'

The decision was really made on Avner's first night back from Tel Aviv, although they continued talking about it during the weeks that followed. Avner wasn't going to do anything yet to make it official, at least, not in the sense of going to the immigration authorities or writing a letter of resignation to Ephraim. As far as he was concerned, there was nothing for him to resign from anyway. He had already resigned two and a half years ago.

He did, however, put down two months' rent for a much larger apartment in Brooklyn. As a surprise for Shoshana, he also bought some very modern Scandinavian furniture, the kind he knew she had always dreamed about having in her living room. He used almost the very last of his money to buy it for her.

'How can we afford this stuff?' she asked, her eyes widening in delight, when Avner took her to the store to see the coffee table and the sofa he had selected.

'Don't worry about it,' Avner replied. 'We can afford it.'

The phone call from Ephraim came before Avner had even had time to move into the bigger apartment and have the new furniture delivered. 'How's the holiday going?' Ephraim asked in Hebrew. Avner recognized his voice immediately.

'Where are you calling from?' he asked.

'I'm in New York,' Ephraim said. 'I'd like to see you.'

'Sure,' Avner replied. 'Why don't you come to my place?'

'No, no,' Ephraim said, 'I don't want to bother you at home. Why don't you come to the hotel?'

They agreed to meet in the lobby the following morning, so that Avner didn't even have to ask Ephraim what name he was using. Although Shoshana's phone was unlikely to be tapped, and Ephraim was no doubt calling from a public booth, the precaution was routine.

'It's good to see you,' Ephraim said the next day, as they sat in his small, rather faded hotel room. 'You're looking rested. Well – there's another job we would like you to do.'

It was not a surprise. Avner had thought about it all night and concluded that this was the most likely reason for Ephraim's wanting to talk with him in New York.

He had also made up his mind in advance how he would respond. But he couldn't bring himself to do it right away. In truth, he was looking for an excuse.

'This other job, what would it entail?' he asked. 'Is it like the one before?'

'No,' Ephraim said, 'it's not like that job at all.' He still had the maddening habit, which Avner remembered from their first meeting, of raising a paper napkin to his face, as if he were about to blow his nose, but then not putting it to any use. 'It's completely different. For one thing, it would be in a different continent. In South America.'

Avner said nothing.

'The only thing that would be the same,' Ephraim continued, 'is that, again, you couldn't take your family with you. That's the only thing. But we'd be able to arrange for you to come home for, oh, two or three weeks, maybe every seven months. Say, twice a year.'

'No,' Avner said. He said it just like this: *no*, very flatly.

Ephraim looked up, in evident surprise. He even gave a little half-hearted laugh. 'Well,' he said. 'Maybe you want to think about it.'

'There's nothing to think about. I don't want to do it.'

Ephraim said nothing for a few seconds. Then he put his hand on Avner's shoulder. 'Look, we're friends,' he said. 'What is the problem?'

Avner had spoken more harshly than he meant to, perhaps because he was a little ashamed of himself. What was he doing? No wonder Ephraim was surprised: it was not usual for an Israeli commando to refuse to go on a mission. 'Okay, we're friends,' he replied, 'that's why I'm telling you. My family relationship will not take another trip like that. And . . . well, I'm not interested in doing it any more.'

Ephraim unfolded himself and walked to the window. He stood there looking out for a few seconds, then turned back to Avner. 'Well, if the answer is no,' he said, 'and I'm really sad to hear that it's no . . .' He broke off, trying a different tone. 'Look, maybe it's my fault. I called you too soon. What you need is some more time to think about it.'

'I don't need time,' Avner replied. 'I'm glad you called, so I could tell you. I don't want to do it. Okay? I'm sorry.'

Ephraim sat down again. 'I understand,' he said softly. 'Maybe you don't think I understand, but I do. Believe me.' He spoke with genuine sympathy in his voice, which made it infinitely worse. What Avner took his tone to mean was: *I understand you have battle fatigue. I understand you have lost your nerve. I understand you just haven't got what it takes in the long run.* Not sarcastically, not as a challenge, but the way a doctor might talk to a patient. A patient with a terminal illness, which wasn't his fault, but for whom the doctor could do nothing more. It was the worst moment in Avner's life.

Going from hero to bum, as Carl would have put it, in ten seconds.

And the next thing Ephraim said was even more devastating, especially with the false heartiness in his voice:

'Listen, don't worry,' he said, 'don't look so glum. It's all right. We'll bring you and your family back to Israel. There's enough work in Israel that you can do. Work that is just as important.'

'I don't want to go back to Israel,' Avner said.

Ephraim stared at him.

'I want to stay in New York for a while,' Avner repeated, speaking slowly.

'What do you mean?' Ephraim asked. 'You can't.'

'What do you mean, I can't?' Avner said, raising his eyes to meet his case officer's. 'I want to stay in New York.'

'But you *can't* stay in New York,' Ephraim said, almost as if he were talking to a child. 'You don't have papers, you don't have work, you don't have anything. What are you going to do here?' He spread his hands, waving the paper napkin in the air. 'What on earth are you talking about?'

'I'm talking about staying here,' Avner said reasonably. 'I don't know what I'm going to do yet, and I don't care. I want to stay with my family, that's all. I don't want to know about anything else.'

Ephraim shrugged and grimaced. 'Well,' he said, 'maybe I caught you at a bad time. I don't even understand what you're talking about – at least, I hope I don't. Are you telling me you're going to be one of those *immigrants*? You're sending me back to your mother and father to tell them? You, *born* in Israel, you're going to leave the country?'

Avner wanted to say 'yes' but he couldn't. He took a deep breath, but the word wouldn't come out. He was too much of a coward. He simply couldn't face Ephraim and say it to him. Not then.

Maybe, in spite of everything he had worked out in his mind, in spite of everything he had discussed with Shoshana, he had not yet made a real decision. Maybe he never would.

Or maybe he'd never have enough courage to look somebody like Ephraim in the eye and tell him.

Or tell somebody like his mother.

'I'm not leaving the country,' he said, glancing away. 'I will, ah, I will probably come back. But for now . . . I just want to stay away. That's all.'

'Oh well,' Ephraim said immediately, 'if you tell me you want to stay for a few months, that's a different story. We can talk about that. But it's better if we don't talk about it now. I have to go to Washington for a few days. Before I go back to Israel, I'll speak to you again. In the meantime, talk to your wife. I'm sure your wife doesn't want to stay in America.' Ephraim laughed again, as if the idea were just too ludicrous for words, then added: 'I didn't mean to speak sharply with you. Forgive me. But I misunderstood you. I thought you were saying you wanted to stay here for good.'

He extended his hand to Avner.

Avner shook his hand, but he still couldn't look Ephraim in the eye. 'Look, I didn't say "for good" but I did mean for a few years. Here, or in Australia, or I don't know. I did mean that.'

'We'll talk, we'll talk,' Ephraim said quickly. 'Later.' He started picking up some papers and putting them in his briefcase, without looking at Avner any more, but Avner couldn't simply leave the room. He felt too angry and too guilty.

'Would you . . . would you like to come and have dinner with us?' he asked Ephraim, getting even more furious with himself.

Ephraim stopped fumbling with his briefcase and looked at him. 'No,' he said coldly. 'Thank you. I have other people to meet.'

There was nothing more to say. Avner did not go straight home. He went for a long walk, strolling all the way from the east side to the Hudson River, oblivious of the Manhattan crowds and the traffic, crossing against a hundred red lights without even looking around. He was trying to think. What should he have said to Ephraim? How could he explain it to him, when he could not even explain it to himself? *Why* did he not want to go back to Israel?

He had always wanted to live in America. Was it because, patriotic as he was about Israel, he could never think of the Middle East as his home? Was it because of the *air*? The heavy, oppressive air that could be cold but never crisp and clean? The air that, humid or dry, carrying stench or fragrance, would only hang over him ominously, burn him, numb him, whip sand into his eyes, but not sustain him, like the air of Europe, with an easy, gentle, neutral grace?

No. It was more than the air.

Was it because he had failed? In his own eyes, at least? Because he, the little Dutch boy, who wanted to be a hero more than anything else, had finally become a hero under false pretences? Because it felt to him like a mockery? Because every time somebody clapped him on the back or pumped his hand he had to wonder why? Had they forgotten about Carl, Robert, and Hans? The leader of a mission coming back without his men – a hero? Without even the *bodies* of his men, when the Israeli army tradition was never to leave a wounded or dead comrade behind, not even if you had to risk a dozen other men to carry him home. A hero, when he had lost most of his men without achieving his main objective? A hero, when the *mechablim* still had the run of Europe?

Maybe that's what he should have explained to Ephraim. But maybe that wasn't the real reason, either. Maybe it was something else.

But even when he understood it, he could still not express it. He tried telling Shoshana about it, but he could see from the look in her eyes that he was not explaining himself clearly enough. Yet by that time he was certain. He was certain, even if he could never make anybody else understand.

As long as he was in Israel, he had to be a little Dutch boy. Just to feel *equal* to everybody else. Maybe this wasn't true for other Israelis, but it was true for him. Who could tell why?

Perhaps because he wasn't a Galicianer. Perhaps because he wasn't like Mother. Perhaps because he always felt more at home in Frankfurt. Or because he wasn't as tough as the kibbutzniks. But unless he was a little Dutch boy, he was nobody. Nobody at all.

But weren't there other countries that did not demand so much? Where a man could simply be himself, live for himself, without feeling second-rate or guilty? Countries that did not expect a citizen to be a hero? A kibbutznik-hero, a pioneer-hero, a soldier-hero? Countries where a man would not have to feel inferior if he did not volunteer for every mission?

It wasn't Israel's fault, of course. Avner never imagined that it was. It was his own fault. Israel had high standards, that was all. Some people could live up to them naturally – like Mother – and many people probably didn't care. Many people might not even realize that there were standards – great, heroic, sacrificial standards – for them to live up to. They could be oblivious to any standards. They could work, vote, yell at one another, do their stint in the army every year, and be perfectly happy in Israel. They didn't have to be heroes.

Avner had to be. As long as he was an Israeli. It was nobody's fault but his own. And it was nobody's fault that he couldn't make it. Because the truth was, he was not a hero. He was just an ordinary guy. Tired of the bullshit. Tired of pretending that he was anything else. As he would have to, in Israel. Being a hero or pretending to be one. Not necessarily as a commando, charging pillboxes, picking up land mines, hunting terrorists forever, but maybe like Mother. Living on a little pension. Sacrificing a family. Retiring to a kibbutz. Asking for no reward. Saying: the Jews have a home, that's your reward. Waiting for the phone to ring.

And watching the Galicianers sharing out the dumplings. No.

He would not do it anymore. He would not be the good little Yekke potz from Nahariya. If anybody tried to push the Jews into the sea again, he'd go back and fight: that went without saying. He'd go back if he was seventy. But in the meantime he'd live with his family like a normal human being. In America.

Ephraim phoned Avner from Washington a few days later. 'While you're thinking about what you're going to do,' he said, 'I want you to think about one other thing.'

'What's that?' Avner asked.

'You're still under contract.'

At first Avner thought he had heard incorrectly. He was in a public phone booth, having called back Ephraim's phone booth number in Washington, and there was a lot of traffic on Queens Boulevard. 'Did you say *contract*?' he asked. 'What do you mean?'

'The piece of paper you signed,' Ephraim said. 'In my office, remember? When you came back in October. You read it and signed it.'

Avner remembered it well. He remembered signing a piece of paper in Ephraim's office after the Yom Kippur War. But he had not bothered to read it.

'You mean,' he asked Ephraim, 'you made me sign a paper to say that I'm working for you guys forever?'

Ephraim laughed. 'It's not as bad as that,' he replied. 'It's only a three-year contract, renewable at our option every year. We renewed it while you were out of the country.'

'Wait a minute,' Avner said. His head was spinning. 'Whatever I signed, how can you renew it while I'm away? Without my permission?'

'What do you mean, permission?' Ephraim said. 'We don't need your permission. It's our option, and all we have to do is notify you.'

'But you didn't. I was out of the country.'

'Well, we notified your file,' Ephraim replied. 'It's all perfectly legal, take my word for it. So just think about that, while you're thinking.'

'You notified my *what*?' Avner said slowly. If Ephraim had spent a lifetime trying, he could not have come up with anything more calculated to rub Avner the wrong way. The fucking Galicianer notified my file, and now he thinks he's got me? Not on his life! 'Tell you what,' Avner said to Ephraim, 'you notified my file. Now you send my file to South America. I'm staying in New York.'

'Don't fly off the handle,' Ephraim said. 'I'm just calling to tell you, that's all. I thought you might like to know.'

'Okay, you told me,' Avner replied. 'Now let me tell you something. I'm not going anywhere, and I'm not going back home.'

'Then you're in breach of your contract,' Ephraim said and hung up.

The following week Avner flew to Geneva.

He did not stay at the Hotel du Midi, since he was using a different passport. However, he had contacted Steve who was back in Europe on a routine mission, and met him at his old favourite Movenpick Restaurant, the morning after he arrived. 'You're in bad shape, chum,' Steve said to him.

'Why?' Avner asked.

'I don't know why,' said Steve, shaking his head. 'But you're in hot water.'

'What are you talking about?'

'Well, I met Ephraim when he was on his way back home,' Steve said. 'He told me he had talked with you in New York. He said he had expected more of you. You were being totally unreasonable, he said.'

'I want out.'

'I know,' Steve said. 'He told me. What are you going to do?'

'I don't know what I'm going to do yet. But I want to take my money and go. We talked about this a long time ago, remember? Even Carl. We said, once it's over, we go. We all said that.'

'Yes, I remember,' Steve nodded. 'We said it, I guess.'

Avner looked at him. 'And what about you?' he asked.

Steve shrugged and looked away. 'I'm a little older than

387

you, chum,' he said finally. He looked back at Avner. 'And even if I wasn't . . . ' He left the sentence dangling, then continued, 'Anyway, that's your business. If you want out, I guess the right time's when you're young. While your kid's not yet in school, and all that. I agree. But they're going to give you a lot of trouble, you know.'

'What are you talking about?' asked Avner. 'What the hell are you talking about? Why should *they* give me any trouble?' He couldn't help noticing that he was using the word 'they' in exactly the same way as his father. 'I've done nothing to them.'

'Don't yell at me,' said Steve. 'All I know is Ephraim was supposed to be your friend, and now he's pissed off with you. That's all.'

'To hell with Ephraim,' Avner said. 'I'm going to the bank.'

They went together. Avner had another safe-deposit box, for which he had the only key, and in which he still had a few odds and ends from the mission, including a couple of extra passports. Now he picked them up to take home, in much the same spirit as some soldiers bring back souvenirs from the wars. Then he told a clerk that he wished to close out one of his accounts.

In a few minutes the clerk returned with some papers and a small envelope. Avner looked at the money inside. It was the equivalent of slightly under three dollars.

'That's impossible,' he said, glancing at Steve. 'Are you sure that's the right account?'

The clerk double-checked. 'Yes, monsieur,' he said. 'That's the account.'

'There must be some mistake,' Avner said, quite casually, because he really believed it. 'That account should have close to a hundred thousand dollars in it.'

The clerk coughed discreetly. 'You're aware, Monsieur, that there is access to this account by another party. There seem to have been some withdrawals . . . Monsieur would like me to check it, perhaps?'

'Would you, please?' said Avner quietly.

During the few minutes the clerk was away from the counter, Steve and Avner exchanged no words.

An older official, wearing a dark suit and a somewhat anxious frown, returned with the clerk. He invited Avner and Steve into an office and offered them a seat. 'You realize, of course,' he said, looking at a ledger, 'that the monies in this account have been deposited by a French company.'

'Yes,' Avner said cautiously. That was the original 'cover'.

The official shrugged. 'Well, of course, along with monsieur, that company also had the right of withdrawal. And four days ago they withdrew almost the entire amount. Look.'

Avner looked.

'I trust that is in order?' the official asked. 'There is nothing wrong?'

'No,' Avner said numbly. 'There's nothing wrong.'

He was about to walk out of the bank when Steve, who seemed even more shaken by what was happening than Avner, said 'Wait a minute,' and then rushed to another clerk to have a look at his own account. Like Avner, he had left the money accumulating in Geneva at the end of the mission. Now he was taking deep breaths, exhaling through his nostrils like a bull, while he waited at the counter for the clerk to return.

But Steve's account was intact. His money, nearly a hundred thousand dollars was neatly noted in the credit column.

'See,' he said to Avner, almost accusingly, probably because he was so relieved, 'it's there! It's all there.'

Avner nodded and walked out of the bank. He kept walking, followed by Steve. At the quay he sat on a bench, staring at the rippling waves of the Rhône. Steve kept saying, 'Don't panic' and 'Don't worry' but Avner only nodded and said nothing. He could hardly breathe. There was a sharp pain in his stomach as though someone had run him through with a thin blade. He looked at his hands as if they belonged to someone else: they were trembling. His lips were trembling. For a few seconds he could feel his entire body quivering. He wanted to cry.

'Can you believe it?' he said to Steve finally, pulling himself together.

'Maybe it's a misunderstanding,' Steve said. 'Maybe they took it out because . . . if you're quitting, maybe they want to give you a cheque. Maybe . . .' He stopped because he sounded foolish, even to himself.

'I wish I knew who took that money out,' Avner said. 'Because I tell you, I'm now going to go and shoot every one of them.'

'Don't get excited,' Steve said.

Avner stared at him. 'Don't get excited?' he asked. 'That money is not theirs!'

'Wait. Don't.' His partner shook Avner by the shoulder. 'Come on, let's think for a second. Why don't you call them? Better still, get on a plane. Right now. Go back and talk to them.'

Avner was beginning to calm down. Yes. Of course. Go back to Israel. That was precisely what they would want him to do. That was what the whole thing was about. 'Do you realize,' he said to Steve, 'that we owe them army service? We're reserve officers. How long since you've done your stint? In my unit it's two months a year.'

'You don't think . . .' Steve started, but Avner interrupted him.

'They could keep me for over a year. Legally. Until I do what they want. Meantime, what is Shoshana going to do in New York with the kid? With no money?'

'I'll go for you,' Steve said. 'I'll talk to them.'

Avner wasn't surprised that Steve should make the offer: they had been partners. 'No,' he said to him. 'Thank you. You shouldn't get involved. You have your relationship with them, and I have mine. Thanks,' he repeated. 'I'll figure something out.'

'Where are you going to go?' Steve asked.

'Back to New York,' Avner said, and he did, taking the first available Swissair flight, and calling Shoshana on the phone from Kennedy airport. He had to call her to pick him up: he did not have enough money for a taxi.

They still had some money in Shoshana's bank account. About two hundred dollars.

It was on the drive back from the airport that he told Shoshana. He had to tell her: it affected both of them. It affected Geula.

'But how can they do that?' Shoshana asked. 'It's not right.'

'I know it's not right,' Avner replied. 'But they did it. Mind you, maybe they didn't. My partner said maybe they're sending the money to me here.' Avner offered this to Shoshana without conviction, just to make things appear less bleak for the moment, but Shoshana wasn't buying it.

'Do you believe they'd give you the money after they took it out of there?' she asked him. 'I don't.'

'No point in getting upset for the moment,' Avner said. 'Anyway, I can always say to Ephraim: you win. Where's the new mission?'

They were still driving when Avner said that, with Shoshana at the wheel. The next thing she did was to swerve to the kerb, braking so hard that Avner nearly smashed his nose against the windshield. 'You say that to Ephraim,' Shoshana said with flashing eyes, 'and the first chance I get, I'll pin your legs against a wall with the car. See how much use you are to Ephraim with a cast up to your hips.'

She meant every word of it. Avner could see that.

'Easy,' he said to her, impressed by the bolt of lightning that she was at that moment, striking so unexpectedly. 'We have to live on something. We have no money, no papers, no jobs. Besides, we're Israelis, we are still at war. Maybe they need me.'

'Not like this,' Shoshana said. 'If you wanted to go, I wouldn't say a word. I never did. I never even asked you a question. Do you think I didn't know – I mean I didn't *know* –

but do you think I didn't know what you were doing? What do you think it was like, waiting for you with the baby? And I said nothing. I'm a *sabra* and I married a soldier, that's what I said to myself.

'But not like this. I'd rather scrub floors. They're not forcing you to go anywhere.'

'Okay, we'll see,' Avner said. 'Just start up the car.'

Shoshana looked at him, and began pulling away from the kerb. 'I mean what I say,' she said. 'You don't know me yet.'

For about ten days Avner heard nothing from anyone and he made no inquiries himself. He wasn't even sure whom to contact or where to start asking questions, short of going back to Israel. In the past he would always have a designated channel of communication: a phone number, a safe deposit box, a station chief somewhere. Now there was only Ephraim in Tel Aviv. There was no point in calling Ephraim except to say that he was giving in. And he was not prepared to do that.

They moved to the new apartment because the first month was already paid for and they had given notice at the old building. As the new place was only a few blocks away, they kept the same phone number.

A couple of days after they had moved, the telephone rang. It was one of the security officers at the Israeli Consulate in New York.

'There's a letter for you here,' the security man said. 'You'll have to come here to read it.'

'Can't you just mail it?' Avner asked.

'No. That letter has to stay here. You come in and read it.'

Maybe Steve was right. Maybe it was a cheque, after all. Avner took the subway to Manhattan the following morning.

It was not a cheque. It was a one-page document that had evidently arrived in a pouch with the rest of the diplomatic mail. It simply stated that although a date had been set for Avner's return to Israel (which, as Avner said immediately to the security man, was a fucking lie) Avner had not returned.

From this omission they concluded, the document continued, that Avner had voluntarily resigned (the document didn't say from what) and that such a resignation amounted to a breach of contract. Under the circumstances there were no monies due to Avner, but they wished him good luck in the future, stamped and signed by someone indecipherable in the personnel department.

Avner turned over the piece of paper but there was nothing on the other side.

The security man reached out and took the document from Avner's hand, then pushed a ledger across to him. 'Just sign here,' he said, 'that you have read it.'

'What do you mean?' Avner asked. 'I need a copy.'

'There are no copies to this,' said the man. 'Just sign here that you have seen it and I'll countersign it.'

'I haven't seen it,' Avner said, his colour rising.

'Come on,' said the security man, 'don't give me heart trouble. I only work here. Just sign it on this line.'

'You make me sign it,' Avner said. The security officer made no move. 'Thanks anyway,' said Avner, and he walked out of the Consulate.

He was going home. There was to be no money, ever. In a curious way, he was actually feeling relieved. He didn't care about the hundred thousand dollars. Had he done what he did for a hundred thousand dollars? If it had been for money, he wouldn't have done it for a million. They didn't have to offer him this deal – or any deal. He had volunteered. He had done it because he was asked by the Prime Minister and the *memune* to go on a historic mission. In the presence of General Sharon, his early hero, who had said to Avner: *I wish they were asking me*. That's why he had said yes. He never asked them for a hundred thousand dollars. He asked them for nothing.

It was Ephraim who had told him what the deal was to be, as he had told Carl, Robert, Hans and Steve. He had said to them: 'Whenever you're in Switzerland, you can look at your account and see it grow.' Ephraim said it. Avner and his

393

partners would never have dreamed of asking him. It would never have crossed their minds.

And even now it wasn't the money. Yes, it would have been nice to let Shoshana keep the new Scandinavian furniture; it would have been a pleasure to look at her face when the Danish kitchen with the icemaker was delivered to her. Yes, he had spent hours looking at it in the window on the avenue Hoche; yes, he had even dreamt about it once. But it didn't matter. He wanted the money only so that he could do what he wanted: stay in America. Or go to Australia or to Europe. So that he wouldn't have to push paper in Israel just to feed Shoshana and the baby. Or chase the *mechablim* in South America or wherever. That was all that hundred thousand dollars was for. Nothing else. And now that he was going to quit anyway, now that both he and Shoshana were resolved to do it, the easy way or the hard way, to do it no matter what: what difference did that money make any more? They'd never had any money before, so they wouldn't have any money now. It was okay. It would take a Galicianer like Ephraim to believe that he could pull Avner like a puppet on a string of money.

Except for one additional problem.

Papers.

Avner had travelled for such a long time on false documents – documents supplied by the Mossad, or purchased on Mossad money, or made up by Hans during the mission – that the idea of legitimate papers and normal immigration procedures, with the endless, cumbersome bureaucracy they entailed, was quite alien to him. Outside the cosy shelter of diplomatic and service passports, in the real world of quotas and work permits and green cards – a world Avner, ironically enough, had never encountered during his travels – the atmosphere was very chilly.

Not being a landed immigrant in America, Avner could not seek employment. Yet the two hundred dollars in Shoshana's bank account would not take the family far in the summer of 1975. He had to earn some money. Like an illegal immigrant from Mexico, Avner had no choice. He joined the thousands of aliens exploited for the most menial tasks in America's vast underground economy.

He never thought of it as exploitation. On the contrary, he was grateful for the opportunity. If he wanted something to which he was not officially entitled – to live in America – for the time being he would have to do it on very unfavourable terms. That was fair enough. He didn't mind driving a cab or painting a house for less money than a landed immigrant; and he didn't mind doing it for longer hours. It was only that, while he was driving taxis or painting houses, he was slowly beginning to realize that he might be doing jobs like that for a lifetime.

After Paris, London and Rome. After the borrowed jet-set lifestyle of an agent. At twenty-eight, the most exhilarating, the most exciting, the most interesting part of his life was over. And he couldn't even talk about it. At the same age that other people would be looking forward to new experiences, new challenges, he would begin a gentle slide into obscurity. What could he ever do in his life to even approach the things he had done before?

It didn't matter. Avner kept telling himself that it didn't matter. But he also kept seeing his father, sitting in his deck chair, half asleep, with flies sitting on the rim of the glass of tepid orange juice beside him. Dozing, sitting, dreaming of rubies. Waiting for the phone to ring.

Avner's casual jobs were coming to him through the two or three contacts he had made on his previous trips to New York – a Jewish businessman in Queens, an *El Al* employee with a cousin in New Jersey – none of whom had the slightest inkling about his past. It was through his contacts that Avner met his immigration lawyer – a shrewd, skilled, elderly man, and not even Jewish – who had hit upon the idea of getting Shoshana's papers first. There would be a better chance to acquire landed immigrant status for her; for one thing, there were no holes in her employment history, the Mossad having arranged a nominal civilian job as a cover for her when she came to New York. Once Shoshana received her green card, it would be easier to get landed immigrant status for her husband.

Meanwhile, even though the risk of detection and deportation by the immigration authorities was slight, it could not be discounted altogether. In a macabre way the thought was even amusing: after years of leading one of the most daring operations in Europe, *Israeli ex-Agent Caught for Pushing Illegal Hack in Manhattan*. It would have been the ultimate irony.

Stubborn and obstinate as Avner was, determined as both he and Shoshana had become not to admit defeat; to stick it out no matter what; to starve rather than crawl back to those who, as far as Avner was concerned, had cheated and betrayed him, he would later admit that during the next seven difficult months he was more than once on the brink of doing just that. If Ephraim had called him again, saying . . . saying anything. *It was a misunderstanding. Do one more job and you'll get your money. Come back to Israel and we'll pay you there.* If Ephraim had held out a carrot it might have worked. It showed weakness, and Avner hated to admit it, but it was the truth.

But Ephraim held out no carrot. Instead, he chose a stick.

It happened in November, after 1 am one night. Avner wasn't yet asleep, but he was already lying in bed beside Shoshana with the lights out. He heard the car stop outside the house, but he thought nothing of it. A few seconds later the doorbell rang.

Shoshana woke up.

Avner put his finger to his lips, so she said nothing, but almost instinctively she got out of bed and went to the cot where Geula was sleeping. Making no noise, Avner approached the window. He did not touch the curtain and did not turn on the light. Squinting, he tried to look into the street through a

396

narrow opening between the curtain and the window frame. Charlie woke up as well but, cleverly taking his cue from the silence of his masters, he did not bark. Instead, he put his paws on the window sill beside Avner, trying to look through the same opening.

The bell didn't ring again. Avner could see a man – evidently the one who had rung the doorbell – getting back into the driver's seat of a small car which had been parked in front of the duplex with its lights on. It was a Japanese car. The man himself looked like – it was hard to tell. He could have been anything. Not Arab, though, not black and not Oriental. He was a Caucasian.

Avner was certain that he did not know him. He was also certain that no one he knew would ring his doorbell at 1 am. The immigration authorities would not send out a lone officer in a foreign car and an immigration officer would definitely ring more than once. It had to be something else.

The Japanese car took off. Whatever the man wanted, Avner thought, he wasn't very clever at his business. He hadn't scouted the street before ringing the bell. If he had, he would have first turned his car around. The duplex happened to be on a dead-end street. The way the man was heading, he would now have to turn around and come back the same way before he could leave the area. Avner could easily intercept him. Get his licence number at least.

He drew back the curtain.

The Japanese car came roaring down the street with its lights out. It seemed that on realizing he had to turn around and drive by again, the man at the wheel at least had the good sense to turn off the illumination on his licence plate. Avner couldn't see the number. The car looked like a late model Toyota.

Five minutes later the telephone rang.

'There's a message for you on the door,' said a male voice when Avner picked up the receiver. The caller hung up immediately. He had spoken in fluent English, but Avner thought he could discern an accent. A familiar accent. It would not have surprised him if the caller's native language had been Hebrew.

Avner decided to play it safe. He did not think the 'message' would explode, but why take chances? Groping around his front door in the dark he would present a perfect target for an ambush, whether by a radio-controlled bomb or by a gun. Why risk it? He could wait until morning to look at whatever the man had left on his door.

'It's nothing,' he said to Shoshana. 'Go back to sleep.'

But he didn't sleep much himself.

When it was daylight and people began to appear in the street, Avner got dressed and left the house through the back door. He walked around the block, observed nothing suspicious, then came back to his front entrance. He could immediately see the small envelope tucked in between the door frame and the door. It looked harmless; too small and thin for a letter bomb. Still, he handled it gingerly. It seemed all right: the paper wasn't spongy, it didn't sweat, it didn't smell of marzipan.

Cautiously, Avner opened it. There was nothing in it but a snapshot of his daughter. Avner recognized the particular picture which he himself had taken sometime in the summer. It was the only print. They had kept the negatives, but for the sake of economy, had had only one set of prints developed to send to Shoshana's parents in Israel. The snapshot in the envelope must have come from that series. There were no other copies.

The picture showed Avner's daughter in a close-up, head cocked to one side, facing the camera quizzically. Two of her fingers were stuck firmly in her mouth.

Someone had drawn four concentric circles over her forehead, with an inky dot in the centre. A perfect target.

His daughter.

Avner tried to remain calm.

It couldn't be the *mechablim*. If they had found him, they wouldn't warn him. There would be nothing to warn him about. They would try to kill him perhaps, or even kill his wife and daughter, but they wouldn't be sending him snap-shots with targets drawn over them.

They couldn't even get hold of this particular snapshot. No one could. No one could, except . . .

This was a snapshot they had sent to Israel. To *Israel*.

He had no choice: he had to show it to Shoshana. 'This is it,' he said to her. 'I'm going back. This will be settled, one way or another.'

'No,' she said. 'I'm not letting you go. We can hide. I don't care. You're not going. I'll make a scandal. I'll call the *New York Times*.'

'Easy,' Avner said. 'Let me think. You know, I don't even think it's *them*. I mean, not my case officer. Maybe some local asshole who wants to be a hero. If I go back and tell them . . .'

'No,' said Shoshana. 'I don't care who it is. Once you're back, you're back. Your case officer, nothing! Maybe he'll say "Sorry, I know nothing about it. But since you're here, we have some unfinished business." You think I don't know them? I know them better than you.'

Avner looked at his wife in amazement. She was right, of course. She was absolutely right. It was exactly what Ephraim would say, whether he was telling the truth or not. Whether it had been his idea, or somebody else's.

'We have to let her go to the kindergarten,' he said. 'We can't keep an eye on her day and night; we both have to work. I don't think they'll try anything, but they might. Not to hurt her, I'm sure, but . . . if they take her back, we'll have no choice. Let me think.

'I'm going to call my brother. I'll have Ber come here and stay with us.'

'But how will you pay for his ticket?' Shoshana asked.

'Don't worry,' Avner said. 'I'll get the money.'

He got the money by the simple expedient of borrowing it from his friend, the owner of the taxi he drove, promising to pay him back in weekly instalments. Little brother, Mother's favourite, was by then twenty-one years old; he had just finished his military service. Avner could hardly think of him in any other way but as the tow-headed scrawny kid *he* was supposed to babysit for while he was doing his stint in the army. He'd come home for a two-day leave, and Mother would say: 'Do me a favour, stay with your brother this afternoon, let me do some shopping. Only for a few hours.'

Ber arrived as scheduled. He looked exactly like Father, Avner thought, the way Avner himself wouldn't have minded looking: blond, blue-eyed, more German than a German. Only he wasn't very tall; Father, in his prime, had been taller. But little brother was in tip-top shape: broad shoulders dropping seven inches to his narrow waist, a cocky grin on his rather thin, arrogant lips. The boy loved New York, still seemed to worship Avner, and didn't mind baby-sitting for Geula.

Two weeks later he came home, not exactly white in the face, but quite shaken. He came home holding Geula tightly by the hand, and told Avner the following story.

As he was waiting for his niece to come out of the kindergarten, only a few steps from the main door, a foreign-made car suddenly pulled up and two young men got out. As Geula came out with the rest of the children and started running towards him, the two young men made a move. One of them stood in front of him, and the other tried to snatch up the little girl.

'Then what happened?' Avner asked, controlling his voice.

'A couple of policemen were coming down the street behind me,' Ber said. 'They had just turned a corner, I didn't even see them. I only knew because the guy in front of me shouted to the other one "Police!" and they both got back into the car.'

'He shouted "Police"?'

'That's the funny thing,' his brother replied. 'The guy shouted "Police!" in Hebrew.'

Neither Avner nor Shoshana had told Ber anything about Avner's problems with the Mossad. He knew nothing. His story could not have been the reaction of an overactive imagination to a known danger. Avner had warned him to watch out for his niece like a hawk only because there was a lot of street crime in New York, including kidnappers and child molesters.

Not the kind of warning to elicit a story about two young men shouting 'Police!' in Hebrew.

It had to be, as far as Avner was concerned, what actually had happened.

There could be only one explanation for it.

And only one response.

Avner started working on it. For the next week he worked, doing everything alone. This was an operation he had to do by himself. He told no one about it, not even Shoshana. He worked slowly, carefully, methodically. He worked exactly as 'they' had taught him to work, leaving no traces, arousing no suspicions, observing everything without being observed. He had never done a better job, and a week later he was ready.

At 10 am on a Tuesday in January, 1976 he walked into the Israeli Consulate.

'You have a nerve,' said the security officer when Avner walked through the door, followed by a protesting secretary. 'You have a nerve to walk in here like this. Or maybe you've come back to give me your signature?'

Avner took an envelope from his pocket and put it on the desk.

'Please let me talk,' he said to the man. 'When I finish you can talk. You can say anything you want. But before you open your mouth, let me finish.

'You guys tried to kidnap my daughter. Maybe you know something about it, maybe you don't. Maybe you had something to do with it because it's a New York operation. Maybe you didn't. I don't care. You're the guy I know. I hold you responsible.'

Avner opened the envelope and took out six snapshots of children. He spread them out in front of the security officer.

401

The kids in the pictures ranged from four to maybe seven. Two of them were boys and four were girls, in black-and-white telephoto action shots, taken in playgrounds, schoolyards and in the street. 'Do you know them?' Avner asked the man. 'You should know one at least, because she is yours.'

The man said nothing. He was staring at the pictures.

'You guys work here,' Avner said. 'You live in nice houses. Your kids go to nice schools. You see, I know where you live and I know where your children go to school.

'I don't much care about myself,' Avner continued, 'but please make sure nothing happens to my daughter. If you're smart, you'll post guards. You make sure nothing happens to her even by accident. Do you understand me? You make sure she doesn't even fall off a swing in the playground. Because I'll hold you responsible. If anything happens to my daughter I will get every one of your kids, and you should know: I'm dead serious.'

The security man found his voice, even if it was a little shaky.

'I know nothing about what happened to your daughter,' he said, spreading his hands. 'Believe me.'

'You believe *me*,' Avner replied. 'You know, you don't know; I don't care. Somebody knows. So do yourself a favour and spread the word. Show the pictures around. Tell them what I said to you.'

Avner stood up, and the security officer rose with him. 'Listen, you're crazy,' the man said. 'You should see a doctor. I'm telling you, you're imagining things.' He kept talking as he followed Avner to the doorway. Avner said nothing, but as he opened the door he turned back.

'You're young,' he said to the security man, 'and you don't know everything. You don't even know me too well. Please tell some other people about this. Don't try to deal with it on your own.'

Avner left the Consulate. He made no attempt to move or change his family's routine. For about another month he

402

received no calls, no letters. There were no further incidents. Then one day he got a phone call from an old acquaintance in *El Al* security. In a past that seemed so distant it might have been a hundred years ago, they had been sky marshals together.

'They asked me to call you,' the man said. 'Can you go to the hotel in Manhattan on Friday? Same room as before, at 10 am? Somebody wants to meet you.'

It had to be Ephraim.

'Yes,' Avner replied. 'Tell him I'll be there.'

Ephraim didn't offer to shake his hand when he opened the door of his hotel room on Friday. He stood aside to let Avner enter, then turned his back on him and walked to the window. 'There is only one reason I wanted to see you,' he said to Avner without turning around. 'I wanted to ask you one question. How low do you think we'd stoop?'

Avner didn't answer. Ephraim turned around to look at him.

'Do you think we kidnap little girls?' he asked. 'Do you think you're talking about the *mechablim*? You're talking about your *country*!'

As far as Avner was concerned, it was a good performance. It was exactly what he had expected.

'Where is my money?' he asked Ephraim.

'Your money!' Ephraim came closer to Avner, looking at him as if he were seeing him for the first time, looking at him in total astonishment. 'It's your money you want to talk with me about? What has happened to you?'

'Maybe I'm getting older,' Avner said. 'Maybe I'm getting a little smarter.'

'I don't believe I'm talking to you,' Ephraim said. 'I don't believe I'm talking to an Israeli, *any* Israeli, never mind a man of your training, your background. A man of your family, a son of your father, your mother. What would your mother say if she could hear you saying such things?'

Avner got angry. 'My mother would talk exactly the way

you talk,' he said to Ephraim, 'because she wouldn't know any better. You do.'

'Excuse me,' said Ephraim, 'maybe I'm very naïve. Maybe I'm a very simple guy, because I don't know any better myself. Maybe I should come to America and learn from you. Maybe every guy should demand some money before he gets into a tank. Maybe we should distribute stock certificates before every parachute jump. Good idea, I'll suggest it. I'll give you credit, I'll tell them it came from you!

'Do you think you were the only guy on a dangerous mission?' Ephraim started pacing, warming to his subject. 'Do you think you did anything special? Do you remember anything about the history of your country? Do you know how many people did far more dangerous things, under far worse conditions? Do you know how many people lost limbs, how many people died?

'Do you think that's what Israel's money is for, to provide for your happy retirement? Your partner doesn't think so, he's still working. Nobody's asking you to be a hero, if you haven't got the guts. Just come back and pull your weight, like everybody else. Then, maybe, we'll talk about money.'

Ephraim fell silent, waiting for Avner to speak, but Avner said nothing. After an interminable silence Ephraim finally said: 'Well – shall we just call it quits?'

'First let me ask you one question,' Avner said. 'Way back, three years ago, why did you select me?'

Ephraim snorted. 'Good question,' he said derisively. 'I wish I knew the answer. But I can tell you what we thought. We thought – that's what the guys in your unit said – that you never give up. That maybe you're not too strong and you're not too fast, but you run forever. When the big guys and the fast guys are lying on their backs, you're still running.

'That's what your commander said. You're obstinate. And we thought maybe we wanted an obstinate fellow.'

'Well, if you thought I was obstinate,' Avner said, 'why did you think I'd stop asking for my money? Why did you

404

think I'd let you cheat me and lie to me, and let you threaten my family? If I'm supposed to be obstinate.'

'There's no talking to you,' Ephraim said, turning red in the face. 'You keep coming back to your money. It turns out you did everything for money.'

'You look me in the eye when you say that,' Avner said, 'because you know I asked for nothing. None of us did. You promised. And now you owe me, that's all. Not because of what I did, but because you promised. I don't know why you did, maybe because you don't have faith in anybody, because you trust no one – isn't that the truth? – but you promised.'

'You promised, you promised,' Ephraim said, 'you're like a five-year-old! I've never met anybody like you. You say you didn't do it for money, so what's your problem? You didn't do it for money and you got none. You should be happy.'

For a second Avner stared at Ephraim, and then he started to laugh. He couldn't help it. What Ephraim had just said was exactly like a joke, an old joke, that he remembered his father telling many years ago, when he was still a boy, when they were still living in Rehovot.

A Galicianer and a Yekke were sharing a plate of cakes and there were only two pieces left, a big one and a small one. 'You choose,' said the Yekke, and the Galicianer took the big piece without hesitation.

'That's typical,' the Yekke said.

'Why, what would you have done?' asked the Galicianer with his mouth full.

'I would have taken the smaller piece, of course,' said the Yekke.

'Well, what are you complaining about?' the Galicianer asked. 'That's what you got.'

That was just an old joke, but this was reality. As far as Avner could see, it was the story of the Galicianers running Israel. There was nothing more to be said. He continued looking at Ephraim, his shoulders shaking with suppressed laughter. 'What are you tittering about?' Ephraim asked, taken aback, but Avner only shook his head.

'I guess that's what happens when we give big jobs to little men,' Ephraim said. He now sounded genuinely offended.

'No, you're wrong,' Avner replied, making towards the door. 'That's what happens when you *cheat* little men. You need really big men to close their eyes when you cheat them. Like my father maybe. Little men are not big enough.'

'I see you're going,' Ephraim said, 'and I will not detain you. Let's just forget about our differences. You don't have to worry about your daughter, your wife. Good luck to you in America, or wherever you end up. We thank you for everything you have done for Israel. *Shalom*.'

'*Shalom*,' Avner replied, closing the door. It was an easy word to say. Peace, peace, but was there to be any peace?

He wished he could see into the future.

EPILOGUE

———————∿∿∿———————

THIS CONVERSATION in the early spring of 1976 was not the last contact Avner would have with his one-time superiors. However, it effectively brought those matters which are the subject of this account to a conclusion. Avner retired from all clandestine activities; changed his name and domicile; and to the best of my knowledge now lives with his family somewhere in North America.

My only information on his surviving partner 'Steve' is that he has, to this day, continued serving his country within the ranks of one of its security organizations.

The three terrorist leaders Avner's team did not succeed in finding in the course of the mission – Ali Hassan Salameh, Abu Daoud, and Dr Wadi Haddad – remained active in the terror network for varying lengths of time. Dr Haddad, whose 1975 split from George Habash's organization may or may not have been genuine, continued masterminding major acts of international terrorism until early 1978. At that time he entered an East German hospital where he died a few months later, reportedly of natural causes. As an organizer he was probably without equal during the terrorist decade. It is possible that his militancy grew to exceed that of his one-time partner Dr Habash, and it resulted in their much-publicized parting of the ways in 1975. It is equally possible that his relationship with Dr Habash had merely turned clandestine in the manner of the relationship between Black September and Al Fatah. There is no evidence that Dr Haddad's death in East Germany was due to anything but its publicly stated cause: cancer.

Abu Daoud (Mohammed Daoud Odeh) was shot in the

lobby of a hotel in Poland, though not fatally, on 1 August, 1981. Published reports have suggested that the man who attempted to assassinate Daoud – and who somehow managed to escape after the attempt – was an Israeli agent. If true, this raises the interesting question of whether the Israeli secret service has become audacious enough to extend its operations – other than information gathering – into Soviet-bloc countries; places that used to be strictly off-limits in the days of Avner's team and consequently safe havens for terrorists. Operating counter-terrorist teams in totalitarian countries, where even ordinary activities such as renting apartments, checking in and out of hotels, and leasing vehicles are minutely scrutinized and often severely restricted, is extremely difficult. Also, if captured, agents cannot expect to rely on legal safeguards and civilized restraints that protect even suspected spies or terrorists in Western democracies. The international repercussions of such operations might also be unusually severe; Soviet retaliation against countries that engineer hostile penetration might be far more forceful than the response of Western nations under similar circumstances.

In the light of this, an unconfirmed report according to which Abu Daoud was indeed shot by an Israeli agent, but one who acted impulsively on noticing the infamous terrorist in a hotel rather than one whose mission in Poland was to assassinate him, makes a certain amount of sense. Though it could be argued that carefully selected and trained agents are unlikely to act outside the perimeters of their missions, there have been enough examples of agents doing so to make this no less likely than a fundamental change of Israeli policy concerning operations inside the Soviet bloc. (It is also possible that the attempt on Abu Daoud's life, in spite of reports to the contrary, was the result of a squabble within the Palestinian movement – the Israelis point the finger at the Abu Nidal's Black June – or that it was set up by the KGB.) The only fact that can be stated with certainty is that Abu Daoud was shot and wounded in Poland.

All published accounts speak with equal certainty about the assassination of Ali Hassan Salameh on 22 January, 1979, in Beirut. Reportedly, attempts on Salameh's life continued throughout the 1970s. Richard Deacon, in his book *The Israeli Secret Service*, described two earlier attempts, one in 1975 and one on 7 October, 1976, the first of which – an Israeli sniper in Beirut firing through a window with a telescopic rifle – succeeded only in putting a bullet through a dummy of a human figure. The 1976 attempt, in Deacon's version, resulted in Salameh being critically wounded; other sources, such as David B. Tinnin, report only the wounding of one of Salameh's friends.

However, on 22 January, 1979, Salameh and several of his bodyguards were blown up when his Chevrolet station wagon passed a parked Volkswagen at 3.30 pm near the corner of Beirut's rues Verdun and Madame Curie. Apparently such an assassination became possible because Salameh, who had been an exceptionally wily target, adopted a more routine lifestyle after his 1978 marriage to the former (1971) Miss Universe: a Lebanese beauty named Georgina Rizak. In accordance with traditional Muslim practice, Salameh did not divorce his first wife, and he began travelling with some predictability between PLO headquarters, the home of his first wife and two children, and Georgina's apartment in the rue Verdun.

What he did not know was that his movements were reportedly observed by an Israeli agent, masquerading as an eccentric cat-loving English spinster under the name of Erika Mary 'Penelope' Chambers. She had taken an apartment not far from Georgina Salameh's in the rue Verdun. Some other Israeli agents rented a Volkswagen, loaded it with explosives, and parked it on Salameh's daily route to his new wife's apartment. Then, according to one source, 'Penelope' planted a small radio transmitter under the fender of Salameh's station wagon or (according to another source) pressed the button on her own radio transmitter when she saw Salameh's car passing the parked Volkswagen in the street below her window. Either way, the Volkswagen blew up, demolishing Salameh's car and the Landrover of his bodyguards following it, as well as killing or injuring several passers-by.

Salameh's death was officially announced by the PLO and duly reported by Israeli television news. His funeral was attended by Yasser Arafat, and the world press gave wide currency to a photograph of the Palestinian leader at the ceremony, standing with his arm around Salameh's exceptionally handsome thirteen-year-old son, Hassan. 'We have lost a lion,' Arafat was quoted as saying. Stewart Steven's *The Spymasters of Israel*, published in 1980, describes Salameh's assassination in some detail, and a 1983 book by the Israeli authors Michael Bar-Zohar and Eitan Haber, *The Quest for the Red Prince*, is partly devoted to recounting the same story.

The facts surrounding the explosion of Salameh's Chevrolet on 22 January, 1979, in Beirut seem beyond dispute. An unconfirmed rumour, however, insists that Salameh did not perish in the explosion for the simple reason that he was not in the car when it blew up. (The explosion resulted in enough mangled bodies to make this at least a theoretical possibility.)

This rumour is most likely to be a continuation of the Salameh legend, expressing only a wishful myth. Such myths often spring up around the memory of a revolutionary figure, especially one whose existence has been shrouded in mystery during his lifetime and who was known to have escaped death on many other occasions. At the same time, if Salameh was not in his station wagon that day (a fairly routine deception), the Palestinians as well as the Israelis would have their own reasons for pretending to a belief in his death. From the Palestinians' point of view, nothing would keep Salameh safer than the Israelis' conviction that they had already succeeded in killing him. The Mossad, for its part, might try to convince the Palestinians that Israel had been successfully misled, so as to give Salameh, if he *is* still alive, a feeling of false security.

Such games of deception have been known to continue between opposing intelligence services *ad infinitum* – though it is also true that, no matter how convoluted reality may be, rumours have a way of being more convoluted still. The only known facts are that Salameh's car did blow up, killing several people travelling in it, and that both Palestinians and Israelis took the public stand that the terrorist leader was among the victims.

In the notes, I have outlined some instances where my information has been at variance with information reported elsewhere. When recounting activities which, by their very nature, had to be conducted in secrecy – and where subsequent information may be freely extended to reporters for the sole purpose of deception – it would be rash to claim greater accuracy for information gathered by oneself than for information gathered by others.

Added difficulties arise when logic or common sense can no longer be relied on to test the truth of any reported event, since even the most illogical or senseless reports can turn out to be factual. This is especially true in the underworld of political terror. To mention only one example, the careful and conscientious French journalist Serge Groussard, no doubt on the basis of information vouchsafed to him by normally reliable sources, held Mahmoud Hamshari responsible for the 'execution' of Wael Zwaiter as part of a Black September operation.[1] Untrue as this piece of information happened to be – and even unlikely on the face of it, given that Hamshari and Zwaiter were comrades-in-arms – it may have appeared perfectly credible in 1973, when Groussard first reported it, given the terrorists' penchant for killing each other in factional squabbles.

It is with this note of caution – and not to contradict other reports but as a matter of interest – that I feel obliged to point out a few further discrepancies.

To begin with, it is my understanding that the code name 'Wrath of God' which the Israelis are alleged to have given to their counter-terrorist operation following the Munich massacre – and which is almost uniformly reported by Western journalists, including Claire Sterling, Edgar O'Ballance, Richard Deacon, Christopher Dobson and Ronald Payne, David B. Tinnin, and others – may have been invented after the fact, either by Western reporters or their Israeli informants. It was not recognized as the code in use at the time of the mission by my sources. (Interestingly, the two Israeli writers, Michael Bar-Zohar and Eitan Haber, do not mention it in their book.)

The code names 'Mike', 'Tamar', and 'Jonathan Ingleby' – one or more of which is used by several writers in describing the Zwaiter and Boudia assassinations as well as the incidents at Lillehammer – are not recognized by my sources. While 'Ingleby' might have been an assumed identity used by an agent in Lillehammer, there was no such false passport in use, either in Rome or in Paris. 'Tamar' – supposedly the beautiful blonde girlfriend of the team leader, described as being involved in the Zwaiter hit and as personally pulling the trigger in Lillehammer – has the aura of pure invention. (Not necessarily by the authors describing her, but by their informants.) My understanding is that the claim of General Zvi Zamir's physical presence during the Zwaiter and Boudia hits is similarly baseless, while his presence in Lillehammer is unlikely. Along with 'Tamar' the blonde hit-woman, the personal attendance of the head of the Mossad at the scene of various assassinations in Europe smacks of out-and-out fiction. It is, however, not uncharacteristic that such audacious fiction should be fostered by the 'public-relations' sections of the Mossad.

In fairness, the difficulty facing the researcher in this field is considerable, and it may even lead to the initial rejection of information that is later proved to be accurate. To use an example from my own research, the name of Wael Zwaiter's Australian woman friend in Rome was originally given to me as 'Jeanette von Braun'. Since the name sounded highly improbable, and it was quoted to me from memory, I decided not to include it in this account unless I could verify it in some way. Finding no trace of the name in the newspaper files, I decided to leave it out. The book was already completed when I found independent verification of von Braun's name, in time to note it here.

Though hardly of earth-shattering importance, such details illustrate the problems all writers face when dealing with matters that cannot be verified by a phone call. With this understanding I add that, according to my information, no one pretended to be a plumber to intercept Hamshari's telephone line; and the bomb was not placed in the base of the telephone in 'full sight' of Hamshari or his bodyguards by someone pretending to be a phone repairman, as reported by one source.

Turning to more important matters, though I have tried to keep my assessment of Avner in the background throughout this book, at this point it may be of some interest to note my own impressions of him.

During our meetings I found him to be a man of two distinct physical moods: an imperturbable, almost indolent calm, alternating – practically without warning – with a sudden, lizard-like agility. For an Israeli he has very few gestures. Talking or listening, he is relaxed and all but motionless; however, when he moves it is with a quick single-mindedness that can best be described as reptilian. The impression is of one who does not think too long before he acts – who leads without turning to check if others are following. ('How would you get into that building?' I asked him once in Europe, pointing to a restricted zone. 'Like this,' he replied, and in the next minute he was walking through the door.) He is meticulous in his personal habits, to the point of having an almost spit-and-polish military air about him, and he tends to be thoughtful and generous in social dealings.

Though he claims to be satisfied with the sedate, peaceful life of the family man, there remains in him a 'craving for the high' (an expression I borrow from the forensic psychiatrist,

Andrew I. Malcolm) that the nine-to-five routine of the ordinary citizen could hardly fulfil. Surreptitious activities may now be against his expressed wishes as well as his considered judgment but there clearly remains in him a longing for experiences filled with tension. Consequently I do not credit his claim that he became a counter-terrorist solely because of the high premium put on patriotism by his peers in the kibbutz, in the army, in his own family and in Israel in general, though I have no doubt that it was a factor.

I do accept that the hope of financial reward was not a motive; nor would he have derived any unhealthy satisfaction from exercising physical force over others. That he readily became a counter-terrorist can be explained by other needs. His innately adventurous personality required an element of danger for simple equilibrium (a personality type commonly observed among sky divers, motorcycle racers, etc.); he also had a high degree of competitiveness which could find no outlet through any other gift or ability.

Such personality traits do not disappear with the opportunity to exercise them. A person who needs to shine, a person who requires tension or danger just to be on an even keel, will not lose these needs when circumstances or his better judgment remove him from the conditions where he can fulfil them, not even if he has lost the nerve or will required to indulge in their fulfilment. The problem is even worse if it arises at an unnaturally early age, as with professional athletes, for instance. In Avner's case, it seems likely to me that his main reason for recounting his experiences was to enable him to relive them.

Avner's present views on his mission are devoid of second thoughts or regrets. He claims not to have ever had any personal feelings of enmity for the men he killed or helped to kill, but continues to regard their physical elimination as something demanded by necessity and honour. He fully supports the decision that sent him and his partners on their mission, and has absolutely no qualms about anything they did.

While as convinced as he ever was about the rightness of

the mission, he no longer has any opinion on its usefulness. He concedes that it has in no way eliminated terrorism or diminished hatreds and tensions in the world, but on the whole he feels that more innocent people would have become victims of terrorist acts in Israel and in Western Europe if his team and other teams had not killed some top terrorist organizers during the 1970s. He regards the shooting of the young *fedayeen* foot soldiers in Switzerland and Spain as regrettable but unavoidable under the circumstances. He has no regrets about the killing of the woman assassin in Holland. If anything, had she not died at the time, he would be ready even today to hunt her down on his own.

Though Avner feels a deep sense of personal loss over the deaths of his partners – and is capable of being moved to tears when recounting the circumstances – he does not feel responsible for what happened to them. The only exception is 'Carl'. In that instance, he believes, his desire to avoid conflict with a much admired senior man could have clouded his judgment as a leader, but he is quick to point out that neither his partners nor his case officer blamed or censured him. As a nominal leader of ranking agents he was not expected to exercise control over their personal affairs. He was merely the first among equals. Owing to the nature of the mission, the leader was not even in sole control of operations. At no time were any risks undertaken by anyone at his orders alone, as they might be in the army, but only through decisions participated in by all.

Though he feels wronged, and his confidence in the honesty of Israel's 'Galicianer' power-elite is thoroughly shaken – he now believes that they demand full loyalty but return none, and cynically use trusting and enthusiastic young people as pawns with no regard for their feelings and welfare – his overall patriotism as an Israeli remains undiminished. Contemplating every conflict, past or present, he unequivocally takes Israel's side. As between Israel and her enemies, he stands squarely with his own country. He even concedes that the power-elite may be guided by equally

415

patriotic impulses, but argues that Israel's real interests are no longer served by their clannish, ruthless and self-seeking ways. He allows that it is perhaps in the nature of all government agencies engaged in clandestine work to be cynical and ruthless – with their own employees as well as with outsiders – and that it was probably foolish of him to expect anything else.

When he has nightmares – very infrequently – they centre around his childhood in the kibbutz. He has virtually no tense dreams about the army or the Six Day War, and none whatever about the mission.

Conditioned as most of us are to the myths that have built up around modern intelligence agencies such as the KGB, the CIA and, especially, the Mossad, the question arises as to why such an ordinary young man was sent to head such an extraordinary operation. In addition to the myths, this feeling is reinforced by fictional representations of super-agents – the James Bonds and Smileys – whose colourful, many-sided, highly accomplished personalities have become part of our cultural expectations. On one level we know that the fictional agent who combined the worldliness of Machiavelli with the knightly virtues of King Arthur is merely the figment of someone's imagination. On another level, if we encounter a person who presumes to operate on James Bond's turf, yet falls noticeably short of his accomplishments, we feel cheated.

Unless he is a monstrous psychopath. That is another archetype we find acceptable. We are conditioned to the cold, inscrutable killer, the Mafia hit-man, the goon. However, while both the brutal goon and the highly sophisticated and superbly motivated top agent may exist in real life, they (especially the latter) are in a minority. Despite the fiction and despite the myth, my fairly systematic reading of the record leads me to believe that most employees of intelligence bureaucracies – including the Mossad, legends notwithstanding – are quite ordinary people. This is routinely borne out by the facts whenever a clandestine operation is brought to light – whether it is Lillehammer or the famous

416

'Operation Suzanna' of the 1950s, where Israeli agents tried to sabotage Western installations in Egypt, hoping to blame it on Egyptian nationalists.

In the light of this it is not surprising that the leader of one of the Mossad's famous 'avenger' teams should turn out to be a person of fairly ordinary tastes, views, motivations and accomplishments. Unlike the KGB, the Mossad as a rule seems not to rely on criminal psychopaths even for its 'wet business' or 'dirty tricks' operations; partly, no doubt, because of the control and support they would require. It would be quite impractical to send five goons with Swiss bank accounts to hunt down terrorists on their own; they would have to be structured and supervised at every turn. At the same time budding Einsteins would not fulfil the role. Exceptional people generally choose to contribute to their societies in different ways – or in different capacities when (rarely) they make intelligence work their career. This leaves average, ordinary people to do the shooting.

Ironically, while they must be loyal and courageous, they may be chosen for their lack of outstanding qualities as much as for the qualities they do possess. It is evidently not desirable for them to be overly imaginative, fanatical or daring: too much imagination is conducive to doubts; too much fanaticism to instability; too much daring to incaution. At the risk of minimizing the problems involved, it seems that a counter-terrorist assassination team has to find answers to only two questions: how to locate the target, and how to get away after the hit. (The third question – how to do the hit – is generally determined by the answers to the first two.) The solution to the first question, almost invariably, comes through informers. The solution to the second question – getting away – represents 90 per cent of the difficulty and requires most of any team's preparatory and organizational skills.

It is mainly owing to the dynamics of modern, especially urban, societies that the second problem can be solved at all. The anonymity, mobility, and crowding of contemporary

417

communities – even outside the major population centres – is such that it breeds an indifference in bystanders and even in the authorities. Almost no one attracts anyone's attention. Coupled with an element of surprise and a reluctance to interfere in what has come to be regarded as somebody else's business, this generally permits surveillance before as well as escape after a hit. Few political killers – other than wilful kamikazes or crazed individuals acting on their own – are ever apprehended at the scene. Then, having withdrawn to their previously prepared places of safety, assassins, like their victims, become vulnerable to little else but betrayal by one of their own associates. Without such betrayal the risk of detection by the authorities is not very great.

In my opinion, the operational genius of the Mossad – and other agencies that act in a like manner – lies in the recognition of the essential simplicity of the task. The Mossad may have been led to this recognition by the terrorists themselves, whose main weapons have been audacity, self-confidence, reliance on surprise and speed, and the discovery that a single minute's time before or after an action – or the distance of a single block from its scene – would permit them to melt into the anonymity of a modern, free and mobile community. What the Mossad has evidently discovered is that these very factors, while they make the prevention of terrorism difficult, make terrorists equally vulnerable to counter-terrorists using the same tactics.

While it is likely that the Mossad has maintained different counter-terrorist teams trying out different methods of penetration, the second stroke of organizational genius seems to have been to use one team – Avner's – as a self-contained unit, supplied with nothing but a hit list and funds, to make its way in the underground of Europe in exactly the same way as any other small terrorist cell. This method has probably imitated most closely the way actual terrorist groups are launched and maintained by the various Arab or Soviet-bloc countries.

This approach – which may well have been experimental –

appears to have resulted in the impressive initial score, leading some researchers to suspect a complex and awesome organization as well as operatives of exceptional personal qualities behind it. The fact, however, seems to be that it was the audacious simplicity of using a few ordinary ex-commandos and agents with liberal funding and near complete autonomy that was responsible for the operation's success.

Turning to the question of the Mossad's treatment of its own agent, rights and wrongs become particularly blurred. Assuming the facts to be accurate, it would seem that, by ordinary standards, the agent was dishonestly treated. But is there not an underlying assumption, of which an agent ought to be aware, that one cannot 'quit' an intelligence service at will? Is there no claim to a higher loyalty? Is there no implied contract of obedience, no implied agreement to serve in minor or boring ways, after one is no longer willing to volunteer for dangerous work? Can an agent not be said to have broken his contract if he refuses? I'm not sure of the answer, but – while in human terms I can sympathize with the agent's disillusionment – I find it a reassuring indication of the Mossad's liberality that such a dispute could arise in the first place. No KGB agent could expect to oppose his masters in this manner – not if he wished to survive to tell the tale.

Beyond questions of right and wrong, a final point of interest may be the utility of counter-terrorism. In the end, did Avner's mission succeed or fail? It is often suggested that counter-terror solves nothing; it exacerbates rather than reduces underlying tensions; it increases rather than decreases terrorist incidents, and so on. These objections may well be true. Certainly almost a decade after Munich, during the period between August, 1980, and November, 1981, at least twenty acts of terrorism had been recorded by Arafat's Al Fatah, Abu Nidal's Black June, Saiqua, George Habash's Popular Front, and the latest 'Fifteenth of May Movement for the Liberation of Palestine', resulting in thirty-six dead and hundreds wounded in Paris, Beirut, Nairobi, Cairo, Buenos Aires, Istanbul, Vienna, Athens, Antwerp, and Rome. Yet it seems to me that the utility of counter-terrorism cannot be decided on the basis of what it solves or fails to solve. A clash of arms never 'solves' anything, short of a decisive military engagement like Waterloo, and even that may only postpone matters for a generation or two.

The tragic fact is that the maps of the world are drawn in blood. No borders have ever been settled except through victory or exhaustion, unless peace has been imposed on the warring parties by a superior force from outside. While the spirit of a struggle is alive, nations have no choice but to fight it every day, regardless of whether a day's battle 'solves' anything or not, because the only other choice is giving up and going under. It is hypocritical of older nations, which have drawn their own maps on the globe with the blood of their forefathers, to apply standards of restraint to younger countries – either of morals or of utility – which, had they been applied to themselves in the past, would have prevented their emergence or survival in the first place.

Saying this could be mistaken for the suggestion that there are no standards of restraint in warfare, but it is not the same thing at all. One can, in terms of moral justification, distinguish between counter-terrorism and terrorism in the same way one distinguishes between acts of war and war crimes. There are standards; terrorism is on the wrong side of them; counter-terrorism is not. It is possible to say that the Palestinian cause is as honourable as the Israeli cause; it is not possible to say that terror is as honourable as resisting terror. Ultimately both the morality and the usefulness of resisting terror are contained in the uselessness and immorality of not resisting it.

TORONTO, VI XVI MCMVXXXIII

NOTES

FOREWORD

[1] For example, the physical descriptions and personal backgrounds of some of the people who appear in the book.

[2] Though two sources represent a self-evidently higher standard than a single source, the method itself can become something of a fetish. In American journalism in recent years it tended to reduce the issue – in the words of Michael Ledeen – to 'not whether something is true, but merely whether two people say it is true'.

[3] The Jerusalem Conference on International Terrorism defined terrorism as 'the deliberate, systematic murder, maiming and menacing of the innocent to inspire fear in order to gain political ends.' (From a statement read at the closing session by US Senator Henry Jackson, reported by the Jonathan Institute, 1979.)

PROLOGUE

[1] The Cuban, Syrian and Bulgarian teams were, in fact, housed at the opposite end of the Olympic village from the Israeli team. However, the total distance between Strassberger Strasse where these teams were located and the building of the Israeli team is not more than perhaps 400 metres or 437 yards.

For a detailed layout of the Olympic village at Munich see Serge Groussard's *The Blood of Israel* (William Morrow, New York, 1975), a meticulously researched account, on which I have relied for several facts in this prologue.

[2] The occupants included five athletes, two medical officers, and, in Apartment 5, Shmuel Lalkin, the head of the Israeli delegation, whom the terrorists had been especially anxious to capture. The point has been made, by Groussard and others, that the Israeli security officers who were known to be travelling with the team seemed absent from their apartment (possibly Apartment 6) on the night of the terrorist attack in Connollystrasse.

[3] According to some sources, the group's leader was 'Tony'. Others assign this role to 'Issa'. Edgar O'Ballance (in *Language of Violence*, Presidio Press, Novato, California, 1979) reports his real identity as Mohammed Masalhad, an architect who worked on the construction of the Olympic village and had been sent from Libya because of his familiarity with the site. O'Ballance also quotes the Arab newspaper *An Nahar* attributing the throwing of the hand grenade to Badran rather than Issa, and the shooting of the hostages in the other helicopter to el-Denawi (*op. cit.* p. 124). As O'Ballance points out, the exact sequence of events as well as the terrorists' full identity is very difficult to establish.

CHAPTER 1

[1] Agaf Modiin – Information Bureau – commonly abbreviated to *Aman*. The military intelligence service of Israel, *Aman* came into being in the summer of 1948 as one of the three branches of the old Sherut Yediot (Information Service) known as *Shai*. For detailed descriptions see Stewart Steven's *The Spymasters of Israel* (Hodder & Stoughton, 1981) and Richard Deacon's *The Israeli Secret Service* (Sphere, 1979).

[2] The kibbutzim, those collective agricultural communities, expressed a great deal about the roots, the basic spirit, the oldest social impulses of Israel. The early immigrants, especially the members of the powerful Second and Third *Aliyah*, arriving between the turn of the century and the mid-1920s, came predominantly from Eastern Europe. They brought with them a set of ideals that were a mixture of several leading trends in nineteenth-century European social and political thought, including nationalism as well as extreme egalitarianism.

The kibbutz movement, embodying many of the early Zionist impulses, reached the zenith of its influence in the 1950s. Though active kibbutzniks constituted a mere 3 to 5 per cent of Israel's population, their habits, beliefs, customs and manners were held up for public adulation, almost in the way of status symbols. The political influence of kibbutzniks in Israel was profound: estimates put it at five to seven times their proportion of the population. According to Amos Elon (see his brilliant study, *The Israelis*, p. 315; (Weidenfeld & Nicolson, 1971) to which I have referred for this and some other facts), in 1969 kibbutzniks held roughly 15 per cent of the top political positions and 30 per cent of all seats in parliament.

Kibbutznik ideals included a cult of toughness, service, self-sacrifice and a mystic bond with the soil. Manual, especially agricultural, labour was revered. The new Israeli citizen was supposed to be direct in speech (often to the point of rudeness) and simple in dress and manners. In a form of inverted snobbery, all personal adornments, all badges of rank or formal habits of speech were frowned upon. Though this was not a mere affectation – kibbutzniks *were* tough, worked unbelievably hard, and often sacrificed ordinary human desires for comfort, material rewards or privacy – the end result was to elevate kibbutznik manners and mores into a new hierarchy of precedence. They became something of an aristocracy, an elite in Israel.

[3] Har-Zion, a third-generation *sabra* born in 1934, became a legendary commando in the Israeli army, at times also venturing into private forays in Arab-held territories and killing Arab soldiers. On one occasion he was arrested by the Israeli authorities (though later released) for killing two Arabs who might have been responsible for the murder of Har-Zion's sister. General Ariel Sharon contributed an enthusiastic foreword to Har-Zion's memoirs, published in 1969.

CHAPTER 2

[1] Italy's Fabrica d'Armi Pietro Beretta is probably one of the oldest manufacturers of firearms, having been founded in 1680. The factory began concentrating on the production of automatic pistols in 1915, and has since produced several million of them in various models and calibres. Two of the .22 calibre models are sold in the United States as the 'Plinker' and the 'Minx' and are quite popular, but the model adapted by the Israelis is based on the 9 mm

'Lungo Parabellum' first designed in 1951 for special detachments of the Italian navy and air force. It has a light alloy ('Ergal') body and a special magazine capacity of ten cartridges. It has been further modified for the Mossad's use.

[2] 'Ortega' is a pseudonym, as is 'Dave'.

[3] Short for *Sherut Habitachon*, sometimes translated as the Department for Security. *Shin Bet* is to the Mossad what the FBI is to the CIA, though the comparison is not exact. The operational and administrative structures of the two Israeli agencies are different in many respects from those of their American counterparts. Both the Mossad and *Shin Bet*, as well as *Aman* and two more agencies (the Special Investigation Division of the Israeli police and the Research Department of the Foreign Ministry) belong to a parent body, the Central Committee of Security Services or *Veada Merkazit Lesherutei Habitachon*, which coordinates their activities.

[4] Yiddish for 'thief'.

[5] Eliahu Cohen, probably the most famous Israeli operative as well as the most successful (at least, of those who were eventually detected), was born in Alexandria in 1924. For three years, between 1962 and 1965, he penetrated the highest government circles of Syria under his cover as 'Kamal Amin Taabet', a Syrian businessman from South America, and from his apartment in Damascus transmitted invaluable intelligence data to Tel Aviv. He was captured and hanged by the Syrians in May, 1965. The most detailed and scholarly account of Eli Cohen's exploits is *The Shattered Silence* by Zwy Aldouby and Jerrold Ballinger, published in 1971 in New York by Lancer Books by arrangement with Coward, McCann & Geohegan.

[6] In *The Spymasters of Israel*, Stewart Steven relates how two or three Israeli agents in Europe were actually reported to the police as 'suspicious characters' because of their inability to blend into the landscape. 'Having lived all of their lives on kibbutzim, never having entered, let alone stayed in, a smart international hotel, they were completely at a loss.' In this context Steven also points out that Isser Harel, the Mossad's first great *memune*, had to include, with some misgivings and reluctance, 'good manners' in the training programme for Mossad operatives. Harel himself was a model Galicianer; not that it diminished his stature as one of the greatest spymasters of the century.

[7] Changing names was an Israeli custom, and still is to some extent. New settlers quickly Hebraize their names, and others select new names almost at will signifying qualities they admire or wish to possess. One joke suggests that the Israeli social register should be called *Who Was Who*.

[8] As-Saiqa (Thunderbolt), Black September, Al Fatah, the Democratic Front for the Liberation of Palestine, the Popular Front for the Liberation of Palestine-General Command, Black June, National Arab Youth for the Liberation of Palestine, etc. are all groups and splinter groups within the complex and ever-changing structure of the Palestine Liberation Organization. To some degree all are Marxist or Marxist-inspired, though they may not accept the Kremlin's interpretation of 'scientific socialism' in every detail. They all endorse some form of terror as acceptable in the fight against Israel. Though they frequently cooperate with one another in the struggle against 'Western imperialism' and Israel, they also accept terror as a means of settling disputes within their own ranks. The table produced in Appendix I, taken from Avrim Yaniv's *P.L.O.: A Profile* (Israeli Universities Study Group for Middle

Eastern Affairs, 1974), represents the organizational structure of the *fedayeen* as it existed during the period covered in this account.

[9] Dr George Habash, often referred to as a 'dentist', did qualify as a doctor at the American University in Beirut. As a Christian Arab, born at Lod (then Lydda), it made sense for Habash to embrace a theory of liberation for Palestine that was Marxist rather than religious in emphasis. The Popular Front grew out of an earlier organization founded by Dr Habash, called *Haraka* (Haraka al-Kuamiyyim al-Arab) or the Arab Nationalist Movement. The Popular Front was decidedly more left-wing and militant than Arafat's Al Fatah (giving Fatah in comparison a rather undeserved credit for 'moderation') though within two years of its founding in 1967 some even more left-wing and more militant groups broke away from it, such as Ahmed Jibril's Popular Front – General Command and Nayef Hawatmeh's Democratic Popular Front. The latter was notable for its lack of both democracy and popularity, as it is estimated never to have had more than about 300 members. For more details on Dr Habash and the origins of the Popular Front see Edgar O'Ballance's *Language of Violence* (*op. cit.*).

The claim has been made by Claire Sterling in *The Terror Network* (Weidenfeld & Nicolson, p. 39) that Dr Habash was 'persuaded' to 'go international' in 1967 by the wealthy Italian publisher-playboy Giangiacomo Feltrinelli, and that it was 'with Feltrinelli's money that Habash sent his first commando into Western Europe in 1968'. If so, the Soviet Union's hand is not far to seek. Feltrinelli, though probably too unstable to control reliably, was known to have been inspired in many of his ideas by the KGB via the Czechoslovakian secret service.

[10] Dr Wadi Haddad, another Christian Arab, was the son of a well-known Arab scholar. In 1952 he set up a medical practice in Amman in partnership with Dr Habash. According to Edgar O'Ballance (*op. cit.*, p. 60) the two doctors 'were reputed to hand out propaganda leaflets with their prescriptions'. A cautious man and by all accounts a brilliant organizer, Haddad remained Dr Habash's operations chief and second-in-command for some years; after breaking away from Habash, he continued organizing the most spectacular terrorist actions of the 1970s until his death.

As pointed out earlier, it is of some interest that three of the most militant Palestinian terrorist leaders, Habash, Haddad and Hawatmeh, are not Muslims. This probably explains why all three have drawn their inspiration from Marxism rather than from the religious concept of the *Jihad* or Holy War against Israel. It is necessarily speculation whether it is an additional factor in the considerable enmity between them and the Muslim factions of the Palestinian struggle. In 1970, for instance, Dr Haddad and his family narrowly escaped death when Fatah fired rockets at their apartment in Beirut, though Haddad would later blame the Mossad for the attempt.

CHAPTER 3

[1] One possible reason for the murder of the eleven Olympic athletes having a more profound emotional impact on most Israelis than the murders of even greater numbers of equally innocent people – e.g. at Lod Airport – might have been the mysterious, symbolic quality of sports figures representing a nation at an international event. A German public relations blunder – an official

government spokesman on live television announcing shortly after midnight that the commando action had been successful and all Israeli hostages had been saved – might also have contributed to the frustration and anger of the Israeli public when the truth was revealed the next day. After that, most Israelis had no confidence that even the captured *fedayeen* would ever be brought to justice by the Germans. They were right: within a few weeks two Black September guerrillas hijacked a Lufthansa 727 on a regular run between Damascus and Frankfurt. Before the day was out, the West Germans had traded the three surviving Munich terrorists for the Lufthansa jet and its passengers at Zagreb's Pleso Airport in Yugoslavia.

[2] According to my information, the 'hit teams' did not 'grow out' of Ariel Sharon's Squad 101, as reported by several sources, except perhaps as a historic tradition. Sharon's original squad, created in the late 1950s and operating in a (perhaps unavoidably) merciless way against the *fedayeen* in the Gaza Strip and other territories on Israel's borders, itself 'grew out' of an earlier tradition of counter-terrorist warfare. But the personnel and organization of the post-Munich assassination teams under General Zamir were entirely different. Though my source reports Sharon's presence during the meeting in Golda Meir's quarters at the start of the mission, it seems to have been a symbolic presence only, possibly aimed at boosting operational morale. By 1972 the original Squad 101, its men and its organization, would have been considerably past their prime in every sense of the word.

[3] It may be far-fetched to suggest that Israel's not having the death penalty may have cost Eli Cohen his life, but it is at least a remote possibility. When, after Cohen's capture, the Israelis offered through unofficial channels to exchange some captured Syrian agents for him, the Syrians reportedly replied with indignation that such an exchange would amount to a poor bargain for Syria. Cohen was facing death in Damascus while the captured Syrian agents were in no danger of losing their lives. Zwy Aldouby and Jerrold Ballinger also make reference to such a Syrian response in a slightly different version (*op. cit.* p. 389).

[4] See also Stewart Steven, *op. cit.*, p. 262.

CHAPTER 4

[1] Apparently on the night of 21 June, 1965, four Israeli commandos penetrated the Jewish cemetery in Damascus in an unsuccessful attempt to retrieve Eli Cohen's body. They disinterred the casket, put it on a truck, and nearly made it to the Lebanese border before being detected. Though the Syrian border patrol could not apprehend the Israelis, they forced the commandos to flee, leaving Cohen's body behind. The incident is described by Zwy Aldouby and Jerrold Ballinger, in *op. cit.*, pp. 425–6.

[2] Israeli doubts about Kanafani's assassination were not the result of any real doubts about his role as a terrorist leader. Apart from the regret for having blown up his teenage niece along with him, killing men like Kanafani, who in their role as writers, intellectuals, and press officers had many personal ties and friendships with Western journalists and opinion-makers, and whose public personalities were often very attractive, raised some questions in Mossad circles about the backlash that such violence might engender. These were

never *moral* doubts; simply the view that assassinating known intellectuals might be counter-productive, regardless of their role in terrorism. However, these doubts did not prevent the Mossad from mailing a letter bomb to Bassam Abou Sharif, Kanafani's successor as a spokesman for the Popular Front, within six weeks of Kanafani's death. The bomb did not kill Sharif, though it permanently disfigured him. (See also *The Hit Team* by David B. Tinnin with Dag Christensen, Future, 1977; Stewart Steven, *op. cit.*, pp. 265–6; and Edgar O'Ballance, *op. cit.*, pp. 87, 90, 145, for further views on the Kanafani affair.)

[3] The answer is known today, whether Ephraim knew it at the time or not. There was without doubt more than one team targeted on at least some of the same terrorist leaders. The practice, which clearly has some advantages as well as disadvantages, is certainly not without historical precedent. For an excellent account of how the Germans sent independent agents from two separate intelligence services, the *Sicherheitsdienst* and the *Abwehr*, to assassinate the Allied leaders at Tehran, see *Hitler's Plot To Kill The Big Three* by Laslo Havas (Cowles, Cambridge, Massachusetts, 1969).

CHAPTER 5

[1] According to Christopher Dobson and Ronald Payne in *The Terrorists* (Facts on File, New York, 1979, p. 132) the Italians escaped the embarrassing responsibility of having to try the Palestinian terrorists who gave their names as Ahmed Zaid and Adnam Ali Hashan by granting them 'provisional liberty' on the grounds that their bomb 'was not adequate to destroy the airliner'. The Italians were not alone. Edgar O'Ballance quotes Israeli Defence Minister Moshe Dayan as saying in 1973. 'Of the 110 terrorists caught so far in the world, 70 have been released after a short time. We do not know how much ransom money had been paid, or what overt or under-the-counter agreements states have entered into with them' (*op. cit.*, p. 185). Dayan was proved to be right in 1978 when the former Italian Prime Minister, Aldo Moro, soon to be murdered by the Red Brigades and already imprisoned by them, pleaded from his captivity in a letter to his Government: 'Liberty (with expatriation) was conceded to Palestinians, to avoid grave risks of reprisals. Not once, but many times, detained Palestinians were released by various mechanisms. The principle was accepted . . .' Moro wrote this from his prison to persuade the Italian Government to let loose captured terrorists from the Red Brigades in exchange for his life. After all, 'the principle was accepted'; the Italian Government had done so before. In 1978, however, it did not, and Moro was killed. (Quoted by Claire Sterling in *The Terror Network, op. cit.*) Incidentally, Ahmed Zaid's and Adnam Ali Hashan's names are also reported as 'Ahmed Zaidi Ben Baghdadi' and 'Adnam Mohammed Ashem'. This may be a good place to mention that the English spelling of Arab (or even Hebrew) names is highly idiosyncratic and is sanctified by few conventions of common usage. This lack of uniformity, coupled with the Arab (and Israeli) penchant for changing names, selecting long names of which only parts are used, nicknames, *noms de guerre*, etc., has often played havoc with the records of Western journalists and intelligence services.

[2] Several books mention Zwaiter's assassination without going into any details. One elaborate description, given in David B. Tinnin and Dag Christensen's *The Hit Team*, is at variance with my information in several respects. Tinnin and Christensen have General Zvi Zamir witnessing the assassination from a car parked nearby. If so, my sources were certainly unaware of it. They offered

'nonsense' as the mildest comment on the idea that the head of the Mossad would expose himself in such a fashion. Tinnin and Christensen have the getaway car abandoned on the Via Bressanone, about 300 yards from the scene of the assassination. The distance is roughly accurate, but my information places the car in the opposite direction along the Corso Trieste, close to the Via Panaro. (There *is* a possibility that Carl, in his role as a sweeper, might have moved the vehicle before the police discovered it, but it is unlikely.) The getaway car was not parked directly in front of entrance C and, though a blonde woman had been sitting in it at one point, she was no longer in the car when the assassins emerged from the doorway. (The 'blonde woman' must have exercised the imagination of witnesses because she crops up in two other accounts, Stewart Steven's *The Spymasters of Israel* and Edgar O'Ballance's *Language of Violence*, as driving away with the two male assassins.) Zwaiter was returning home *from* his lady friend, according to my sources, and not *with* her, as in O'Ballance's account. My understanding is that the Israeli commandos did not drive directly to the airport and catch a midnight flight out of Rome, as in Tinnin and Christensen's book, and that their total time in Italy had been considerably longer than five hours. Stewart Steven's contention that the assassins, 'though Mossad-trained and recruited, were not full-time intelligence officers' does coincide with my information, at least in a technical sense. But Steven's view that this assassination was the work of a team specially recruited for this particular action does not coincide with my information.

[3] Apparently Robert did pick up one ejected shell, though later he could not find it in his pocket, and concluded that he might have left it on the seat of the getaway car. This may be the shell Tinnin and Christensen report in their book as having been found in the car, though they describe it as 'an unfired .22 cartridge' (*op. cit.*, p. 81).

CHAPTER 6

[1] There are, in fact, no claims of the Mossad ever having made this particular type of error. Mistakes of other kinds have been made, of which more later.

[2] Though Belgium still played a role, by the 1970s it was by no means the focal point for illicit arms that it had been before World War II. The Soviet-bloc countries, certain Middle Eastern countries like Libya, some African states, as well as some 'non-aligned' Communist countries like Yugoslavia or Cuba had become much more important suppliers of arms, even if often only in the role of middlemen. However, the nature of this arms market was considerably different from the old-fashioned illicit market which made its wares available to privateers. In the modern market, though possession of the arms may be illicit on the part of the end-users, the vendor is almost always government-controlled. In this sense France, the US, South Africa, Israel and others also contribute to an illicit weapons market, though probably not on the scale of the Soviet-bloc countries, and not invariably as an expression of government policy.

[3] I do not mean that from the early 1960s to this day every person who smoked pot, opposed the Vietnam war, protested against pollution, demanded equal pay for women, tried to preserve endangered species and so on was at the same time, consciously or unconsciously, furthering the foreign policy interests of the Soviet Union. Rather, that: a) every one of these movements has served as a staging area for tiny violent minorities to disrupt Western societies or change their nature by provoking repressive measures – an ancient Communist tactic –

and, b) that substantially larger minorities within these movements joined them in the belief that their pet peeves, from linear thought to the killing of whales, were plots by, or problems peculiar to, the free enterprise system.

This created a climate in the West, especially between 1965 and 1975, where every Western policy had to be carried out with reference to the special interests and beliefs of these groups, even when doing so was evidently injurious to the larger interests of Western society as a whole. In talking about the consequences of the efforts of only one of these groups – the environmentalists – Paul Johnson, former editor of the *New Statesman*, had this to say in his book *Enemies of Society*: 'The precise economic effects, in terms of human misery and death, of the eco lobby's *coup* will never be known . . . The only gainer was the archetypal totalitarian state, the Soviet Union, which saw its own prestige rise, and its effective military and political power enhanced, as the wealth of the West fell and its self-confidence evaporated.' (*Enemies of Society*, Weidenfeld & Nicolson, London, 1977, p. 101.)

[4] Quoted by Claire Sterling, *op. cit.*, p. 274.

[5] 'It has always been very striking to me,' notes Harvard history professor Richard Pipes, 'that these terrorist groups, among whom there are many anarchists who detest the Soviet Union as much as they do the Western capitalist countries, have almost *never* struck at Soviet objectives. This is to me added evidence that the Russians exercise a very considerable controlling influence over these movements.' (The Jonathan Institute's report, p. 14, italics in the original.)

[6] Few things show more clearly Soviet Russia's disinterest in ideology when it comes to a chance to destabilize the West and its allies than its support of the various neo-Fascist 'black' terrorist groups, either directly or through proxies, throughout the world. For some examples see, *inter alia*, Claire Sterling, *op. cit.*, especially pp. 113–18.

[7] On some of the facts coming to light during the 1970s, see Claire Sterling, *op. cit.*, pp. 286–92. A book written by Klaus Reiner Rohl, the husband of the German terrorist leader Ulrike Meinhof, also makes very interesting reading in this respect (*Fünf Finger sind keine Faust*, Kiepenheuer and Witsch, Cologne, 1977). 'Public knowledge' in this sense meant only that the information was becoming available and some of it would be printed from time to time, mainly in scholarly and specialized publications.

Mass-market publications, almost without exception, wouldn't touch the subject until the late 1970s, and editors – as I know from personal experience – might accuse a writer of 'bias' or 'cold war mentality' for submitting documented accounts of Russia's role in international terrorism. Soviet Russia's role in terrorism had been surrounded by what author-journalist Robert Moss termed at the 1979 Jerusalem Conference 'a conspiracy of silence'. (The Jonathan Institute report, p. 23.)

[8] In the words of Jean François Revel, 'The CIA and the KGB working together, with all the gold of the Transvaal, would not be enough, at least in the present state of things, to establish a military dictatorship in the Netherlands or Sweden.' (*The Totalitarian Temptation*, Penguin, 1978, p. 243.)

[9] Claire Sterling mentions the example of Libero Mazza, the prefect of Milan, who had raised the alarm about young Italians going to Czechoslovakia for guerrilla training. 'His report was buried and his reputation ruined', Ms

Sterling writes. 'He was held up in the left-wing press as a horrible example of unregenerate reaction, or worse.' (*Op. cit.*, p. 289.) One might add that the officials who buried Mazza's report in 1970 would bury many of their own numbers – and eventually Aldo Moro – within the next eight years, as the fully trained Italian terrorists started returning from Czechoslovakia.

[10] Swiss and West German intelligence officers were familiar with Lenzlinger, whom they described as 'a miniature Feltrinelli', though he was never charged with any offence. He died under mysterious circumstances in 1976.

[11] Terrorism is expensive; in 1975 estimates for Al Fatah's budget alone ranged from 150 million (Israeli sources) to 240 million dollars (Syrian sources) according to Walter Laqueur. (*Terrorism*, Weidenfeld & Nicolson, 1977, p. 90.) Soviet Russia, notoriously short on foreign exchange, has always been loath to waste precious American dollars or Swiss francs on foreign terrorists; such hard currency as Russia has for the purposes of destabilization and espionage is needed by the KGB itself.

On the contrary, Soviet Russia prefers to *earn* hard currency through the sale of weapons and services. Most of the actual funds for terrorism come from oil-rich Arab countries like Libya; 'taxes' on the earnings of Palestinians in such countries; donations from wealthy sympathizers such as Feltrinelli, and collections taken up for the terrorists, often under the guise of humanitarian, refugee relief or nationalistic purposes, from the general population. (Dobson and Payne report 600,000 dollars raised in 1972 from Irish-Americans for the Provisional IRA through dances and raffles, while various Western church organizations are known to have raised money for African terrorists.) Last but not least on the list is common crime, such as bank robberies and kidnappings for ransom, which have been the methods favoured by German, Italian and South American terrorist groups. (See *inter alia*, Christopher Dobson and Ronald Payne, *The Terrorists*, pp. 83–100; Claire Sterling, *op. cit.*, especially pp. 258–71.)

CHAPTER 7

[1] See also Serge Groussard, *op. cit.*, p. 107.

[2] For an excellent description of the Ishutinites see Tibor Szamuely, *The Russian Tradition*, Secker & Warburg, 1974, pp. 247–49.

[3] Fakhri al-Umari, a leading Black September terrorist. Edgar O'Ballance describes him as 'the head of its "Killer section" ' (*op. cit.*, p. 107).

[4] Mohammed Daoud Odeh, known as 'Abu Daoud', became one of Black September's top leaders from its inception.

[5] Ironically enough, Ali Hassan Salameh and Abu Daoud were later reported to have been in Geneva during the last days of September 1972, while the team was holding its first meetings at the Hotel du Midi. The city being relatively small, they could have met by chance, turning a corner.

[6] The well-known models: 'Star', 'Astra' and 'Llama'. The revolver is the 'Ruby'.

[7] Stewart Steven reports that Hamshari 'was surrounded by bodyguards. They were posted outside his flat, at his front door and in the street below.' (*Op. cit.*, p. 269.) This does not coincide with my information, but it agrees with the

initial data the team received on Hamshari. which later turned out to be erroneous.

[8] Dr Ami Shachori, an agricultural attaché, killed as he was sitting at his desk on 19 September, 1972. The fatal injury was caused by a splinter from the desk

[9] Hamshari lingered for another month. He finally succumbed to his injuries on 9 January. 1973.

CHAPTER 8

[1] For some years in the early 1970s the KGB's operational centre for Arab terrorist activities was in Cyprus. (See also Richard Deacon, *op. cit.*, esp. p. 249.) Edgar O'Ballance quotes Cypriot President Makarios as saying: 'Cyprus has its own problems; we do not want our territory to be used as a battlefield in the Arab-Israeli conflict.' (*Op. cit.*, p. 194.)

By 10 April, 1973, when President Makarios made this remark, more than half a dozen assassinations, attempted hijackings, and so on, had been carried out by the Arabs as well as the Israelis on Cypriot territory. Though the KGB eventually moved its liaison centre with Arab terrorists to Damascus, Cyprus continued to be a battleground, partly because of its geographical location. One of the worst incidents occurred as late as February, 1978, when Palestinian gunmen, having murdered an Egyptian editor, landed in a hijacked Cyprus airliner in Nicosia. Egypt sent a commando force to Cyprus to seize the terrorists but, possibly because of an error in communications between the Egyptian commandos and the Cyprus National Guard, fifteen commandos died in the ensuing firefight.

[2] Travelling on a Syrian passport, under the name of Hussein Bashir.

[3] According to my sources, the envelope contained a thousand dollars in US currency. If, as some writers report, al-Chir 'was actually being financed by the KGB' (Richard Deacon, *op. cit.*, p. 255) the modest amount underlines Russian frugality in these matters.

CHAPTER 9

[1] Since an agent's main job is to furnish information for his country, his wilful failure to do so, for whatever reason, would appear to be a serious dereliction of duty. Yet the records of intelligence agencies are filled with examples of data being purposely withheld or stopped at one level or another instead of being passed up the line. The reasons – apart from simple treachery – vary from negligence to considerations of personal advancement within a bureaucracy. An agent might prefer to gain credit for doing a task rather than risk its being given to another agent or department.

Another example may be data conflicting with a pet theory or philosophy held by a section of the agency, which is therefore suppressed. Before the Yom Kippur War a junior officer by the name of Siman Tov, attached to Southern Command Intelligence, submitted a situation analysis indicating that the Egyptians were preparing for hostilities. His report – according to the post-war public inquiry of the Agranat Commission – never got further than his superior's desk. It is by no means a rare example. Shocking as it may sound to

430

outsiders, it is not surprising that the team considered the idea of not reporting the Beirut intelligence, though it is to their credit that they did report it in the end.

2 For instance, on 1 March, 1973 – less than three weeks before the Geneva meeting between the team and their case officer – Black September terrorists shot two American diplomats and the Belgian Chargé d'Affaires during a takeover of the Saudi Arabian embassy in Khartoum. Mossad agent Baruch Cohen was killed in January in Spain. During the same period there was a Black September attempt to sabotage the Schonau Castle refugee camp for Russian Jews in Austria.

3 At that time there was a weekly meeting for top Mossad officials routinely scheduled for Thursdays.

4 The notoriety of Tannous and Halesh may have had more to do with their looks than with the success of their exploits. They were both Christian Arab nurses of sultry good looks who, with two male companions, commandeered a Belgian airliner and flew it to Israel, demanding the release of Israeli-held Arab prisoners in exchange for the plane and hostages. Israeli commandos attacked, killing the two male terrorists and capturing Tannous and Halesh. They were both sentenced to life imprisonment in Israel in 1972. For a detailed description of this operation see Edgar O'Ballance, *op. cit.*, pp. 110–15.

5 Most sources associate al-Kubaisi with George Habash's Popular Front for the Liberation of Palestine rather than with Yasser Arafat's Al Fatah – that is, Black September. My own sources agree with this. Since the Munich massacre is regarded as having been a Black September operation, al-Kubaisi's inclusion in the team's hit list underlines that Israel's policy of counterstrikes against terrorists was considerably wider than a mere revenge action against individuals responsible for Munich.

6 The idea that facing their victims somehow diminishes their moral burden is common to many political assassins. In an interview, telecast over the Canadian *Global* network on 13 March, 1983, one of the Phalangist assassins who took part in the massacre of civilians in the Palestinian refugee camps in the summer of 1982 insisted to the interviewer that he had 'never shot anyone from behind'. Evidently, in the assassin's own eyes, this made his actions less reprehensible. It is possible that non-political killers have similar beliefs, but I'm not aware of any research on the subject.

7 In their book *The Quest for the Red Prince* (William Morrow, New York, 1983), the Israeli authors Michael Bar-Zohar and Eitan Haber claim that al-Kubaisi's assassination on the night of 6 April was delayed by some twenty minutes because al-Kubaisi happened to be picked up by a prostitute driving by in her car just as he was about to be shot. The assassins decided to wait, hoping that the hooker would drive her customer back to the same spot where she had picked him up, and she did so twenty minutes later. Though this makes a very good story, it does not coincide with my understanding of these events.

8 The eyewitnesses followed no one. In fact, they did not even notice Robert, who had stopped a little distance away on the other side of the street when the shooting started. All eyewitness accounts in the papers mention two assassins, not three (e.g. see *Le Figaro*, 7 April, 1973).

CHAPTER 10

[1] Some of these aliases – as well as some others of which my sources have been unaware – are reported by Richard Deacon in *op. cit.*, pp. 257–8. The time sequence noted in Deacon's book slightly differs from my information.

[2] Edgar O'Ballance notes that a Frenchman by the name of François Rangée was sentenced to death in 1974 by a Beirut court for allegedly collaborating with the Israeli raiders (*op. cit.*, p. 174). My sources have no information on this. *Le Group* did end up cooperating with the team in the attack on the PLO in Beirut (see below) but all participating operatives were said to have withdrawn with the Israelis immediately after the raid.

[3] After Yasser Arafat, head of Al Fatah, and Saleh Khalif (known as Abu Iyad) who was the deputy head of Fatah and the head of Black September.

[4] This figure may be exaggerated. Christopher Dobson and Ronald Payne report seventeen Arab guerrillas killed, which appears to be a more realistic figure (*op. cit.*, p. 212).

[5] Sources vary slightly on the number of Israeli dead and wounded. Some reports suggest that the helicopters were not part of the operation as originally planned, but the need for helicopters developed because a large number of documents found at PLO headquarters had to be evacuated along with some casualties. According to these reports, the original idea was to keep Israeli involvement a secret and blame the entire episode on a fight between rival Palestinian factions, and this plan was abandoned only because the helicopters had to be deployed. (See David B. Tinnin, *op. cit.*, p. 96; Stewart Steven, *op. cit.*, p. 247.) My information is that the planned deception had only the limited scope of keeping Lebanese forces away from the scene of the fighting, in keeping with their tradition of non-interference with Palestinian rivalries, and Israel had no intention of keeping the operation a secret after its successful conclusion.

[6] The Beirut raid and its significance are discussed in considerable detail in other works. Perhaps the only thing that need be added is that the raid proved the validity of small commando operations – at least in certain situations – by causing nearly as much damage to the PLO as the Israeli army's invasion of Lebanon did nine years later. Moreover, it did so at a fraction of the cost in material, money, and in Israeli, Palestinian and Lebanese lives. Instead of hurting, it enhanced Israel's reputation. Undeniably, the benefits of the Beirut raid for Israel were short-lived – but whether the 1982 Lebanese invasion will provide more lasting benefits still remains to be seen.

[7] See *Le Figaro*, 10 April, 1973.

[8] The KGB resident in Athens would probably have made no particular effort to keep his contact with Muchassi a secret. It is worth repeating that the Soviet Union (while it did make some public statements of disapproval of certain terrorist actions such as Munich) on the whole tried less to conceal its own role of support for terrorism than the détente-struck Western governments and press did during that period. It is an entirely different matter that the KGB would not have wished to have a direct confrontation with the Mossad, just as the Mossad would not have wanted to tangle with the KGB. For instance, no team would have considered an attempt to assassinate a PLO terrorist while he was riding in his Russian contact's car.

432

[9] For some reason, while most sources I have consulted agree on the major particulars (such as the time and the place) of other Mossad counter-terrorist acts, reports on Muchassi's assassination are quite contradictory. Richard Deacon, for instance, reports it as having occurred in Cyprus on 9 April (*op. cit.*, p. 256). Stewart Steven has it on 7 April in Cyprus, and even elaborates on the 9 April attack on Israeli ambassador Timor's residence as being the Palestinians' revenge for Muchassi's death (*op. cit.*, p. 271). But the Palestinians would have been unlikely to avenge an act that was not to occur for another three days. Edgar O'Ballance's date and place (Athens, 12 April) agree with my information, though the name of the victim does not (*op. cit.*, p. 178). I could find no report on the wounding or killing of a KGB operative (or any Russian) in any published accounts.

CHAPTER 11

[1] Richard Deacon rates Boudia's involvement very high in Baruch Cohen's death. 'Within an hour he [Cohen] had been shot dead: his killer was none other than Mohammed Boudia, the man he was hunting down' (*op. cit.*, p. 256). Other sources don't go quite as far, either in terms of Boudia's involvement or in terms of the business that took Baruch Cohen to Spain. In a general sense the two men *were* hunting each other as part of the shadowy war among all agents of terror and counter-terror, but it is not confirmed that they were specifically hunting each other on the day of Cohen's death, in January, 1973.

[2] For a detailed description of Feltrinelli's career see Claire Sterling, *op. cit.*, pp. 25–48. It is a chilling, unforgettable portrait of the neurotic playboy-revolutionary.

[3] See *Le Figaro*, 29 June, 1973. The contradictory information on Boudia's movements and whereabouts on the night preceding, and on the morning of his death added to the confusion. Christopher Dobson and Ronald Payne report that Boudia's Renault 'had been parked all night in the rue des Fossés Saint-Bernard' and that '[f]or some convoluted reason, another of Boudia's friends told [the police] that he had spent the night with her on the other side of Paris.' (*The Carlos Complex*, Coronet, 1978, p. 25.)

My information is that the girl in question told the police the truth. Boudia *had* spent the night in the rue Boinod in the 18th *arrondissement*, and drove his Renault to the rue des Fossés Saint-Bernard in the early hours of the morning, where he left it parked while visiting another girl who lived nearby. The explosive device was planted during this period. When Boudia came back from his morning visit with his second girlfriend, around 11 am, the hit took place.

CHAPTER 12

[1] Golda Meir's actual words: 'I cannot promise that the terrorists will let us live in peace. But I can, and do, promise that every government of Israel will chop off the hands of those who want to cut short the lives of our children' are quoted by Edgar O'Ballance in *op. cit.*, p. 233. The words were spoken in response to the Democratic Popular Front's leader Naif Hawatmeh's boast of responsibility for the atrocity at Maalot in which twenty-two Israeli children lost their lives. It is of interest to note that Golda Meir, whose initial opposition to

counter-terrorism was well known, and seemed to be based not only on fear of possible error and diplomatic entanglements but on general considerations of civilized conduct, adopted a much harder line in her later pronouncements on the subject. For instance, she reportedly told the Knesset after the Beirut raid: 'It was very marvellous. We killed the murderers who were planning to murder again.' (Quoted by David B. Tinnin in *op. cit.*, p. 96.)

[2] However, a sinister rumour, which is probably unfounded, attributes Alon's murder to an internecine struggle within the Israeli power structure. I regard the rumour as untrue, more because there has never been a shred of evidence of Israelis assassinating one another than because the Palestinians have claimed 'credit' for Alon's killing. What many Palestinian factions – and possibly even the Israelis – have done on some occasions is to claim 'credit' for terrorist acts they did not, in fact, commit. On the principle of 'kill one, frighten a hundred' this makes sense: if the real purpose of terror is to strike fear in the opponent's heart, it can be accomplished by stealing 'credits' as easily as by earning them. However, the rumour concerning Alon's death is probably more indicative of an attempt at misinformation.

[3] In the spring of 1973 – while posing as a Baader-Meinhof comrade from Germany – Avner had spent two nights in a safe house with Carlos. It was a kind of commune in Paris on the Left Bank, where people of all kinds – most of them hippies, sympathizers, and camp followers rather than terrorists – kept coming and going, some crashing in corners, with no one asking any questions of anybody else. Avner even chatted with Carlos, without much interest, as the pudgy Venezuelan didn't impress him unduly and he took him to be some anarchist of no particular concern to Israel. Presumably Carlos was similarly unconcerned about Avner.

[4] Richard Deacon reports their names as Abdel Hadi Nakaa and Abdel Hamid Shibi (*op. cit.*, p. 262). However, other sources claim that the explosion was not caused by Mossad agents, and that 'the Rome police put the cause down to unstable detonators' that the two men were carrying in their car when it blew up in the Piazza Barberini (Edgar O'Ballance, *op. cit.*, p. 225). Of course, the Italian authorities had a marked preference for closing the files on acts of terrorism by attributing them to accidental causes, which would not only save them the rigours of an investigation but also some diplomatic entanglements. At the same time, as pointed out above, neither side in the Middle East conflict has been above claiming 'credit' for accidents or acts committed by a faction on the opposing side. My sources report only that *they* had nothing to do with the action in Rome in June, 1973; and that at the time they also believed that it was carried out by a Mossad counter-terrorist team. The truth may never be known.

[5] David B. Tinnin and Dag Christensen – whose information in other respects is at considerable variance with my sources – provide a fascinating account of the Lillehammer fiasco in their book *The Hit Team*. Many major details in their story sound completely authentic. There are some exceptions, such as the use of a female agent as one of the hit squad which, according to my information, is highly unlikely (though she is also mentioned in other accounts); and the presence of General Zvi Zamir, the head of the Mossad, in Norway during the assassination, which my sources regard as a 'fairy tale'.

[6] The lines from Nizar Qabbani's poem in this chapter are from his book *Political Works*, published in 1974, quoted by Elie Kedourie in Bernard Lewis' *Islam and the Arab World*. The other fragments are from the anthology, *Enemy of*

the Sun: Poetry of Palestinian Resistance, edited by Naseer Aruri and Edmund Ghareet (Drum and Spear Press, New York, 1970).

[7] There is no question that Zionist extremists have also used the weapon of political assassination against statesmen and diplomats, as well as indiscriminate acts of terrorism against non-combatants. It is true that many moderate Zionists have clearly and unequivocally condemned Zionist extremists – but Arab nationalists have also condemned Arab terrorists on numerous occasions. The fact remains that between 1944 and the end of 1948, Zionist terrorists assassinated Lord Moyne, the British resident minister for the Middle East; Count Bernadotte, the Swedish UN mediator for the Middle East; Rex Farran, the brother of British anti-terrorist officer Major Roy Farran (by a parcel bomb sent to England); and attempted to send letter bombs to other British statesmen, including Clement Attlee, the Prime Minister.

They also blew up the King David Hotel in Jerusalem, killing ninety-one people, including fifteen Jews, and massacred 254 old men, women and children at the Arab village of Deir Yassin. These acts of terrorism were in addition to the bombing and killing of British soldiers, officers and installations (including recreational facilities) in Palestine. It goes without saying that in no sense could Zionist acts of terrorism provide justification for subsequent (or contemporaneous) acts of *fedayeen* terror; but it also indicates that moral lapses of the most horrible kind are not exclusive to any one nation or movement.

[8] The phrase is Claire Sterling's (*op. cit.*, p. 117).

[9] The Haganah was a Jewish self-defence force before the establishment of the State of Israel. In those years Papa Salameh was known for such exploits as the killing of the Arab businessman Ahmed Latif in the main street of Jaffa, then disinterring the body and putting it back in the street as a warning to those who would collaborate with the Jews. 'This traitor got his just reward,' Salameh's henchmen warned passers-by. 'Let him rot here, and may the dogs eat his corpse.' (Recounted by Michael Bar-Zohar in *Spies In the Promised Land*, Davis-Poynter, 1972.)

[10] See Claire Sterling, *op. cit.*, pp. 118–19. But in addition to Communists and neo-Nazis, it has been suggested that Salameh – especially in the later years of his career as Fatah's security chief – may have collaborated with the CIA, at least in some limited way. (See David Ignatius in the *Wall Street Journal*, 10 February, 1983.) Though it is highly unlikely that Salameh was ever a CIA agent – or was even used by the CIA in isolated operations – it is possible that he, as a shrewd and sophisticated man, tried to insure his own security against his Israeli enemies by doing certain favours for individual CIA operatives or for American diplomats. Without any question, Salameh's help to Americans on Middle East missions could have been invaluable on certain occasions, and they might have reciprocated at times by helping to keep Salameh one step ahead of the Mossad. However, all this is highly speculative.

CHAPTER 13

[1] Hilarion Capucci, the Greek Catholic Archbishop of Jerusalem, smuggled weapons for the PLO. Arrested in July, 1974, he was later sentenced to twelve years by an Israeli court. The Mossad had been aware of Capucci's involvement with terrorism before capturing him red-handed, as it were. Nor did

Capucci offer any defence other than a claim of 'diplomatic immunity' and a rejection of the Israeli court's jurisdiction over him. But no church – Protestant, Catholic or Orthodox – has been immune to attempts at Soviet infiltration, mainly through the promotion of some kind of ideological alliance between religion and Marxism.

[2] I could find no record in the German-language Swiss press of the incident. (On this subject, see also note 2, Chapter 18.)

CHAPTER 14

[1] David B. Tinnin quotes Prime Minister Meir as saying: 'You can't guarantee me that some day there won't be a mistake. Some day, some of our people will get caught. Then, you tell me: what are we going to do?' (*op. cit.*, p. 29). Though this quote seems to express a greater concern about the political consequences for Israel than for the lives of bystanders, it is probable that the two considerations were equally present in Golda Meir's mind. In fact, in the course of Israel's history, several Israeli spies and saboteurs were caught in foreign countries; Israel did nothing, and nothing much happened. A lot of countries spy, sabotage and terrorize, are caught, and suffer no great consequences. A few diplomats are expelled once in a while, and there may be some sharp notes exchanged, along with mild economic sanctions for limited periods of time. Israel had no reason to believe that she would be treated differently.

CHAPTER 15

[1] When push comes to shove, many male terrorists die fighting. So do a few female terrorists. Most women, however, have enough sense to give up at the last minute, or not to pull the pin on the grenade that would blow them up along with their attackers and victims. Khaled, Halesh and Tannous were captured alive in situations where their male companions were not. I am aware of no example of a male terrorist being captured alive while his female comrades died fighting.

The female leader of an attempt to hijack a Japan Air Line 747 blew herself up by accident in the cocktail lounge of the plane while grabbing her purse which contained a hand grenade. (As Christopher Dobson and Ronald Payne remark, accurately if somewhat unkindly, in their book: '[she] should have paid more attention to her grenade and less to her champagne.' *The Carlos Complex*, p. 176.) In fact, female terrorists die in action mainly through self-inflicted wounds or in situations where the attacking forces do not give them an option to surrender.

CHAPTER 16

[1] In fairness to Pepe, few men would have been even marginally suitable to be an agent's *husband*. It is a common experience of intelligence agencies that female agents cannot count on the kind of unquestioning support from their spouses that male agents can. Therefore, almost invariably, female agents are single or else work with their husbands. At the very least, the husband will be an intelligence officer.

[2] Perhaps Hans wasn't altogether paranoid. Whatever *Le Group* did and whatever forces were behind it, the KGB may well have set up a privateer group, in some respects not unlike Papa's organization, which operated in France until 1978. Called *Aide et Amitié*, it allegedly provided aid and friendship to international terrorists. (See Claire Sterling, *op. cit.*, pp. 49–69.)

[3] This is the perennial problem of all clandestine operations. It is impossible to seek information without giving away the fact that one is seeking it; it is impossible to meet an informer without being met by him; it is impossible to see without being seen. Precautions can be taken only to minimize the risk; it cannot be eliminated altogether. An agent could be perfectly secure only if he made no attempt to find out anything. Which, indeed, is the reason why 'sleepers' or 'moles' can exist undetected sometimes for decades: they do nothing, only wait to be activated by their masters. The minute they are, their lifetime as agents becomes very finite.

Relying on 'regular' informers instead of privateers like *Le Group* doesn't reduce the risk. Reportedly, Baruch Cohen was shot while sitting in a sidewalk café with an Arab informer known to him, who was reaching into his pocket for what Cohen believed was a list of names. Instead of the list, the Arab produced a gun and shot Cohen four times. (See Christoper Dobson and Ronald Payne, *The Carlos Complex*, p. 25.)

[4] Between November, 1971, and September, 1973, Black September – the terrorist group responsible for Munich – claimed responsibility for at least fourteen acts of terrorism, most of them in Western Europe. However, after the fall of 1973, there were no more Black September attacks in Europe, and only one – an attempt to assassinate King Hussein in Rabat on 11 October, 1974 – in the Middle East. While it is impossible to tell whether the cessation of Black September activities in Europe was due to the loss of nine top organizers between October, 1972, and June, 1973 – it is a better guess that it was primarily due to internal PLO politics following the Yom Kippur War – it is also true that Avner's team could justifiably conclude from it that their operation was having an effect. Especially since that was what they wanted to believe.

CHAPTER 17

[1] Such psychological consequences are probably the inevitable trade-off for increased security whenever a team is sent on a mission with no regular contact to its home base. Not having to communicate diminishes the chances of detection and – for skilled operatives – autonomy may enhance efficiency. However, this may be offset by feelings of insecurity and lack of direction when things go wrong. The history of behind-the-lines commando operations is filled with examples of doubts, psychological pressure, feelings of inadequacy or of having done wrong. Such self-condemnation may be justified, but it is also reported when – from the point of view of the objective observer – the agents have done the only thing they could in terms of their mission.

[2] I could find no record of the incident in the Spanish press. As in the Glarus case, considerations of security precluded a direct inquiry from the authorities. My sources agreed to cooperate on condition that no police or security forces would be alerted to research being done on the subject. As a result, I can back up certain contentions in this account only by my faith in sources whose accuracy I could verify in other respects.

[3] Along with the fire-bombing of the Pan American jetliner in Rome on 17 December, 1973, resulting in the death of thirty-two passengers. this marked the appearance of Abu Nidal as the terrorist leader with the highest body count. Abu Nidal, a renegade from Black September, and Yasser Arafat had reportedly 'sentenced' each other to death, though as of this writing neither 'sentence' has been carried out. In 1983, when Arafat's close associate, Dr Issam Sartawi, was assassinated in Portugal, the Western press attributed the murder to Abu Nidal, though Arafat himself blamed Israeli intelligence. (*Time* magazine, 25 April, 1983.)

CHAPTER 18

[1] General Zvi Zamir had retired in the fall of 1974 to be replaced by General Yitzhak Hofi. For reasons of security Israel never reveals the identity of the *memune* – or of certain other top security officials and army or military intelligence commanders – until their retirement. As with many security shibboleths, this makes more sense on paper than in reality. The identity of top officials, well hidden from Israeli citizens, journalists and others, seldom remains a secret from the KGB or the terror network, as subsequent events often show. For instance, Soviet spy Israel Beer (arrested in 1962) would have been fully aware of the identities of the top intelligence officials in Israel as he himself rose to the position of deputy head of *Aman*. This clearly means that the identity of the first great *memune*, Isser Harrel, was known all along to Israel's enemies – though perhaps not to her friends. Since General Hofi's identity had also been known during his tenure (from the fall of 1974 to roughly the end of 1982), owing to a slip-up at the time of his appointment, only two *memunim*, Zamir and his predecessor Meir Amit, seem to have successfully concealed their identities while holding office. (The man who had been groomed to be General Hofi's successor died under somewhat mysterious circumstances during the 1982 campaign in Lebanon. The current *memune*'s identity has so far been kept a secret.)

EPILOGUE

[1] Serge Groussard, *op. cit.*, p. 107

CHRONOLOGY

5 September, 1972	Black September terrorists massacre eleven Israeli Olympic athletes at Munich.
16 October, 1972	Wael Zwaiter is shot dead in the lobby of his Rome apartment building.
8 December, 1972	In Paris, Mahmoud Hamshari is fatally injured by a bomb in his telephone.
24 January, 1973	Abad al-Chir is blown up in his hotel room in Nicosia, Cyprus.
6 April, 1973	Basil al-Kubaisi is shot dead in a street in Paris.
9 April, 1973	Kamal Nasser, Mahmoud Yussuf Najjer, and Kemal Adwan are assassinated in their apartments in Beirut.
12 April, 1973	Zaid Muchassi is killed in an explosion in his Athens hotel room. A man, assumed to be a KGB operative, is also shot outside the hotel.
28 June, 1973	Mohammed Boudia is blown up in his car in Paris.
12 January, 1974	Three armed unidentified Arabs are shot in a church near Glarus, Switzerland.

21 August, 1974	The woman 'Jeanette' is shot dead in her houseboat near the Dutch town of Hoorn.
11 November, 1974	A young, armed, unidentified Arab is shot in a garden in Tarifa, Spain.

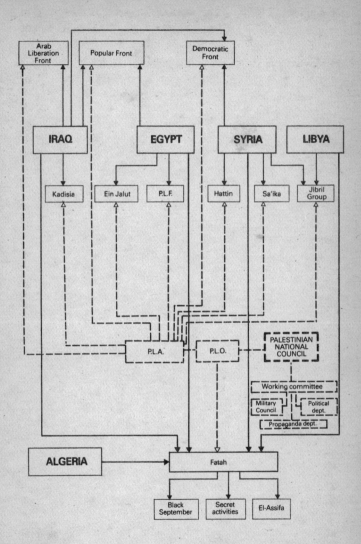

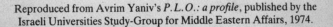

Reproduced from Avrim Yaniv's *P.L.O.: a profile*, published by the
Israeli Universities Study-Group for Middle Eastern Affairs, 1974.

441

BIBLIOGRAPHY

Zwy Aldouby & Jerrold Ballinger *The Shattered Silence*, Lancer Books, by arrangement with Coward, McCann & Geohegan, New York, 1971.

Shlomo Avineri *The Making of Modern Zionism*, Weidenfeld & Nicolson, 1981.

Ralph Baker *Not Here, But In Another Place*, St Martin's Press, New York, 1980.

Michael Bar-Zohar *Spies in the Promised Land,* Davis-Poynter, 1972.

Michael Bar-Zohar & Eitan Haber *The Quest for the Red Prince*, William Morrow, New York, 1983.

Jillian Becker *Hitler's Children*, Lippincott, New York, 1977.

Eli Ben-Hanan *Our Man in Damascus*, New York: Crown, New York, 1969.

Richard C. Clark *Technological Terrorism*, The Devin-Adair Co., Old Greenwich, 1980.

Richard Clutterbuck *Guerrillas and Terrorists*, Faber and Faber, 1977.

Gabriel and Daniel Cohn-Bendit *Obsolete Communism: The Left-Wing Alternative*, Penguin, 1969.

Michael Davitt *Within the Pale*, c. 1903.

Richard Deacon *The Israeli Secret Service*, Sphere, 1979.

Regis Debray *Revolution in the Revolution*, Greenwood Press, 1980.

Christopher Dobson & Ronald Payne *The Carlos Complex*, Coronet, 1978.

Christopher Dobson & Ronald Payne *The Terrorists*, Facts on File, New York, 1979.

Amos Elon *The Israelis*, Weidenfeld & Nicolson, 1971.

Frantz Fanon *The Wretched of the Earth*, Penguin, 1970.

Serge Groussard *The Blood of Israel*, William Morrow, New York, 1975.

Laslo Havas *Hitler's Plot to Kill the Big Three*, Cowles, Cambridge, Massachusetts, 1969.

Chaim Herzog *The Arab-Israeli Wars*, Methuen, 1982.

Paul Johnson *Enemies of Society*, Weidenfeld & Nicolson, 1977.

Leila Khaled *My People Shall Live*, c. 1973.

John Laffin *Fedayeen*, Cassell, 1978.

Walter Lacqueur *Confrontation: The Middle East and World Politics*, Quadrangle, New York, 1974.

Walter Laqueur *Terrorism*, Weidenfeld & Nicolson, 1977.

Bernard Lewis *Islam and the Arab World*, McClelland and Stewart, Toronto, 1976.

Benjamin Netanyahu *International Terrorism: The Soviet Connection*, The Jonathan Institute, 1979.

Edgar O'Ballance *Language of Violence*, Presidio Press, Novato, California, 1979.

Shimon Peres *From These Men*, Wyndham, 1979.

Kim Philby *My Silent War*, Granada, 1969.

Jean-François Revel *The Totalitarian Temptation*, Penguin, 1972.

Michael Selzer *Terrorist Chic*, Hawthorn Books, New York, 1979.

Claire Sterling *The Terror Network*, Weidenfeld & Nicolson, 1981.

Stewart Steven *The Spymasters of Israel*, Hodder & Stoughton, 1981.

Tibor Szamuely *The Russian Tradition*, Secker & Warburg, 1974.

Alan M. Tigay *Myths and Facts 1980*, Near East Report, 1980.

David B. Tinnin with Dag Christensen *The Hit Team*, Futura, 1977.

Jessica Stirling
The Deep Well at Noon £2.50

From the heady jubilation of Armistice Day 1918, young Holly Beckman is drawn out of the grey Lambeth slums and into the rich and corrupt society of Mayfair's Smart Set. Part-owner of a Pimlico antique shop, she is determined to reach the top . . . from the whitewashed mews of Mayfair to the murky back parlours of underworld pubs, she carves out her career, driven by burning ambition but hindered by her own fiery passions.

The Blue Evening Gone £1.95

The years have taken the Beckman family far from the Lambeth slum world of their father Leo. Holly – left a widow at the death of Christopher – is now married to Kennedy King, her partner in the art business. Brother Ritchie has forged, literally, his own career in the trade. Maury, now a wealthy builder, is still the trusted and despised older brother. As the skies once again darken with war clouds, the Beckmans are swept into family turmoil, threatening all they have won from the struggling years.

Beloved Sinner £1.75

First UK publication of the magnificent new novel from the author of *The Spoiled Earth*.

Escaping with her governess from the clutches of a domineering stepmother, the lovely Sophy Richmond found herself in the arms of a young Hussar – learning the terrible price of illicit love. The fiery affair ended, and she met and married Leon de Nerval, a wealthy businessman. It seemed that happiness was hers, until she was threatened by the haunting shadow of a past passion that would never let her escape . . .

Jessica Stirling
The Gates of Midnight £1.75

A widow once more, Holly Beckman faces the dark years of
a new world war. Her son Chris is thrust into the front line
with the RAF, her antique business holds no more interest
for her, and suddenly David, the lost lover of two decades, is
back in England. If Holly falls again under his irresistible
charm, can she trust him, so many years after? Across the
Channel, her brother Ritchie sees his art business crumble
under the advancing invader. He enlists the aid of an old
adversary and a roguish friend to outwit his mendacious wife
and her Nazi friends. A new generation of Beckmans finds
love in the shadow of conflict. Their chronicle comes full
circle . . .

Hugh Walpole
Rogue Herries £2.50

The history of a divided family that mirrors eighteenth-
century England – magnificent fiction set against the wild
and beautiful scenery of the Lake District, crowded with fairs,
revels, witches, murder, strolling players and Jacobite agents.
Dominating all is proud, intolerant Francis Herries – the dark
Angel of Borrowdale – who despised his wife and sold his
mistress at a public fair, yet came to love sixteen-year-old
Mirabell Starr above life itself . . .

Vanessa £2.50

Everyone said that Benjie was no good . . . At fifteen,
Vanessa had Benjie in her blood: she would never betray
him. This absorbing novel portrays the lives of successive
generations of Herries – from the triumph of Judith Paris's
hundredth birthday in the 1870s to the disillusionment of the
1930s. The author's understanding of love is matched by his
masterly descriptions of the wild Cumberland countryside –
where the past was never dead and the spirit of Rogue
Herries lived on . . .

Susan Howatch
The Rich are Different £3.50

A great fortune and the struggle to control a worldwide business empire; an ambitious and beautiful woman who is one of the most provocative heroines in fiction; a love that spans ecstasy and anguish and a story that reaches from the quiet Norfolk countryside across the ocean to the New York of the Roaring Twenties.

'Love, hate, death, murder and a hell of a lot of passion...'
DAILY MIRROR

The Sins of the Fathers £3.50

From Wall Street to the quiet of an English country churchyard, Susan Howatch's magnificent narrative traces the fortunes of the Van Zale dynasty through two decades of wealth, ambition and struggle, until the sins of the fathers are finally visited upon the next generation.

The Shrouded Walls £1.75

Although it was a marriage of convenience, Marianne finds herself falling in love with Axel, the husband she hardly knew ... Until he takes her to Haraldsdyke, the lonely house on the Kent marshes, where the atmosphere is oppressive with witchcraft and murder ... Alone, bewildered, and friendless, Marianne is soon terrified for her life.

Daphne du Maurier
Jamaica Inn £1.95

The cold walls of Jamaica Inn smelt of guilt and deceit. Its dark secrets made the very name a byword for terror among honest Cornish folk.

Young Mary Yellan found her uncle was the apparent leader of strange men who plied a strange trade. Was there more to learn? She remembered the fear in her aunt's eyes . . .

'An exciting brew . . . for a late evening's reading' SATURDAY REVIEW

The King's General £1.95

A brilliant re-creation of the love shared by Sir Richard Grenvile – at once the King's General in the West and the most detested officer in his army – and Honor Harris of Lanrest, as brave as she was beautiful, during the years when Cornwall echoed to the brisk tattoo of Royalist drums and the alien challenge of rebel bugles.

The Loving Spirit £1.95

A powerful exuberant romance of Cornwall, through three generations of passion and drama, of sailing ships and the glory of wind and sea.

Janet Coombe was born with the loving spirit, and passed it on to her son Joseph. When it reappears in her great-granddaughter Jennifer, the barrier of the years breaks down as they are carried beyond all prudence in their need to love and be loved.

'Miss du Maurier creates on the grand scale . . . a rich vein of humour and satire, observation, sympathy, courage, a sense of the romantic are here' OBSERVER

Fiction

☐	**The Chains of Fate**	Pamela Belle	£2.95p
☐	**Options**	Freda Bright	£1.50p
☐	**The Thirty-nine Steps**	John Buchan	£1.50p
☐	**Secret of Blackoaks**	Ashley Carter	£1.50p
☐	**Hercule Poirot's Christmas**	Agatha Christie	£1.50p
☐	**Dupe**	Liza Cody	£1.25p
☐	**Lovers and Gamblers**	Jackie Collins	£2.50p
☐	**Sphinx**	Robin Cook	£1.25p
☐	**My Cousin Rachel**	Daphne du Maurier	£1.95p
☐	**Flashman and the Redskins**	George Macdonald Fraser	£1.95p
☐	**The Moneychangers**	Arthur Hailey	£2.50p
☐	**Secrets**	Unity Hall	£1.75p
☐	**Black Sheep**	Georgette Heyer	£1.75p
☐	**The Eagle Has Landed**	Jack Higgins	£1.95p
☐	**Sins of the Fathers**	Susan Howatch	£3.50p
☐	**Smiley's People**	John le Carré	£1.95p
☐	**To Kill a Mockingbird**	Harper Lee	£1.95p
☐	**Ghosts**	Ed McBain	£1.75p
☐	**The Silent People**	Walter Macken	£1.95p
☐	**Gone with the Wind**	Margaret Mitchell	£3.50p
☐	**Blood Oath**	David Morrell	£1.75p
☐	**The Night of Morningstar**	Peter O'Donnell	£1.75p
☐	**Wilt**	Tom Sharpe	£1.75p
☐	**Rage of Angels**	Sidney Sheldon	£1.95p
☐	**The Unborn**	David Shobin	£1.50p
☐	**A Town Like Alice**	Nevile Shute	£1.75p
☐	**Gorky Park**	Martin Cruz Smith	£1.95p
☐	**A Falcon Flies**	Wilbur Smith	£2.50p
☐	**The Grapes of Wrath**	John Steinbeck	£2.50p
☐	**The Deep Well at Noon**	Jessica Stirling	£2.50p
☐	**The Ironmaster**	Jean Stubbs	£1.75p
☐	**The Music Makers**	E. V. Thompson	£1.95p

Non-fiction

☐	**The First Christian**	Karen Armstrong	£2.50p
☐	**Pregnancy**	Gordon Bourne	£3.50p
☐	**The Law is an Ass**	Gyles Brandreth	£1.75p
☐	**The 35mm Photographer's Handbook**	Julian Calder and John Garrett	£5.95p
☐	**London at its Best**	Hunter Davies	£2.95p
☐	**Back from the Brink**	Michael Edwardes	£2.95p

☐	**Travellers' Britain**	} Arthur Eperon	£2.95p
☐	**Travellers' Italy**		£2.95p
☐	**The Complete Calorie Counter**	Eileen Fowler	80p
☐	**The Diary of Anne Frank**	Anne Frank	£1.75p
☐	**And the Walls Came Tumbling Down**	Jack Fishman	£1.95p
☐	**Linda Goodman's Sun Signs**	Linda Goodman	£2.50p
☐	**Scott and Amundsen**	Roland Huntford	£3.95p
☐	**Victoria RI**	Elizabeth Longford	£4.95p
☐	**Symptoms**	Sigmund Stephen Miller	£2.50p
☐	**Book of Worries**	Robert Morley	£1.50p
☐	**Airport International**	Brian Moynahan	£1.75p
☐	**Pan Book of Card Games**	Hubert Phillips	£1.95p
☐	**Keep Taking the Tabloids**	Fritz Spiegl	£1.75p
☐	**An Unfinished History of the World**	Hugh Thomas	£3.95p
☐	**The Baby and Child Book**	Penny and Andrew Stanway	£4.95p
☐	**The Third Wave**	Alvin Toffler	£2.95p
☐	**Pauper's Paris**	Miles Turner	£2.50p
☐	**The Psychic Detectives**	Colin Wilson	£2.50p
☐	**The Flier's Handbook**		£5.95p

All these books are available at your local bookshop or newsagent, or can be ordered direct from the publisher. Indicate the number of copies required and fill in the form below   11

....

Name_____

(Block letters please)

Address_____

_____

Send to CS Department, Pan Books Ltd, PO Box 40, Basingstoke, Hants
Please enclose remittance to the value of the cover price plus:
35p for the first book plus 15p per copy for each additional book ordered
to a maximum charge of £1.25 to cover postage and packing
Applicable only in the UK

While every effort is made to keep prices low, it is sometimes
necessary to increase prices at short notice. Pan Books reserve
the right to show on covers and charge new retail prices which
may differ from those advertised in the text or elsewhere